DIM
WIT

DIM WIT

THE STUPIDEST QUOTES OF ALL TIME

ROSEMARIE JARSKI

Ulysses Press

To Richard Madeley—The Gaffer

Published in the United States by:
ULYSSES PRESS
P.O. Box 3440
Berkeley, CA 94703
www.ulyssespress.com

First published in the United Kingdom in 2008 by Ebury Press,
an imprint of Ebury Publishing, A Random House Group Company

ISBN: 978-1-56975-722-2
Library of Congress Control Number: 2009902016

U.S. Editors: Sayre Van Young, Lauren Harrison
U.S. Production: Abigail Reser
Interior design: seagulls.net
Cover design: Double R Design

1 3 5 7 9 10 8 6 4 2

Printed in Canada by Transcontinental Printing

If stupidity got us into this mess, then why can't it get us out?

Will Rogers

CONTENTS

Introduction 17

THE WORD

Names 30

Questions 33

Words 34

New Words 37

Languages...38

Pronunciation 41

Freudian Slips 43

Daffynitions..45

Grammar & Punctuation 47

Literally 48

Idiotic Idioms 49

New Proverbs 51

Silly Similes..54

Mangled Metaphors 55

Misprints & Typos 58

Actual Medical Misprints.....................................60

Actual Clerical Misprints.....................................61

Spelling..62

Malapropisms..64

Spoonerisms 69

Goldwynisms 71

Signs & Notices...72

CONTENTS

Actual Warnings 73

Nominal Warnings 75

Homophones, Eggcorns & Slips of the Ear 76

Mondegreens—General 79

Mondegreen Lyrics (Misheard Lyrics)..............................80

Misheard Musical & Song Titles 83

Mondegreen Christmas Carols & Songs............................83

Film & TV Subtitles 87

Writer 88

Bad First Drafts of Famous Lines 90

Books 91

Book Titles That Didn't Quite Make It 95

Autobiography 96

Poetry 97

Journalism & News..98

Headlines..99

Corrections...100

HUMANITY

Gender..104

Gay...106

Lesbian...107

Race 109

Attraction 110

Dating 113

Kiss...115

Sex...116

Romance 121

Love 122

Marriage..123

Wedding 126

Battle of the Sexes 128

Cheating..129

Divorce...131
Family—General...132
Family Planning..133
Baby 136
Mother 138
Father 139
Children 140
Sex Education..142
Home 143
Domestic Work..144
DIY 145
Class & Snobbery..146
Ego 147
Manners & Etiquette...149
Insults...151
Advice 152
Communication...154
Mistakes 156
Insurance Claims 158
Car Insurance Claims 160
Learning & Lessons...161
Work 162
The Office 166
Awards 166
Winning & Losing...168

SPORTS & LEISURE
Sports—General 171
Water Sports...172
Athletics 174
Basketball 176
Baseball 178
Tennis...180

CONTENTS

Football 181

Golf 183

Boxing 185

Horseracing 187

Hunting 188

Chess 189

Leisure Pursuits 190

Gambling..192

Shopping 193

Useless Products 195

Holiday 196

Christmas & Holidays..197

Party..199

Gifts 200

THE NATURAL WORLD

Animals—General 203

Cat 205

Dog 206

Birds 208

Insects..209

Nature 209

Weather 211

The Environment...212

ARTS & ENTERTAINMENT

Culture 216

Art...216

Popular Music 219

Classical Music...222

Opera 224

Musical Instrument...225

Dance 225

Film & Hollywood 226
Shakespeare 230
Actors & Acting 232
Fame & Celebrity 233
Television..236
Radio..237
Comedy 238

SCIENCE & TECHNOLOGY
Science..242
Astronomy...243
Mathematics 246
Statistics 247
Technology 248
Computer 249
Internet...251
Inventions 252
Letters & E-mails 253
Telephone 254
You Can't Argue with That! 257

SOCIETY & POLITICS
Politics..261
Politicians 266
Dimwit Politicians: What They Say about Them 267
George W. Bush in His Own Words 269
George W. Bush: What They Say about Him...........270
Royalty..273
Crime 274
Police..278
Law & Lawyers...281
In Court: Actual Transcripts from
    Official Court Records 282

CONTENTS

Doctors' Expert Witness Statements:
  Actual Transcripts from Official Court Records..............289
Lawyers' Questions and Statements:
  Actual Transcripts from Official Court Records..............291
Sentencing 292
Capital Punishment 293
Prison 293
Judge 295
War & Peace 295
Violence...299
Terrorism...301
The Armed Forces 303
Weapons 304
Business 306
Advertising 308
Money 309
Tax 311
Rich...312
Poor...312
Charity 313

TRAVEL & COUNTRIES
Geography...317
Travel & Tourism..319
Countries—General 322
Great Britain...324
Ireland 325
America 326
Transport—General..327
Bus 328
Car 329
Train..333
Air Travel 334
Boat...338

THE UNIVERSE

The World 341

Life 342

Beliefs 343

American Credo 344

Astrology & Superstition.................................345

The Supernatural 347

God 348

Religion—General 349

Christianity..350

The Bible 351

Biblical Bloopers..352

Catholic 353

Jew 354

Atheist 355

Immortality 356

Afterlife 356

Reincarnation 357

History 358

The Future..361

THE BODY

Appearance—General.......................................363

Hair..364

Height 367

Beauty 367

Ugly..369

Cosmetic Surgery..369

Fashion...371

Health & Medicine 374

Nurse: Actual Extracts from Nurses' Exam Papers 377

Dentist..379

CONTENTS

Doctor 379

Hospital 383

Addiction & Drugs 386

Alcohol—General 388

Wine 390

Drunk 391

Hangover 393

Smoking 393

Food & Drink 395

Vegetarian 400

Restaurant 401

Weight 404

Diet 405

Exercise 406

Disability 408

Retirement 411

Age 411

Death & Dying 414

Suicide 418

Funeral 419

Epitaph 422

THE BRAIN

Education 424

School 425

Teacher 426

Exams & Tests 427

Report Cards 429

College 429

Intelligence 430

Thinking 433

Genius 434

Illogical Logic 435

Philosophy 438
Truth 440
Lies 440

THE MIND
Fear & Paranoia 443
Madness & Therapy..445
Memory..446
Time 449
Punctuality 451
Happiness..452

MISCELLANEOUS 453

INDEX 458

INTRODUCTION

Mark Twain once said, "Better to remain silent and be thought a fool, than to speak out and remove all doubt." But who listens to wise advice? A fool and his words are soon parted, and *Dim Wit* is here to prove it with a double hernia's–worth of the dumbest things ever said.

If you're thinking that sounds like a pretty dumb premise for a book—a trivial undertaking for the trivial minded—you may be surprised to hear that there is a long and illustrious tradition for such collections. Gustave Flaubert, the author of *Madame Bovary*, compiled one, as did the celebrated American satirist, H. L. Mencken. There's even a dedicated literary term: A collection of stupid remarks is known by the French word *sottisier*.

The French may have supplied the word, but when it comes to *la stupidité*, our Gallic cousins can't hold a candle to English-speakers. Infinitely rich in words, metaphors, proverbs, similes and slang, endlessly malleable and notoriously inconsistent, the English language is fraught with linguistic traps ready to trip up the unwary at every turn. One little word out of place and you can find yourself suffering from foot-and-mouth disease—I mean foot-in-mouth disease. See what I mean?

But one man's blunder is another man's belly laugh, and this *sottisier* aims to maximize mirth by covering verbal, written and even the odd behavioral blooper. So strewn with verbal banana skins are these pages that the book might very well be designated a health and safety hazard. Don't say you haven't been warned!

Of all the verbal mishaps, the "mondegreen" is surely the most delightful. If you aren't familiar with the term, the best way to explain it is to tell the charming story of how it came by its unusual name. The word was coined by American writer Silvia Wright. Growing up, she learned an old Scottish ballad, "The Bonnie Earl of Murray," which contains the couplet:

> They have slain the Earl of Murray
> And laid him on the green.

But what young Silvia heard was this:

> They have slain the Earl of Murray
> And Lady Mondegreen.

The sad death of Lady Mondegreen touched Sylvia's childish heart, and it wasn't until many years later when she encountered the poem in written form that she realized she'd misheard the words. And so the "mondegreen" was born.

Relatives of Lady Mondegreen pop up in the most unexpected places and have even been known to bumble into our cherished Christmas carols. There's a Wayne in a manger; Round John Virgin in "Silent Night" (as in, "Round John Virgin, mother and child"); Buddy Holly in "Deck the Halls with Buddy Holly"; and let's not forget Good King Wence's lass who looked out on the feet of heathens.

Song lyrics are the natural home of the mondegreen, or, at least, they were until record companies started including the words of songs on record sleeves, thereby enabling us to discover that what we'd always known as "Scare a moose, scare a moose, will you do the damn tango?" was, in fact, "Scaramouche, Scaramouche, will you do the fandango?" Not that we were any the wiser in that particular instance.

I can't help thinking it was more fun when we had to rely on our own interpretations. As a child, I honestly believed that "Super Trouper" by Abba opened with the legend, "I was sick and tired of everything when I called you last night from Tesco." What Agnetha and Frida were doing in those days hanging around the U.K.'s answer to Wal-Mart, I didn't like to ask, but I was shocked when I finally found out that they were actually calling from the city of Glasgow.

Glasgow, shmasgow, I prefer my version. And I also prefer the version of a Prince song I heard my sister belting out as it played on the car radio: "She wore a raspberry soufflé …" Maybe it's hereditary, this susceptibility to mondegreens, because my entire family suffers from it.

I was in two minds whether to give any room to malapropisms, having long felt toward them the way other people feel about puns, or Céline Dion records (you know that feeling when you're chewing the silver-paper wrapper from a chocolate bar on a tooth with a cavity?). A malapropism is a confusion of words that sound alike (think, affluent/effluent), and my antipathy dates from a school trip to see a play called *The Rivals*. Written by Richard Sheridan in 1775, this Restoration "comedy" features the character Mrs. Malaprop after whom the verbal slip is named. I vividly recall this preposterous bewigged and bepowdered old bat strutting around the stage shrieking things like this:

> He is the very pine-apple of politeness!
> She's as headstrong as an allegory on the banks of the Nile!
> She might know something of the contagious countries!
> It gives me the hydrostatics to such a degree!

I'd been told these malapropisms were the original and the best, "the height of hilarity," but they didn't raise so much as a titter from me, or my classmates or, indeed, the rest of the audience for the simple reason that none of us had a clue what the "correct" words were. I have since noticed that when these "classic malapropisms" appear in anthologies, most editors take no chances: They provide the correct word in parentheses after each malapropism. To my mind, that's like explaining the joke. What's the point?

Call me heretical, but the "immortal" Mrs. M. and her worn-out old chestnuts have been consigned to the box marked "Jokes Past Their Amuse-By Date." In their place is a selection of freshly minted malapropisms, and I can confidently say, without fear of contraception, that the only nerve they'll hit is your funny bone. See if this hits the spot: "A few years ago when there was a solar eclipse in England, I overheard my neighbors wisely advising a friend not to look directly at the sun as it would burn the back of their rectums." Ouch. Pass the Preparation H.

As Mrs. Malaprop gave her name to the malapropism, so Reverend Spooner gave his name to the spoon, I mean spoonerism—a slip of the tongue in which the initial letters or sounds of two or more words are switched (think, nosy cook/cosy nook). As he was both a real-life Oxford lecturer and man of the cloth, it might be argued that this Victorian gentleman already enjoyed an unfair advantage in the inanity stakes. Apparently he was prone to riding through the city of "Spreaming Dires" on his "well-boiled icicle" and addressing the students at New College thus:

> You have hissed all my mystery lectures, and were caught
> fighting a liar in the quad. Having tasted two worms, you will
> leave by the next town drain.

Jesus, did no one ever think to check the level in the old codger's claret decanter? Let us raise our glasses to the queer old dean, I mean, dear old … dear me, it's catching! Which of us hasn't got our words in a mucking fuddle—especially when we've had a drink?

But I count myself lucky. Only the taxi company I call for a cab home at the end of a long night on the sauce is witness to my embarrassment ("I'm red as a sheet," as Yogi Berra would say). Broadcasters and presenters who have a lingual malfunction have to suffer their blushes in front of an audience that may be in the millions. Their humiliation may be compounded if their blunder is then posted on a video-sharing website such as YouTube. As a courtesy to cybersurfers, where a blooper is available to hear or see on the net, it will be indicated by the letters "YT" in the credit line. Just do a simple word search to find the clip and savor the fluff in its full aural glory.

While verbal errors are understandable—we're only human, after all—you might think that technological advances would have all but wiped out the written error, given that most of us now use computers equipped with spellcheck and autocorrect facilities. Not a chance. Technology, far from eradicating mistakes, is actually *adding* to the error quotient. IT expert Sandy Reed has even coined a new word, "technopropism," to describe those mistakes that occur "when language and the tools of technology collide." A prime example involved a newspaper journalist who autocorrected the word "black" to "African American" in an article, then forgot to re-check the final copy. The published article included a description of a dog with "African American spots."

Sometimes you don't know whether the blame lies with the computer or the person operating it. A while ago, I was on the phone with an American acquaintance and happened to mention that I'd been given a box set of *Carry On* films. The other day I received an e-mail from him in which he asked if I've watched any of my "carrion movies." Now, I'm hoping this is a technopropism because, if not, it means he actually believes I am a fan of some weird film genre dedicated to the decaying flesh of dead animals.

Within these pages you'll find a glittering cast of Densa members that includes reality TV stars, sports commentators, high court judges as well as unsung idiots plucked from villages the world over. Together they cover the full speculum of stupidity—from the dippiness of Alice Tinker (she had a Teletubbies-themed wedding) to Jessica Simpson's reality checks (lest we forget the Chicken of the Sea incident).

Figures from real life rub shoulders with figures from fiction. On a single page, you may find Keith Richards from The Rolling Stones batting a line to Ali G who, in turn, volleys it to Tallulah Bankhead who then smashes it to Saffy from *Absolutely Fabulous*. Now there's a mixed doubles you never thought you'd ever see. Diverse as these characters are, they all occupy the same virtual space in our heads, so they sit comfortably beside each other—worryingly so, in certain cases. Take George W. Bush and Homer Simpson. Talk about bosom buddies. Cover their credit lines and you'd be hard pressed to tell whose line is whose: "I'm a commander guy ... We'll continue to enhance protection at ... our nuclear power pants." Are these the words of the dumbest dunderhead in America—or Homer Simpson?

Stupid remarks both intended and unintended are given equal billing. This won't please purist purveyors of blooperology whose strict code requires that all slips be "accidental." It's a stupid requirement, though, not only because it rules out some of the funniest lines but also because it's impossible to police. Even when the foolish remarks are made by real people, you can't be one hundred percent sure they were made unwittingly. And unless you were there to hear it or the event was recorded, you can't even be sure a line was uttered by the person credited.

A case in point is Samuel Goldwyn. He was the Polish immigrant who won fame as the producer of such unforgettable Hollywood movies as *Wuthering Heights, Stella Dallas* and *The Best Years of Our Lives* (for which he won an Oscar), but these days he's equally famous for his word-manglings known, imaginatively, as "Goldwynisms." What you may not know is that many of the best Goldwynisms were dreamed up by his press agents, most notably Ben Sonnenberg. Ironically, Sonnenberg was originally hired in order to keep a lid on the mogul's verbal goofs, which Goldwyn feared were making him a laughing stock in Tinseltown. What Sonnenberg discovered was that far from tarnishing his image, these eccentric turns of phrase were actually enhancing it. The wily publicist promptly performed a U-turn and went into production manufacturing new ones.

The upshot is that 70-odd years later it's virtually impossible to tell a genuine Goldwynism from a fake. That said, I do believe my own personal favorite is 24-carat Goldwyn because screenwriter Jean Negulesco swears he was there at the time. The story goes that the two were strolling in Negulesco's garden when Goldwyn spotted something. "Ah, that's my new sundial," says Jean. "Every day the sun casts a shadow from the piece of metal at the top. Since the shadow changes all through the day, you can tell what time it is." Goldwyn throws up his hands in astonishment. "My God!" he cries. "What will they think of next?"

Ah, bless his heart. "It is so pleasant to come across people more stupid than ourselves. We love them at once for being so," as Jerome K. Jerome wrote. Somebody else's blunder may give us a reassuring feeling of superiority, or an unnerving feeling of "There but for the grace of God go I," but, either way, it endears the blunderer to us by making them seem more human.

Politicians, always keen to seem more human, have caught on to this, and the roll call of those accused of trying to wheedle their way into our affections by "dumbing down" includes Silvio Berlusconi, the Italian Prime Minister, Bertie

Ahern, the Irish Taoiseach and Boris Johnson, the mayor of London. The latter plays on his clown's image to keep his citizens guessing: "Beneath the elaborately constructed veneer of the bumbling buffoon," he jests, "there may well be a bumbling buffoon." As a former journalist, he is fully aware of the useful publicity such tomfoolery generates, but could it also be a skillful ruse to deflect attention away from unpopular policies and the sometimes shady shenanigans of his personal life? Certainly there are those, like Jeremy Hardy, who sense darker forces at work beneath the greasepaint grin: "Boris Johnson may seem like a lovable buffoon but you know he wouldn't hesitate to line you all up against a wall and have you shot."

There are those who would say the same thing about George W. Bush. "The widespread suspicion he may be a dim bulb really lets Bush off too easily," argues Michael Kinsley. "It's not that he is incapable of thinking through the apparent contradictions in his own alleged core philosophy. It's that he can't be bothered." Jay Leno suspects a double bluff: "Bush is smart. I don't think that Bush will ever be impeached, because unlike Clinton, Reagan or even his father, George W. is immune from scandal. Because if George W. testifies that he had no idea what was going on, wouldn't you believe him?" Having spent many hours sifting the words of the President, my own feeling is that Ann Richards, herself a former Texas governor, comes closest to the truth: "Poor George, he can't help it—he was born with a silver foot in his mouth."

"There's no rehab for stupidity," as Chris Rock observes. Until such time as medical science can offer "brain jobs" or "gray matter enhancements," no amount of moolah can buy your way out of the idiocracy. Paris Hilton is heiress to the fortune of a famous hotel chain whose name escapes me (I'll check my towels when I get home). She has had the best education money can buy ("Use your spark of genius to build a better world," goes the motto of the private school she attended in New York, whose alumni include writer Truman Capote and artist Roy Lichtenstein). Yet despite enjoying the best blessings of existence, she will never escape her heirhead image. While her detractors assure us she really is as brainless as she behaves ("Like the state of Kansas: flat, white and easy to enter," quips Conan O'Brien), she and her supporters argue that it's all part of her "dumb blonde" schtick: "It's not how I am, it's the character I play."

Having spent many hours sifting through the celebutante's words, what's struck me is just how *little* she says. The common perception is that she is constantly putting her perfectly pedicured foot in her perfectly lipglossed mouth, but, actually, she's extremely guarded. Her "conversation" is, for the most part, innocuous and noncommittal, limited to a series of inane catchphrases, simpering squeals and grating giggles: "That's hot ... ewwww ... soooo grosss ... ha-ha hee-hee ... whatever." What the heck does that mean? Well, it means whatever you want it to mean. And that's the beauty of it as far as she is concerned. She is a blank slate onto which we can project our own meaning, and that, crucially, makes her ideal for marketing purposes.

Paris Hilton's intelligence may be just a notch above that of Tinkerbell (her pet Chihuahua, not Peter Pan's fairy friend, who is *wayyyyy* smarter), but when it comes to marketing, the gal is nothing short of a genius. Guided by the best business brains money can buy, she has built a multi-million dollar brand with perfume, fashion and jewelery lines, book deals, nightclub franchises, reality TV series and even a starring role in a Hollywood movie—a remake of Ingmar Bergman's *Cries and Whispers*. Just kidding. It's a romantic comedy called *The Hottie and the Nottie*, described by one discerning critic as, "about as funny as anal rape." "I'm laughing all the way to the bank," says Paris.

Paris Hilton is frequently held up as the epitome of our dumbed-down society, which worships vapid and vacuous celebs and makes them into role models for the young. Endless surveys tell us that kids today think Hitler's first name was "Heil" and that B.C. means "Before Cable." But The Stupid have always been with us. Two hundred years ago, an equivalent survey would have found that kids thought Nelson's first name was Half and Pompeii was destroyed by an overflow of larva.

The question is, Has idiocy become the *dominant* force in today's society? Have we made a cult of stupidity? In the past, there was a stigma attached to stupidity but there is no longer any shame in admitting that you've never read a book or finished school. Stupidity is now worn like a badge of honor. It's all the rage. "Stupidity is the new black!" screams the style section of *The Sunday Times* like it was the latest must-have accessory. Slogans on T-shirts that used to boast "I'm with Stupid" now boast "I am Stupid." On *The Simpsons*, Lisa catalogs the cultural and intellectual decline: "We are a town of lowbrows, no-brows and ignorami. We have eight malls, but no symphony; 32 bars but no alternative theater; 13 stores that begin with Le Sex ..."

And now there are bookstores pedalling books glorifying stupidity! Without condoning what William Gaddis calls "the deliberate cultivation of ignorance," perhaps there *is* something to be said for stupidity. Oscar Wilde certainly thought so:

> There is more to be said for stupidity than people imagine.
> Personally I have a great admiration for stupidity.
> It is a sort of fellow-feeling ...

It's true; there is a kinship. For all her fame and money, it's easier to identify with the no-talent that is Paris Hilton than, say, the über-talented ice queen Gwyneth Paltrow whose "blonde moments" are limited to two things: child-naming and choice of diet. Similarly, Princess Diana was a privileged, pampered princess, yet millions related to her because she was, as she herself put it, "as thick as two short planks." She left school without any qualifications except an award for Best Kept Hamster. And in the 2000 Presidential election, many preferred Dubya for his stumbling, "homespun" speeches to "automatons" like Al Gore who delivered slick and polished performances.

Stupidity is not only bonding, it's also essential to progress. Stupid people are, by definition, those with less sense and ability to reason. But their irrationality and illogicality may be the very qualities that make them more imaginative and creative. The ability to look at the world differently, to think outside the box, is crucial to innovation. Even brainiacs acknowledge this. Albert Einstein said, "I never came upon any of my discoveries through the process of rational thinking." And another egghead, Ludwig Wittgenstein, observed, "If people did not sometimes do silly things, nothing intelligent would ever get done."

The kind of stupidity celebrated in this collection is not rank ignorance; rather, it is "nonsense" in the tradition of Edward Lear and Lewis Carroll. It shares the same spirit of illogical logic, the same silly flights of fancy and the same playful delight in the quirks and quiddities of language *per se*. Sections like "Mangled Metaphors" and "New Proverbs" are delirious romps through Looking Glass territory where you can revel in the verbal pyrotechnics of the English language in all its whiz-bang vibrancy and versatility. Read it forward or backward, there's not a cliché in sight. Perhaps a more appropriate subtitle for this treasury would have been "Adventures in Blunderland."

"Stupidity has its sublime as well as genius, and he who carries that quality to absurdity has reached it," wrote Christoph Martin Wieland. So, who achieves the "sublimity of stupidity"? Certainly Groucho Marx, Woody Allen and Steven Wright. These comic philosophers can say something that sounds just plain stoopid but, on further contemplation, is seen to contain a deep existential truth. Such artful artlessness is a fiendishly difficult trick to pull off, a fine balancing act where the words are tottering on a tightrope between the profound and the ridiculous.

It's a helluva lot easier when it comes naturally—as with Lawrence "Yogi" Berra. He's a national treasure, fêted for his brilliance both as a baseball player for the New York Yankees and a phrase-maker. As his friend and fellow ballplayer, Joe Garagiola explains, "Yogi puts words together in ways nobody else would ever do. You may laugh and shake your head when Yogi says something strange like, 'It ain't over 'til it's over,' but soon you realize what he actually said makes perfect sense. And you find yourself using his words yourself because they are, after all, the perfect way to express a particular idea."

We all ought to keep some corner of our mind that is forever stupid. What better insulation against the woes of the world? There's a Peanuts cartoon in which Snoopy is performing one of his madcap dances while misery-merchant Lucy looks on disapprovingly. "You wouldn't be so happy if you knew about all the troubles in this world," she snipes. But the beagle is impervious to her doom mongering. "Don't tell me!" he counters, skipping blithely on. "I don't want to know!" And then, ears pert and grinning widely: "I'm outrageously happy in my stupidity."

That's the smartest thing I've heard all day.

FOOTNOTE: If you're wondering about the correct words to Mrs. M.'s malapropisms, they are: pinnacle; alligator; contiguous; hysterics. If you guessed them all correctly, you're either lying or did the play for your theater final at Harvard.

STOP THE PRESSES! Just got home and checked the towels in my linen closet, so I can now reliably inform you that the name of that famous hotel chain whose fortune Paris Hilton is heir to is Marriott.

THE
WORD

NAMES

I hate ridiculous names.
Peaches Honeyblossom Michelle Charlotte
Angel Vanessa Geldof, English socialite

Well, now that you're here, we may as well get to know each other. My name is Peabody. I suppose you know yours.   **Mr. Peabody, *The Bullwinkle Show***

My name is Les Dawson. That's a stage name, actually. I was christened "Friday Dawson" because when my father saw me he said to my mother, "I think we'd better call it a day."   **Les Dawson**

Are you called Cat because you bury your own poo?
          Frank Skinner, to television personality Cat Deeley

—Could I have your name?
—Well, you could, but it would be an incredible coincidence.
          Police officer and Kip Wilson, *Bosom Buddies*

I love my name. Paris is my favorite city. And Paris without the P is "heiress," isn't it?   **Paris Hilton, *Confessions of an Heiress***

Most people call their dogs Fergie. I'm kind of proud. You hear it in the park: "Fergie, come here!"   **Sarah Ferguson, The Duchess of York**

—Surely you can't be serious?
—I am serious … and don't call me Shirley.
          Ted Striker and Dr. Rumack, *Airplane!*

What's your name, Kate?   **Simon Bates, BBC Radio**

Well, I was born Mary Patterson, but then I married and naturally took my husband's name, so now I'm Neil Patterson.
          Stephen Fry, *A Bit of Fry and Laurie*

No, my name is Mike.   **Mike Hampton, Atlanta Braves pitcher, when asked by a schoolchild if he was rich**

Tom.   **Tom Nissalke, former Houston Rockets coach, when a reporter asked him how to pronounce his name**

—What do you call a Frenchman wearing sandals?
—Felipe Felop.

Anon.

I'll phone up [the Hilton hotel, Paris] and say, "Hi, it's Paris Hilton," and they'll say, "Yes, this is the Paris Hilton." So I'm like, "Yes, I know, I'm Paris Hilton." It can go on for hours like some bad comedy film.

Paris Hilton

What if the 1972 Democratic National Committee headquarters had been located [not in the Watergate Hotel but] in the Mayflower Hotel? Journalists would think it exceedingly clever to add the word "flower" to the end of any scandal: Iranflower, Whitewaterflower, Monicaflower, Flowersflower.

Jerry Pannullo

You can't call a child Arthur! Every Tom, Dick and Harry is called Arthur.

Sam Goldwyn

I called my son Jett, and I wanted to call my daughter Qantas, but my wife wouldn't let me.

John Travolta

Frank Zappa named his daughter Moon Unit. And everybody knows that's a boy's name.

John Hinton

When he heard your daughter's name was Portia, he said, "Why did they name her after a car?"

Wanda Gershwitz, *A Fish Called Wanda*

—Why did you choose Apple as a name for your little girl?
—I don't know … we just loved it … We thought it was a unique name but we didn't expect the media onslaught … It's not like calling a little girl Shithouse …
—Was Shithouse on the list?

Jonathan Ross and Gwyneth Paltrow, *Friday Night with Jonathan Ross*

That cartoon character, Asterix.
I wonder how rude his real name is.

Jimmy Carr

One was called "Whitey" for no reason at all. To be fair, his name was White.

Hank Marvin

People started calling me "Fiery" because "Fiery" rhymes with "Fred" just like "Typhoon" rhymes with "Tyson."

Fred Trueman, cricketer

I am going to name my first wife after him.

Captain Benjamin "Hawkeye" Pierce, *M*A*S*H*

—Shaw?
—Positive.   **Gladys Flynn and George Bernard Shaw**

In giving my details to a Spanish website, I found that it was compulsory to give
a middle name, which I lack. The best I could do was to put "none" in the
appropriate space. This the system recognized and helpfully translated. I now get
letters addressed to David Nada Stevenson.   **David Stevenson**

I am the only man in the world whose first and second names are both
synonyms for "penis."   **Peter O'Toole**

Danger could be my middle name—but it's John.   **Eddie Izzard**

—Let me start with Terry. What was his full name?
—I don't know … It was, like, a weird Greek name. Like Douglas.
                                                     Interviewer and Paris Hilton

I meet so many people. I don't even know some of my friends' names.
                                                                   Paris Hilton

A tourist once stopped to admire a North Carolina mule. He asked the mule's
owner what the animal's name was. The farmer said, "I don't know, but we call
it Bill."   **Samuel James Ervin Jr., former North Carolina senator**

It's a colugo, or flying lemur, although this is something of a misnomer since it
doesn't actually fly and it certainly isn't a lemur.
                                              Sir David Attenborough, *Planet Earth*

We have a cat called Ben Hur. We called it Ben until it had kittens.
                                                                   Sally Poplin

"Jimmy"—isn't that the name of a baby kangaroo?
                                              Helen Adams, *Big Brother 2* (U.K.)

—A rose by any other name would smell as sweet.
—Not if you called 'em stenchblossoms.
—Or crapweeds.   **Lisa, Bart and Homer Simpson, *The Simpsons***

I think they named the orange before the carrot.   **Demetri Martin**

QUESTIONS

Ignorance is bliss. Oedipus ruined a great sex life
by asking too many questions.
Stephen Colbert

—Can I ask a dumb question?
—Better than anyone else I know.
Rose Nylund and Dorothy Zbornak, *The Golden Girls*

—Where were you born?
—Goa.
—Goa, that wonderful former Portuguese colony. Tell me, have you ever been
there? **Bob Monkhouse and contestant, *Bob's Full House***

Where were you first born? **Jools Holland**

The stupidest question I've ever been asked is whether Hermione Gingold is my
real name. Now I just say, "Not really. I was born Norma Jean Baker."
Hermione Gingold

If you were a tree, what kind of tree would you be?

Barbara Walters, to Katharine Hepburn

What vegetable would your husband most like to sit on?
Bob Eubanks, *The Newlywed Game*

—Which kitchen utensil would you most like to be?
—Um ... a butter knife, so I could cut and spread ...
Interviewer and recording artist Nelly

... and how long have you had this lifelong ambition? **Gary Davis**

Why, why, why ... I know you're a talk-show host, but why all the questions?
Janice Dickinson, to Jonathan Ross,
Friday Night with Jonathan Ross

Yesterday I saw a chicken crossing the road. I asked it why. It told me it was
none of my business. **Steven Wright**

—What grows in the marsh, baby?
—Marshmallows?

www.overheardatthebeach.com

Do you have blacks, too?

George W. Bush, to Brazilian President Fernando Cardoso

When did you start to next intend to look—let me strike that. It seems so bad that it was almost Shakespeare.

Lawyer, actual transcript from official court records

I'm asking a question. It's rather long. But since I was confused before, I want to make sure that my confusion is clear.

Lawyer, actual transcript from official court records

How fatal is it?

Mike Morris

WORDS

I will use big words from time to time, the meanings of which
I will only vaguely perceive, in hopes such cupidity
will send you scampering to your dictionary:
I will call such behavior "public service."
Harlan Ellison

—Sam, I have dire news.
—Good or bad?

Diane Chambers and Sam Malone, *Cheers*

—Lascivious adulterer!
—Don't you dare call me that again until I have looked it up!

Anna and Fritz Fassbender, *What's New Pussycat?*

K.O.

Mork, *Mork & Mindy*

—What's a castrati?
—I don't know, but I'm sure it's spicy.

Bart and Marge Simpson, *The Simpsons*

I've decided to skip "holistic." I don't know what it means, and I don't want to know. That may seem extreme, but I followed the same strategy toward Gestalt and the twist, and lived to tell the tale.   **Calvin Trillin**

—I know you can be underwhelmed, and you can be overwhelmed, but can you ever just be, like, whelmed?
—I think you can in Europe.
Chastity and Bianca Stratford, *10 Things I Hate About You*

I always get nominated to do all the press interviews because I'm so eloquent and Liam is the opposite of it—whatever that is.
Noel Gallagher, of Oasis

I can remember a reporter asking me for a quote, and I didn't know what a quote was. I thought it was some kind of soft drink.
Joe DiMaggio

—Are you a volatile player?
—Well, I can play in the center, on the right and occasionally on the left side.
Reporter and David Beckham

—Can you give me an anagram for the word "on"?
—No.   **Joseph Romm**

What's the plural of "ignited"?   **Gaby Roslin**

—He's trying to make a mountain out of a molehill.
—He wants you to wear a padded bra?
Diane Chambers and Carla Tortelli, *Cheers*

Adebayor and Fabregas are almost telepethetic ... they're telepephatic ... they're pepathic ... they're pathetic ... in fact they're not, they're really good.
Graham Taylor, British soccer coach

The idea of putting gondolas on Blessington Lake to boost tourism is well and good in theory, but tell me this, who is going to feed them?
Councillor, County Wicklow, Ireland

Who ever thought up the word "mammogram"? Every time I hear it, I think I'm supposed to put my breast in an envelope and send it to someone.
Jan King

—Hey, what does "apprehensive" mean?
—It means you're scared—with a college education.
Moe and Larry (The Three Stooges), *Merry Mavericks*

If the English language made any sense, "lackadaisical" would have something
to do with a shortage of flowers.
Doug Larson

—Gone? What do you mean, gone?!
—Are you just panicking, or do you really not know the meaning of the word?
Joe Hackett and Lowell Mather, *Wings*

I wonder what the most intelligent thing ever said was that started with the
word "Dude." "Dude, these are isotopes." "Dude, we removed your kidney.
You're gonna be fine." "Dude, I'm so stoked to win this Nobel Prize. I just
wanna thank Kevin and Turtle and all my homies."
Demetri Martin

Bunsen burner: A lot of you are just surprised you heard that word again, aren't
you? Nobody mentions it. It just doesn't come up in the real world, does it?
Jimeoin

The allegations were denied as the police continue to question the allegators.
Reporter, television news

—Don't be facetious!
—Oh, keep politics out of this!
Sal Van Hoyden and Chester Hooton, *Road to Utopia*

I asked my teacher what an oxymoron was, and he said, "I don't know what an
'oxy' is, bastard."
Arthur Smith and Chris England

—I'm doing this competition on the cereal packet. You have to write in ten
words what cornflakes mean to you. So I wrote: "Cornflakes, Cornflakes,
Cornflakes, Cornflakes, Cornflakes, Cornflakes, Cornflakes, Cornflakes,
Cornflakes."
—Pathetic. You'll never win. That's only nine words.
—Oh, yeah … "Cornflakes."
Vyvyan Basterd and Rick, *The Young Ones*

NEW WORDS

A truck containing hundreds of copies of *Roget's Thesaurus* overturned on the highway. The local newspaper reported that onlookers were "stunned, overwhelmed, astonished, gobsmacked, amazed, bewildered and dumbfounded."
Anon.

I've coined new words, like "misunderstanding" and "Hispanically."
George W. Bush

"Arbolist" ... look up the word. I don't know, maybe I made it up. Anyway, it's an arbo-tree-ist, somebody who knows about trees.   **George W. Bush**

I don't think we need to be subliminable about the differences between our views on prescription drugs.   **George W. Bush (YT)**

This is what I'm good at. I like meeting people, my fellow citizens, I like interfacing with them.   **George W. Bush**

—Have you always lived in Beaumont since you came off the farm?
—No, I lived in Orange before I married and demarried.
Lawyer and witness, actual transcript from official court records

I put confidence in the American people, in their ability to sort through what is fair and what is unfair, what is ugly and what is unugly.   **George Bush Sr.**

The boom times are getting even more boomer.   **Bertie Ahern, Irish Taoiseach**

I can't be dishappy with that.   **Elizabeth Tweddle, gymnast**

I don't know what happened, but there was a major malmisorganization problem there.   **Murray Walker, sports commentator**

It's simply beyond words. It's incalculacable.   **Michael Scott, *The Office***

They said, "You know, this issue doesn't seem to resignate with the people."
And I said, "You know something? Whether it resignates or not doesn't matter
to me ..."
                                                                    George W. Bush

After the bombing, most Iraqis saw what the perpetuators of this attack were
trying to do.   George W. Bush

He's completely unoverawed ...   James Hunt, racecar driver

We have leadership—there's just no followership.
                                            George Danielson, former congressman

I resent your insinuendoes.   Richard J. Daley, former mayor of Chicago

This is untoward. This is not toward!
                                                            Tracy Jordan, *30 Rock*

I am a person who recognizes the fallacy of humans.
                                                                    George W. Bush

When something is so, so sick, it's risiculous. It's sick and ridiculous. Risiculous.
See, I have my own dictionary.   Fergie

—So, we should totally take a consensuous on that with the entire team.
—Consensus.
—What?
—Consensus.
—[*laughing*] I should totally carry around a thesaurius with me!
                        Manager and employee, www.overheardintheoffice.com

LANGUAGES

In Paris they simply stared when I spoke to them in French;
I never did succeed in making those idiots understand
their own language.
Mark Twain

Spain is going to be difficult for me. I've never had to learn a language and now
I do.   David Beckham

—Can you speak Spanish?
—I don't know, I've never tried.
P. G. Wodehouse, *Ring for Jeeves*

—I can speak French: *Sí, sí, señor*.
—That's Spanish.
—Gee, I can speak Spanish, too!
Sid Silvers and Jack Benny

—Seamus, do you understand French?
—I do if it's spoken in Irish.
Anon.

The Dutch boxer Regilio Tuur can speak four languages, which is amazing for someone so short.
Commentator, NBC

Oh, you're speaking German. I'm sorry, I thought there was something wrong with you.
Basil Fawlty, *Fawlty Towers*

Do they speak Portuganese in Portugal? I thought Portugal was in Spain.
Jade Goody, British TV personality

She speaks 18 languages and can't say "no" in any of them.
Dorothy Parker

As the French say, I have that certain "I don't know what."
Dr. Evil, *Austin Powers: The Spy Who Shagged Me*

They speak all the languages of the rainbow here.
Jackie Stewart

Listen! Someone's screaming in agony. Fortunately I speak it fluently.
Spike Milligan

—How's your Latin?
—*Comme ci, comme ça.*
—Good!
Mike Allen and caller, *Talk Radio*

I can't even spell "spaghetti," never mind talk Italian. How could I tell an Italian to get the ball—he might grab mine.
Brian Clough, on the influx of foreign soccer players to the U.K.

Pepsi Brings Your Ancestors Back from the Grave!
Chinese translation of the slogan "Come Alive with Pepsi"

"Eureka" is Greek for "This bath is too hot!"
Dr. Who

Everybody's talking French. I don't understand.

Geoffrey Boycott during his trial for assault in France

It's always a mistake trying to speak French to the Frogs. As Noël Coward once remarked, "They don't understand their own language."

Robert Morley

Boy, those French, they have a different word for everything.

Steve Martin

He thought lacrosse was what you found in la church.

Robin Williams

"Buffet"—a French word that means, "Get up and get it yourself."

Ron Dentinger

It's déjà vu all over again.   **Yogi Berra**

Interpreter! Interpreter! How do you say the opposite of *"Vive La France"*?

Winston Churchill, exasperated by Charles de Gaulle

I was in a Dunkin' Donuts in Canada, and the menu was in French—the whole thing. And I asked the woman for a coffee, and she only spoke French. Now, I've taken a lot of drugs in my time, but I've got to say that the single most frightening experience of my life was thinking, "I could have swore I was in fuckin' Canada when I got off that tour bus. And now I'm in … am I? No, I don't know." And then I said to the woman, "You can speak English, can't you?" And I think she was getting annoyed that I was being a bit rude by that point, because she was only speaking French. I was going, "I know you can speak English. We're in Canada. And I know you understand what I'm saying." I may have brought up something about the war and then left.

Noel Gallagher, of Oasis

Julio Cesar Chavez speaks English, Spanish and he's bilingual, too.

Don King

I bought a self-learning record to learn Spanish. I turned it on and went to sleep. During the night, the record slipped. The next day I could only stutter in Spanish.

Steven Wright

I speak Esperanto like a native.   **Spike Milligan**

I speak 12 languages—English is the bestest.

Stefan Bergman, mathematician

English? Who needs that? I'm never going to England!

Homer Simpson, *The Simpsons*

—Don't you know the Queen's English?
—Of course he knows she's English.

Boycie and Marlene, *Green, Green Grass*

There are certain words in our society that have changed totally. I was in America, where a very good friend of mine—an academic, highly intelligent—and was walking across Central Park, and he says, all of a sudden, "Ah, shit! I've stood in some dog's doo-doo!" Now, "doo-doo" is shit. "Shit" is not doo-doo. So you have this word, which has lost its total meaning … The Americans use "shit" for everything now except shit.

Dave Allen

The BBC first spoke to another nation in an experimental broadcast to the United States in 1923. At the time it was questionable that we spoke the same language; it took a team of translators a week to figure out that "bangers and mash" were not some veiled British threat.

Bill Clinton

It is of interest to note that while some dolphins are reported to have learned English—up to 50 words used in correct context—no human being has been reported to have learned dolphinese.

Carl Sagan

PRONUNCIATION

Never eat anything you can't pronounce.
Erma Bombeck

—I wouldn't mind a quickie.
—It's pronounced quiche.

Kirk Sutherland and Norris Cole, *Coronation Street*

—[*reading*] The Grand Pricks takes place in Silverstone.
—It's Grand Prix. You pronounce it "pree."
—Well, it says "pricks" here.   **Little girl and TV host**

Platypus? I thought it was pronounced "platy-ma-pus." Has it changed?
Jessica Simpson

—How do you do, Margot?
—The "t" is silent, as in Harlow.   **Jean Harlow and Margot Asquith**

In a recent interview, Governor Arnold Schwarzenegger said, "Cannabis is not a drug." Of course, when Arnold said it, it sounded like, "Cannibals need a hug."
Conan O'Brien

I once sat through a lecture about voluntary service overseas given by a dour Swiss Red Cross official that would have been bum-numbingly boring were it not for the fact that all the way through he pronounced "U.S. Peace Corps" as "U.S. Peace Corpse."   **Rosemarie Jarski**

I was once paged at JFK airport as "Mr. No One."

Peter Noone

That e-mail was from Ann On.
DJ, reading an e-mail from "anon" (anonymous)

A pissometer?
Prince Philip, being shown a piezometer, a device for measuring water depth in soil, on a visit to a cotton farm in New South Wales

The award was presented post-humorously.

Showbiz **reporter**

Back in 1981, Tom Harkin, a senator from Iowa, was asked to make a speech on health-care reform. He instructed his speechwriter to draft something that would show he was "in touch" with everyday folks. The speechwriter dutifully slotted in a reference to *ER*, the top-rated television medical drama at the time. The senator's speech went swimmingly—right up until he reached *ER*, which, alas, he'd never heard of, and duly pronounced, "Errrr."
Rosemarie Jarski

That was "Dennis, Dennis" by Blondie.
Radio DJ, on "Denis, Denis"

General de Gaulle and his wife were at a state banquet in Paris attended by the British Prime Minister Harold Macmillan and his wife. Macmillan asked Madame de Gaulle, "What are your hopes and wishes for the future?" "A penis," she replied without blinking an eye. The awkward silence was broken when the general leaned over and said, "I think the word is pronounced 'happiness.'"

Paul Ellis

FREUDIAN SLIPS

Pardon me, your Freudian slip is showing ...
Anon.

Okay, there you get two different views of what this election is about, and some say this erection is—this election—is about Iraq and Iraq only.

Jim Angle, Fox News (YT)

We have to introduce another player, and with a great deal of pleasure, we present Karen Lesko. Hi Karen! Doesn't she have pretty nipples—er, pretty dimples ...

Gene Rayburn, *Match Game* (YT)

She lost her tittle thanks to—her TITLE ... the former Miss Nevada could take Donald Trump to court in a quest to get her tiara back ...

News anchor, Fox News (YT)

Right after the break, we're going to interview Eric Weihenmayer, who climbed the highest mountain in the world—Mount Everest, but—he's gay, I mean, he's gay, excuse me, he's blind, so we'll hear about that coming up ...

Cynthia Izaguirre, BBC News (YT)

J.Lo's new song, "Jenny From the Block," all about Lopez's roots, about how she's still a neighborhood gal at heart, but folks from that street in New York, the Bronx section, sound more likely to give her a curb-job than a blow-job ... er, a b-block-party.

Shepard Smith, Fox News, November 4, 2002 (YT)

The Deputy Police Chief says six officers were killed, including the district's top cock ... top cock ... COP ... after the vehicle they were riding in was sprayed with bullets.

Jane Skinner, Fox News (YT)

And later we'll have action from the men's cockless pairs.

Sue Barker, commentating on a rowing race

I would like to spank—*thank*— Spike Jonze.

Meryl Streep, misreading a faxed British Academy of Film and Television Arts acceptance speech (YT)

Isn't Halle Berry the most beautiful woman? I have a film I'd like to be in her with—I mean, I'd like to be with her in.

Ewan McGregor

Who is Heather Mills shagging—suing?   **Reporter, Radio Scotland**

At Oxford Crown Court, Donald Neilson denied he was the Pink Panther ... Black Panther.   **Reporter, BBC Radio**

As I was telling my husb— as I was telling President Bush ...

Condoleezza Rice, unmarried National Security Advisor

The best way to defeat the totalitarian of hate is with an ideology of hope—an ideology of hate—excuse me—with an ideology of hope.

George W. Bush

National Hunt Service—National Health Service.

Queen Elizabeth II, in her annual speech to Parliament, 2003

The United States has much to offer the Third World War.

Ronald Reagan, in a speech about the Third World. The error was repeated nine times in the same speech.

Mr. Ronald Reagan has lost his head over President Carter ... er, I beg your pardon ... Mr. Ronald Reagan has lost his lead over President Carter.

Newsreader, BBC World Service

Facts are stupid things.

Ronald Reagan, misquoting John Adams, "Facts are stubborn things."

For seven-and-a-half years I've worked alongside him. And I'm proud to have been his partner. And we'd have triumphs. We've made some mistakes. We've had some sex—uh, setbacks …

George Bush Sr., on working with Ronald Reagan (YT)

We recognize that these cunts in defense medical services have gone too far.

John Spellar, Junior Defense Secretary, talking about cuts in services, in the British House of Commons

And tonight northern areas can expect incest and rain—I'm sorry, incessant rain.

Weather forecaster

We'll be back with the recap after this message.

Ralph Kiner, broadcaster

DAFFYNITIONS

A chair is a piece of furniture. I am not a chair because no one has ever sat on me.

Ann Widdecombe, on the call for gender-neutral Parliamentary language in the U.K.

Depends what your definition of "is" is.   **Bill Clinton**

[*writing lines on the blackboard as a punishment*] No one cares what my definition of "is" is.   **Bart Simpson, *The Simpsons***

Abbreviate: the cheese we had yesterday   **Hank Levinson**

À la carte: Muslim wheelbarrow   ***I'm Sorry I Haven't a Clue***

Aloof: top of a Chinese house   **Alan Burke**

Antediluvian: one who is against the support of Paris museums

Marvin Goodman

Antipasto: weight-watchers   **Bernard H. Cohen**

Aquarium: lava lamp with feces   **David Corrado**

Aquarium: interactive television for cats   **Anon.**

Autoeroticism: necking in cars — Peter De Vries

Bacillus: Roman god of germs — Carol Drew

Balloon: bad breath holder — Demetri Martin

Benign: what you can't wait to do when you're eight
Jeffrey Rich

Bicentennial: sexually confused 100-year-old — Paula Drechsler

Bidet: D-Day minus two — Albert G. Miller

Bigamy: a large, small person — William Honig

Bilious: in debt — David R. Scott

Bricklayer: confused chicken — Anon.

Brouhaha: the joy of cooking — J. B. Hapgood

Buffet: a gay shoeshine boy — Hilary Solomon

Buttress: a long strand of derrière hair — Jennifer Hart

Dichotomy: operation performed on lesbians to make them normal
Kenneth Tynan

Fallacy: cocky — *I'm Sorry I Haven't a Clue*

Feckless: celibate in Ireland
Jeremy Hardy, *I'm Sorry I Haven't a Clue*

Flabbergasted: appalled over how much weight you have gained
Michelle Feeley

Ignoranus: a person who is both stupid and an asshole
Victor Lewis-Smith

Negligent: describes a condition in which you absent-mindedly answer the door in your nightie — Sandra Hull

Oyster: a person who sprinkles his conversation with Yiddish expressions

Meg Sullivan

Paper clips: the larval stage of wire coat hangers

Jerry Scott & Jim Borgman

Racket: a small pair of breasts   **Jerry Pannullo**

Seersucker: one who spends all her money on fortune-tellers

Peter De Vries

Shelf-gratification: thumbing through the men's magazines at a newsstand

Chris Doyle

Spatula: a tiff among vampires   **Anon.**

Willy-nilly: impotent   **Beth Benson**

GRAMMAR & PUNCTUATION

In the social sciences, articles that have titles with colons have a
higher acceptance rate than those without colons.
The Australian *magazine*

The goals of this country is to enhance prosperity and peace.
George W. Bush, at the White House Conference on Global Literacy

I'm from the southern states. I asked this northern woman, "Where are y'all from?"
and she said, "I'm from a place where we don't end our sentences with
prepositions." So I said, "OK, where are y'all from, bitch?"
Charlene Stillfield, *Designing Women*

And I want to say anything is possible. Comma. You know.
Frank Bruno, former boxing champion

Should "anal retentive" have a hyphen?   **Anon.**

And with an alphabetical irony, Nigeria follows New Zealand.

David Coleman, sportscaster

Grammar school never taught me anything about grammar.

Isaac Goldberg

I thought the conjugation of verbs meant saying, "Drink, drank, drunk." I asked Kaplan to conjugate "fail," and he said, "Fail, failed, bankrupt."

Leo Rosten

I am the Roman emperor, and am above grammar.   **Emperor Sigismund**

LITERALLY

Literally: the sound a human rectum makes when trying to pronounce the word "figuratively"
The Devil's Dictionary X

Klaus is the son of a man who buys, sells and breeds horses. So he was literally born in the saddle.

Derek Thompson, horseracing commentator

When those stalls open, the horses are literally going to explode.

Brough Scott, horseracing commentator

Princess Anne's horse is literally eating up the ground.

Peter Bromley, horseracing commentator

My grandfather, King George VI, who had literally been catapulted onto the throne …   **Prince Edward**

You can row down the river, literally, following in Constable's footsteps.

The Travel Show, BBC

I'm telling you that Porsche was literally right up my arse in the fast lane of the motorway.   **Elaine Roberts**

Dido was our secret weapon until she literally exploded onto the scene with one swift blow.   **Mohd Firhad, record executive, on singer Dido**

Then she met a bloke called Fritz—literally. That was his name.

Simon Bates

Rangers have been so far ahead. Now they've gone onto, literally, another planet.

Geoff Webster, sportscaster

After that goal you could literally see Arsenal's players deflating.

Micky Quinn, former British soccer coach

And as Mansell comes into the pits, he's quite literally sweating his eyeballs out.

Commentator, ITV (U.K.)

I was one of the boys, literally.

Rachael Heyhoe-Flint, cricketer

And Greg LeMond has literally come back from the dead to lead the Tour de France.

Phil Liggett, sports commentator

She literally wiped the court with her opponent.

Wimbledon tennis commentator

Perhaps the most picturesque use of "literally" was that of a writer who asserted that "for five years Mr. Gladstone was literally glued to the Treasury Bench."

E. W. Fordham

The overlarge vicarage of a Westmorland parish was described at a local meeting as "literally a white elephant round the neck of the incumbent."

E. M. Bullock

I went back to the Isle of Man quite literally with my tail between my legs.

J. P. Donleavy, Irish author

IDIOTIC IDIOMS

I think modern science should graft functional wings on a pig,
simply so no one can ever use that stupid saying again.
Anon.

You can't turn a sow's ear into a rose—or a flower.

Mike Parry

You've really put your finger on the nail there.   Brenda Ellison

Let's hope it's not a case of sore grapes.   Alan Brazil

They can't afford to take their minds off the gas.   Andy Townsend

We should turn a blind ear to that.   Alan Mason

Been there. Done there.   David Genser

He will need every tool in the book today.   Andy Townsend

You're barking up the wrong dog there.   Alan Webb

It's the stupid economy.   Robin D. Grove

There's an old saying in Tennessee—I know it's in Texas, probably in
Tennessee—that says, "Fool me once, shame on—shame on you. Fool me—you
can't get fooled again."
                        George W. Bush, trying to say, "Fool me once, shame on you;
                                     fool me twice, shame on me." (YT)

What a waste it is to lose one's mind, or not to have a mind is being very
wasteful. How true that is.
                        Dan Quayle, trying to make reference to the motto of the
                    United Negro College Fund, "A mind is a terrible thing to waste."

Is the Pope a Cadillac?   Jennifer Hart

He's treading on dangerous water there.   Ron Atkinson

Tom has—we all have—the right to practice how we feel. It finally becomes
unfair. Don't judge someone until they have tossed your salad.
                                              John Travolta on Tom Cruise

I want to hear it so quiet we can hear a mouse dropping.
                                     Gregory Ratoff, film director and actor

If you can't stand the heat in the dressing room, get out of the kitchen.
                                                    Terry Venables

Before the game, our dressing room was like Dunkirk before they went over the
trenches.   **John Sillett, British former soccer coach**

There wasn't room to swing a rat.   Serena Martins

That's just the tip of the ice cube.

Neil Hamilton, former member of Parliament

He's a wolf in cheap clothing.

Jack Browne

They've got old shoulders on their heads.

J. P. R. Williams

This could well be the goose that killed the golden egg.

City council member

It's like finding a haystack full of needles.

Leo Rosten

It was a Catch 50-50 situation, really.

Dean Willey

We're still as sharp as a button here.

David Vine, sportscaster

As the old saying goes, people in glasses shouldn't throw stones.

Alan Smith

Does a high-ranking religious figure evacuate his bowels in a wooded area?

Mambo, *Duckman*

An eye for a tooth.

Hermine Stover

Nigel and I hit it off like a horse on fire.

Tony Britton

This is the icing on the gravy.

Lucas Glover

Well, we'll be back again tomorrow, all bright and bushy-eyed.

David Vine, sportscaster

As they say in Italy, it's Goodnight Vienna.

Reporter, Century FM Radio (U.K.)

NEW PROVERBS

Wise men make proverbs, but fools repeat them.
Samuel Palmer

Romeo wasn't built in a day.

Ryan Potts

Where there's smoke, there must be someone smoking.

Tagline, *Easy Living*

Once bread becomes toast, it can never go back.

Ajax, *Duckman*

In the City of the Bald, barbers are beggars.

T. Griffiths

People who live in *châteaux* shouldn't throw *tomateaux*.

J. B. Morton

People who live in glass houses shouldn't walk around in their underwear.

Bill Cosby

People who live in glass houses have to answer the bell.

Bruce Patterson

The hand that turns the doorknob opens the door.

D. H. Anderson

Don't get mad, get angry.

Edwina Currie

Never the bride, always the bridegroom.

Peter Jones

You don't have to have been a horse to be a jockey.

Arrigo Sacchi

Two heads are better than none.

Jean Green

A big mouth is good for cooling soup.

Pete Finnerty

Gloves make a poor present for a man with no hands.

George Van Schaick

Even the finest shoe makes a terrible hat.

Japanese proverb

It is better to wear out your slippers dancing than to have your feet cut off.

Hermine Stover

Who has legs must wash two knees.

Wendy Cope

Many hands make a tall horse.

Michael Russell

You can lead a horse to water, but before you push him in, just stop and think how a wet horse smells.

George Gobel

A nose that can see is worth two that sniff.

Eugéne Ionesco

A dill pickle makes a soggy bookmark.

Anon.

You can't make a silk purse out of a sow's ear, but there's nothing to stop you making a lovely pork pie.　　　　　　**Humphrey Lyttelton**

When you see the writing on the wall ... you're in the toilet.

Redd Foxx

The hand that wears the boxing glove cannot lift the vol-au-vent to the lips.

Bill Greenwell

A bird in the hand makes it difficult to blow your nose.

Richard Betten

When an owl comes to a mouse picnic, it's not there for the sack races.

Thomas Banacek, *Banacek*

It's always darkest just after the lights go out.

David Robinson

A person with false teeth may still speak the truth.　　　　　　　**V. Earnest Cox**

Truth is seldom like a howling pancake.

Jonathan R. Partington, mathematician

A slug in mucus wins few friends.　　　　　　**Jan Rut-Brown**

He who drinks borsht with a cross bear may carry home salt, but he will limp.

Sanford Meschkow

If only rich men could have ugly daughters, the czar would be a woodcutter.

Sanford Meschkow

Never shake hands with a stricken cat.　　　　　　**Mark Greitzer**

If auntie had a moustache, he'd be an uncle. ·　　　　　　**Polish proverb**

You can lead a herring to water, but you have to walk really fast or he'll die.
Rose Nylund, *The Golden Girls*

It ain't over till the fat lady eats.

John Kammer

SILLY SIMILES

In comparison, there's no comparison.
Ron Greenwood

John and Mary had never met. They were like two hummingbirds who had also never met.
Russell Beland

She walked into my office like a centipede with 98 missing legs.

Jonathan Paul

She grew on him like she was a colony of E. coli and he was room-temperature Canadian beef.
Brian Broadus

He fell for her like his heart was a mob informant and she was the East River.
Brian Broadus

He was deeply in love. When she spoke, he thought he heard bells, as if she were a garbage truck backing up.
Susan Reese

She jerked away from me like a startled fawn might, if I had a startled fawn and it jerked away from me.
Raymond Chandler

The sunset displayed rich, spectacular hues like a JPEG file at 10 percent cyan, 10 percent magenta, 60 percent yellow and 10 percent black.
Jennifer Hart

He was as tall as a six-foot-three-inch tree.

Jack Bross

His fountain pen was so expensive it looked as if someone had grabbed the Pope, turned him upside down and started writing with the tip of his big pointy hat.
Jeffrey Carl

The plan was simple, like my brother-in-law Phil. But unlike Phil, this plan just might work.

Malcolm Fleschner

And Keegan was there like a surgeon's knife … bang!

Bryon Butler

No cow's like a horse, and no horse like a cow. That's one similarity anyhow.

Piet Hein, scientist

Like peas in a pub.

Father Dougal, *Father Ted*

It looked like something resembling white marble, which was probably what it was: something resembling white marble.

Douglas Adams

The little boat gently drifted across the pond exactly the way a bowling ball wouldn't.

Russell Beland

You're walking through this competition like a piece of cake. Mike Read

I'm always thinking one step ahead, like a … carpenter … that makes stairs.

Andy Bernard, *The Office*

I want to pay tribute to everyone at the magazine who has helped with its current success … I have been propelled by their talents, as a fat German tourist may be transported by superior alpinists to the summit of Everest.

Boris Johnson, departing *Spectator* magazine editor

MANGLED METAPHORS

It's a strange world of language in which skating on thin ice can get you into hot water.

Franklin P. Jones

We didn't have metaphors in my day. We didn't beat about the bush.

Fred Trueman

Gentlemen, the apple of discord has been thrown into our midst; and if it be not nipped in the bud, it will burst into a conflagration which will deluge the world.

Sir Boyle Roche, Member of Parliament

It's really got up his goat.

Sarah MacDonald

He's got too many cats in the fire.

Joan Roach

There comes a time in the affairs of man when he must take the bull by the tail and face the situation.

W. C. Fields

So before a storm in a teacup brews, nip it in the bud.

Russell Grant, astrologer

I don't think it helps people to start throwing white elephants and red herrings at each other.

Bertie Ahern, Irish Taoiseach

Jerusalem wasn't built in a day.

Robert Maxwell, media magnate

If you let that sort of thing go on, your bread and butter will be cut right out from under your feet.

Ernest Bevin, British Foreign Minister

It's dog eat dog in this rat race.

John Deacon

And this is the real carrot at the end of the rainbow.

Paul Lyneham

I have a feeling everyone is putting two and two together and making four.

Alan Smith

It doesn't take a lot to figure that out. It's not rocket salad.

Bill Green

Smoke and daggers ...

Bertie Ahern, Irish Taoiseach

He can't have it both ways. He can't take the high horse and then claim the low road.

George W. Bush

It looks like the cows have come home to roost.

Lieutenant Frank Drebin, *The Naked Gun 2½: The Smell of Fear*

He's not the sharpest cookie in the jar.

Mark Jones

He's a big clog in their machine.   Yogi Berra

The phrase "can of beans" comes to mind.
John Humphreys, *Today*, BBC Radio (YT)

The window of opportunity will be blown completely out of the water.
Geraldine Kennedy

I think you've hit the nose on the nail there.
Kevin Greening

He's been burning the midnight oil at both ends.
Sid Waddell

The boys' feet have been up in the clouds since the win.
Alan Buckley, British soccer coach

If we start counting our chickens before they hatch, they won't lay any eggs in the basket.   Bobby Robson

He put all his eggs in one basket and pulled out a cracker.
Dennis Taylor

That's 35 yards if it's a day ...   Des Lynam, sports commentator

I suppose, if you let this genie out of the bottle you'd get, to continue the allusion, a whole lot of butterflies out of Pandora's box.
Pru Goward, Australian politician

We have really opened a worm's nest.   Simon Bates

Water is a burning issue.   Ieuan Owen

I'm glad two sides of the cherry have been put forward.
Geoffrey Boycott, BBC Radio

He's got the Midas touch right now—everything he touches turns to silver.
Richard Keyes

It's been a real gravy train for a long time; now the gravy has really come home to roost on the shirt.   Robbie Vincent

I've been up and down so many times that I feel as if I'm in a revolving door.
Cher

We have slammed shut the revolving door we found open.

Bertie Ahern, Irish Taoiseach

This kind of thing has happened since Kingdom Come.

Peter Lush

The foot's on the other hand now ...   **Ted Striker, *Airplane!***

You buttered your bread. Now sleep in it!

Jiminy Cricket, *Pinocchio*

This isn't a man who is leaving with his head between his legs.

**Dan Quayle, on the resignation of
Chief of Staff John Sununu**

We'll be there till the fat lady freezes over.   **Philip Cardwell**

She's as safe as an olive.   **David Coleman**

And finally she tastes the sweet smell of success.   **Ian Edwards**

MISPRINTS & TYPOS

In the 9/11 Commission Report, they say it was Iran—not Iraq—that was helping al-Qaeda. So apparently we invaded the wrong country because of a typo.
David Letterman

Baby Luke weighed in at 6 pounds 13 ounces. His father said, "It's terrific! I don't even know what lay it is!"   *Daily Mail*

To inquire about midwifery training, write to this address: The Royal College of Madwives ...   *Nursing Newsletter*

The new exhibition will feature dozens of paintings and pints by this promising young artist.   *Valley Newsletter*

W. H. Auden and Cecil Day-Lewis, the Poet Laureate, are expected to nominate Roy Fuller, the much respected poet (and solicitor), whose respected slimy volume *New Poems* was received with something approaching rapture.
The Times

Sir Malcolm Sargent was a master in controlling almost impossibly large chairs.
West Lancashire Visitor

Chamber Music: Adagio for Clarinet and Springs.   *Daily Telegraph*

Before Miss Jenkinson concluded by singing, "I'll Walk Beside You," she was prevented with a bouquet of red roses.   *Sussex Press*

Sid Scott made his stage debut at a reggae concert—and stopped a riot when soufflés broke out in the huge crowd.   *Daily Star*

Geek Dancing   **Sign in a Greek taverna**

Pimps No. 1 or Pimps No. 2   **Sign in a restaurant**

Get ready, in the desserts of Iraq, for its last huzzah.   *Guardian*

WE ARE READY FOR HOLLY WAR
Islamic banner, seen during protest march,
The 25 Most Nonsensical Protest Signs (YT)

CIA Reportedly Sought to Destroy Domestic Flies
San Francisco Chronicle

Playboy Enterprises estimates that removing ornamental pants from its offices will save $27,000 a year.   **Knight News Wire**

8:30—"I Love Christmas"—a treat for nostalgia lovers ... featuring clips from such film classics as *The Snowman* and *Chitty Chitty Gang Bang*.
Sutton Coldfield Observer

Conrad's job, according to Gillespie, is to serve as a "raving ambassador for general aviation."   *Sunday Patriot News*

The breaking down of most prejudices and discriminations has lifted women from mental work to important management and top professional positions.
The Scranton Tribune

GET A BRAIN! MORANS!   *The 25 Most Nonsensical Protest Signs* (YT)

The conference's attitude was indicated by the almost total lack of applause after Mr. Wilson's 30-minute speech while Engineering Union leader Bryan Stanley was greeted with sustained crapping when he put the anti-common-market case.

The Zambian Times

Man Breaks Leg in Fall off Bride

St. Louis Post-Dispatch

DEATHS: James G. Stahlman, former publisher and president of *The Nashville Banner*, died Saturday, of a massive strike.   *The New York Times*

ACTUAL MEDICAL MISPRINTS

A lamp was seen in the patient's groin—it was even more prominent when he coughed.

Obese muddle-aged women are prone to diabetes.

Diabetic comma is a serious sign.

The woman complained of a pain in her left beast.

The surgeon may order the bloody pressure to be taken.

A vomit bowel should be placed by the patient's bedside.

A light male is given at 6 p.m. and then nothing by mouth until after the test.

The patient was washed all over with warm soupy water.

The patient's moth was cleaned with glycerine of thymol solution and then treated with glycerine and lemon.

The doctor noticed that the patient's pupils were diluted.

The patient should be given one table to suck before going to theater, this will render the throat insensitive.

Smoke can be a serious treat to health.

Each patient was given his drag as ordered by the doctor.

The patient's lover was enlarged and causing him some embarrassment.

A blond diet should be given to the patient suffering from a gastric ulcer. This helps to allay his suffering.

The needle should be driven into the tissue by an angel of about 45 for a subcutaneous injection.

The patient was a little bugger compared with his size a year previously.

The patient must be given a soothing and bland duet and he must have it often.

The patient is left quietly in bed so that he can rust as much as possible.

The patient was continually sneering and Sister told him he must cover his face when he did this.

The urine must be tasted by the staff nurse daily. If there is any doubt the Sister and Doctor must also do this.

The response to cold varies from person to parson.

ACTUAL CLERICAL MISPRINTS

Thou shalt commit adultery.
The Bible, 1631, nicknamed "The Wicked Bible"

For the first time for 17 years confirmation services were hell at Holy Trinity Church, Woodgreen, on Tuesday evening, when the Bishop of Dorchester officiated.
Church News

When parking on the north side of the church, please remember to park at an angel.
Church Bulletin

An Italian sinner will be served at 5:30 p.m. at the Essex Centre United Methodist Church.
The Vermonter

Appropriate music was played on the organ by Mr. G. F. satin with pearl trimming. The bride looked becoming with white Goods. Her train was that on Earth do Dwell. The hymns sung were All people of silver lace.
Church News

As they moved up the central aisle past the chair of St. Augustine, one was reminded of the erotic titles some of them bear. Here were the bishops of The Arctic, Cariboo, Fond du Lao, Omdurman ...
Daily Telegraph

Top-hated bishops stole the show at the village fête.
Salisbury Journal

The Rev. John Macaskill, who was Church of Scotland minister at Kinlochbervie, North-West Sunderland, for 50 years, died yesterday at his home there at the age of 88. A native of Harris, he went to Kinlochbervie as an assistant. He is survived by his wife and one sin.
Church News

SPELLING

It's a damn poor mind that can only think of
one way to spell a word.
Andrew Jackson

—Everybody, I'd like you to meet my date, Dr. Lilith Sternin, MD, PhD, EdD, APA.
—Boy, it sure isn't spelled like it sounds.
Frasier Crane and Woody Boyd, *Cheers*

—My name's Brandee—with two *e*'s.
—Brandee with two *e*'s? [*reading the label on a liquor bottle*] Can you believe, big company like this, they spell it wrong!
Brandee and "Coach" Ernie Pantusso, *Cheers*

—I'm Candi with an *i*. I used to spell it with a *y* but nobody ever took me seriously, so then I switched it to an *i*, you know, like Gandhi.

— Yes, yes, I understand that's why he did it too.

Candi Pearson and Frasier Crane, *Frasier*

A chrysanthemum by any other name would be easier to spell.

William J. Johnson

Whenever I try to spell "banana" it makes me feel stupid because I don't know when to end it. How many "nas" are on this thing? Bana—keep going ... Bananana—damn!   **Demetri Martin**

—How d'you spell "emphysema"? I need a sick note for school.

—Look in the dictionary.

—But I don't know how to spell it!   **Carl and Debbie Gallagher, *Shameless***

[*watching a student spell the word "potato" on the blackboard*] Add one little bit on the end. [*The child, against his better judgement, adds an* e *to spell the word "potatoe."*] There you go!

Dan Quayle "correcting" a student's spelling during a visit to a school in New Jersey (YT)

It took me five years to learn to spell Chattanooga—and then we moved to Albuquerque.   **Joe Morrison, football coach**

Carlotta was the kind of town where they spell trouble T-R-U-B-I-L, and if you try to correct them, they kill you.

Rigby Reardon, *Dead Men Don't Wear Plaid*

This is just a note to wish you luck toomorrow ... Best of luck to you and, of course, to Ipswich Town in toomorrow's big game ... I hope there are two good results for Ipswich toomorrow.

Tony Blair, handwritten note to the opposing candidate in a special election

—And that spells cash with a capital ...

—K!

—You should go back to school.

—No way. I hated teaching.

Roland T. Flakfizer and Jacques, *Brain Donors*

My wife ... pleased me by laughing uproariously when reading the manuscript, only to inform me that it was my spelling that amused her.

Gerald Durrell, writer

MALAPROPISMS

A colleague of Charlotte Edmunds recently came out with what may be the first ever malapropism for malapropism. Having described another colleague as "a vast suppository of information," he became aware of his error and apologized for having committed a "Miss Marple-ism."
New Scientist

Tonight, we're honoring one of the all-time greats in baseball, Stan Musial. He's immoral!

Johnny Logan, singer, introducing Musial at a banquet

Also Sally Rose Lee is here. This name may go down in the anals of ... anals ... I believe that's annals ...

Jay Leno, *The Tonight Show with Jay Leno*

Paula Radcliffe has been absolutely castrated by the media.

Commentator, BBC Radio

[*looking in the mirror*] I look like God's gorilla!

Jade Goody, *Big Brother 3* (U.K.)

Later in life, my mother developed a great gift for malapropisms. I remember, one early July afternoon, her ringing up and saying, "Oh, darling, darling, isn't it wonderful, Virginia Woolf's just won Wimbledon!"

Jilly Cooper

I once performed with a group of singers. The son of one of the other singers, just before a performance, encouraged his mother with, "Break an egg!"

Heidi Gerkin

I can't be doin' with Donny Osmond and that bunch of Morons.

Bert Fletcher

You must come to Lumley Castle. It's castrated all over with enormous flying buttocks!
Lady Serena James

My nan was complaining of chest pains. I said, "Are you all right, Nan?" She said, "I think I've got vagina."
Peter Kay

My elderly neighbor came round in a panic. "Oh dear," she said, "my toilet's overflowing. There's water everywhere. If you could come round and have a look I'd be internally grateful."
Bert Cole

Anything that man says you've got to take with a dose of salts.
Sam Goldwyn

[The question is] too suppository.
Alexander Haig, Secretary of State, declining to answer a question at a Senate committee hearing

"Ooh, it smells lovely in here today," I said, sniffing the air, as I entered my mum's living room. "Yes," she said, "when I was in town yesterday, I bought some of that pope pourri."
Sharon Gough

When a work colleague was asked about the decor in his new flat, he replied that all the walls were "painted in Mongolia."
Al Sansome

Peter Crouch is absolutely centrifugal to England's World Cup chances.
Mike Parry

Play captains against each other, create a little dysentery among the ranks.
Christopher Moltisanti, *The Sopranos*

They say I have tic tacs ... or is it tactics?
Jade Goody, *Big Brother 3* (U.K.)

I'm not going to be an escape goat for anyone.
Jade Goody, *Big Brother 3* (U.K.)

Do you remember when he was doing that PhD? She used to do all his typing and sit up all night helping him with his feces.
Bill Duffield

That was a real tour de France!
Rose Nylund, *The Golden Girls*

Your ambition, is that right, is to abseil across the Channel?
Cilla Black

I used to have a friend who said that if she didn't have breakfast she would be ravished by 11 o'clock.   **Maureen Gourlay**

It's her birthday ... so she'll be going out for a coffee and a nice Vietnamese pastry—what am I saying, *Viennese* pastry.   **Mo Dutta, BBC Radio**

My nan said, "While you're at the shops, be a love, and pick me up a pint of that semi-skilled milk."   **Melanie Blake**

I could murder a cup of decapitated coffee.   **Gladys Rogers**

Being invited to some affair which required black tie, I dressed in same and was walking through the kitchen ... Our housekeeper took a look at me and said, "Oh, you look so extinguished!" All I could say was, "Thank you!"
                                                            Brian A. Fahey

He's had so many romances, he's a regular Don Coyote.   **Leo Rosten**

My mother-in-law employed a Mrs. Malaprop who suffered from "very close veins," and regularly visited her "choir practor."   **Cindy Winn**

A friend told us his wife couldn't have a baby because her fluorescent tubes were blocked.   **Colin Hulford**

Looking at a new baby in its pram, my nan said, "Ahh, it makes you come over all nocturnal."   **"Nanecdotes,"** *The Russell Brand Show*

She hasn't been herself since she had the baby. I think she's got postmortem depression.   **Lilian Blake**

Do I have to mow the lawn yet again? Why can't we just cover it in concrete and lay down some afroturf?   **Elaine, overheard,**
                                                        The Graham Norton Show

He was lying on the stretcher in hospital and I saw a black puncture mark right below, I guess you call it, the uterus of the eye.
                        Witness, actual transcript from official court records

A few years ago when there was a solar eclipse in England, I overheard my neighbors wisely advising a friend not to look directly at the sun as it would burn the back of their rectums.   **Rykan**

The scepter of unemployment stalking the North East ...
                                        John Prescott, Member of Parliament

I fired my attorney for gross incontinence.

Angelica, *Rugrats*

[*reattaching kernels of corn to a cob*] Oh, this is hard. Look, I'm cock-handed.
Brian Belo, *Big Brother 8* (U.K.)

It just came to me in a dream, like St. Paul on the road to Domestos.
Brian Potter, *Phoenix Nights*

When I began teaching many years ago in a primary school, I began to keep examples of the children's malapropisms: "We are all human beans"; "A young fox is called a fox cube"; "You put your votes in a ballet box."
W. R. Violen

I once taught in a school where the principal broadcast over the intercom system after completing a successful fire drill, "Congratulations, students, you excavated the building in three minutes."
Marty Sutton

In answer to the question, "What does a butterfly become after the caterpillar stage?" one of my students wrote, "A syphilis."
P. J. Conner

A 13-year-old recently wrote, "We should not take everything for granite."
Stanley Burroway

Floods of molten lager, flowing down the mountainside ...
Reporter, BBC Radio

Nearly 200,000 people have been forced from their homes by a huge tycoon in the Philippines.
Newsreader, BBC Radio

My friend was chatting about her daughter, "Chloe's taking a year off before university," she explained. "She's going to Israel to work on a kebab."
Caroline Toms

The first time I went to Africa I said to my mum, "Look at these people—they're so emancipated."
Andrea McLean, *Loose Women*

I asked my seventh-grade English class to write a paragraph on an exciting moment in their lives. One student wrote, "I'll never forget the time my brother choked at dinner and my father gave him the Hemlock Remover."
Annette Fine

My gran was raving about a film she'd seen called *Arsenal and Old Lace*.

Tracy Phillips

She's getting on now, my nan, but she's still got all her facilities.

Jackie Briggs

My great aunt disliked "sympathetic" cream. She always used "Presbyterian" crossings in town.

Gill Wright

I'm on the brink of an abscess.

Sam Goldwyn

I'm on the horns of a Dalai Lama.

Dick Vosburgh

This is unparalyzed in the state's history.

Gib Lewis

My friend said, "It was an absorbent price."

S. Booth

Oh, my God, it's the abdominal snowman!

Rufus Kline

Last week in Russia, we saw the name "McCoist" spelt in the Acrylic alphabet. Quite a sight.

Alistair Alexander, Radio Scotland

[They are] trying to upset the apple tart.

Bertie Ahern, Irish Taoiseach

I'm just a prawn in this game.

Brian London

We've got to nip this thing in the butt.

Ellen Blake

Mike's got a whole new set of bannisters.

Don King, on Mike Tyson's trial

I loved him like a brothel.

S. J. Perelman

—Maybe he's agoraphobic.
—Jack? Scared of fighting? I don't think so!

Father Ted and Father Dougal, *Father Ted*

I've got bigger fish to fly.

Archie Bunker, *All in the Family*

It will take some of the lust off the All-Star game.

Pete Rose

I cannot tell you how grateful I am. I am filled with humidity.

Gib Lewis

Everything's back to Norman.

Tommy, *Rugrats*

SPOONERISMS

—How is Bill Oddie like the Reverend Spooner?
—One is a bird watcher, the other is a ...
Anon.

President Union will address the nation on the state of the Bush.   Anon.

I'll stop my startwatch.   Murray Walker, car racing commentator

If the terriers and bariffs are torn down, this economy will grow.
George W. Bush

Holy crip, he's a crapple!   Peter Griffin, *Family Guy*

May I sew you to your sheet?   Rev. William Archibald Spooner

This pie is occupewed.   Rev. William Archibald Spooner

I'm just killing Mom before time gets here.
Kate O'Brien, *The Drew Carey Show*

—Do you feel like some breakfast?
—Indood I dee! A suggestion to warm the hartles of my—cockles of my heart.
Wife and Ronnie Barker, "Sketcherism Spoon"

Two teas and a couple of lemon turd carts, please.   Terry-Thomas

Have another piece of Grace, your cake.
Curate, to Cosmo Lang, Archbishop of Canterbury

Your cook is goosed.   Paul Clarke

The lance has been boiled.   Sky News reporter

I'd rather have a bottle in front of me than a frontal lobotomy.
Dorothy Parker

Through a dark glassly ...   Rev. William Archibald Spooner

Also keeping an eye on the Woodstock Rock Festival was New York's Governor Rockin Nelsenfeller.

News reporter

Princess Margaret, wearing an off-the-hat face ...

Max Robertson

Aristotle Onassis—the Greek shitting typhoon ...

Radio commentator

I'd like to introduce Marshall Field Montgomery ...

Sam Goldwyn

—How is a piece of lawn furniture like a talkative nanny?
—One is a patio chair; the other is a chatty au pair.

Helen & Miriam Dowtin

When I was teaching English, I once made a reference to that classic, *Fuckleberry Hinn.*

Clare Cross

Lady Loverly's Chatter.

Peter De Vries

A woman said to me, "Do you know who I love—that Winifred Oprah."

Paul O'Grady

The Lord is a shoving leopard.

Rev. William Archibald Spooner

Ladies and gentlemen, the President of the United States—Hoobert Herver!

Harry von Zell

Viv Anderson has pissed a fatness test.

John Helm, TV commentator

I guess that's a bear we've all got to cross.

Corporal Walter "Radar" O'Reilly, M*A*S*H

—William, I'm leaving you.
—Leaving me after 20 years of bedded wiss?

Wife and Ronnie Barker, "Sketcherism Spoon"

Where pacifically in the specific are you going?

Sharon Strezlecki, *Kath & Kim* (U.K.)

Oh, why can't we break away from all this, just you and I, and lodge with my fleas in the hills—I mean, flee to my lodge in the hills.

Groucho Marx, *Monkey Business*

And next time, we'll be looking at blind dogs for the guide.

Simon Groom

GOLDWYNISMS

Sam Goldwyn created a caricature of himself
and then wore it as a disguise.
Ben Sonnenberg, Goldwyn's PR representative

Give me a smart idiot over a stupid genius any day.

I'll give you a definite maybe.

I can answer in two words: um-possible.

Avoid clichés like the plague.

A verbal contract isn't worth the paper it's written on.

We're overpaying him, but he's worth it.

It's more than magnificent, it's mediocre.

They say it's not as bad as they say it is.

We've all passed a lot of water since then.

We'll jump off that bridge when we come to it.

It's spreading like wild flowers.

Don't count your chickens before they cross the road.

You gotta take the sour with the bitter.

Gentlemen, include me out.

Yes, but that's our strongest weak point.

Directors are always biting the hand that lays the golden egg.

Never let the bastard back in my office again—unless I need him.

SIGNS & NOTICES

When she saw the sign "Members Only," she thought of him.
Spike Milligan

Warning! Pears falling!

Sign on a pear tree in Cripplegate Park, Worcester, England

Give way to trains.

Notice at an unmanned East Anglian, England, railway level crossing

Beer—Wine—Guns—Ammo—Picnic Supplies

Sign at a roadside convenience store in south Texas

It is forbidden to walk on the grass. But it is not forbidden to fly over the grass.

Augusto Boal

Shoe Rental: Adults: $2.00. Seniors and Children: $2.00.

Bowling alley, Texas

Massive Shoe Sale: Buy One, Get One Free!!   **South London store window**

Push or Pull   **Door of a Dorset, England, convenience store**

I hate it when I see one of those road signs that says "Draw Bridge Ahead" and I don't have a pencil.   **Lou Chiafullo**

I live near Holland Park. There's a sandpit about 8 feet by 10 feet with a sign saying "DOG LAVATORY." I do not know of any dog in the world that can read English.   **Dave Allen**

I once saw this sign on an Irish lift: "Please do not use this when it is not working."   **Spike Milligan**

Is forbidden to steal towels, please. If you are not person to do such, please not to read notice.   **Tokyo hotel**

Please do not bathe outside the bathtub.   **Sri Lanka hotel**

If you wish breakfast, lift the telephone and our waitress will arrive. This will be enough to bring up your food.   **Tel Aviv hotel**

Depositing the room key into another person is prohibited.

Tokyo hotel

No tools kept inside at anyone time.

Notice on the back of a maintenance van

I live near a graveyard which actually has a sign that says, "Do not use the footpath to the crematorium—it is for patrons only." **Dave Allen**

Last chance for fuel. Next three stations are mirages.

Gas station, Serengeti, Tanzania

Out for lunch. If not back by 6:00 out for dinner also.

Sign in grocery store window

Shop closed due to shop closure.

Sign in a shoe store window

ACTUAL WARNINGS

At the San Diego Zoo ... there's a display featuring half a dozen life-size gorillas made out of bronze. Posted nearby is a sign reading CAUTION: GORILLA STATUES MAY BE HOT. Everywhere you turn, the obvious is being stated. CANNON MAY BE LOUD. MOVING SIDEWALK IS ABOUT TO END. To people who don't go around suing each other, such signs suggest a crippling lack of intelligence ... It's hard trying to explain a country whose motto has become, "You can't claim I didn't warn you."
David Sedaris, Me Talk Pretty One Day

Packet of peanuts: Contains nuts.

Garden wheelbarrow: Not intended for highway use.

Cardboard sun visor for car: Do not drive with sun visor in place.

Washing machine: Do not drink the water inside this machine.

Iron-on patch: Do not iron on while wearing shirt.

Bottle of bleach: Do not look down the nozzle while squeezing the bottle.

Bottle of hair dye: Do not use as an ice cream topping.

Hair dryer: Do not use in shower. Never use while sleeping.

Packet of AA batteries: Do not microwave.

Christmas fairy lights: For indoor and outdoor use only.

Bottle of red wine: Serving suggestion: Best served with or without food.

Bikini: Do not expose to direct sunlight.

Hotel pool, Sri Lanka: Do not use the diving board when the swimming pool is empty.

Microwave oven: Do not use for drying pets.

Chainsaw: Do not try to stop chain with hands.

Blowtorch: Not to be used for drying hair.

Box of household nails: Do not swallow. May cause irritation.

Dog shampoo: Do not feed contents to fish.

Camera: This camera only works when there is film inside.

Aerosol spray can: Warning: Death may occur without warning!

Safety campaigners have repeated their warnings about the dangers of fireworks after a prankster tried to launch a powerful rocket from his backside. The 22-year-old man suffered serious internal injuries when the black cat thunderbolt rocket ignited during the bonfire-night stunt at Monkwearmouth in Sunderland.
John Marsh, BBC Radio, *Radio Bloopers U.K. 2007 #1* (YT)

NOMINAL WARNINGS
(but it can only be a matter of time before these, too, become reality ...)

Box of shoes: Average contents: 2

Harry Pike

Odor Eaters: Do not eat.

Chuck Smith

Grand piano: Harmful or fatal if swallowed.

Peter Fay

Pantyhose: Not to be used in the commission of a felony.

Judith Daniel

Cup of McDonald's coffee: Allow to cool before applying to groin area.

Elden Carnahan

Magic 8 Ball: Not advised for use as a home pregnancy test.

Chuck Smith

Wetsuit: Capacity: 1.

J. Calvin Smith

Infant's bathtub: Do not throw baby out with bath water.

Gary Dawson

Coconut Shampoo & Conditioner: Not recommended for washing coconuts.

Rosemarie Jarski

Disposable razor: Do not use this product during an earthquake.

Jim Gaffney

Fisherman's Friend throat lozenges: Not meant as substitute for human companionship.

Tom Witte

Handgun: Not recommended for use as a nutcracker.

Art Grinath

Tube of Super Glue: In case of accidental ingestion, consult a mortician.

The Simpsons

HOMOPHONES, EGGCORNS & SLIPS OF THE EAR

The intellectual is invariably yolked to the stupid.
Guardian

Pete Doherty fled the home of his girlfriend Kate Moss this morning after an almighty bust-up ... Heroine addict Pete, 27, accompanied 32-year-old Kate to her £3 million home after Babyshambles' performance at Brixton Academy.
Evening Standard

We put chlorine in vast quantities into water and apart from bleaching your heir, it would have no effect.   *Guardian*

The patient's hare was carefully wrapped in a triangular bandage.
Nurse's examination paper

—What symptoms were the patients displaying?
—The patients' four heads were bathed in sweat.
Nurse's examination paper

He could sneak away with a rye smile.   *Guardian*

The tradition goes back to the Romans, who would eat just about anything, including door mice.   *Guardian*

She always dressed impeccably, with such personal flare even though she did not have a lot of money to spend on clothes.
Guardian

I made a comment to a newspaper about therapists saying that people should not become dependent on them and it got printed as, "The rapists say ..."
Oscar Levant

LANDLORDS: We have ten ants looking for good-quality homes.
Advertisement, *County Down Spectator*

We were talking to Karl once about bringing back a mammoth to life ... and he went, "Really?" He was too interested. "A man moth?" I went, "Not a man moth! What were you thinking of when you thought it was a man moth?" He said, "I thought it was a moth with a bloke's head bumping into a lamp."

Ricky Gervais, on Karl Pilkington, radio host

I was once majestically written to by a colleague as James Hay, "Solicitor and not a republic."

James N. D. Hay, British solicitor and notary public

During a book signing in Sydney in 1964, the British writer Monica Dickens had a woman come up to her with a copy of her novel, saying, "Emma Chisit." Only after dutifully signing "To Emma Chisit, Monica Dickens" in the flyleaf did she realize that the woman had been asking, "How much is it?"

David Fickling

—Describe your year in five words ...
—Wait a second—my urine? Describe my urine in five words. I don't think I can do it in five. Oh—my year!

Erik Hedegaard and Eva Longoria, *Rolling Stone*

When I was doing a radio program recently, it included playing requests for listeners, and one old lady phoned in asking for the song "Edelweiss," and the producer received a letter of thanks ... She wrote, "Thank you for the lovely 'Anal Vice.' All my neighbors thought it was the best thing on the show!" and obviously she is totally unaware of the error.   **Kenneth Williams**

Of course, there's always the company that offers "the ultimate inconvenience." I've heard this in radio ads not once, but twice.   **Vicki Blier**

In a fashion note, we referred to "correspondence shoes." We should have said "co-respondent's shoes." The reference is to the co-respondent in a divorce case.

Guardian

—I'm exhausted after only two days into the course.
—I beg your pardon?
—I'm exhausted and we're only two days into the course.
—Oh, I see. I thought you said "after two day's intercourse."

Friend and Nicola Weller

Our local hairdresser was called "Hair Events." Without seeing the written form, "Hairy Vents" seemed a pretty unusual name for the business.

Frances McCunnie

A little girl wrote home from summer camp, explaining that she had developed "dire rear."

Dan Harrison

After my suggestion of the topic, "Euthanasia," I once got an oral presentation on "Youth in Asia."

David Cox, teacher

My son wrote a school paper all about his visit to Washington, D.C., where he enjoyed his visit to the "Aaron Space Museum."

Claire Schwarz

A child returned from San Francisco with excited descriptions of "Fisherman's Dwarf."

Hank De Sutter

A few months ago, my five-year-old son informed us that he thought he was "black toast intolerant." Michael Brunelle

My daughter said she'd heard about a book by J. D. Salinger called *Catch Her in the Rhine*.

Greg Merkley

I really like that Thomas Hardy novel, *Tess of the Dormobiles*.

Jack Malloy

During the Gulf War, when the U.S. was bombing Baghdad and it was in the newscasts every day, an acquaintance overheard his young son explaining things to a little friend, about how the Good Dads have to go over and fight the Bad Dads.

Cathy Julien

For many years, I believed that communist China was presided over by two elderly dictators, named Chem and Mao ... Oddly, there was never a picture of Chem. Only when Mao died in 1976, and I was 13, did I discover to my embarrassment that Chairman Mao was one person.

Ben Macintyre

I could have sworn I heard on the news that the Chinese were producing new trombones. No, it was neutron bombs.

Doug Stone

As a civil servant in the 1950s, I heard of an official who received a memo from his boss's secretary inviting him to attend a "haddock-stirring committee." The puzzled official's superior had dictated "ad hoc steering committee."

Gerry Hanson

I once said, "To quote Clough, 'Say not the struggle nought availeth,'" and found it transcribed as, "To quote fluff, 'Up the struggle naughty bailiff.'"

Sir Anthony Jay

A public park, which will open next summer, is dedicated to raising awareness of children with cystic fibrosis. The park will be called "Sixty-Five Roses," a name derived from the way one five-year-old pronounced his disease.

The Oregonian

I'm 85. My memory's not what it was. I think I've got old timer's disease.

Florence Powell

Some years ago, a Scottish friend of my mother mentioned casually to her that the Countess of Ayr was coming for tea the following day. It turned out to be the county surveyor.

Keith Kemp

Years ago, when my children were small and we were leaving for an out-of-town trip, my babysitter's father was supposed to come to the house to pick up the spare key for her. We had never met him before. Around dinner time, when the doorbell rang, I opened the door and found a clergyman standing there who said, "A man's dead." While I was processing this, I gave him, I'm sure, one of my blankest what-are-you-talking-about looks. He repeated himself. When it dawned on me, I was embarrassed and went to get him the key. What he had actually said was, "I'm Ann's dad."

Sue Frank

MONDEGREENS— GENERAL

I think that printing the lyrics is embarrassing, and it's like having a close-up of your zit on the inside of your album cover.
Bradford Cox, of Deerhunter

Our Father, who art in heaven, Halloween be thy name.

Josie Cliff

Malachy McCourt's memoir … *A Monk Swimming* is a whimsical evocation of the way its author as a child misheard "Hail Mary, full of grace, the Lord is with thee, blessed art thou amongst women" as "Blessed art thou, a monk swimming."

Christopher Lehmann-Haupt

When I was a young boy back in Ireland, I always used to think that the words spoken by the priest at a funeral were, "In the name of the Father, the Son and into the hole he goes." It made sense to me at the time. I suppose, in a way, it still does.

Dave Allen

The line is, "Cause I'm saving all my love for you" … Well, the woman who wrote in saying that she'd misheard the song thought it said, "Cause I'm shaving off my muff for you." I don't know what muff is. Is it a bad word? Is it? Okay. Sorry. Is it a bad word and I just don't know it? Am I about to get fired? Let's move on.

Lori Wilson, TV anchor, WCAU-TV, Philadelphia (YT)

MONDEGREEN LYRICS (MISHEARD LYRICS)

Abba: Chiquitita
Chicken tikka, you and I know …

Madonna: Like a Virgin
Like a German, touched for the thirty-first time …

Wham!: Wake Me Up before You Go-Go
Wake me up to pour you cocoa …

Bob Dylan: Knockin' on Heaven's Door
Knock, knock, knockin' on Kevin's door …

Simon & Garfunkel: Mrs. Robinson
We'd like to know a little bit about your far-off isles.

Dusty Springfield: Son of a Preacher Man
The only boy who could ever reach me was the son of a pizza man.

Kenny Rogers: Lucille
You picked a fine time to leave me, Lucille, four hundred children and a box of oatmeal …
You picked a fine time to leave me your seal, four hundred children and the cops in the field …

The Rolling Stones: You Can't Always Get What You Want
You can't always get a Chihuahua ...

Elton John: Tiny Dancer
Hold me closer, Tony Danza ...

Neil Diamond: Forever in Blue Jeans
I'd much rather be the Reverend Blue Jeans.

Queen: Bohemian Rhapsody
Is this the real life, is this just Battersea?
Scare a moose, scare a moose, will you do the damn tango?
Spare him his life and his lone slice of cheese.

Simon & Garfunkel: The Sound of Silence
Silence like a casserole ...

James Taylor: Fire and Rain
Obscene fire and obscene rain ...

Crystal Gayle: Don't It Make Your Brown Eyes Blue
Donuts Make Your Brown Eyes Blue

John Travolta & Olivia Newton-John: You're the One That I Want
I got chimps, they're multiplying ...
Meditate, mad erection, feel yahweh ...

Shania Twain: That Don't Impress Me Much
I can't believe you kiss your cock at night ...

Hot Chocolate: You Sexy Thing
I've been eating marigolds ...

Sting: So Lonely
Sue Lawley ...
Salami ...

Maria Muldaur: Midnight at the Oasis
Midnight after you're wasted ...

Eagles: Desperado
I've been outright offensive for so long now ...

Madonna: Erotic
Bill Oddie, Bill Oddie, put your hands all over my body ...

Elaine Paige: Don't Cry for Me, Argentina
Don't cry for me Marge and Tina ...

John Denver: Country Roads
West Virginia, mount yer momma ...

Brian Adams: Summer of '69 ...
Got my first real sex change ...

The Beatles: Lucy in the Sky with Diamonds
The girl with colitis goes by ...

Bob Dylan: Blowin' in the Wind
The ants are my friends, they're blowin' in the wind ...

Queen: Killer Queen
She keeps a mower and shovel in a pretty cabinet ...
Let them meet Kay, she says, just like on my Internet ...

Robert Palmer: Addicted to Love
Might as well face it, you're a dick with a glove ...

Desmond Dekker and the Aces: The Israelites
Oooh, oooh, me ears are alight ...

Bonnie Tyler: It's a Heartache
It's a hard egg, nothing but a hard egg ...

Jimi Hendrix: Purple Haze
'Scuse me while I kiss this guy ...
'Scuse me while I zip my fly ...

Carly Simon: You're So Vain
Your head strategically twitched below one eye, your tropic was Africa ...

Frank Sinatra: I Love Paris
I love parrots in the springtime, I love parrots in the fall ...

MISHEARD MUSICAL & SONG TITLES

The Kind and Di

South Specific

"The London Derrière"

Elgar's Enema Variations

The Dream of Geronimo

Beethoven's Erotica Symphony

"Rap City in Blue"

Beethoven's Pathetic Sonata

Haydn's Cremation

Handel's "Let the Bride Seraph Him"

MONDEGREEN CHRISTMAS CAROLS & SONGS

GOOD KING WENCESLAS
Good King Wenceslas looked out on the feast of Stephen ...
Good King Wence's lass looked out on the feet of heathens ...

HARK, THE HERALD ANGELS SING
Hark, the herald angels sing ...
Hark, the Herod angels sing ...

Joyful, all ye nations rise ...
Joyful, all lean Haitians rise ...

With th'angelic host proclaim ...
With Anne's jelly toast proclaim ...

God and sinners reconciled.
Garden centers recycled.
Goddamned sinners wrecked a child.

ANGELS WE HAVE HEARD ON HIGH

Gloria in Excelsis Deo!
Gloria in eggshells cease day-o!

JOY TO THE WORLD

Joy to the world, the Lord is come!
Joy to the world, the Lord has gum!

WE THREE KINGS

We three kings of Orient are ...
We three kings of glory and tar ...
We three kings of Oregon are ...

THE HOLLY AND THE IVY

The holly and the ivy, when they are both full grown ...
The Harley and the ivy, when they are both full chrome ...

O TANNENBAUM

O tannenbaum, O tannenbaum ...
O Taliban, O Taliban ...
O atom bomb, O atom bomb ...

AWAY IN A MANGER

Away in a manger ...
Howay in a manger ...
A Wayne in a manger ...

Away in a manger, no crib for a bed,
The Little Lord Jesus laid down his sweet head ...

Away in a manger, no crib for a bed,
The little Lord Jesus lay down his wee ted ...

The cattle are lowing, the baby awakes ...
The cattle are blowing the baby away ...

THE FIRST NOEL
Noel, Noel, Noel, Noel,
Born is the king of Israel ...

Noel, Noel, Noel, Noel,
Barney's the king of Israel ...

SILENT NIGHT
Round yon Virgin, mother and child ...
Round John Virgin, mother and child ...

Holy infant so tender and mild,
Sleep in heavenly peace, sleee-eeeep in heavenly peace ...
Holy infant so tender and mild,
Sleep in Beverly Hills, sleee-eeeep in Beverly Hills ...
Sleep in heavenly peas, sleee-eeeep in heavenly peas ...

O HOLY NIGHT
Fall on your knees, oh hear the angel voices!
Fall on your niece, oh hear the angel voices!

DECK THE HALLS
Deck the halls with boughs of holly, fa la la la la, la la la la ...
Deck the halls with Buddy Holly, fa la la la la, la la la la ...

GOD REST YE MERRY GENTLEMEN
God rest ye merry gentlemen ...
Get dressed ye merry gentlemen ...

LET IT SNOW
Let us know, let us know, let us know!

WINTER WONDERLAND
In the meadow we can build a snowman, then pretend that he is Parson Brown …
In the ghetto we can build a snowman and pretend that he is partly blind …

Later on we'll conspire as we dream by the fire …
Later on, we'll perspire, as we dream by the fire …

RUDOLPH THE RED-NOSED REINDEER
All of the other reindeer used to laugh and call him names …
Olive, the other reindeer, used to laugh and call him names …
Adolf, the other reindeer, used to laugh and call him names …

Rudolph, the red-nosed reindeer, you'll go down in history.
Rudolph, the red-nosed reindeer, you'll go drown in Listerine.

I SAW MOMMY KISSING SANTA CLAUS
I saw Mommy kissing Santa Claus underneath the mistletoe last night …
I saw Mommy kissing Santa Claus underneath the missing toe last night …

JINGLE BELLS
Dashing through the snow in a one-horse open sleigh …
Dashing through the snow with one whore, soap and sleigh …

Bells on bobtail ring, making spirits bright …
Bells on Bob's tail ring, making spirits rise …

What fun it is to ride and sing a sleighing song tonight …
What fun it is to ride and sing a slaying song tonight …

SANTA CLAUS IS COMING TO TOWN
He's making a list and checking it twice, he's gonna find out who's naughty and nice …
He's making a list o' chicken and rice, he's gonna find out who's snoring at night …

He sees you when you're sleeping
He'll seize you when you're sleeping …

SLADE: MERRY CHRISTMAS EVERYBODY
Does your granny always tell you that the old songs are the best ...
Does your granny always tell ya that the old socks are the best ...

BAND AID: DO THEY KNOW IT'S CHRISTMAS?
The greatest gift they'll get this year is life ...
The greatest gift they'll get this year is lice ...

WE WISH YOU A MERRY CHRISTMAS
Now bring us some figgy pudding and a cup of good cheer ...
Now bring us some friggin' pudding and bring it right here ...

FILM & TV SUBTITLES

I must apologize to the deaf for the loss of subtitles.
Angela Rippon, BBC News

I'm the puff, and you are the straight man.
I'm the puff, and you're normal.

Confetti (Spanish translation)

It was a ball to shoot.
It was like filming a dance scene.

Seabiscuit (Spanish DVD translation)

She died in a freak rugby accident.
She died in a rugby match for people with deformities.

Unidentified TV show

Hungarian swimmers ...
Hung Aryan Swimmers ...   **U.S. TV sportscaster, during the Olympics**

The Conservative Party is in favor of a tax on houses.
The Conservative Party is in favor of attacks on houses.

BBC TV

Benedict XVI.
Ben Debit XVI.   **BBC TV**

They're all here because of Michael Owen.
They're all here because of my cologne.

TV Sports

WRITER

The reason why so few good books are written is that so few people
who can write know anything.
Walter Bagehot

I was going to chuck it all, burn my bridges and go off to Paris to write my
novel, but I didn't have enough frequent-flier miles.

David Sipress

I never think at all when I write. Nobody can do two things at the same time
and do them both well.

Don Marquis

I have read that the Rev. C. R. Maturin (the author of Gothic novels), when in
the throes of composition, used to be seen with a red wafer stuck on his
forehead, a sign to his numerous family that he was not to be spoken to.

Frederick Locker-Lampson

Dan Brown has painted a fascinating picture of the bizarre-sounding home life
the childless couple lead. Blythe, we learnt, encourages Dan's habit of rising at 4
a.m. seven days a week to begin writing. When writer's block sets in he hangs
upside down, bat-like, until the ideas start flowing again.

Vanessa Allen

I'm writing a sequel to *The Da Vinci
Code*. It's called *I Know What You Did
Last Supper*.

Paul Lyalls

Nick Kochan has written a book about money laundering called *The Washing
Machine*. He's on the line now.

Sarah Montague, BBC Radio

I can boil an egg and burn toast for breakfast, but because I love to eat, it made
sense to write a book.

Sarah Ferguson, on her book *Dining with the Duchess*

Fresh from playing the central character in the Bridget Jones novels, actress Renée Zellwegger, 33, said she planned to write "fiction, non-fiction, whatever I'm feeling when I pick up the pen."

Metro magazine

I'm not going to say I sit there with a pen and paper—I don't think anyone does that. I haven't got time for a typewriter.

Katie Price aka Jordan, British TV personality, on her novel *Angel*

I could copy out the Yellow Pages and they would still publish it simply because I'm a celebrity.

Hugh Grant

Fiction writing is great. You can make up almost anything.

Ivana Trump

Some people have a way with words. Other people ... not have way.

Steve Martin

I haven't read the book because it's full of words.

Robbie Williams, on the book he coauthored with Mark McCrum, *Robbie Williams: Somebody Someday*

—My second novel is coming out soon.
—What's it called?
—I don't know.

Kerry Katona and Jonathan Ross, *Friday Night with Jonathan Ross*

—You could be another Brontë sister.
—But I can't sing.

Morecambe and Wise

Well, there are things I don't really know about, like sentence structure, a beginning, a middle, and an end.

Pamela Anderson, on getting help writing her novel

You may remember that the Dial Press had been asking me for some years for a manuscript, but when I sent the [manuscript] of AF [*Animal Farm*] they returned it, saying shortly that "it was impossible to sell animal stories in the U.S.A."

George Orwell

My new book has got pedophilia, September 11 and lots of black people in it. I'm moving on, we've got to progress.

Jilly Cooper

I'm writing a book about Siamese twins that are attached at the nose. It's called *Stop Staring at Me!*

Zach Galifianakis

My next opus will be an index to the dictionary.   Leo Rosten

I've always wanted to write a book, but unfortunately I don't have a pen.
                                                     Tom Baker, *Little Britain*

BAD FIRST DRAFTS
OF FAMOUS LINES

Scrambled eggs, oh, my baby, how I love your legs.
                                            Paul McCartney, "Yesterday"

Wow, this is, like, so totally not a movie set in the Nevada desert.
                                            Evan Golub, after Neil Armstrong

How do I love thee? Let me get back to thee on that ...
                                 George Friedman, after Elizabeth Barrett Browning

Call me Ishmael the sailor man, toot toot.
                                            Brad Suter, after *Moby Dick*

I have nothing to offer but blood, sweat and phlegm.
                                      Chuck Smith, after Winston Churchill

I have a feeling ...
                             Tracy Jordan, after Dr. Martin Luther King, *30 Rock*

The unexamined life is like a box of chocolates.
                                            Joseph Sisk, after Socrates

And God saw that it was scrumdiddlyumptious.
                                      Kevin Mellema, after Genesis 1:10

Go ahead, punk. Enrich my life!
                                      Scott Campisi, after *Dirty Harry*

You know how to whistle, don't you, Steve? You juthst thtick two fingerth in
your mouf like thith and ... blow.
                                            Joel Knanishu, after Lauren Bacall
                                            in *To Have and Have Not*

BOOKS

I like a thick book because it will steady a table, a leather volume because it will strop a razor, and a heavy book because it can be thrown at a cat.
Mark Twain

Reading is the basics for all learning.

George W. Bush

You teach a child to read, and he or her will be able to pass a literacy test.

George W. Bush

I gave my nephew a book for Christmas. He's spent six months looking for where to put the batteries.

Milton Berle

At Barnes & Noble, I overheard a teenager say to her friends, "You know how you can rent DVDs? Well, there should be a place where you can rent books."

Miley

We Have Books About TV!

Sign outside Springfield Library, *The Simpsons*

You see, I don't believe that libraries should be drab places where people sit in silence, and that's been the main reason for our policy of employing wild animals as librarians.

Monty Python's Flying Circus

One of the great things about books is sometimes there are some fantastic pictures.

George W. Bush

A bit of advice: Never read a pop-up book about giraffes.

Sean Lock

I always had my nose in a book. My parents couldn't afford Kleenex.

Joe Hickman

The other night I was reading the dictionary. I thought it was a poem about everything.

Steven Wright

I got to page 1,264 of *War and Peace*. It was really hotting up, but unfortunately I lost my copy.

Boris Johnson, mayor of London

I read part of it all the way through.

Sam Goldwyn

On the bus home I would even read every detail of the bus ticket, I just love words so much.

Sheila Quigley

—You're in a pretty good mood tonight.
—Why not? Last night I was up till two in the morning finishing off Kierkegaard.
—I hope he thanked you for it.

Sam Malone and Diane Chambers, *Cheers*

—Do you like Kipling?
—I quite like the fruit slice.

Ralph and Ted, *The Fast Show*

Howard's End? Sounds filthy, doesn't it?

Rita, *Educating Rita*

—Have you ever read *Of Human Bondage*?
—No, I'm not really into porn.

Eddie and Buffy Summers, *Buffy the Vampire Slayer*

I haven't read *Lolita* yet. I'll wait six years, when she'll be 18.

Groucho Marx

The staff who run the website had never heard of *Lolita*, and to be honest, no one else here had either. We had to look it up on Wikipedia.

Spokesman for Woolworths, who were forced to withdraw a children's bed named "Lolita" after mothers objected to it

A children's book you will never see: *Mommy and Daddy Are Getting a Divorce and It's All Your Fault.*

Michael Farquhar

FOR SALE: Rare work on cannibalism. Good condition. Ten plates.

Catalog, New York bookseller

—What's the best thing you read this year?
—You mean like a book?

Reporter and Justin Timberlake, *Rolling Stone*

—I'm reading *Chicken Soup for the Soul*.
—You should read *Tomato Sauce for Your Ass*. It's the Italian version.

Irina and Tony Soprano, *The Sopranos*

The Stray Shopping Carts of Eastern North America: A Guide to Field Identification
Julian Montague, book title

I thought it was pretty good, for a book.
David Sipress

I love books. At the moment I'm reading *My Life* by Bill Clinton, which freaked me out 'cause I didn't know he knew anything about my life.
Tim Vine

—I'm giving John Wayne a book for his birthday.
—He's got a book.
Peter Bogdanovitch and John Ford

In my teens I conducted a whole conversation on the assumption that a man called Tristram Shandy wrote a book called *Laurence Sterne*.
Lady Antonia Fraser

She thinks *Candide* is a toenail polish.
Diane Chambers, *Cheers*

—Are you familiar with the *I Ching*?
—Sure. That's why I switched to boxers, my friend.
Wilson W. Wilson and Tim Taylor, *Home Improvement*

Once in a swimsuit and once in evening dress.
The All-England "Summarise Proust" Competition, *Monty Python*

Dickens originally wrote the role of Nancy for a 17-year-old.
Contestant, *I'd Do Anything*

I'm a great fan of hers, but I haven't read any of her books. I just don't have the time.
Kate Winslet, on Iris Murdoch

Harry Potter this ... Harry Potter that ... I'd never even *heard* of Harry Potter till the book came out!
Caller, BBC Radio

Books are useless! I only ever read one book, *To Kill a Mockingbird*, and it gave me absolutely no insight on how to kill mockingbirds!
Homer Simpson, *The Simpsons*

He thought "Moby Dick" was a venereal disease.
Marlin Borunki, *The End*

Do you have a copy of *Moby Dick*? I don't mind who it's by.

Customer in bookstore

War and Peace? Forget it. No one can read four ounces a day.

"Coach" Ernie Pantusso, *Cheers*

I took a speed-reading course, and read *War and Peace* in 20 minutes. It's about Russia.

Woody Allen

I read a book twice as fast as anybody else. First I read the beginning, and then I read the ending, and then I start in the middle and read toward whichever end I like best.

Gracie Allen

I bought a book called *How to Hug*. Imagine my disappointment when I got it home and found it was Volume VI of the *Encyclopedia Britannica*.

Anon.

In 1989, the famous American playwright Arthur Miller was invited to speak at the literary festival in Hay-on-Wye. "Hay-on-Wye?" he queried. "Is that some kind of sandwich?"

Robert Sims

Is that all you guys do ... read these books? You ought to get a life!

Donald Rumsfeld, Secretary of Defense, to reporters during a press briefing

Mostly I read menus and traffic signals and that's about it.

David Yow

The last time we were in a restaurant together, she slammed the menu down on the table and screamed, "I hate reading. Someone please tell me what's on the menu."

Pamela Anderson, on Paris Hilton

The only thing Californians read is the licence plate in front of them.

Neil Simon

I don't read books because if they're any good they're gonna be made into miniseries.

Ouiser Boudreaux, *Steel Magnolias*

Tales from Wessex, by Thomas Hardy, is a collection of six classic tales from a superb English writer. Even if they had not turned them into TV plays, they would still be well worth reading. *Daily Mirror*

All my good reading, you might say, was done in the toilet … There are passages in *Ulysses* which can be read only in the toilet—if one wants to extract the full flavor of their content. Henry Miller

I got news for you—if it wasn't for the toilet, there would be no books. George Costanza, *Seinfeld*

BOOK TITLES THAT DIDN'T QUITE MAKE IT

Who's Afraid of Virginia Wade?	John Brenchley
A Farewell to Elbows	E. O. Parrott
The Prunes of Wrath	Pete Landells
A Burnt-out Satchel	Ralph Pearce
The Hunchback of West Ealing United Reform Church	Michael Green
Doctor Finlay's Bookcase	E. Duvall
The Rabbit of the Baskervilles	Wandryn J. Bonso
East of Sweden	Joan Herniman
In the Flip-Flops of the Fisherman	Chris Bond
Zen and the Art of Taking the Bike to the Garage	Gill Breenllew

AUTOBIOGRAPHY

I've given my memoirs far more thought than any of my marriages.
You can't divorce a book.
Gloria Swanson

—Chris, have you ever thought of writing your autobiography?
—On what?
Dennis Pennis and Chris Eubank

—So your autobiography is out in paperback. What's it about?
—Myself.
Jeremy Vine and Lord Longford, BBC Radio

My autobiography is straight from the horse's mouth. Not that I'm saying I'm a horse.
Victoria Beckham

I thought "autobiography" was a history of motor cars.
Gill Murray

I'm writing an unauthorized autobiography. I'm warning family and friends not to talk to me.
Steven Wright

I don't think anyone should write his autobiography until after he's dead.
Sam Goldwyn

—I enjoyed your autobiography. Who wrote it for you?
—I wrote it myself. Who read it to you?
Humphrey Bogart and Ilka Chase

This is my novel: "Once upon a time there was a lovely little sausage called Baldrick, and it lived happily ever after." It's semi-autobiographical.
Baldrick, *Blackadder the Third*

Do you find yourself reminiscing a great deal in your autobiography?
Gloria Hunniford

He'd love to discuss the book in detail; there's only one problem—he hasn't read it yet.

**Simon Hattenstone, interviewing Pete Bennett,
winner of *Big Brother 7* (U.K.), about his autobiography**

One man, I'm told, asked the bookseller for a packet of condoms because he was too embarrassed to ask for a copy of my autobiography, *Mustn't Grumble*.

Sir Terry Wogan

I was misquoted.

Charles Barkley, on his autobiography

POETRY

I wish you would read a little poetry sometimes. Your ignorance cramps my conversation.

Anthony Hope

—Have you heard of Walt Whitman?
—No, who's he play for?

Annie Savoy and Ebby Calvin LaLoosh, *Bull Durham*

—Do you know your Shelley, Bertie?
—Oh, am I?

P. G. Wodehouse, *The Code of Woosters*

A limerick fan from Australia
Regarded his work as a failure:
His verses were fine
Until the fourth line ...

Anon.

My favorite nursery rhyme is: One, two, three, buckle my shoe.

Robert Benchley

Poems to Break the Tedium of Riding a Bicycle, Seeing One's Friends, or Heartbreak Verses Demonstrating That No Man Can Be Unhappy Amid the Infinite Variety of this World, and Giving the Reader Choice of Several Titles, the Author's Favorite Being, "Some Play Golf and Some Do Not"

Samuel Hoffenstein, title of poetry collection

My favorite poem is the one that starts "Thirty days hath September" because it actually tells you something.

Groucho Marx

My son writes poetry. I know it is good for I cannot understand a word of it.

Eliza Goodge

I recently bought a book of free verse. For $12.

George Carlin

JOURNALISM & NEWS

Perhaps there are not as many stupid things said
as there are set down in print.
Goncourt brothers

Ever noticed that no matter what happens in one day, it exactly fits the
newspaper?

Jerry Seinfeld

I read the newspapers. I mean, I can tell you what the headlines are. I must
confess, if I think the story is, like, not a fair appraisal, I'll move on. But I know
what the story's about.

George W. Bush

If I was to read everything that I read about myself in the papers, I wouldn't
have time to do my job.

John Prescott

CNNNN: More Ns than any other network.
Home of newstainment.
We report, you believe.
Because opinion matters more than fact.
No one has more news because no one has more desks.
We don't just cover wars, we win them.
Now with 20 percent more chimp stories.

Slogans, *CNNNN* (Australian TV satire of CNN)

Of course, for many years I did work in the field. I remember being in Somalia
once and this poor, wounded kid crawled up to me—and he touched me. And I
looked down, and there was a bit of blood on my suit. It was that moment that
I realized: I'd prefer to work in the studio from now on.

Craig Reucassel, *CNNNN* (Australian TV satire of CNN)

HEADLINES

Lesbian Japanese Monkeys Challenge Darwin's Assumptions

Daily Telegraph

Alien Giant Hailstones Made Me Gay and Pregnant Claims Elvis Lookalike

Weekly World News

War Dims Hope for Peace *Wisconsin State Journal*

As Violence Falls in Iraq, Cemetery Workers Feel the Pinch

McClatchly News Service

Red Tape Holds Up New Bridge *Milford Connecticut Citizen*

Bar Trying to Help Alcoholic Lawyers *Seattle Times*

Headless Blonde Found in Thames *Chicago Tribune*

Twelve on Their Way to Cruise Among Dead in Plane Crash

Dallas Morning News

Man Survived 17 Days Adrift on Flying Fish

Los Angeles Times

Hitler Used to Sell Potato Chips *New Mexican*

Sharon to Press His Suit in Israel *Oregonian*

Sisters Reunited after 18 Years in Checkout Line at Supermarket

Arkansas Democrat

Teenage Prostitution Problem is Mounting *Tonawanda News*

Prostitutes Appeal to Pope *Eugene Register*

Crowds Rushing to See Pope Trample Six to Death

Peoria Journal Star

Joint Chiefs Head Will Be Replaced *Courier-Journal*

Helping Hurt Children is Reward Enough	*Charlotte Observer*
Dr. Tackett Gives Talk on Moon	*Indiana Evening Gazette*
New Vaccine May Contain Rabies	*Newport Daily Press*
Bishop Defrocks Gay Priest	*New York Post*
Late Bus Conductor Remembered	*New London Connecticut News*

CORRECTIONS

An error doesn't become a mistake until you refuse
to correct it.
Orlando A. Battista

Corection.   *The New York Times*

An article about President Clinton's State of the Union Message rendered a word
incorrectly in a quotation from the President. He advocated making government
"leaner, not meaner"; he did not say "and" meaner.
The New York Times

Contrary to what we said in a column headed "Return of the Living Dead"
yesterday, HMS *Hampshire* did not sink after hitting a land mine. They are
rarely found at sea.   *Guardian*

In the Review section's special summer reading issue of 2 July 2000 we wrongly
ascribed a reading list to Roddy Doyle, the celebrated Irish author.
Unfortunately, owing to a misunderstanding, the "Roddy Doyle" we spoke to,
and who gave us a very interesting selection of summer reading, was a computer
engineer from north London.   *The Observer*

In last week's issue of *Community Life*, a picture caption listed some unusual
gourmet dishes that were enjoyed at a Westwood Library party for students
enrolled in a tutorial program for conversational English. Mai Thai Finn is one
of the students in the program and was in the center of the photo. We
incorrectly listed her name as one of the items on the menu.
Pascack Valley Community Life

The recipe for the "Bacon and Egg Breakfast Tower" on page 6 of "Kick-Start Your Cooking" serves 12 people not 1.

Weight Watchers meeting booklet

An article about the Dominican Republic referred incorrectly to the legendary creatures called "ciguapas." They are beautiful women—not men—who lure men into their homes at the bottom of mountain rivers.

The New York Times

In a report last week of a court case involving Mr. Edward Brien of Scottes Lane, Dagenham, we wrongly stated that Mr. Brien had previously been found guilty of buggery. The charge referred to was, in fact, one of burglary.

Dagenham Post

We apologize for the error in last week's paper in which we stated that Arnold Dogbody was a defective in the police force. We meant, of course, that Mr. Dogbody is a detective in the police farce.

Ely Standard

The Pacific Rim column in yesterday's BusinessExtra section should have read that *Fine Boys* is a leading Japanese fashion magazine for guys, not gays.

San Francisco Chronicle

At Oxford, C. B. Fry's party trick was to leap backward from carpet to mantelpiece from a standing fart.

Guardian, **first edition**

At Oxford, C. B. Fry's party trick was to leap backward from carpet to mantelpiece from a standing tart.

Guardian, **second edition**

At Oxford, C. B. Fry's party trick was to leap backward from carpet to mantelpiece from a standing start.

Guardian, **third edition**

A photo caption incorrectly identified Phyllis Diller as Lucille Ball's guest on Columbia Broadcasting Company's *Here's Lucy* show. The picture was actually of Jim Bailey, who is noted for his impersonation of Miss Diller.

The New York Times

Faradisation was a form of electrotherapy and not as we said ... "better known as electrocution" ... death by electric shock.

Guardian

I realize that the translation of religious documents is open to interpretation, but when I said that the Good Samaritan was "moved to get off his ass" I feel it translates better using the word "donkey."

Ron Burke, letter to the *Newbury Weekly News*

Heather Mills's charitable donations, recorded in the part of the divorce case judgment released to the public, are £627,000 and not £627.   ***Guardian***

In yesterday's issue, The New York Times did not report on riots in Milan and the subsequent murder of the lay religious reformer Erlembald. These events took place in 1075, the year given in the dateline under the nameplate on Page 1. The Times regrets both incidents.   ***The New York Times*, 1975**

Millwall's chant, "Everybody hates us and we don't care" … is a misquotation. The celebrated defiance of the Millwall fans is, "No one likes us. We don't care."

The Independent

Statements made by Sylvester the Cat were erroneously attributed to Daffy Duck.

Boston Globe

A caption misidentified a drag queen shown standing behind Quentin Crisp. The performer was Brandywine, not Lady Bunny.

The New York Times

Apropos "The Godfathers": Sam Giancana can only be said to have "died peacefully in Chicago" if the definition includes being shot dead. He was murdered.   ***Guardian***

Instead of being arrested, as we stated, for kicking his wife down a flight of stairs and hurling a lighted kerosene lamp after her, the Reverend James P. Wellman died unmarried four years ago.

Unidentified American newspaper, noted by Edward Burne-Jones

HUMANITY

GENDER

It takes all sorts to make a sex.
Saki

The most important job is not to be governor, or First Lady in my case.
George W. Bush

Karyn is with us. A West Texas girl, just like me. **George W. Bush**

You are a woman, aren't you?
Prince Philip, accepting a gift from a native woman in Kenya

—I'm a transvestite.
—Could've fooled me, you haven't even got an accent.
Beverly LaSalle and Archie Bunker, *All in the Family*

—Is Tiny Tim a boy or a girl?
—I don't think so.
Alan Sues and Goldie Hawn,
Rowan & Martin's Laugh-in

I'm not actually half girl/half boy. I've worked this out. I'm sort of all boy, plus extra girl.
Eddie Izzard

Last time [I was on the show], I said that England rugby player Danny Cipriani once dated Larissa Summers, a girl who used to be a man. Well, Larissa's been in touch and apparently she didn't used to be man, so apologies for that.
Nick Ferrari, *The Alan Titchmarsh Show*

You have to understand that just because I have a penis that doesn't make me any less a woman than any other woman.
Darlene, a transvestite, *Mr. Miss World*

I get fan mail from women. I don't know why. Even Helen Keller would get the gist. I think they see me as a challenge—like Mount Kilimanjaro.
Alan Carr, gay comedian

You're bisexual, John. So, who would you sleep with first, me or Judy?
Richard Madeley, to John Barrowman, *Richard & Judy*

—Ken [Livingstone] said he thinks we're all bisexual. Do you agree?
—I'm a polymorphous pervert. That's what Freud would say.
Johann Hari and Boris Johnson, *Attitude* magazine

Bisexual? I just called it "whoring." I was terrible. If it wasn't nailed down …
Me poor mother. I remember her shouting up the stairs one time, "Who've you
got up there? A fella or a woman?"
Paul O'Grady

All that's bi about me these days are my bifocals.
Paul O'Grady

—I understand you have a little lad of 12.
—Yes, that's right.
—Is he a boy or a girl?
—A boy.
Richard Madeley and caller, *Richard & Judy*

My daughter, a eunuch?
Erronius, *A Funny Thing Happened on the Way to the Forum*

To be truthful, I missed my penis.
**Charles Kane, the first person to have had
a sex-change operation—who then had it reversed**

My wife had half a dozen sex-change operations, but couldn't find anything she liked.
Woody Allen

When I was 12, oh what a joy, Mom told me I was a boy!
Peter Potter, *Son of Paleface*

—Here's your giraffe, little girl.
—I'm a boy!
—That's the spirit. Never give up.
Homer Simpson and Ralph Wiggum, *The Simpsons*

GAY

There's nothing wrong with being gay.
I have plenty of friends that are going to hell.
Stephen Colbert

I was very naïve before I got married. I didn't even know what a homosexual was until I met my husband.

Mary Drury

—Have you ever had sex with a man?
—Not yet.

Reporter and Boris Johnson, mayor of London

—Tell me, Mr. Gardener, have you ever had sex with a man?
—No ... I don't think so.

Dennis Watson and Chance the gardener, *Being There*

—Ben's hot, but I think he's gay.
—No way. Why?
—He asked if my carpet matches my drapes.

Two girls, www.overheardinnewyork.com

I have known several homosexuals quite well—in fact, I used to go to bed with a young Turkish boy called Abdul when I was stationed in Cyprus. Most obliging lad ... but anyway he, it later turned out, was, in fact, homosexual. I had to stop seeing him once I'd found out, naturally.

Hugh Laurie, playing an army officer

Are you telling me the man who tried to put a rubber fist in my anus was a homosexual?

Borat Sagdiyev, *Borat*

He wasn't an obvious homosexual. I mean, he didn't push it down people's ... er ... noses.

Valerie Edwards

—Plato was gay.
—Mickey Mouse's dog was gay?
—Goofy was his lover.

Jodie Dallas and Jessica Tate, *Soap*

If I didn't know me, I'd probably think I was gay too.

Sisqó

—One day I just clicked. I said, "Mom, Dad, Boss, I'm gay."
—So what happened?

—My mom cried for exactly ten seconds, my boss said, "Who cares?" and my dad said, "But you're so tall!"

Peter Malloy and Howard Brackett, *In & Out*

Bart is gay? Marge, it's all your fault. Why did you have to be so feminine around him?

Homer Simpson, *The Simpsons*

We've all got a feminine side, but I was told that we've all got a bit of a gay side, too. So I thought, "All right, I'm going to be gay." I was walking down the street trying to look at men, but I just like women too much.

Benjamin Zephaniah

An Irish queer is a fellow who prefers women to drink.

Sean O'Faolain

My son is gay, and that's his boyfriend— he's gay too.

Roy Biggins, *Wings*

We had gay burglars the other night. They broke in and rearranged the furniture.

Robin Williams

I don't understand homophobia myself ... Mathematically, in the great race of life, homosexual people have ruled themselves out of the competition for women, so what's to dislike?

Boris Johnson, mayor of London

I have nothing personally against homosexual men, but I wouldn't want my daughter to marry one.

Hugh Laurie, playing an army officer

You know what's *so* wrong about gayness? If there are two men, who has the vagina?

Stanley Smith, *American Dad!*

In Iran, we don't have homosexuals like in your country.

President Mahmoud Ahmadinejad, lecturing at Columbia University, New York

And I'm not homophobic, all right? Come round, look at my CDs. You'll see Queen, George Michael, Pet Shop Boys. They're all bummers.

David Brent, *The Office* (U.K.)

—Howard, do you want gay men to be labeled?
—Yes, that would be fantastic!

Jane Christie and Howard, *Coupling*

—Damn! You can't go nowhere now without seeing faggots. I saw two brothers holding hands on the train the other day. It's like they were coming out of the closet on the train.
—There ain't no closet on the train.

Two guys, www.overheardinnewyork.com

As of last month we have gay bishops, official. I wonder if this will filter down into the game of chess? Those bishops can make all the same moves, but can only be taken from behind.

Jason Wood

LESBIAN

Lesbian: just another damn woman trying to do a man's job.

Anon.

Women can't be gay. Because if men were gay and women were gay they'd cancel each other out.

Danny Dallas, *Soap*

I'm in love with a woman now, but I don't think that makes me a lesbian.

Samantha Fox, former model

You have a high voice for a lesbian.

Bertha Vanation, *Torch Song Trilogy*

She looked like a lesbian with doubts about her masculinity.   Peter De Vries

Nobody Knows I'm a Lesbian   Slogan on a T-shirt

Labels can be misleading. I saw a news report about a lesbian protest march, and the report said, "Coming up next, a lesbian demonstration." My first thought was, "Cool. I always wondered how those things work."

Michael Dane

Oh, wouldn't that be great … being a lesbian. All the advantages of being a man, but with less embarrassing genitals. Plus every time you have sex, there's *four* breasts—two guest breasts and two you can take home afterward.

Jeff Murdock, *Coupling*

RACE

I'm a white male, aged 18 to 49. Everyone listens to me, no matter
how dumb my suggestions are.
Homer Simpson, The Simpsons

Caucasian? It was on my army draft card. I thought it meant "circumcised."
Elvis Presley

—You're colored!
—Yes, I am!
—You didn't sound colored on the phone.
—That's 'cause I used the white telephone.
Archie Bunker and Chester Byrd, *All in the Family*

Everybody's colored or else you wouldn't be able to see them.
Captain Beefheart

I'm not against the blacks, and a lot of the good blacks will attest to that.
Evan Mecham, governor of Arizona

I got one of those forms for jury duty, you gotta fill it out. Omigod, I don't
wanna do jury duty so my friend says, "Why don't you just write something
racist on the form like, 'I hate Chinks.'" And I said, "I don't want people to
think I'm racist, I just wanna get out of jury duty." So I filled out the form and I
wrote, "I love Chinks." **Sarah Silverman**

Personally, I prefer to be called a "person of paleness," if you must refer to my
race. **Dan Henry**

Bigotry started a long time ago—nobody knows where. Personally, I think the
French started it.
Johnny Fever, *WKRP in Cincinnati*

The thing about xenophobia is it's a Greek word.
Al Murray, as The Pub Landlord

—What do you call a black man who flies a plane?
—A pilot, you racist.
Anon.

My girlfriend isn't Asian. She's Thai.

Drew Gooden, NBA forward

I hope I stand for anti-bigotry, anti-Semitism, anti-racism. This is what drives me.

George Bush Sr.

[speech on immigration broadcast live on Sky TV]
—Let me outline the action that a Conservative government would take. As we've seen, some of the increase in population size results from natural change—birth rates, death rates. Here our policy should be obvious ...
—*[overheard, off camera]* Extermination!

David Cameron and Julie Etchingham, presenter, Sky News (U.K.) (YT)

I believe in equality. Equality for everybody. No matter how stupid they are or how superior I am to them.

Steve Martin

So, if this show teaches you anything, it should teach you how to respek everyone: animals, children, bitches, spazmos, mingers, lezzers, fatty boombahs and even gaylords. So, to all you lot watching this, but mainly to the normal people, respek!

Ali G, *Da Ali G Show*

ATTRACTION

Men seldom make passes at girls who wear glasses.
Dorothy Parker

Hi, I'm Moe, or, as the ladies used to call me, "Hey, you behind the bushes!"

Moe Syzslak, *The Simpsons*

Our eyes met, and the ground lurched beneath my feet and bells rang out. My God, I thought, I've finally found her! Then I remembered we were in an elevator.

Charlie Acord and Melinda Dalehite

—Mary Kelly thinks you're a complete idiot.
—Then why does she keep looking at my arse when we're talking?
— She's lip-reading.

Sally Harper and Patrick Maitland, *Coupling*

I wouldn't touch that with a 10-foot pole. Maybe an 8-foot Hungarian …

Johnny Carson, *Rowan & Martin's Laugh-in*

Even hookers want to know why we can't "just be friends."

Ray Aragon and Cynthia Coe

—Mother, what do I have to do to please a man?
—Remember to always use lots of scent and never let him see you brush your teeth.   **Joan and Iris Wyndham**

—What do blondes put behind their ears to attract men?
—Their feet.   **Anon.**

She said, "Would you like to see me in something flowing?" I said, "Yes, the River Thames."   **Morecambe and Wise**

—You're all right to play around with … but we're intellectual opposites.
—What do you mean?
—Well, I'm intellectual and you're opposite.

Cleo Borden and Ivan Valadoff, *Goin' to Town*

I've been chased by women before but not while I was awake.

Peter Potter, *The Paleface*

When we first got together, one of the things me and Judy had in common was a passion for the correct use of the apostrophe.

Richard Madeley, *Richard & Judy*

You know, you two girls have everything. You're tall and short and slim and stout and blonde and brunette. And that's just the kind of a girl I crave.

Groucho Marx

There she was … a delicately beautiful face and a body that could melt a cheese sandwich from across the room.

Lieutenant Frank Drebin, *The Naked Gun 2½: The Smell of Fear*

Her hair glistened in the rain like nose hair after a sneeze.   **Chuck Smith**

Is that your own hair or did you scalp an angel?

Larry Haines, *My Favorite Blonde*

—Those are some long legs!
—I just had them lengthened. Now they go all the way up.
Topper Harley and Ramada Thompson, *Hot Shots*

—I'm not wearing a bra, Johnny.
—Yeah? Well, that makes two of us.
Chorus Girl and Johnny Kelly, *Johnny Dangerously*

—You know what's wrong with Susan, don't you?
—Thrush?
Kurt McKenna and Brian Steadman, *Teachers*

To try to draw her attention, I set fire to myself. It moved her: She fried an egg on me.
Seagoon, *The Goon Show*

A lot of weather we've been having lately.
Oliver Hardy, chatting up a lady, *Way Out West*

Some day, you'll have my children. In fact, they're in the car now if you want them.
Roland T. Flakfizer, *Brain Donors*

An American girl hit on me in a club and asked me to make her an Egyptian princess. So I threw a sheet over her head and told her to be quiet.
Ahmed Ahmed

If a black guy fancies you, you know straight away. If a white guy fancies you, he'll ask you if you know where the toilet is.
White girl, *White Girls Are Easy*

Soon I hope to take you on a Caribbean cruise, where we can hold hands on a soft summer's evening and watch that old Jamaican moon. Why that old Jamaican will be mooning us, I have no idea.
Roland T. Flakfizer, *Brain Donors*

You know, if I were a single man, I might ask that mummy out. That's a good-looking mummy.
Bill Clinton, on an excavated Inca mummy

DATING

I think, therefore I'm single.
Lizz Winstead

Hey babe, you wanna come up and see my coffee sometime?
Larry (The Three Stooges), *I Can Hardly Wait*

All my friends started getting boyfriends. But I didn't want a boyfriend.
I wanted a 13-color biro. **Victoria Wood**

—What's your new boyfriend like?
—Did you ever see *An Officer and a Gentleman*?
—Yeah ....
—Well, he's kinda like the guy I went to see that with.
Rachel Green and Phoebe Buffay, *Friends*

Excuse me, haven't you seen me somewhere before?
Richard Burton, *What's New Pussycat?*

—Carla, who do I know who would be a good match for Diane?
—What about that guy you used to play ball with—Fred Wilson?
—Fred's dead, Carla.
—So she has to drive ... **Sam Malone and Carla Tortelli,** *Cheers*

I once dated a waitress. In the middle of sex she'd say, "How is everything? Is
everything okay over here?" **David Corrado**

After eating, you should wait half an hour before dating a lifeguard.
Will Truman, *Will & Grace*

I went out with a promiscuous impressionist. She did everybody.

Jay London

I used to go out with a lot of wolves, but now I'm down to about a pack a
night. **Jo Anne Worley,** *Rowan & Martin's Laugh-in*

—So, are you one of those really, really high-maintenance girls?
—In terms of, like, what?
—Maintenance.
Dale Howard and Jennifer Clark, *Big Brother 9* (U.K.)

My girlfriend told me I should be more affectionate. So I got two girlfriends.

Rodney Dangerfield

It's really hard to maintain a one-on-one relationship if the other person is not going to allow me to be with other people.

Axl Rose, of Guns N' Roses

You know, when we're not fighting, we get along just fine.

Jim Rockford, *Rockford Files*

I was seeing this girl for about six weeks, until someone took my binoculars.

Larry the Cable Guy

Girls are like pianos. When they're not upright, they're grand.

Benny Hill

—Er, you don't happen to know how much polar bears weigh, do you?
—Polar bears? No.
—Neither do I, but it breaks the ice. Would you like to dance?

Scott Fields and a girl in a disco, *Love Life*

—Don't go near my daughter again. Don't try to see her. Don't write her and don't phone her.
—Can I use her underwear to make soup?

Jimmie-Sue's father and Rigby Reardon, *Dead Men Don't Wear Plaid*

People wonder why I go out with models with nothing between their heads.

Simon Le Bon, of Duran Duran

It is relaxing to go out with my ex-wife because she already knows I'm an idiot.

Warren Thomas

I really quite like being single. Except for the bit about not having a man.

Jane Christie, *Coupling*

Our kid was courting a lass in her car. "Do you want to want to get in the back seat?" she said. "No," he said, "I'd sooner stay in the front with you."

Les Dawson

Likes going out for meals—or staying in for meals. Skin color: not essential.
Cheryl Carroll, personal ad, *The Royle Family*

I have a friend who subscribes to a dating website. The other day she got very excited when she thought she'd found a chap with his own "chocolate laboratory." It had to be pointed out to her that the abbreviation "choc lab" meant he'd got a "chocolate Labrador."
John Blackwood

He said he couldn't go through with the date as the photograph wasn't "representative." Okay, it was an old photo, but have I really changed that much in 15 years?
Dawn, *Gavin & Stacey*

—The thing is, Dil, you're not a girl.
—Details, baby, details.
Fergus and Dil, *The Crying Game*

Howard Hughes was never able to stay with one woman because he looked at them like airplanes. He wanted to get a sleeker plane with bigger turbines.
Leonardo DiCaprio

If you don't think women are explosive, drop one.
Gerald F. Lieberman

Dumping me? Just give me a reason. You think I'm unemotional, don't you? I can be emotional. Jesus, I cried like a child at the end of *Terminator 2*.
Tim Bisley, *Spaced*

There are other fish in the sea, and I'm now married to a pike.   **Les Dawson**

KISS

Never let a fool kiss you or a kiss fool you.
Joey Adams

—Doug! I think I just felt your tongue in my mouth.
—It's called a French kiss.
—But I thought you were from Nebraska!
Marcia Brady and Doug Simpson, *The Brady Bunch Movie*

—I was thinking, later, you could kiss me on the veranda.
—Lips would be fine.

Rosita and Dusty Bottoms, *Three Amigos!*

I didn't know it was against the rules.

Cleberson Souza Santos, Brazilian soccer player, after being booked for kissing the referee during a soccer match (YT)

—Lips that touch liquor shall never touch mine.
—Your lips?
—No, my liquor.

Dick Martin and Jo Anne Worley, *Rowan & Martin's Laugh-in*

People who throw kisses are hopelessly lazy.

Bob Hope

—Where did you learn to kiss like that?
—I used to play a bugle in the boy scouts.

Claribel Higg and Eddie Pink, *Strike Me Pink*

I've kissed so many women, I could do it with my eyes closed.

Henny Youngman

So I kissed Lucy, and was very surprised to feel her tongue pop out. It was my first real snog and I loved it. You can imagine that I fell in love instantly. Sadly, the next year Lucy developed distemper and had to be put down.

Hugh Laurie, *A Bit of Fry and Laurie*

I wasn't kissing it. I was trying to bite it off.

Denis Healey, denying that he once kissed the hand of Margaret Thatcher

SEX

We English have sex on the brain, which is a very unsatisfactory
place to have it.
Malcolm Muggeridge

Someone once came up to me and asked, "If you could sleep with anyone living or dead, who would it be?" And I said, "Anyone living."

Jimmy Carr

I admit I have a tremendous sex drive. My boyfriend lives 40 miles away.

Phyllis Diller

I hated having sex with the optometrist. He kept asking me, "Is this better, or is this better?"

Carol Leifer

I'm an experienced woman. I've been around—well, all right, I might not have been around, but I've been ... nearby.

Mary Richards, *Mary Tyler Moore*

—You're just looking for casual sex.
—Casual sex? What are you talking about? This is, like, my best suit.

David Morgan and Kathy, *Cross My Heart*

I'm a nice girl. I hate it on the first date when I accidentally have sex.

Emmy Gay

Once you have sexual intercourse, you are no longer a virgin.

Ivana Trump, writing an advice column

What man desires is a virgin who is a whore.

Karl Kraus

Would I be bad in bed? Well, I once referred to the "missionary position" as the "military position," so that says a lot.

Luke Marsden, *Big Brother 9* (U.K.)

The first time we ever made love I said, "Am I the first man who ever made love to you?" She said, "You could be. You look damn familiar."

Ronnie Bullard

—I don't know how I lost my virginity to that man. He must have slipped me something.
—Apparently. **Dorothy Zbornak and Sophia Petrillo, *The Golden Girls***

—How did you lose your virginity?
—I had sex. **Interviewer and L. L. Cool J, *Spin* magazine**

And I'll tell you another thing: I faked every orgasm!

Lieutenant Frank Drebin, *The Naked Gun*

Is it wrong to fake orgasm during masturbation? **Lotus Weinstock**

What is orgasm, after all, except laughter of the loins?

Mickey Rooney

I've never heard of this Greek chap, Clitoris, they're all talking about.

Lord Albemarle

I first mentioned it to Joe, sitting in the front room one night. I said, "Joe, have you ever heard of the clitoris?" He didn't even look up from his paper. "Yeah," he said, "but it doesn't go as well as the Ford Escort."

Shirley, *Shirley Valentine*

I bought my wife a sex manual but half the pages were missing. We went straight from foreplay to postnatal depression.

Bob Monkhouse

Anal sex? No thanks. I want a shag more than once a year.

Lou Clarke

Men, on average, think about sex once every eight minutes. I make a point of thinking about sex every four seconds. That makes me 120 times more manly than the rest of you.

Simon Munnery

—I don't think we should make love, all right?
—OK, we'll just have sex.

Harris K. Telemacher and Sandee, *L.A. Story*

I make it a policy never to have sex before the first date.

Daisy Morgan, *Surrender*

My mother is 60, and her whole life she only ever slept with one guy. She won't tell me who.   Wendy Liebman

I went to a meeting for premature ejaculators. I left early.

Jack Benny

I believe in safe sex. My bed's got a handrail.   Ken Dodd

You know, we talk a great deal about "safe sex." By that I don't mean "making love to a strong box."   Stephen Fry

I'm shooting a commercial for safe sex. How ironic. Because I don't have that.

Tila Tequila

If you ain't careful, sex can lead to some terrible fings: herpes, squat rot, or even worse, somefing called "a relationship."

Ali G, *Da Ali G Show*

At a meeting of nuns in the convent, the Mother Superior announced that there was a case of gonorrhea in the convent. "That sounds like good news to me," said one of the nuns. "I was getting tired of that Chardonnay."

Anon.

—What is syphilis?
—Syphilis is a venerable disease.

Nurse's exam paper

Syphilis is a sociable disease.

Peter De Vries

Our research found that one in ten men thinks chlamydia is a flower.

Genevieve Clark, of the U.K. HIV/AIDS charity the Terrence Higgins Trust

In bed, my wife's favorite position is back-to-back.

Chuck Smith

As for that topsy-turvy tangle known as *soixante-neuf*, personally, I have always found it to be madly confusing, like trying to pat your head and rub your stomach at the same time.

Helen Lawrenson

—People forget that the brain is the biggest erogenous zone.
—On you maybe.

Jackie Treehorn and Jeffrey Lebowski, *The Big Lebowski*

If you want a healthy sex life, the key word is communication. If you're making love to your partner, for heaven's sake tell them.

Ivor Dembina

During sex I fantasize that I'm someone else.

Richard Lewis

—We think that your friend, Monette, might be practicing the world's oldest profession.
—You think that Monette is a carpenter?

Mary Jo Shively and Charlene Stillfield, *Designing Women*

You're a hooker? Jesus, I forgot! I just thought I was doing great with you!

Arthur Bach, *Arthur*

—Is she a prostitute?

—Oh, no! She's an actress who's researching the part of a prostitute, going on ... 14 years now.

Drew Carey and Nigel Wick, *The Drew Carey Show*

You wanna hear my personal opinion on prostitution? If men knew how to do it, they wouldn't have to pay for it.   **Roseanne Barr**

The thing I love most about my S&M mistress is that she doesn't care whether I'm Baptist, Jewish, Catholic or Methodist. She's a non-denominatrix.

Woody Walker

I went to see a go-go dancer. But she'd gone.   **Harry Hill**

I didn't suspect it was an orgy until three days later.   **S. J. Perelman**

Let's not call them orgies, let's just say it was seven or eight people in love.   **Ronnie Hawkins**

Sign of an incompetent phone-sex operator: "I'm 39 and sort of dumpy, wearing a pink housecoat ..."

Marc Liebert

I tried phone sex and got an ear infection.   **Richard Lewis**

—I have been married for two years and our marriage is going through a difficult phase. My wife wants children and we haven't had any. I want sex and we haven't had any. What do you advise? Going to a marriage guidance counsellor?

—Not really. I don't suppose you'll get any sex with a marriage guidance counselor.

Miles Kington

Of course, this isn't the first case I've come across of a man seeking sexual gratification with his vacuum cleaner, but this guy obviously didn't know his model well. If he had, he'd have known that right under where the hose attaches, there's a revolving blade for pushing the dust into the collection bag. It just goes to show, you should always read your appliance instruction manual before turning it on.

Doctor Louis Napolento

Guys, I've got to tell you something: I'm omnipotent.

Michael Kelso, *That '70s Show*

An Englishman sucked his Viagra tablet instead of swallowing it. He wound up with a stiff upper lip.

Ken O'Callaghan

They should make Viagra for women, so men aren't the ones having to wait an hour.

Bill Strider

An Irishman was having sex with a Jewish girl. "You're not very tight for a Jewish girl," says the Irishman. "You're not very thick for an Irishman," she replies.

Anon.

ROMANCE

You're worse than a hopeless romantic. You're a hopeful one.
Hannah Warren, California Suite

It's all about romance. And chapstick.

Mitch Leery, *Dawson's Creek*

What do you know about romance? Your idea of foreplay is finding a dark place to park.

Faith Yokas, *Third Watch*

Doorbell rang the other day. I answered the door and there was a delivery boy with two dozen roses. I opened the card, and it said, "Love from your boyfriend, Ernie." I was having tea with my girlfriend, Clementine, at the time and I said, "Clementine, do you know what this means? For the next two weeks I'm going to be flat on my back with my legs wide open." Clementine said to me, "What's the matter, you ain't got a vase?"

Bette Midler

I'll meet you tonight under the moon. Oh, I can see you now, you and the moon. You wear a necktie so I'll know you.

Groucho Marx

—It was so romantic, Mr. Rigsby: champagne, soft lights, Tchaikovsky in the background …
—Oh, was he there too?

Miss Jones and Mr. Rigsby, *Rising Damp*

I even hired a sky-writer to write "Brian loves Alex" across the sky, but he ran out of smoke. It came out Brian loves Al.

Brian Hackett, *Wings*

—Arthur, take my hand.
—But that would only leave you with one!

Arthur Bach and Susan Johnson, *Arthur*

—My, what a fiery nature!
—Let's throw another log on it!

Sal Van Hoyden and Chester Hooton, *Road to Utopia*

LOVE

—But Mortimer, you're going to love me for my mind too!
—One thing at a time.

Elaine Harper and Mortimer Brewster, Arsenic and Old Lace

That is a *babe*! She makes me feel kinda funny, like when we used to climb the rope in gym class.

Garth Algar, *Wayne's World*

Love is being able to squeeze your lover's spots.

Zoë Ball

I'm the Hiroshima of love.

Sylvester Stallone

Love can sweep you off your feet and carry you along in a way you've never known before. But the ride always ends, and you end up feeling lonely and bitter. Wait. It's not love I'm describing. I'm thinking of a monorail.

Jack Handey

My husband is thoughtful. I can't stand getting into a cold bed, so every night, he plugs in the electric iron. While I am undressing, he irons my side of the bed, then I get in, and iron his side.

Letter, *Daily Mirror*

When you find your soulmate, you could sleep under their armpits.

Heather Mills

I decided to give each and every one of my Beanie Babies a hug, even the ones that have lost 90 percent of their value.

Art Grinath

Love's not a potato, you can't throw it out the window.

Russian proverb

Love is eternal as long as it lasts.

Henri de Régnier

—I love you! I love you!
—Oh, say it in French. Please, say it in French.
—I don't know French ... what about Hebrew?

Fielding Mellish and Nancy, *Bananas*

I love horse manure ... for all the things it can do and for the smell of it.

Dame Helen Mirren

Forget love—I'd rather fall in chocolate!

Sandra J. Dykes

MARRIAGE

Plans, marriages and journeys appear to me just as foolish
as if someone falling out of a window were to hope
to make friends with the occupants of the room before
which he passes.
Jean Cocteau

Please, Marabelle, if you'll marry me this once, I promise I'll never ask you again.

Moe (The Three Stooges), *Uncivil War Birds*

—Are you married?

—No, engaged.

—What, engaged to your fiancée?

Peter Powell and radio listener, BBC Radio

The closest I ever got to an altar was when my uncle tried to sacrifice me to the corn gods to make the crops grow.

Lewis Kiniski, *The Drew Carey Show*

I would love to have a wife I feel comfortable with. But it has to be the right person, where you're both independent to a point where you can go off to Alaska at a moment's notice with your friends and it won't be an issue.

Leonardo DiCaprio

I married a suicide bomber but she went off with someone else.

Jeff Green, *The A-Z of Being Single*

I never want to marry. I just want to get divorced.

Natasha, *Love and Death*

—Didn't I tell you I was going to get married?
—Who to?
—Why, a woman, of course. Did you ever hear of anybody marrying a man?
—Sure.
—Who?
—My sister.

Oliver Hardy and Stan Laurel, *Beau Hunk*

If gay marriage was OK—and I was uncertain on the issue—then I saw no reason in principle why a union should not be consecrated between three men, as well as two men; or indeed three men and a dog.

Boris Johnson, mayor of London, *Friends, Voters, Countrymen*

I think that gay marriage should be between a man and a woman.

Arnold Schwarzenegger

I always wanted to be a June bride.

Gene Robinson, gay bishop who entered into a civil union with his long-time partner, Mark Andrews, on June 9, 2008

I don't see what the big deal is about same-sex marriages. Every married couple I know has the same sex all the time.

Jim Rosenberg

Heterosexual marriage is just wrong. I mean, if God had meant men and women to be together, he would have given them both penises.

Jack McFarland, *Will & Grace*

With men and women, does you think that men should marry only one woman? Does you believe in mahogany?

Ali G, *Da Ali G Show*

Oh, go on, marry him, even if you have to sign one of those prenatal agreements.
Rose Nylund, *The Golden Girls*

—So, how long have you known this guy you're marrying?
—It'll be two months—in three weeks.

Liz Lemon and Cerie, *30 Rock*

—Are you married?
—Am I not a man? And is not a man stupid? I'm a man. So I married. Wife, children, house, everything. The full catastrophe.
Basil and Alexis Zorba, *Zorba the Greek*

—When did you get married?
—[*turning to his publicity agent*] When did I get married?
Interviewer and Tyrone Hill, basketball star

—You never met my wife, did you?
—Yes, I never did.
Oliver Hardy and Stan Laurel, *Helpmates*

—Do you have to ask your wife everything?
—Well, if I don't ask her, I wouldn't know what she wanted me to do.
Oliver Hardy and Stan Laurel, *Sons of the Desert*

Tie yourself up with some chick and pretty soon she's gonna be making you eat with a knife and fork.
Juan Epstein, *Welcome Back, Kotter*

—How did you meet your husband?
—At a travel agency. I was looking for a holiday and he was the last resort.
Anon.

—So, when was the last time you had sex?
—With each other?
Marriage counsellor and Ari Gold, *Entourage*

My ex-husband tricked me into marrying him. He told me I was pregnant.
Carol Leifer

My psychiatrist said my wife and I should have sex every night. Now we never see each other.
Rodney Dangerfield

Remember, marriage is a two-way street. I don't know what that means, but remember it.

George Burns

I don't want to be married. It sounds crazy, but in my mind, it's all connected. You get married, you have kids, you grow old, and then you die. Somehow, it seems to me, if you didn't get married, you wouldn't die.

John Burns, *Taxi*

—If I died, would you marry again?
—We'll talk about it when it happens.

Claire and Cliff Huxtable, *The Cosby Show*

I would rather have a baby through my penis than get married again.

Eminem

I have tried both marriage and single life, and I cannot recommend either.

John W. De Forest

Jerry Hall says that to keep your husband keen, you must be "a maid in the parlor, a cook in the kitchen and a whore in the bedroom." I recently decided to follow her advice. I kept the house very clean, I prepared delicious meals every night, and I allowed dozens of fat businessmen to have sex with me for money in the marital bed. Surprisingly, my husband left me.

Pauline Riley, *Viz* magazine

—My wife's an angel.
—Lucky bastard. Mine's still alive.

Anon.

WEDDING

I learned a long time ago never to trust anybody wearing a
wedding gown, especially a woman.
Sam Malone, Cheers

Before you can get divorced in Britain, you need to get married. For Harvey and Jane, the big day has arrived ...

Tom Baker, *Little Britain*

I told a friend I was getting married, and they said, "Have you picked a date yet?" I said, "Wow, you can bring a date to your own wedding? What a country!"

Yakov Smirnoff

You're going to have a big wedding whether you like it or not. And if you don't like it, you don't have to come!

Agnes Hurley, to her daughter, Jane, *The Catered Affair*

"Daddy, Daddy," shouted my six-year-old son Jack ... "I'm going to be a paperboy at Auntie Josie's wedding!"

Eamonn Holmes

—How are you coping with pre-wedding jitters?
—I have two words for you: champagne.

Interviewer and Pamela Anderson

—Weddings take a lot of organizing. We're having a champagne toast.
—You have toast made of champagne? Wicked! You posh people have thought of everything.

Carrie Davis and Chris Moyles, *The Chris Moyles Show*

The bride arrived in a full-length white mink coat ... over a red sequinned knee-length party dress. The groom wore dark glasses.

The Times, on the wedding of
Liza Minnelli and David Gest

The bride is on the right.

TV commentator, as Lady Diana Spencer
set off down the aisle on her father's arm
to marry Prince Charles

Our dog wasn't really the ring-bearer. He just had a wee bag round his neck; he walked from A to B then we took the rings out.

Ashley Jensen, on her wedding in California

—I never understand why people throw rice at weddings.
—Because tomatoes leave stains.

Sophia Petrillo and Dorothy Zbornak, *The Golden Girls*

Is it kissomary to cuss the bride?

Rev. William Archibald Spooner

He doesn't have any holiday time left, so his employer's given him passionate leave for his honeymoon.

E. F. Holmes

My wife and I were setting off on our honeymoon in the evening, and an elderly relative, on hearing that we had quite a distance to travel, inquired, "Will you be going all the way tonight?"

Matthew Cochrane

A honeymoon couple go into a hotel and ask for a suite. "Bridal?" asks the desk clerk. "No, thanks," says the bride, "I'll just hang on to his shoulders."

Anon.

BATTLE OF THE SEXES

If a man does something silly, people say, isn't he silly? If a woman does something silly, people say, aren't women silly?

Doris Day

I always take my wife morning tea in my pajamas. But is she grateful? No, she says she'd rather have it in a cup.

Eric Morecambe

Who wears the trousers in this house? I do. And I also wash and iron them.

Denis Thatcher, husband of Margaret

When my sister and I were growing up, there was never any doubt in our minds that men and women were equal, if not more so.

Al Gore

In my house I'm the boss. My wife is just the decision maker.

Woody Allen

I'm not a chauvinist. Women just aren't as good as men at anything—well, in sport, anyway.

Eric Bristow

—He hates women.

—So he's a misogynist?

—No, a choreographer.

Two guys, www.overheardinnewyork.com

—Men and women have different brains.

—Yes, it was in the *Daily Mail*. Women can't fold maps, and men can't get interested in headboards.

Stan Meadowcroft and Dolly Belfield, *Dinnerladies*

CHEATING

The grass looks greener ... but it's Astroturf.

Anon.

With my wife, I don't get no respect. The other night there was a knock on the front door. My wife told me to hide in the closet.

Rodney Dangerfield

A husband opens his hotel room and discovers his wife in bed with her arms around another man. "What are you doing in bed with my wife?" he exclaims. The other man looks at him, looks at the woman, looks back at him and then back at the woman. "You're right," the man says to the woman. "He is stupid!"

Dave Allen

—It was an accident.

—Oh, so you were walking by and just happened to fall into her vagina?

Keith Charles and David Fisher, *Six Feet Under*

Follow me around. I don't care. I'm serious. If anyone wants to put a tail on me, go ahead. They'd be very bored.

Presidential candidate Gary Hart to the press, who soon exposed his extramarital affair with model Donna Rice aboard a yacht called *Monkey Business*

I have not had an affair with Petronella. It is complete balderdash. It is an inverted pyramid of piffle. It is all completely untrue and ludicrous conjecture. I am amazed people can write this drivel.

Boris Johnson, then member of Parliament, on an alleged affair with journalist Petronella Wyatt, later confirmed

I'm making absolutely no comment—and no, I did not.

> **Boris Johnson, when asked if he deliberately misled Michael Howard, who fired him for lying about his extramarital affair**

—He's seduced my Freda like one of those things that lure sailors onto the rocks—what are they called?
—Icebergs?   **Bert Fry and David Archer, "The Archers," BBC Radio**

—You know, my wife doesn't understand me.
—Oh, you married men are all the same.
—No, I mean it. She doesn't understand me. She's Swahili.

> **Tim Conway and Eileen Brennan, *Rowan & Martin's Laugh-in***

—Gary, when I was away, did you sleep with a woman?
—How do you mean, "woman"?
—A woman. You know, the ones with what you and Tony call "shirt potatoes."

> **Dorothy and Gary Strang, *Men Behaving Badly***

—Have you been sleeping with Rose Flamsteed?
—Not a wink.   **Peter De Vries, *The Glory of the Hummingbird***

"Why go out for burger when you've got steak at home," says Paul Newman about his lovely wife Nanette, and he should know.

> **Mrs. Merton, *The Mrs. Merton Show***

I think a man can have two, maybe three affairs, while he is married. But three is the absolute maximum. After that, you're cheating.

> **Yves Montand**

I wouldn't trust my husband with a young woman for five minutes, and he's been dead for 25 years.   **Kathleen Behan**

You've got to believe me, Edith, nothing was ever constipated.

> **Archie Bunker, *All in the Family***

Since the day I married you 13 years ago, there's *never* been a man in my life!

> **Bea Benaderet**

A drunk finds out that his wife is having an affair, so he confronts her: "I-I heard about your infidelity. You, you've betrayed me. I-I'm going to put an end to it all!" He takes out a revolver, loads it, and puts it up to his head. His wife just sits in the corner laughing. "Don't laugh," he says. "You're next!"

> **Dave Allen**

DIVORCE

The real genius for love lies not in getting into
but getting out of love.
George Moore

After her divorce from Sir Paul McCartney, I see Heather Mills is footloose
around town again.
Nadine Barber

The West Surrey Committee recorded the case of a man who wished to take
divorce proceedings but later withdrew the application "in case his wife got to
hear about it." **Annual Report of the Law Society (U.K.)**

The court was told she threw the frying pan at him in the bedroom.
She said she kept it on her dressing table to hold cosmetics.
Daily Telegraph

"The wife threw almost every form of domestic utensil at her husband," said
Mr. Justice Karminsky in the Divorce Court. But she was not cruel, he decided,
for on almost every occasion she missed.
Evening Standard

A 31-year-old Carlisle man who stripped his wife, stuffed some of her clothes
into her mouth, tied her hands behind her back and struck her, was making a
desperate attempt to show her that their marriage was not over, Carlisle City
magistrates were told. *Cumberland News*

—You were married twice, right?
—Married three times.
—Three times. How did the marriages end?
—Ended up with me being single.
Lawyer and witness, actual transcript from official court records

I'm enjoying having my own space and being able to shut the front door, turn
the furniture upside down, and pour raspberry jam on it, and no one's going to
tell me, "That's aesthetically unsatisfactory."
Salman Rushdie

—How did that marriage end?
—Real fast.

—Did it end from divorce?
—Yeah.
—Do you have any kids from that marriage?
—No. I didn't, but she did.

Lawyer and witness, actual transcript from official court records

We divided the house equally. She got the inside, I got the outside.

Anon.

FAMILY—GENERAL

Clever father, clever daughter; clever mother, clever son.
Russian proverb

Families is where our nation finds hope, where wings take dream.

George W. Bush

If more families were like us, the world would be a better place.

Kelly Osbourne, daughter of Ozzy and Sharon

I owe a lot to my parents, especially my mother and father.

Greg Norman

My parents have been there for me, ever since I was about seven.

David Beckham

—Is there any insanity in your family?
—Well, I have a sister.

Interviewer and J. L. Carr, at a job interview

My grandmother was insane. She had pierced hearing aids, and unscented perfume. It came in an empty bottle.

Steven Wright

One time my grandmother said to me, "Steven, come over here. Here's $5 and don't tell your mother I'm giving this to you." I said, "It'll cost you more than that."

Steven Wright

I come from a stupid family. My father worked in a bank. They caught him stealing pens.
Rodney Dangerfield

My mother is Welsh, my father is Hungarian. Which makes me well-hung.
Billy Riback

—What irritates you most about your family?
—They're Welsh.
—Why does that irritate you?
—Because that makes me Welsh.
Audience question, *Punt & Dennis*

—[*to guest, Ruth Jones*] My brother-in-law's passionate, too, because he's from South Wales …[*to Judy*] You know Pete, don't you?
—[*exasperated*] I'm your WIFE! You're talking about your BROTHER-IN-LAW!
Richard Madeley and Judy Finnigan (married over 20 years), *Richard & Judy*

He has waited 62 years to meet the brother he never knew he had.
Reporter, *BBC News*

Are you any relation to your brother, Marv?
Leon Wood, to Steve Albert

My brother was adopted. Somebody left him on the back doorstep when he was a baby. We found him when he was 16. We didn't use that door.
Wendy Liebman

My brother thinks he's a chicken; we don't talk him out of it because we need the eggs.
Groucho Marx

FAMILY PLANNING

The family you come from isn't as important as the family you're going to have.
Ring Lardner

It's one of the great urban myths that people get pregnant in order to have children.
Sir Menzies "Ming" Campbell

I'd get pregnant if I could be assured I'd have puppies.
Cynthia Nelms

I'm not gonna do a Britney and pop out some kids. I'm not a Happy Meal. My husband's got the burger, but he's not getting the fries and shake to go with it.

Pink

I thought oral contraception was when you talked your way out of it.

Pauline Lacy

She said, "The diaphragm is a pain in the ass." I said, "You're putting it in the wrong way."   **Carol Montgomery**

I won't say it, but it rhymes with "shmashmortion."   **Jonah,** *Knocked Up*

On the law that requires women to wait 24 hours before they are permitted to have an abortion: I think it's a good law. The other day I wanted to go get an abortion. I really wanted an abortion, but then I thought about it and it turned out I was just thirsty.   **Sarah Silverman**

Did you hear about the really popular Polish abortion clinic? There's a one-year waiting list.   **Anon.**

Abortion is advocated only by persons who have themselves been born.

Ronald Reagan

A friend of mine confused her Valium with her birth control pills. She had fourteen children but didn't give a shit.   **Joan Rivers**

If we can just get young people to do as their fathers did, that is, wear condoms.

Richard Branson

Condoms aren't completely safe. A friend of mine was wearing one and got hit by a bus.   **Bob Rubin**

The most common reason for condoms being ineffective in developing countries is that men wear condoms on their finger. The most common pitfall with the pill is that men take it instead of women.

United Nations report

During an AIDS-awareness campaign in South Africa, thousands of government-issued "safe-sex packs" were distributed. They included not only health information necessary for the practicing of safe sex, but also condoms. And, to keep the literature and condoms from being separated, both were connected with a staple gun, which punctured holes in basically each and every prophylactic, making them useless.   **Andrew J. Hewett**

Condoms, they're useless, aren't they?… They're ineffective and they burst, and your stomach just can't cope with the sudden impact of two kilos of cocaine.

Ardal O'Hanlon

The Irish wear two contraceptives, to be sure to be sure.

Kevin McAleer

My mom and dad were Catholics and used the rhythm method of birth control. At the end of eight years they had their own rhythm section.

Steve Wolski

We don't think our 17-year-old daughter is ready for the pill, so we've been slipping her a placebo.

Jonathan Katz

A friend asked me if a woman should have children after 35. I said that I thought 35 children is enough for any woman.

Gracie Allen

The birth rate has shown a decline over time and a main cause is the difficulty of making ends meet.

The Observer

If your parents never had children, chances are you won't either.

Dick Cavett

—Our surrogacy fee is $100,000.
—It costs more to have someone born than to have someone killed!
—It takes longer.

Chaffee Bicknell and Angie Ostrowiski, *Baby Mama*

When Margaret [Thatcher] was deposed … I went to tea with her in her temporary home in Eaton Square … "I've never liked to ask you before," I ventured, "but do you use HRT?" … "Yes, dear, I have a patch," she replied, tapping her bottom—as if to indicate that it was in place … "But I've only had it for 18 months … You see, no one told me to come off the pill." I was startled. Women usually give up the pill in their 50s, but Margaret was 65 … Did someone forget to tell her?

Teresa Gorman, *No, Prime Minister!*

BABY

A toast to the baby: with Marshall as the father it's sure to have brains;
with Carla as the mother it's sure to have need for them.
Diane Chambers, Cheers

Pregnant?! Yeah but no but yeah but no but, no, because I've never had sex apart from that one time eight months ago, but apart from that I'm a complete virgin.
Vicky Pollard, *Little Britain*

Are you one of those ladies who doesn't realize she's pregnant until she's sitting on the toilet and the kid pops out?
Debbie, *Knocked Up*

—What's it like being pregnant?
—Everything's twice the size it was nine months ago and I'm growing another head inside me.
Tony Smart and Dorothy, *Men Behaving Badly*

They all think they have something in their belly—my three-year-old thinks she has pigs ... and my four-year-old boy thinks he has monkeys.
Angelina Jolie, when pregnant with twins

I was born nine months premature.
Jay London

Of course, he should be there at the birth of his first child. It's something he'll experience two, three, or maybe four times in his life.
Stephen Brierly

I remember so clearly us going into hospital so Victoria could have Brooklyn. I was eating a candy bar at the time.
David Beckham

We'd known that the baby was a boy right from the beginning. And at first it was quite a disappointment, because I found it very unnatural, being a woman and having a boy with all his boy-bits inside me.
Victoria Beckham, *Learning How to Fly*

Having a baby is one of the hardest and most strenuous things known to man.
Anna Raeburn, advice columnist

My feet are in stirrups, my knees are in my face, the door is open facing me …
and my gynecologist does jokes, "Dr. Schwartz at your cervix!" "I'm dilated to
meet you!" **Joan Rivers**

They kept trying to sponge down my face with cool water and all I could do
was shout, "Be careful of my hair," because I didn't want it to go all curly.
Katie Price aka Jordan, British TV personality

—What is it, Del?
—It's a little baby!
Rodney and Del Boy Trotter, *Only Fools and Horses*

Twins?! Are you sure they're both mine? **Gussie, *The Big Trail***

We were born ten minutes apart, Adrian first. She always said she was the real
baby, and I was a kind of backup.
Adair Lara

I was born in the early hours of the morning and had breakfast in bed.
Richard Armour

I've breast-fed myself, and it's not easy. **Jane Garvey**

My obstetrician was so dumb that when I gave birth he forgot to cut the cord.
For a year that kid followed me everywhere. It was like having a dog on a leash.
Joan Rivers

—Babies are meant to look like their grandfathers, aren't they? Do you think she
looks like Mr. Horton?
—No, not really. He's much taller, isn't he?
Rev. Geraldine Grainger and Alice Tinker, *The Vicar of Dibley*

—The baby said her first words … She said "goo."
—At three months? You don't think she might just be making baby noises?
—No, no, no. We looked it up, it's a proper word—GUE. It's a sort of violin
played in the Shetland Islands.
Alice Tinker and Rev. Geraldine Grainger, *The Vicar of Dibley*

When I was born, I was so surprised I couldn't talk for a year and a half.
Gracie Allen

I'm happy to say I lost the weight after the baby. Of course, it took me four years, and we adopted.

Andrea Henry

A tip to all new mothers: Don't put your baby in bed with you, because you might fall asleep, roll on it and put your back out.

Harry Hill

The other day, I was pushing the baby through the park, and he was crying. Because I forgot the stoller.

Emo Philips

—You don't like babies, do you?
—Not when they're young, no.

Jean and Lionel, *As Time Goes By*

MOTHER

You may observe mother instinct at its height in a fond hen sitting on china eggs—instinct, but no brains.

Charlotte Perkins Gilman

I'll be a real good mother. I've been called one.

Wendy Liebman

When you give birth, a little bit of your heart grows. And that part cries all the time.

Céline Dion

I didn't realize how much motherhood sucks out of you. I thought I was getting Alzheimer's because I couldn't remember simple words such as "carrot." I was calling it a "thingle."

Alex Kingston

My mother blames me. She says I'm the reason she can't sit down. She blames me for the entire ruination of her body. This is a woman who attempted a tummy tuck in the eighth month of pregnancy.

Ruby Wax

Olivia, my five-year-old niece, was delighted when her mother returned from hospital with her new baby brother. "Where are they?" I asked when I went to visit. "Mummy's in the living room milking the baby," she helpfully explained.

Carol Platt

It's not easy being a mother. If it were easy, fathers would do it.
Dorothy Zbornak, *The Golden Girls*

We understand the importance of bondage between a mother and child.
Dan Quayle

The titular head—that's the mother, ain't it?
Archie Bunker, *All in the Family*

It must have been tough on your mother, not having any children.
Ann Lowell, *42nd Street*

I'm very loyal in relationships. Even when I go out with my mom I don't look at other moms and think, "Wow, I wonder what her macaroni cheese tastes like."
Garry Shandling

So thank you for reminding me about the importance of being a good mom and a great volunteer as well.
George W. Bush

If your mother were alive, she'd turn over in her grave!
Lou Carbone, *Jungle Fever*

FATHER

This is my father. Try what you can with him!
He won't listen to me, because he remembers what a fool
I was when I was a baby.
George Bernard Shaw

I remember the day my son, Lowell Junior, was born. It's an easy day to remember, it's his birthday.
Lowell Mather, *Wings*

Nothing can compare with the arrival of your first child. Not even winning Wimbledon.
Tim Henman, Wimbledon semifinalist

You can't understand it until you experience the simple joy of the first time your son points at a seagull and says, "Duck!"
Russell Crowe

I was raised by just my mom. My father died when I was eight years old—at least, that's what he told us in the letter.

Drew Carey

He'll be like a father figure to him.
Jamie Redknapp, on Peter and Kasper Schmeichel, who are father and son

My dad was a coalman; he was playful. What other father would fit wooden wings to his son's bike and drive it off the top of a haystack? He really did that.
Ken Dodd

My dad used to say, "Always fight fire with fire," which is probably why he was thrown out of the fire brigade.   **Harry Hill**

Sign your family is nuts: You're 42 but your dad still makes you watch the parade from his shoulders.   **David Letterman**

I always used to hate it when my father carried me on his shoulders. Especially when we were in the car.   **Ardal O'Hanlon**

As long as he has eight fingers and eight toes, he's my son.
Homer Simpson, *The Simpsons*

I would have respected my father more if he had never had me.
Peter De Vries

—Tell me about my dear, dear daddy! Is it true that he's dead?
—We hope so. They buried him.
Lola Marcel and Stan Laurel, *Way Out West*

I just became a godfather. I had my brother killed.   **Auggie Cook**

CHILDREN

When talking to kids, you've got to pretend
that you don't know much—and a few seconds later,
you realize you're not pretending.
Bill Cosby

I don't have any kids. Well, at least none I know about.

Cathy Ladman

I have three kids, one of each.

Rodney Dangerfield

—You were an only child. Do you know why?
—My parents didn't have any other children.

Professor Anthony Clare and Uri Geller,
In the Psychiatrist's Chair, BBC Radio

My brother was an only child.

Jack Douglas

Are you two twins or just brother and sister?

Judy Finnigan, to Monica and Gabriela Irimia,
The Cheeky Girls, *Richard & Judy*

Tragically, I was an only twin.

Peter Cook

—How old is she?
—Three-and-a-half.
—Is it "The Terrible Twos," then?

Chris Tarrant and caller, Capital Radio (U.K.)

What a childhood I had! My parents sent me to a child psychiatrist. The kid didn't help me at all.

Rodney Dangerfield

I don't want to be an orphan. I saw *Annie*. Orphans have to eat gruel and tap dance with mops.

Alf, *ALF*

I was explaining to my five-year-old daughter that our neighbor, Pam, would be coming round to babysit for her and her baby sister. She looked crestfallen. "But, Mummy," she cried, "I don't want Pam to sit on the baby!"

Ann Rees

Then we figured out we could just park them in front of the TV. That's how I was raised and I turned out TV.

Homer Simpson, *The Simpsons*

Gladys, let's play house! You be the door and I'll shut you.

Abner Kravitz, *Bewitched*

This is my sandbox. I'm not allowed in the deep end.

Ralph Wiggum, *The Simpsons*

When I played cowboys and Indians as a kid, I always had to be the post the cowboys tied their horses to.
David Kleinbard

I had earwax as a child. My father stood me in a saucer and used me as a night light.
Les Dawson

—Oh, Kelly, *please*, I'm begging you … *don't* get a tattoo. You'll regret it, you really will, because—
—Dad, I already have a tattoo.
Ozzy and Kelly Osbourne

SEX EDUCATION

Telling a teenager the facts of life is like giving a fish a bath.
Arnold Glasgow

—Mom, where do babies come from? I heard a hideous story about it once in the schoolyard.
—Oh. Well, it's true, I'm afraid.
Lisa and Marge Simpson, *The Simpsons*

—Do you have sexual relations, Mommy?
—Well, yes, dear, I do.
—Can we go and visit them some time?
Young daughter and mother

All my mother told me about sex was that the man goes on top and the woman underneath. For three years my husband and I slept in bunk beds.
Joan Rivers

If my teacher could have influenced my sexuality, I would have turned out to be a nun.
George Carlin

My sex education … I was so nervous—all the girls would go in one classroom and talk about periods, then Mr. Brent would come in and show the boys how to put a condom on, which was really embarrassing … waiting for him to go hard … He had to move schools in the end.
Alan Carr

I remember when someone first mentioned the word "masturbate," I raced home to look in the dictionary and it said "to abuse oneself." I thought, What, like shout "You twat" at the mirror?
Jarvis Cocker

Gary doesn't understand periods. He thinks they're something to do with the moon.

Dorothy, *Men Behaving Badly*

Where do babies come from? Well, son, do you remember in *9½ Weeks* when Mickey Rourke has Kim Basinger up against that wall ...

Dave George

I learned about sex the hard way—from books.

Emo Philips

My favorite book when I was eight was *Everything You Always Wanted to Know about Sex—But Were Afraid to Ask*. I was not afraid to ask.

Drew Barrymore

When I was a little kid I asked my mother where babies come from and she thought I said "rabies." She said you get them from a dog bite. The next week, a woman on my block gave birth to triplets. I thought she'd been bitten by a Great Dane.

Miles Monroe, *Sleeper*

I actually learned about sex watching neighborhood dogs. It was good. I think the most important thing I learned was never let go of the girl's leg no matter how hard she tries to shake you off.

Steve Martin

A maiden aunt in our family bought a house in the country to retire and start a poultry farm. She went off to acquire her stock of poultry and came back quite pleased with herself, having ordered 60 hens and 60 cocks.

Max Bemrose

HOME

I sold my house last week. Got a pretty good price for it,
but it made my landlord mad as hell.
Garry Shandling

[*entering a friend's apartment*] Wow, you go to a garage sale and you wonder who buys all that crap ...

Oswald Lee Harvey, *The Drew Carey Show*

Here it is, Coconut Manor, 42 hours from Times Square by railroad, 1,600 miles as the crow flies, 800 as the horse flies.

Groucho Marx

The potting shed. Is that where they smoke pot?

Jade Goody, British TV personality

—Everything in this high-tech pad works on a voice command.
—Bugger me! Noooooooooooooo!

Dave Allen

DOMESTIC WORK

Domestic work is the most elementary form of labor. It is suitable
for those with the intelligence of rabbits.
Rebecca West

—Get this house cleaned up! Do you know that my wife will be home at noon!
—Say, what do you think I am? Cinderella? If I had any sense I'd walk out on you.
—Well, it's a good thing you haven't any sense!
—It certainly is!

Oliver Hardy and Stan Laurel, *Helpmates*

I was cleaning out the attic the other day with the wife. Filthy dirty and covered with cobwebs—but she's good with the kids.

Tommy Cooper

—Mummy, where does dust come from?
—Cremated fairies.

Jil Evans

—Let's have a garage sale!
—Can't we get in trouble having a garage sale? I mean, we're not actually selling a garage.

Blanche Devereaux and Rose Nylund, *The Golden Girls*

DIY

We'll fix today what your husband mended for you last week.
Sign on a repair truck

I was doing some DIY at home, so I went to the library and said, "Have you got any books on … shelves?"   Ivor Dembina

I was doing some painting, so I went to get my stepladder. I don't get on with my real ladder.   Harry Hill

Does that screwdriver really belong to Phillip?   George Carlin

Women don't need conventional tools, we'll use anything that's handy. But when pounding a nail, don't use a shoe—shoes cost $40 a pair. A package of frozen hamburger costs $2. Use the hamburger.

Jeannie Dietz

I got an odd-job man in. He was useless. Gave him a list of eight things to do and he only did numbers one, three, five and seven. Had to get an even-man in to finish it off.   Stephen Grant

—I had the electrical cords shortened. This one's for the iron, and that one's for the lamp.
—Why did you shorten them?
—To save electricity.   Gracie Allen and George Burns

There are three ways to wire a light switch, two of which will kill and I forget the other one.   P. J. O'Rourke

You can find electrical wires in the wall by drilling at random with a power drill—this will always hit an electrical wire. (It's also a good way to find water pipes.)   P. J. O'Rourke

How many people does it take to screw in a lightbulb? One. Me. Cause I'm the only one that does anything around here anyway.

Vyvyan Basterd, *The Young Ones*

Vyvyan, Vyvyan, Vyvyan! Honestly, whenever anything explodes in this house, it's always, "Blame Vyvyan!"   **Vyvyan Basterd,** *The Young Ones*

CLASS & SNOBBERY

There is always more brass than brains in an aristocracy.
Oscar Wilde

If you're not sure which class you are, simply pull back your foreskin, where you'll find the word "lower," "middle" or "upper."

Tom Baker, *Little Britain*

I went to an exclusive kennel club. It was very exclusive. There was a sign out front: No Dogs Allowed.   **Phil Foster**

Ladies and gentlemen will not, others must not, pick the flowers.

Notice in public gardens, Belgravia, London

—Why do you have to fly first class? —I have a medical condition: I'm a snob. Mimi Bobeck and Mr. Wick, *The Drew Carey Show*

The Duke of Marlborough, having lost to the war effort the services of a valet whose duties included placing toothpaste on the ducal toothbrush, emerged from his bathroom roaring, "What's the matter with my toothbrush? The damned thing won't foam any more!"

Judith Martin

Sir Charles Mendl told me that before roasting a leg of lamb, one must drag it behind one's yacht for 24 hours.   **Mrs. Philip Barry**

She said that she'd never eaten a parsnip before!

Derek Laud, on a fellow housemate, *Big Brother 6* (U.K.)

My wife and I are not really Rolls-Royce people and are happy with a Jaguar.
Angus Ogilvy

They think they're so high and mighty, just because they never got caught driving without pants.
Moe Syzslak, *The Simpsons*

I don't dally with riff-raff these days, and he's a pretty riffy kind of raff.
Turkey Jackson, *Road to Morocco*

You might be a redneck if you've ever removed a wart with a firearm.
Jeff Foxworthy

You might be a redneck if you see a sign that says "Say No to Crack" and it reminds you to pull your jeans up.
Jeff Foxworthy

You might be a redneck if anyone in your family ever died right after saying, "Hey, y'all, watch this!"
Jeff Foxworthy

I'm ghetto. I live in the hood—with me mum.
Kieron "Science" Harvey, *Big Brother 6* (U.K.)

I don't live in the hood; I live in a cul-de-sac.
Craig Coates, *Big Brother 6* (U.K.)

Is it too much to ask for a conservatory and a peach bidet?
Vera Duckworth, *Coronation Street*

EGO

Egotism is the anesthetic that dulls the pain of stupidity.
Frank Leahy

We're not arrogant, we just believe we're the best band in the world.
Noel Gallagher, of Oasis

I'm sorry if I sound arrogant ... I have won the Champions League. I'm not one who comes straight out of the bottle. I'm a special one.
José Mourinho

I never cease to amaze myself. I say this humbly.

Don King, boxing promoter

I have never seen so much enthusiasm for an election campaign. It is like I am a rock star. I had to stop wearing a tie because I thought I might get choked in the crowds.

Silvio Berlusconi, campaigning to become prime minister of Italy, 2008

Ooh, I wish I was a girl so I could fight over me.

Stanley Snodgrass, *Here Come the Girls*

I've never met anyone like me and I don't think the world could cope with another person like me.

Paul Tulip, *The Apprentice* (U.K.)

Sometimes I wish I could be you, so I could be friends with me.

Angelica, *Rugrats*

We're more popular than Jesus now.

John Lennon, on The Beatles, 1966

I want to be like Gandhi and Martin Luther King and John Lennon ... but I want to stay alive.

Madonna

You know, I've always reminded myself of Grace Kelly ...

Jenna Maroney, *30 Rock*

I've outdone anyone you could name—Mozart, Beethoven, Bach, Strauss. Irving Berlin, he wrote 1,001 tunes. I wrote 5,500.

James Brown, The Godfather of Soul

I am the most well-known homosexual in the world.

Elton John

There's nothing better than to know I can be taking a bath at home and at the same time someone is watching me in Brazil.

Barbra Streisand

I can be too entertaining.

Leo Sayer

On occasions I have been big-headed. I think most people are when they get in the limelight. I call myself "Big Head" just to remind myself not to be.

Brian "Old Big Head" Clough

There's nobody in the world like me. I think every decade has an iconic blonde, like Marilyn Monroe or Princess Diana, and right now I'm that icon.

Paris Hilton

[I'm] the most 25th inferlential person in the world.

Jade Goody, British TV personality

I would love to gather all the fans together to say goodbye, but they would crush me with their love.

José Mourinho, British soccer coach, on leaving Chelsea

And I realized, at last, that it's time for a nice long swim in Lake Me.

Kelly Hyson

MANNERS & ETIQUETTE

I always treat fools and coxcombs with great ceremony; true good breeding not being a sufficient barrier against them.

G. K. Chesterton

—How do you do, Miss West?
—How do you do what?

Red Skelton and Mae West

Women say hello and then put their hands down my trousers. I thought it was my hand they were supposed to shake.

Simon Cowell

Lord Wemyss, a delightful old gentleman of 90, had a "Mona Lisa" which he insisted was the real one. The one in the Louvre, he said, was a copy. We were all polite and agreed with him.

Ethel Barrymore

One of my worst moments was when I drank my finger-dipping bowl at a royal party. I thought it was soup. Not only did I drink it, I also asked for the recipe.

Tara Palmer-Tomkinson, British TV personality

—Which hand should you use to stir the soup?
—Neither. You should use a spoon.

Anon.

—Do you always talk with your mouth full?
—Only when I'm eating.

Felix Unger and Oscar Madison, *The Odd Couple*

They say that good manners cost nothing. Bollocks. I sent my daughter to a posh finishing school in Switzerland and it cost me 20 grand.

J. Morgan, *Viz* magazine

On a New York subway you get fined for spitting, but you can throw up for nothing.

Lewis Grizzard

Isn't it embarrassing when you cough up a hairball and it isn't your color?

Harry Hill

I have expressed a degree of regret that can be equated with an apology.

Des Browne, U.K. Defense Secretary

—George Bush doesn't have the manhood to apologize.
—Well, on the manhood thing, I'd put mine up against his any time.

Walter Mondale and George Bush Sr.

You do not pee on someone unless they ask you to.

Mother to little boy, www.overheardatthebeach.com

—What will the neighbors think?!
—We are the neighbors and we don't think.

Ned Flanders and Lisa Simpson, *The Simpsons*

My mother never used to say the word "fart." She used to say, "Whose bottom squeaked?" ... My father also had a way of getting round the word. He would say, "Who whispered?" And we totally accepted the euphemism in our house until, one day, my granny said, "Come on, David, and whisper in Granny's ear."

Dave Allen

POLITE EUPHEMISMS FOR RELIEVING A WEDGIE

Attending to a debriefing.

Sandra Hull

Saying no to crack.

Tara Kennedy

Quelling the Boxer Rebellion.

Chuck Smith

Helping a jockey come from behind.

Ralph Scott

Pickin' cotton in the Deep South.

Jean Sorensen

INSULTS

Can you really afford to give anybody a piece of your mind?
Henny Youngman

—Penny for your thoughts, Sophia?
—You're an idiot, and that's on the house.

Rose Nylund and Sophia Petrillo-Weinstock, *Empty Nest*

I think you're the biggest moron I've ever met in my life. And living round here, that's really saying something.

Ian Beale, *EastEnders*

[He] called me a "rapist recluse." I'm not a recluse.

Mike Tyson

—Why you, you ...
—Don't you call me a you-you!

Oliver Hardy and Stan Laurel, *One Good Turn*

Did he just talk to me like I'm *ugly*?

Cerie, *30 Rock*

Billy is the only person I knew who could hear someone giving him the finger.

Mickey Mantle

—You're a tyrannical fascist!
—Did he just call me a dinosaur?

Randy and Tim Taylor, *Home Improvement*

Tweedledum, Tweedledee and Tweedletwat!

Kieron "Science" Harvey, *Big Brother 6* (U.K.)

—Every morning I wake up glad I'm not you.
—Me too.

Steve Taylor and Jeff Murdock, *Coupling*

—I've changed my mind.
—Does it work any better?   **Big Bill Barton and Tira,** *I'm No Angel*

—I didn't come here to be insulted.
—Where do you normally go?
                    Robin Day and Eric Morecambe, *Morecambe and Wise*

—Where you going?
—To clear my mind.
—Shouldn't take long. One good sneeze
ought to do it.   **Joe Hackett and Lowell Mather,** *Wings*

Rearrange these words: Bugger and Off. I mean, Off and Bugger.
                    Detective Inspector Derek Grim, *The Thin Blue Line*

So I said, "Why don't you shove it where the sun don't shine?" and so he did.
He put it in the cupboard under the stairs and it hasn't been mentioned since.
                    Stephen Fry, *A Bit of Fry and Laurie*

ADVICE

I don't believe this! You're taking advice from Oswald? Oswald who
once swallowed a sponge to soak up all the beer, so he wouldn't
get drunk?
Kate O'Brien, The Drew Carey Show

If you can't stand the heat, get out of the oven.   **Forrest Gump,** *Forrest Gump*

Never floss a stranger.   **Joan Rivers**

Don't cry over skimmed milk.   **Forrest Gump**

Never, ever put an electrical device in your pants.
                              Tim Taylor, *Home Improvement*

Never moon a werewolf.   **Mike Binder**

Never let an aardvark near your cocaine.   David Corrado

Never work before breakfast; if you have to work before breakfast, eat your breakfast first.   **Josh Billings**

Act ditzy. Lose things. It throws people off and makes them think you're "adorable," and less together than you really are.

Paris Hilton, *Confessions of an Heiress*

If you're frightened of the fat, then stay out of the fire.

Alastair Macauley, Sky News (U.K.)

If you're embarking around the world in a hot-air balloon, don't forget the toilet paper. Once, we had to wait for incoming faxes.

Sir Richard Branson

If you are ever lost in the desert and all of a sudden you come across another person, it's probably best not to drink any of their water. Catching a cold would only compound the problem.   **John Maclain**

If you're out on a ship during a thunderstorm, don't sit under a tree.

Spike Milligan

Although no man is an island, you can make quite an effective raft out of six.

Simon Munnery

Try not to have bosses if you can avoid them. Or have your manager deal with them.

Paris Hilton, *Confessions of an Heiress*

Never talk to strangers unless you know them really, really well.

Lowell Mather, *Wings*

I always tell a young man not to use the word "always."

Robert Walpole

Do not suck your thumb—or anybody else's, for that matter.

Forrest Gump, *Forrest Gump*

If the shoe fits, get another one just like it.

George Carlin

Never do your shoelaces up in a revolving door.

Adeye Churchill

Don't own nothin' if you can help it. If you can, even rent your shoes.

Forrest Gump, *Forrest Gump*

If you come to a fork in the road, take it.   **Yogi Berra**

When the horse dies, get off.   **Kinky Friedman**

If you're going to rape, pillage and burn, be sure to do things in that order.

P. J. Plauger

If you're ever on fire, I think it's best not to look in a mirror, because that will really get you in a panic.   **Jack Handey, *Deep Thoughts***

[*in a crisis*] Keep looking shocked and move slowly toward the cakes.

Homer Simpson's brain, advice to Homer, *The Simpsons*

I'm not so good with the advice. Can I interest you in a sarcastic comment?

Chandler Bing, *Friends*

COMMUNICATION

She had lost the art of conversation but not, unfortunately, the
power of speech.
George Bernard Shaw

—Alice, can I share a private thought with you?
—Oh, certainly, Vicar—as long as it isn't about tampons, 'cause I don't
understand them at all.   **Rev. Geraldine Grainger and Alice Tinker, *The Vicar of Dibley***

I promise you I will listen to what has been said here, even though I wasn't here.

George W. Bush

And I interrupt myself to bring you this ...   **Murray Walker**

—I haven't got a brain ... only straw.
—How can you talk if you haven't got a brain?
—I don't know ... But some people without brains do an awful lot of talking,
don't they?   **The Scarecrow and Dorothy, *The Wizard of Oz***

Shut up and talk!   Bridgette Berra

I want to talk to the organist, not the monkey grinder.
                                                    Brian Potter, *Phoenix Nights*

— So he's like, "nuh uh," and I'm like, "uh huh," and he's like, "nuh uh," and
I'm like, "um … uh huh," and he's like, "nuh uh."
—No way!
—Way.   **Two teenagers, www.overheardatthebeach.com**

I could not fail to disagree with you less.   **Boris Johnson, mayor of London**

I have opinions of my own—strong opinions—but I don't always agree with
them.   **George Bush Sr.**

Look, the point is … er, what is the point?
                                                    Boris Johnson, mayor of London

I would explain, my dear, but I fear you wouldn't understand—blessed as you
are with a head that is emptier than a hermit's address book.
                              Ebeneezer Blackadder, *Blackadder's Christmas Carol*

I never said I had no idea about most of the things you said I said I had no idea
about.   **Elliot Abrams, Assistant Secretary of State**

Every time I open my mouth, I put my tongue in it. I never said all the things I
said.   **Yogi Berra**

I didn't even know he had gave a thingy.   **Paris Hilton**

It was impossible to get a conversation going; everyone was talking too much.
                                                                    Yogi Berra

If you chopped off my head, I'd still carry on talking, because the head stays
alive for a bit. I've seen that in films.
                                          Jade Goody, British TV personality

That's why I don't talk. Because I talk too much.
                                                          Joaquin Andujar

There may be a reason I can't think of but the problem with that reason is that I
can't think of it now.   **Boris Johnson, mayor of London**

Of course you don't understand me. I'll bet Mrs. Einstein didn't understand
Albert either.   **Bill Hoest**

I won't say anything because no one ever listens to me anyway. I might as well
be a Leonard Cohen record.
                                      Vyvyan Basterd, *The Young Ones*

MISTAKES

The probability of someone watching you is proportional to the
stupidity of your action.
Hartley's First Law

Unless I'm very much mistaken … I AM very much mistaken …
                                                    Murray Walker

You know how they say the wisest people learn from the mistakes of others? I
am one of the others.   **Bob Monkhouse**

The only time he opens his mouth is to change feet.
                                      David Feherty, on Nick Faldo

It's a guaranteed disaster. Like eating a burrito before sex.
                                      Jack Donaghy, *30 Rock*

My friends, as I have discovered myself, there are no disasters, only
opportunities. And, indeed, opportunities for fresh disasters.
                                      Boris Johnson, mayor of London

— After 9/11 what would your biggest mistake be, would you say, and what
lessons have you learned from it?
—I wish you would have given me this written question ahead of time, so I
could plan for it … I'm sure historians will look back and say, gosh, he could
have done it better this way, or that way. You know, I just—I'm sure something
will pop into my head here in the midst of this press conference, with all the
pressure of trying to come up with an answer, but it hasn't yet.
                                      Reporter and George W. Bush

—That's the first mistake we've made since that fellow sold us the Brooklyn Bridge.

—Buying that bridge was no mistake. That's going to be worth a lot of money to us some day.   **Stan Laurel and Oliver Hardy, *Way Out West***

At the opera in Milan with my daughter and me, Needleman leaned out of his box and fell into the orchestra pit. Too proud to admit it was a mistake, he attended the opera every night for a month and repeated it each time.

Woody Allen

Yeah, I know James Bond wouldn't lock his keys in his car. Don't tell anyone, please.   **Pierce Brosnan, to a security guard who helped him break into his own car outside MGM Studios**

I married a few people I shouldn't have, but haven't we all?

Mamie Van Doren

I've learned from my mistakes and I'm sure I can repeat them exactly.

Peter Cook

If I tried hard the whole time to exude gravitas, I feel that I would fall on my face even harder.   **Boris Johnson, mayor of London**

I was at an audition. There was a woman singing on stage; her voice was so awful that I turned to the man sitting beside me and remarked upon it. He replied very frostily, "That is my wife." Pink with confusion, I hastily stammered, "I didn't mean her voice was awful, only the song she was singing." To which he replied, "I wrote it." I slunk away.

Michael Bentine

If I have offended any Croatians, then they have my deepest apologies.
    Tony Henry after singing, in Croatian, "My penis is a mountain" during his rendition of the Croatian national anthem at Wembley Stadium in London. He should have sung "How we love your mountains."

—Help! The baby just swallowed the house key. What should I do?

—Climb in through the window.
                    Ruth Buzzi and J. J. Barry, *Rowan & Martin's Laugh-in*

But she could not even get her head through the doorway. "And even if my head would go through," thought Alice, "it would be of very little use without my shoulders."   **Lewis Carroll, *Alice in Wonderland***

I left the room with silent dignity, but caught my foot in the mat.

George and Weedon Grossmith, *The Diary of a Nobody*

Veronica would manage to find something to tumble over in the desert of the Sahara.

Jerome K. Jerome, *They and I*

There is no dilemma compared with that of the deep-sea diver who hears the message from the ship above, "Come up at once. We are sinking."

Robert Cooper

I know! If I sink to the bottom, I can run to shore.

Homer Simpson, *The Simpsons*

As I swam ashore, I dried myself to save time.

The Goon Show

This is the dumbest thing Brian's ever done, and he once painted me blue.

Joe Hackett, *Wings*

We're in a sticky situation all right. This is the stickiest situation since Sticky the Stick Insect got caught on a sticky bun.

Edmund Blackadder, *Blackadder Goes Forth*

—What are we going to do?
—I saw this on *The Twilight Zone* one time: All we have to do is ... stop time.

Helen Chapel and Brian Hackett, *Wings*

I never make stupid mistakes. Only very, very clever ones.

John Peel

—[*takes out a can of gas, pours it over the bar and throws a lighted match on it*] Well, this is the only way I can recoup from this ...
—Um, aren't you supposed to get insurance first?
—Oh, crap.

Moe Syzslak and Carl Carlson, *The Simpsons*

INSURANCE CLAIMS

To your dinner guests you say, "Flambé," to your insurance agent
you say, "Short in the house wiring."

P. J. O'Rourke

Intending to test her new smoke detector, the tenant lit a match beneath the device. It worked. Unfortunately, she then threw the lit match into a trash container, igniting the contents. Total damage is estimated at $50,000.

I got up in the morning to go to work. I went into the bathroom and was spraying my hair with hairspray when the sprayer stuck open. I could not get it to quit spraying, so I held the can over the toilet and expelled the rest of the spray. Then I threw the can away. Later my husband came home, sat down on the toilet and lit a cigarette. He was blown into the bathroom wall, breaking his collar bone, for which we are entering a claim.

The Insured was vomiting in the toilet when the lid fell down on her, breaking her nose. We told her there was no coverage for this.

The Insured was fishing at Cold Springs Harbor and hooked a large fish. The fish, however, swam off with her rod and reel. Her claim is for theft.

The Insured reports that birds near her house have been getting drunk on mountain ash berries. Two drunken birds crashed through the bedroom window and stayed just long enough to ruin her bedspread. Does Home Owner Policy cover birds and bedspreads?

The Claimant was wearing her leopard-skin coat in the parking lot of the Southeastern Shopping Centre. She says that an ocelot jumped out from behind a pickup truck, attacked the coat and ran off.

The squirrel broke into my house and apparently was unable to find food. So it chomped up my window moldings and spit them all over the place before drowning itself in the toilet.

The Claimant stated he was giving a speech at a convention before several hundred people. While walking around on the stage, his pants zipper fell, allegedly causing him extreme embarrassment and loss of prestige. Our Insured manufactured the slacks.

The Claimant reported there was a bug on his leg, so he drew his pistol and shot it. Unfortunately, he also shot a hole in his foot.

The Claimant has filed for reimbursement on behalf of her husband who expired due to an alleged heart attack while on business for his company. Investigation and evidence reveal, however, that the deceased actually expired while attempting to make love to a Shetland pony.

CAR INSURANCE CLAIMS

The Insured insists his car was parked outside in the sun most of the day, and with the sun beating down on it, the car shrank, causing many dents to appear in the body and frame. Investigation continuing.

Our investigation indicates that just prior to the accident, Ms. Johnson, while driving: 1) placed her right hand upon the dashboard in order to receive a manicure from the passenger; 2) began brushing her teeth with her left hand; 3) attempted to steer the vehicle with her left elbow. Investigation continuing.

Whenever I get angry, I close my eyes and count to ten. I was mad at my brother while driving on the expressway and closed my eyes. The next thing I knew there was a terrible crash.

The telephone pole was approaching. I attempted to move out of its way, but it hit me.

The Driver explained that she was trying to make an "O" turn. When the [claims] adjuster looked mystified she explained, "That's a 'U' turn where you change your mind."

I pulled away from the side of the road, glanced at my mother-in-law, and headed over the embankment.

I thought my window was down, but I found it was up when I put my head through it.

I didn't think the speed limit applied after midnight.

I knocked over a man. He admitted it was his fault as he has been run over before.

Coming home I drove into the wrong house and collided with a tree I don't have.

Q: What caused the collision?
A: A cow.
Q: What warning was given by you?
A: Horn.
Q: What warning was given by the other party?
A: Moo.

Q: Could either driver have done anything to avoid the accident?
A: Traveled by bus?

I had been driving for 40 years when I fell asleep at the wheel and had an accident.

LEARNING & LESSONS

All that I've learned, I've forgotten.
The little I still know, I've guessed.
Nicolas de Chamfort

That program was so interesting ... I learned things I never even knew.
Adrian Love

This taught me a lesson, but I'm not sure what it is.   **John McEnroe**

Why waste time learning, when ignorance is instantaneous?
Calvin, *Calvin and Hobbes*

My act is very educational. I heard a man leaving the other night saying, "Well, that taught me a lesson."   **Ken Dodd**

I hope this has taught you kids a lesson: Kids never learn.

Chief Wiggum, *The Simpsons*

What a great title for my new book: *Things I've Learned after It Was Too Late.*

Snoopy, Peanuts

—Well, we've all got to live and learn, you know.
—Yeah, but you just live!

Stan Laurel and Oliver Hardy, *The Dancing Masters*

My mother used to tell me, "You live and learn. Then you die and forget it all."

George Foreman

Careful. We don't want to learn from this.

Calvin, *Calvin and Hobbes*

WORK

What is wrong with everyone nowadays? Why do they all seem to think they are qualified to do things far beyond their actual capabilities?
Prince Charles

I really could have been a brain surgeon because I was a very bright child.

Cilla Black

VACANCY FOR SIOUX CHEF: Experience and excellent references required.

Notice in the window of a restaurant in Liverpool, England

I have no training as a cook. Greed is the only important motivation.

Nigella Lawson, celebrity chef

I always thought I'd like to be a travel writer—if I ever went anywhere or was a good writer.

Ellen DeGeneres

I would either like to be rich and famous, or a speech therapist in Spain.

Chanelle Hayes, *Big Brother 8* **(U.K.)**

I love to take care of people, so I think I'd be a good vet.

Jennifer Love Hewitt

If you enjoy working with people, why not become a mortuary technician?

Dorset Echo

You know me as a wine expert, but in another life I would have been a bishop or a dry cleaner, or a dry-cleaning bishop.

Oz Clarke

I'd rather do glue, cut off my sexual organs and be called Enid for the rest of my life than do another sales job.

Pierre South, *Apply Immediately*

When I finished school, I took one of those career-aptitude tests, and based on my verbal ability score, they suggested I become a mime.

Tim Cavanagh

I used to be a narrator for bad mimes.

Steven Wright

When I was filming, I must confess that I developed a real regard for the work of Anthea Turner. Walking and talking at the same time is very hard.

Sir Richard Eyre

FUNERAL OPERATIVES REQUIRED. 35-40 hours per week. Good rates of pay and staff discount.

Colchester Gazette

—I'm willing to start at the bottom.
—You're aiming too high.

Brian Flanagan and job interviewer, *Cocktail*

—So, what do you do?
—I'm an electrician.
—What's that in layman's terms?

Simon Bates and interviewee, BBC Radio

I used to have a job in the Kotex factory. I thought I was making mattresses for mice.

Ray Scott

I was picked for my motivational skills. Everyone always says they have to work twice as hard when I'm around.

Homer Simpson, *The Simpsons*

I got a hot date tonight. I told him I was an ombudsman. I only have 12 hours to figure out what the hell that is.

Jack McFarland, Will & Grace

—I'm a college professor. What did you think when I said I taught Hemingway?
—I thought you were old.

Miles Webber and Rose Martin, The Golden Girls

My favorite ad from an Ulster newspaper: "WANTED: Man and woman to look after two cows, both Protestant."

Frank Carson

The pollen count ... that's a difficult job. Especially if you've got hay fever. One sneeze, you have to start all over again.

Milton Jones

—What do you do?
—I'm a housewife and mother.
—Do you have any children?   Max Bygraves and contestant, Family Fortunes

Sign of an incompetent accountant: Uses only Roman numerals.

Barry Blyveis

—Arthur, honey, we're gonna have to become a two-income family.
—What? You're going to get a second job?

Linda and Arthur Bach, Arthur 2: On the Rocks

I worked as a receptionist for a while, but I couldn't get the hang of it.
I kept answering the phone by saying, "Hello, can you help me?"

Caroline Rhea

My next job was director of pharmaceutical research at ICI ... All I could think of to say was that the pills ought to be oblong instead of round, and after a couple of years they threw me out.

Hugh Laurie, A Bit of Fry and Laurie

How about that? You kiss ass at a drug company for 15 years, you let one little strand of bacteria slip that causes a major disease, and suddenly, it's goodbye lab coat, hello mop.

Lewis Kiniski, The Drew Carey Show

Before I became an actor I had a number of jobs. I was once hired as an "efficiency expert." My first day, I couldn't find the office.

Peter Falk

My father was in the lumber business but only in a small way. He used to sell toothpicks.

Stan Laurel, *One Good Turn*

The hardest part about working in a peanut butter factory is keeping everything from sticking to the roof.

John Maclain

When a great many people are unable to find work, unemployment results.

Calvin Coolidge

And so the fact that they purchased the machine meant somebody had to make the machine. And when somebody makes a machine, it means there's jobs at the machine-making place.

George W. Bush, visiting a cable company in Arizona (YT)

The General Secretary of the National Union of General and Municipal Workers denied the charge that leaders were out of touch with the rank and file, and said it was the rank and file that was out of touch with the leadership.

Guardian

My wife came from a poor family. Her father was a professional carol singer.

Ronnie Barker

I didn't pass my astronaut application. I failed everything but the date of birth.

Navin R. Johnson, *The Jerk*

I thought I wanted to be a fireman. But as it turns out, I just like breaking windows with axes.

Buzz Nutley

If at first you don't succeed, then bomb disposal probably isn't for you.

Murphy's Law of Combat

[I have] stared death in the face many times.

Raef Bjayou, extract from his resumé, *The Apprentice* (U.K.)

My dad always said, "The day I can't do my job drunk is the day I turn in my badge and gun."

Lewis Kiniski, *The Drew Carey Show*

THE OFFICE

I think housework is the reason most women go to the office.
Heloise Cruse

Mr. Oxley's been complaining about my punctuation, so I'm careful to get here before 9:00.
Lois Laurel, *Monkey Business*

—If you're not here on time, I'll have to get another secretary.
—Another secretary? Do you think there'll be enough work for both of us?
George Burns and Gracie Allen, *A Damsel in Distress*

I type at 101 words a minute, but it's in my own language.　　**Mitch Hedberg**

—What is our Vision Statement?
—It says here, "Our vision is always to be true to our vision."
Coworkers, www.overheardintheoffice.com

Attention, everyone, it's time for a fire drill. Johnson, you're fired!
Jay Clemens, *The Drew Carey Show*

AWARDS

The Oscar statuette is the perfect symbol of the picture business: a powerful, athletic body clutching a gleaming sword, with half of his head—the part that holds the brains—completely sliced off.
Frances Marion

I'm a grateful grapefruit.
Björk, accepting Best Female International Artist at the Brit Awards

I just want to thank everyone I met in my entire life.
Kim Basinger, on winning the Best Supporting Actress Oscar for *L.A. Confidential*

Lindsay will always keep growing. She'll do a film and get an Academy Award, and no one will remember her boobs.
Dina Lohan

Baffy waff! Baffy-waffy-wim-wam! Wim-wam-baffy-waff! Waff-waff, wiffy-waffy-wafta!

Harry Hill, extract from his acceptance speech after winning the British Academy of Film and Television Arts for Best Entertainment Program for *Harry Hill's TV Burp*, 2008

I'd like to thank my parents for not practicing birth control.

Dustin Hoffmann, on winning the Best Actor Oscar for *Kramer vs. Kramer*

I took part in the International Suntanning Championships. I got bronze.

Milton Jones

I took part in the International Burglary Championships. I got silver.

Milton Jones

And that bronze medal is worth its weight in gold.   David Coleman

Who was it who said your blonde hair color would stop you winning an enema—an Emmy?

Paul O'Grady to actress Sharon Gless, *The Paul O'Grady Show*

It's about time a transvestite potter won the Turner Prize.

Grayson Perry, transvestite potter, accepting the Turner Prize, the British award for contemporary art, 2003

Usually when someone is given an evening like this, they're way too dead to say thank you.

Billy Crystal, accepting the Mark Twain Prize for American Humor, 2007

I'm only sorry I can't be with you tonight …

Paul Merton, onstage collecting a Comedy Award

I didn't know Malcolm Sargent had been knighted. It was only yesterday he was doctored.

Sir Thomas Beecham

Some breaking news here at the Sky News Center: Howard—Harold Pintus … the play-writer Harold Pinter has just died—has won the Nobel Prize for Literature, apologies for that.

News anchor, Sky News, 2005 (YT)

I'd kill for a Nobel Peace Prize.

Steven Wright

Knocking down a house in Dublin recently, the workmen found a skeleton with a medal on a ribbon round its neck. The inscription read: Irish Hide and Seek Champion, 1910.

Frank Carson

I used to play sports. Then I realized you can *buy* trophies. Now I'm good at everything.

Demetri Martin

WINNING & LOSING

Anybody can win unless there happens to be a second entry.
George Ade

They have three options: They could win or they could lose.

Kevin Keegan

I'm not going to predict what I'm gonna do, but I'm gonna come out there the winner.

Frank Bruno

A winning formula is not something you can write an equation for.

Maggie Brown

I was in a no-win situation, so I'm glad I won rather than lost.

Frank Bruno

Not that people had written you off, but they didn't think you'd win anything.

Archie Macpherson

We were overwhelming underdogs.

Yogi Berra

Winning isn't the end of the world.

David Pleat

This would have been his third win in a row had he won the two before.

Murray Walker

But now he has to consummate the lead ... and that's not always easy.

Mark Cox

England might now be the favorites to draw this match.

Vic Marks, BBC Radio

England were beaten in the sense that they lost.   Dickie Davies

In terms of the Richter scale, this defeat was a force eight gale.

John Lyall

Even Napoleon had his Watergate.   Danny Ozark

Defeated but victorious.   Commentator, Sky Sports (U.K.)

You wouldn't have won if we had beaten you.   Yogi Berra

The reason we lost is because we made too many wrong mistakes.

Yogi Berra

It's disappointing to have lost—that's the bee's knees of it.

Tim Henman

—Who won the Bangkok marathon?
—It was a Thai.   Anon.

Always root for the winner. That way you won't be disappointed.

Tug McGraw

SPORTS & LEISURE

SPORTS—GENERAL

Why are Australians so good at sport? Good food and diet, open-air life, juicy steaks, sunshine and the total absence of any kind of intellectual distraction.
Dame Edna Everage

Man, I'm so bad at sports, they used to pick me after the white kids.
Caretaker, *The Longest Yard*

Life without sport is like life without underpants.
Brent "Billy" Bowden, New Zealand cricket umpire

Ten-pin bowling is a very difficult sport, but it is easier than eleven-pin bowling.
Tom Baker, *Little Britain*

I don't know the rules. Isn't it to put the ball through the hoop and beat the other bugger?
John Prescott, on croquet

If horseracing is the sport of kings, then drag racing must be the sport of queens.
Bert R. Sugar

I went bobsleighing this Christmas. I killed Bob Holness and Bob Carolgees.
Alex Walsh-Atkins, *Viz* magazine

Extreme curling: This already exciting sport is taken to the nail-biting limit when the ice in the path of the slowly sliding stone is cleared by high-tech vacuum cleaners.
Kyle Hendrickson

Street hockey is great for kids. It's energetic, competitive and skillful. And, best of all, it keeps them off the streets.
Reporter, BBC Radio 1

Don't worry about that, Doc. If it happens, I could always come back as a forward.
Harold Snepsts, advised by a doctor to wear a helmet when playing ice hockey to avoid brain damage

—It's funny. I thought you'd never wanna see another hockey game after you got smacked in the head with that puck.
—I played hockey?
Drew Carey and Lewis Kiniski, *The Drew Carey Show*

It's rugby by numbers—A, B, C.   Dewi Morris

Horrocks-Taylor came toward me with the ball. Horrocks went one way, Taylor went the other and I was left holding the hyphen.

Tony O'Reilly, Irish rugby player

Next week we'll be looking at the Tour de France—all those bicycles roaring through the countryside.   Andy Peebles

He's a favorite for the Tour de France—well, an outsider anyway.

Phil Liggett

The Tour de France is a totally different ball game from English cycle racing.

Sidney Bennett

I was watching what I thought was sumo wrestling on the television for two hours before I realized it was darts.

Hattie Hayridge

Darts really can help with literacy.   **Ray Stubbs**

Would she climb to the top of Mr. Everest again? Absolutely!

Misprint, *Houston Chronicle*

I climbed Mount Everest—from the inside.   **Spike Milligan**

WATER SPORTS

You don't drown by falling into the water.
You drown only if you stay there.
Zig Ziglar

I was on water skis, stripped to the waist, skiing fast across the top of the surf, my hair back. My wife was in the boat ahead of me, rowing frantically ...

Woody Allen

Mom said she learned to swim when someone rowed her out in the lake and threw her off the boat. I said, "Mom, they weren't trying to teach you how to swim ..."

Paula Poundstone

Swimming is a confusing sport, because sometimes you do it for fun, and other times you do it to not die. And when I'm swimming, sometimes I'm not sure which one it is. I gotta go by the outfit: pants—uh oh. Bathing suit—OK. Naked—we'll see ...

Demetri Martin

—You trained and trained and trained to swim the Atlantic, which very few people have succeeded in doing.
—Not the Atlantic, the Channel ...

Richard Madeley and David Walliams, *Richard & Judy*

—Ten miles he swam—the last three were agony ...
—They were over land.

Greenslade and Seagoon, *The Goon Show*

The swimmers are swimming out of their socks.

Sharron Davies

Swimming pools in Britain have very strict rules: no bombing, no petting, no ducking and no fondue parties.

Tom Baker, *Little Britain*

—Water polo? Isn't that terribly dangerous?
—I'll say! I had two ponies drowned under me.

Sugar Kane Kowalczyk and Joe, *Some Like It Hot*

I can't see who's in the lead, but it's either Oxford or Cambridge.

John Snagge, commentator, The Oxford and Cambridge Boat Race

If Oxford had been in front, the position would have been reversed.

Commentator, The Oxford and Cambridge Boat Race

Ah, isn't that nice, the wife of the Cambridge president is kissing the cox of the Oxford crew.

Harry Carpenter, commentator, The Oxford and Cambridge Boat Race

ATHLETICS

It's only jumping into a sandpit.
Jonathan Edwards,
on setting the new triple jump world record, 1995

Kris Akabusi, do you have to plan your tactics before the race or do you just try and run faster than the other blokes?   **Mrs. Merton**

If this boy keeps his head and keeps running, the sky's at his feet.
George Blackburn

Harvey Glance is the black American sprinter with the white top and the black bottom.   **Ron Pickering**

A very powerful set of lungs, very much hidden by that chest of his.
Alan Pascoe

McKeen will sit on Cram's shoulder and hope to be lifted by the crowd.
Commentator

Panetta was silver medallist in the European championships, when he led all the way.   **David Coleman**

And this all-British field means that we will, of course, see a British winner in the men's 400 meters this evening.   **Jim Rosenthal**

This could be a repeat of what will happen at the European Games next week.
David Coleman

There's nothing athletes like—or indeed hate—more than hanging around like this.
David Coleman

A fairly casual start this, from Abdi Bile. He always rushes to the back of the field.   **Steve Ovett**

He's doing well ... he's letting his legs do all the running.

Brendan Foster

Watch the time—it gives you a good indication of how fast they're running.
Ron Pickering

There goes Juantorena down the back straight, opening his legs and showing his class.

Ron Pickering

That's the fastest time ever run—but it's not as fast as the world record.

David Coleman

And the line-up for the final of the women's 400-meters hurdles includes three Russians, two East Germans, a Pole, a Swede and a Frenchman.

David Coleman

She's not Ben Johnson, but then who is?

David Coleman

Ben Johnson! He's like Concorde! Off the blocks like a caged lion.

Stuart Hall

Let's be honest, I ran like a lemon—and lemons don't run.

Daniel Caines

The hammer-throwing competition is a fascinating duel between three men.

David Coleman

The news from the javelin is that it was won by that winning throw we saw earlier.

David Coleman

She's dragged the javelin back into the twentieth century.

Ron Pickering

There is a better sport than javelin: discus.

Simon Munnery

We have some great activities in our village games, like the 100-meter hurdles, which are a bit stupid because none of us can jump that high.

Bennett Arron

A guy goes to the Olympics and sees a man carrying a long pole. The guy asks, "Are you a pole vaulter?" "No," he says, "I'm German. But how did you know my name is Walter?"

Anon.

Olympic athletes—disguise the fact that you've taken anabolic steroids by running a bit slower.

Viz magazine

My doorbell didn't work.

Mark Lewis-Francis, on why he missed a drug test

At one point, Pete Doherty offered to carry the Olympic torch, but only because he thought it was a giant spliff.

Jack Dee, *Have I Got News for You*

Within a few hours, the Olympic flame will have been put into cold storage for another four years.   Gordon Clough

BASKETBALL

What is so fascinating about a group of pituitary cases trying to
stuff the ball through a hoop?
Woody Allen

To win, you've got to put the ball in the macramé.

Terry McGuire

—You're seven feet two inches. Do you play basketball?
—No, I wash giraffe ears.   **Spectator and Artis Gilmore**

I have a God-given talent. I got it from my dad.

Julian Winfield

If Stanford is a number 12 seed, then I'm a left-handed ham sandwich.
Wimp Sanderson, Alabama basketball coach, on NCAA tournament seeding

We're going to turn this team around 360 degrees.   **Jason Kidd**

I've had to overcome a lot of diversity.

Drew Gooden, NBA forward

It's almost like we have ESPN.

**Magic Johnson, on how well he and
James Worthy work together**

My game is like the Pythagorean theorem: No one has an answer.
Shaquille O'Neal, on a Lakers victory over the Nets

I've won at every level, except college and pro.
Shaquille O'Neal, on his lack of championships

Any time Detroit scores more than 100 points and holds the other team below 100 points, they almost always win.

Doug Collins, former Detroit Pistons coach

Because there are no fours.

Antoine Walker, NBA forward, after being asked why he shoots so many "threes," or three-point shots.

We can't win at home. We can't win on the road. As general manager, I just can't figure out where else to play.

Pat Williams, Orlando Magic general manager, on his team's 7-27 record

My career was sputtering until I made a 360-degree turn and got headed in the right direction.

Tracy McGrady, Houston Rockets shooting guard

I told him, "Son, what is it with you. Is it ignorance or apathy?" He said, "Coach, I don't know and I don't care."

Frank Layden, Utah Jazz president, on a former player

We have a great bunch of outside shooters. Unfortunately, all our games are played indoors.

Weldon Drew

I'm tired of hearing about money, money, money, money, money. I just want to play the game, drink Pepsi, wear Reebok.

Shaquille O'Neal

I don't want to shoot my mouth in my foot, but those are games we can win.

Sherman Douglas

Everything is magnetized by 10.

Al Harrington, NBA forward, on handling the playoff pressure

Yeah, I'm a little surprised. But nowadays, with snipers and Bin Ladens running around, don't nothing really surprise me anymore. Kind of messed up to say, but, somebody told me they seen a flying monkey. There is flying monkeys, too! Flying squirrels and all kinds of shit. Doesn't nothing surprise me these days.

Kevin Garnett, on whether he was surprised that the Timberwolves didn't sell out against Michael Jordan and the Wizards

BASEBALL

They're not the smartest people in the world, baseball players. They
have a diamond diagramming where they have to go. And they still
have coaches on first and third telling them which way to go.
Otherwise, these guys would run all the way to the warning track.
Benny Ricardo

Who is this Babe Ruth and what does she do?   **George Bernard Shaw**

I told Roland Hemond to go out and get me a big-name pitcher. He said, "Dave
Wehrmeister's got 11 letters. Is that a big enough name for you?"
Eddie Eichorn, White Sox owner

Left hand, right hand, it doesn't matter. I'm amphibious.
Charles Shackleford

Things you never knew about the New York Mets: "Mets" is short for
"Metrosexuals."   **David Letterman**

If we're going to win the pennant, we've got to start thinking we're not as smart
as we think we are.   **Casey Stengel**

Ninety percent of the game is half mental.   **Yogi Berra**

Slump? I ain't in no slump. I just ain't hitting.   **Yogi Berra**

I'm the most loyal player money can buy.   **Don Sutton**

—Do you prefer grass or Astroturf?
—I dunno. I never smoked Astroturf.   **Interviewer and Tug McGraw**

If people don't want to come to the ballpark, how are you going to stop them?
Yogi Berra

They shouldn't throw at me. I'm the father of five or six kids.
Tito Fuentes, former San Francisco Giants second baseman,
after getting hit by a pitch

Baseball is ninety percent mental. The other half is physical.
Yogi Berra

You have two hemispheres in your brain—left and a right side. The left side controls the right side of your body and right controls the left half. It's a fact. Therefore, left-handers are the only people in their right minds.

> Bill Lee, left-handed former MLB pitcher

Well, that was a real cliff-dweller.

> Wes Westrum, former major league catcher, manager and coach, on a close game

There's one word in America that says it all, and that word is, "You never know."

> Joaquin Andujar, former MLB pitcher

How can I play baseball if I'm stupid? If I was stupid I wouldn't have pitched in the World Series. I'd be playing ball in Mexico or Yugoslavia or on Pluto.

> Joaquin Andujar, former MLB pitcher

It was like Samson and Goliath.

> Mark "The Bird" Fidrych, former Detroit Tigers pitcher, after allowing the Detroit Tigers Wives Club to cut his hair for charity

I was the worst hitter ever. I never even broke a bat until last year when I was backing out of the garage.

> Lefty Gomez, former New York Yankees pitcher

I want all the kids to do what I do, to look up to me. I want all the kids to copulate me.

> Andre Dawson, Chicago Cubs outfielder

I made a game effort to argue, but two things were against me: the umpires and the rules.

> Leo "The Lip" Durocher, MLB manager

I've never criticized my players in public, and I'll never do it again.

> Bobby Valentine, former manager of the New York Mets

When I was in high school, I spent a lot of time on my knees playing with balls. I guess it was only natural that I became a catcher.

> Mike Piazza

Winfield goes back to the wall, he hits his head on the wall and it rolls off! It's rolling all the way back to second base. This is a terrible thing for the Padres.

> Jerry Coleman, announcer

TENNIS

A traditional fixture at Wimbledon is the way
the BBC TV commentary box fills up with British players eliminated
in the early rounds.
Clive James

The game of tennis was invented in 1982 by Dr. Jonathan Tennis, when he had the idea of fusing the popular sports of badminton and swingball.

Tom Baker, *Little Britain*

The serve was invented so the net could play. **Bill Cosby**

Deuce is used so you don't have to count so high. **Bill Cosby**

While listening to Radio 5 Live a few weeks ago, I heard the reporter say that the Wimbledon Tennis Championships were just around the corner. Imagine my disappointment when I walked to the end of my street, only to find a dog being sick under an abandoned Ford Escort.

Stitch Mitchell, *Viz* **magazine**

The Gullikson twins are here. An interesting pair—both from Wisconsin.

Dan Maskell

Steffi has a tremendous presence when you're standing right next to her.

Virginia Wade, on Steffi Graf

She puts her head down and bangs it straight across the line.

Ann Jones

Lendl has remained throughout as calm as the proverbial iceberg.

Dan Maskell

—Who are they going to play in the final? Do we know yet?
—This *is* the final.

Max Robertson, tennis commentator, BBC Radio (YT)

FOOTBALL

The NFL, like life, is full of idiots.
Randy Cross

I want to rush for 1,000 or 1,500 yards, whichever comes first.
George Rogers, former New Orleans Saints running back

I used to have this slight speech implement and couldn't remember things before I took the Sam Carnegie course.
Bill Peterson, former Florida State football coach

Defensively, I think it's important for us to tackle.
Karl Mecklenburg, former Denver Broncos linebacker

You cannot change the stripes of a leopard.
Emmitt Smith, former NFL running back and ESPN analyst, on New England Patriots wide receiver Randy Moss

We're not attempting to circumcise the rules.
Bill Cowher, former Pittsburgh Steelers coach

I am not allowed to comment on lousy officiating.
Jim Finks, former general manager of the New Orleans Saints, when asked what he thought of the referees after his team lost a game

We've got to find a way to win. I'm willing to start cheating.
Marv Cook, New England tight end

I only have two things going for me: my arms, my legs and my brain.
Michael Vick, former Atlanta Falcons quarterback

I'm really happy for Coach Cooper and the guys who've been around here for six or seven years, especially our seniors.
Bob Hoying, quarterback, upon winning a Big Ten title for Ohio State

You guys line up alphabetically by height.
Bill Peterson, former Florida State football coach

Probably the Beatles' *White Album.*

Steve Largent, former Seattle Seahawks receiver, when asked
which of his records he'd treasure the most after retirement

I feel like I'm the best, but you're not going to get me to say that.

Jerry Rice

Baseball is the only game left for people. To play basketball, you have to be 7
feet 6 inches. To play football, you have to be the same width.

Bill Veeck

Hawaii doesn't win many games in the United States.

Lee Corso, football analyst

We can't run. We can't pass. We can't stop the run. We can't stop the pass. We
can't kick. Other than that, we're just not a very good football team right now.

Bruce Coslet

He treats us like men. He lets us wear earrings.

Torrin Polk, University of Houston receiver, on coach John Jenkins

But the real tragedy was that 15 hadn't been colored yet.

Steve Spurrier, University of Florida football coach, telling Gators fans
that a fire in Auburn's football dorm had destroyed 20 books

We didn't lose the game; we just ran out of time.

Vince Lombardi

Football is an incredible game. Sometimes it's so incredible, it's unbelievable.

Tom Landry

I didn't know Elvis was from Memphis. I thought he was from Tennessee.

Drew Gooden, Memphis Grizzlies draft pick, answering
a reporter who asked if Drew planned to see Graceland

Al, he just learned a valuable lesson. He just learned that he could get a guy off
in this league using only his mouth!

Boomer Esiason to Al Michaels, when new Cleveland Browns quarterback Tim Couch
got the Dallas Cowboys to go offsides in a preseason game

GOLF

Golf appeals to the idiot in us and the child.
Just how childlike golf players become is proven by their frequent
inability to count past five.

John Updike

For me the worst part of playing golf, by far, has always been hitting the ball.

Dave Barry

There he stands with his legs akimbo.

Peter Alliss

That shot is impossible! Jack Nicholson himself couldn't make it!

Homer Simpson, *The Simpsons*

Ninety percent of short putts don't go in.

Yogi Berra

My golf is improving. Yesterday I hit the ball in one!

Jane Swan

The hardest shot in golf is a mashie at 90 yards from the green, where the ball
has to be played against an oak tree, bounces back into a sand trap, hits a stone,
bounces on the green and then rolls into the cup. That shot is so difficult I have
made it only once.

Zeppo Marx

Bad Golf Made Easier

Leslie Nielsen, title of video

I read the greens in English, but I putt in Spanish.

Chi Chi Rodriguez

—Why do golfers wear two pairs of socks?
—In case they get a hole in one.

Anon.

—Oh no, my shot's gonna go in the water!
—Come on, Yogi, don't be like that. Think positively.
—OK, I'm positive my shot is going into the water!

Yogi Berra and Kevin Carroll

Once when I was golfing in Georgia, I hooked the ball into the swamp. I went in
after it and found an alligator wearing a shirt with a picture of a little golfer on it.

Buddy Hackett

I've lost balls in every hazard and on every course I've tried. But when I lose a ball in the ball washer, it's time to take stock.

Milton Gross

One of the reasons Arnie Palmer is playing so well is that, before each final round, his wife takes out his balls and kisses them—oh, my God, what have I just said?   U.S. golf commentator

No one's ever won the Open three times. It's been won four times and two times, but never in its history has it been won three times.

U.S. golf commentator

At least Gerald Ford can't cheat on his score because all you have to do is look back down the fairway and count the wounded.

Bob Hope

I would like to deny all allegations by Bob Hope that during my last game of golf...I hit an eagle, a birdie, an elk and a moose.

Gerald Ford

I don't think anywhere is there a symbiotic relationship between caddie and player like there is in golf.   Johnny Miller

I told the caddie I wanted a sand wedge and he brought me a ham on rye.

Chi Chi Rodriguez

They say, "Trevino is wondering whether to play a five- or six-iron to the green," when all the time I'm gazing at some broad in the third row of the gallery, wondering where the hell my wife is.

Lee Trevino

My dear, did you ever stop to think what a wonderful bunker you would make?

Walter Hagen, to a buxom opera singer

If Tiger Woods married Jeremy Irons, would they be a Full Set?

John Held

I owe everything to golf. Where else would a guy with an IQ like mine make this much money?   Hubert Green

BOXING

Prize fighters can sometimes read and write when they start—but
they can't when they finish.
Martin H. Fischer

Boxing's all about getting the job done as quickly as possible, whether it takes
10 or 15 or 20 rounds.   **Frank Bruno**

Boxers don't have sex before a fight. Do you know why that is? They don't
fancy each other.   **Jimmy Carr**

Frank Bruno will definitely fight Mike Tyson—that's a fact of life.
Mickey Duff

—So, how far do you think you can go in boxing?
—Well, I've been to Africa.
Interviewer and young boxer, Manchester Piccadilly Radio (U.K.)

—Who's been your greatest inspiration outside boxing?
—Er … I think Joe Louis.   **David Frost and Frank Bruno**

I've had 16 fights and I won all of them but 12.
Kevin, *Mighty Aphrodite*

Born in Italy, most of his fights have been in his native New York.
Des Lynam

I've only ever seen Errol Christie fight once before, and that was the best I've
ever seen him fight.   **Mark Kaylor**

I only hope people will come along in peace and enjoy a good fight.
Mickey Duff

So over to the ringside—Harry Commentator is your carpenter.
BBC announcer

Round One … start of the fight, in fact.   **Des Lynam**

I'm concentrating so much I don't know what I'm doing half the time.
Mark Kaylor, boxer

All the time he's boxing he's thinking. All the time he was thinking, I was hitting him.

Jack Dempsey, on Benny Leonard

Honey, I just forgot to duck.

Jack Dempsey, after losing the world heavyweight title

The referee is the most important man in the ring besides the two fighters.

George Foreman

To be honest, it was a very physical fight.

Jim Watt

The stubble on his chin even hurts you.

Glenn McCrory, on Mike Tyson

Sure there have been injuries and deaths in boxing—but none of them serious.

Alan Minter

—Did you bite your opponent?
—No, I'm a vegetarian.

Reporter and Wali Muhammad

My head has got regrets, but I haven't.

Frank Bruno

If you hadn't been there it wouldn't have been much of a fight.

Harry Carpenter, to Ken Norton
after he lost to Muhammed Ali in 1976

A boxer makes a comeback for one of two reasons: either's he's broke or he needs the money.

Alan Minter

I'll fight Lloyd Honeyghan for nothing if the price is right.

Marlon Starling

I used to be a boxer but I gave it up. I was on the canvas more times than Rembrandt.

Bob Hope

To me, boxing is like ballet, except there's no music, no choreography and the dancers hit each other.

Jack Handey, *Deep Thoughts*

Why does Prince Naseem get a gong just because he's good at punching people? I'm brilliant at it, but the most I've ever got is 200 hours community service.

A. Woodward, *Viz* magazine

Fear was absolutely necessary. Without it, I would have been scared to death.
Floyd Patterson, former heavyweight boxing champion

I would like to retire with my brains still in contact.
Errol Graham

You can sum up this sport in two words: You never know.
Lou Duva

HORSERACING

What must a horse think after a race is over?
They must get to the end and go,
"We were just here. What's the point of that?"
Jerry Seinfeld

A race horse is not like a machine. It has to be tuned up like a racing car.
Chris Pool

This is really a lovely horse. I once rode her mother.
Ted Walsh

The horse sadly died this morning, so it looks like he won't be running in the Gold Cup.
Charlie McCann

He was going all right until he fell at the first.
**John Cullen, riding in the British Grand National
on The Bunny Boiler**

And it's a photo finish between Gold Prospect and Shareblank, and third is probably just in behind those two.
Sir Peter O'Sullevan

I've had an interest in racing all my life—or longer really.
Kevin Keegan

I've not enjoyed 12 minutes so much for a long time. I think sex is an anticlimax after that.
**Mick Fitzgerald, jockey, on winning the
British Grand National riding Rough Quest**

The press were writing him off, and that acted as a spur for him.
**Richard Burridge, after Desert Orchid won
the British national King George VI Chase**

My horse was in the lead, coming down the home stretch, but the caddie fell off.
Sam Goldwyn

HUNTING

It takes up to 40 dumb animals to make a fur coat. It only takes one to wear it.
Anti-fur advertisement

Do you know how many polyesters died to make that shirt?

Steve Martin

—Did you shoot that thing on your wall?
—Nope, the elk just ran through the wall and got stuck.

Neighbor and Bill Engvall

Stuffed deer heads on the wall are bad enough, but it's worse when they are wearing dark glasses, and have streamers in their antlers because then you know they were enjoying themselves at a party when they were shot.

Ellen DeGeneres

I'm against hunting, in fact, I'm a hunt saboteur. I go out the night before and shoot the fox.

Tim Vine

Opponents of foxhunting foolishly suggest that drag hunting would be an adequate replacement for our sport. Well, I for one would take no pleasure from hunting foxes dressed in women's clothing.

E. B. Poole, *Viz* **magazine**

Driving in today, I saw a dead fox, and I thought, "What a terrible way to die."

Otis Ferry, pro-hunting protester

I remember the guts steaming, and the stag turds spilling out on to the grass from within the ventral cavity ... Then they cut out the heart ... we cooked it up with a bit of flour ...

Boris Johnson, *Lend Me Your Ears*

One morning I shot an elephant in my pajamas. How he got in my pajamas I don't know.

Groucho Marx

Just remember it's the birds that's supposed to suffer, not the hunter.

George W. Bush

The grouse are in absolutely no danger from people who shoot grouse.

Prince Philip

Lord Ripon killed 200 rabbits at one shot.

Misprint, noted by A. C. Benson

We've already hunted the gray whale into extinction twice.

Andrea Arnold

The hunting was awful. I didn't bag a damned thing. Duke and I sat there for two days just waiting for something to happen. It's like when Frasier took me to see *Nicholas Nickleby*. Thank God this time I had a gun!

Martin Crane, *Frasier*

Two dumb guys go bear hunting. They see a sign saying "Bear left," so they went home.

Henny Youngman

CHESS

To play chess requires no intelligence at all.
José Raúl Capablanca, World Chess Champion

I had lunch with a chess champion the other day. I knew he was a chess champion because he took 20 minutes to pass the salt.

Eric Sykes

See that chess game over there? When I was four years old, I played ten people all at once—blindfolded. I lost every game.

Charley McCaleb, *China Seas*

I failed to make the chess team because of my height.

Woody Allen

She found [him] seated at the table, playing chess with himself. From the contented expression on his face, he appeared to be winning.

P. G. Wodehouse, *Money in the Bank*

—[*seductively*] Do you know how we keep warm in Russia?
—[*seduced*] I can guess, baby ...
—We play chess.
—I guessed wrong.

Ivana Humpalot and Austin Powers,
Austin Powers: The Spy Who Shagged Me

We played strip chess. She had me down to my shorts and I fainted from tension.

Victor Skakapopulis, *What's New Pussycat?*

Learn to Mate

Slogan for a Canadian chess club

Check and mate! Now king me!

Homer Simpson, *The Simpsons*

LEISURE PURSUITS

Collecting interest does not count as a hobby.
Citibank U.K. advertisement

—You're a fisherman, aren't you?
—Yes.
—What do you fish for?
—Fish.

Jim Bowen and contestant, *Bullseye*

We used to laugh at Grandpa when he'd head off and go fishing. But we wouldn't be laughing that evening when he'd come back with some whore he picked up in town.

Jack Handey, *Deep Thoughts*

—Are you flyin' a kite?
—Nope. Fishin' for birds!

Passerby and Bill Engvall

With his practical concern for animals, Colonel Forbes's main interests are sporting—shooting, fishing, hunting and racing.

***Cotswold Life* magazine**

As so few nowadays understand Greek, the Toxophily Society will henceforth be entitled the Archery Society.

***Eton College Chronicle*, 1973**

I collected butterflies as a kid. The irony was that moths got into the collection and ate them all.

Bill Bailey, *QI (Quite Interesting)*

We hear about one sad case of a man with a model railway who gets up at seven o'clock every morning to send off the first workman's train.

Daily Express

From the earliest age, I have enjoyed being sat on. I would try to worm my way under the cushions of an armchair or sofa, wait for someone to sit down, and savor the sensation of being pinned to the under-springs and almost crushed beneath the weight of the adult above.

Matthew Parris, *Chance Witness*

I used to walk backward to school just to see if it could be done.

Ken Dodd

—I enjoy picking my nose in the car.
—What is it about nose-picking that's so enjoyable?
—Discovery. You never know what you're going to find.

Miriam Margolyes and Andrew Denton,
Enough Rope with Andrew Denton

I love blinking, I do!

Helen Adams, *Big Brother 2* (U.K.)

—This is a jigsaw.
—It's broken!
—That's the object. You have to put it together.
—Why? I didn't break it!

Willie Tanner and Alf, *ALF*

Remember that dirty great 5,000-piece jigsaw of Tower Bridge you did? Took you under ten minutes, hammering pieces in with your fist. Looked nothing like it when you'd finished—it had three skies to my knowledge.

Tony Hancock, *Hancock's Half Hour*

I just spent two weeks doing a 100-piece jigsaw. I was quite pleased with myself because on the box it said "6–8 years."

Les Blake

[*doing a crossword*] A four-letter Italian word for "goodbye" … hmm … Bang!
B-A-N-G.   **Archie Bunker, *All in the Family***

—[*doing a crossword*] Heating device.
—Radiator.
—Five letters.
—Rdatr.   **Ross Geller and Phoebe Buffay, *Friends***

My dad used to keep Eskimos and alligators. He bred escalators. We got a lot of
funny stairs.   **Marek Larwood**

I wanted something to do.   **Les Stewart, who set a world record by typing**
out every number from one to one million, in words.
It took him 16 years, typing for 20 minutes per waking hour.

Incest—a game the whole family can play!   **Anon.**

GAMBLING

Horse sense is something a horse has that prevents it
betting on people.
W. C. Fields

It's foolish to bet on a horse without talking to him first. I know it seems silly to
ask a horse who's going to win a race—but it's no sillier than asking anyone else.
Gracie Allen

That horse had better win, or else we're taking a trip to the glue factory—and he
won't get to come.   **Homer Simpson, *The Simpsons***

Lady Godiva put everything she had on a horse.

W. C. Fields

I backed a horse today—20 to 1. It came in 20 past 4.

Tommy Cooper

—How about a little gin rummy?
—I don't drink it, thank you. Never touch it.
Mr. Jones and Doctor, *Sullivan's Travels*

I used to be a heavy gambler. But now I just make mental bets. That's how I lost my mind.   **Steve Allen**

I like to play blackjack. I'm not addicted to gambling. I'm addicted to sitting in a semicircle.   **Mitch Hedberg**

SHOPPING

Only a fool thinks price and value are the same.
Antonio Machado

I was in a bookstore the other day. There was a third off all titles. I bought *The Lion, The Witch* ...   **Jimmy Carr**

I need to go shopping for clothes to shop in.   **Carmen Berra**

I went into a clothing store, and the lady asked me what size I was. I said, "Actual. I'm not to scale."   **Demetri Martin**

When people in Britain want to buy a pet, they go to a pet shop. If they want to buy a pet shop, they go to a pet shop shop. If they want to buy a pet shop shop, well, they're just being silly.   **Tom Baker,** *Little Britain*

I like going into newsagents and saying, "Excuse me, is that Mars bar for sale?" When they say, "Yes," I say, "I might be back later, I still have a few others to look at."   **Michael Redmond**

What is it about people who repair shoes that makes them so good at cutting keys? "A pair of shoes and a key, please—and a trophy, why not?!"
Harry Hill

I was in a convenience store reading a magazine when the clerk comes up to me and says, "This isn't a library." So I say, "All right, I'll talk louder, then."
Mitch Hedberg

Did you hear about the Irishman born with two left feet? He went out one day to buy some flip-flips.   **Anon.**

I wanted to buy a candleholder, but the store didn't have one. So I got a cake.
Mitch Hedberg

Until I bought that baby oil it just kept sticking to the pan.   **John Maclain**

Bought a cordless extension cord.   **Steven Wright**

Buy thermometers in the wintertime. They're much lower then.

Soupy Sales

Wal-Mart. What's that? Do they, like, make walls there?   Paris Hilton

Oh, I just love it here. So many things and so many things of each thing.
Homer Simpson in "Sprawl-Mart," *The Simpsons*

A stupid practice that a supermarket might perpetrate: Sell each produce item in a different novel way. Grapes: 4 cents each. Coconuts: $7.23 per cubic decimeter.   **Russell Beland**

Bags of frozen vegetables should have a little sticker on every pea and carrot to show the country of origin.   **Thomas L. Schwarz**

A stupid practice that a supermarket might perpetrate: Replace the candy in the checkout lane with kittens and puppies.

Stanley Halbert

The sign said "Eight Items or Less," so I changed my name to Less.

Rod Schmidt

—Mom, we couldn't find any garlic gloves.
—No, honey, I meant cloves.
—Oh, so you mean we were sniffing gloves for nothing?
Randy and Jill Taylor, *Home Improvement*

My wife will buy anything that's marked down. She brought home two dresses and an escalator.   **Henny Youngman**

—There you go again, wanting something that you haven't got.
—I do not. I just want to see what I haven't got that I don't want.
Ricky and Lucy Ricardo, *I Love Lucy*

—I thought we agreed to consult each other before any major purchases.
—Well, you bought all those smoke alarms, and we haven't had a single fire.
Marge and Homer Simpson, *The Simpsons*

I know a guy who called up the Home Shopping Network. They said, "Can I help you?" and he said, "No, I'm just looking."

George Miller

If you don't find it in the index, look very carefully through the entire catalog.

Sears store catalog

You can't have everything; where would you put it?

Steven Wright

USELESS PRODUCTS

Cream of Mushroom Slurpee — Ken Krattenmaker

Mobius toilet paper — Buddy Baker

Seeing-eye giraffes — Blair Thurman

Birthday candle snuffers — Linda K. Malcolm

Ankle watch — Sarah Worcester

Silicone thigh implants — Jerry Pannullo

Garfield condolence cards — Paul A. Sone

Scrabble—special dyslexics' edition — Linda K. Mlacoml

Intermittent headlights — Mark Lesko

Nymphomaniac Repellent — Twink Ruffing

Kosher communion wafers — Joe Shepherd

A transparent colostomy bag — Stephen Dudzik

Nuclear hand grenades. — David T. Harrison

VACATIONS

No man needs a vacation so much as the person
who has just had one.
Elbert Hubbard

BRONTË COUNTRY: 17th-century luxury cottage. Ideal honeymoon. Sleeps
2–5.   *The Times*

We can go away right now. I pack light. Everything we need is right here in my
pants.   **Ryan Harrison, *Wrongfully Accused***

Do you still tan if you don't lie down?
Ditzy girl, www.overheardatthebeach.com

—The other day I went in the water, and I forgot my cellphone was in my
pocket. It doesn't work any more.
—Was it on?
—Yes.
—Well, you should have turned it off before you went in.
Two guys, www.overheardatthebeach.com

—[*holding a crab*] Oh, Daddy, it's so cute! Can I keep it?
—No, honey, it's too small.
—No, Daddy, I want it for a pet.
—It has to live in the ocean, honey. We have to let it go.
—But, Daddy, I love it. Can't I keep it?
—No, baby.
—Daddy?
—Yes, honey?
—Can I step on it?   **Father and small daughter, Goleta Beach,**
California, www.overheardatthebeach.com

—Murray! Cover up! Your business is hanging out of your bathing suit!
—That business closed down years ago.
Wife and husband, www.overheardatthebeach.com

—[*through a megaphone*] Attention, beach-goers, due to the sunset, you must
get out in five minutes or else we will turn the waves off!
—Oh, my God! Is he serious?
Lifeguard and girl, www.overheardatthebeach.com

A young girl who was blown out to sea on a set of inflatable teeth was rescued by a man on an inflatable lobster. A coastguard spokesman commented, "This sort of thing is all too common."   *The Times*

Make bathtime as much fun for kiddies as a trip to the seaside, by chucking a bucket of sand, a bag of salt, a dog turd and a broken bottle into the bath with them.   *Viz* magazine

CHRISTMAS & HOLIDAYS

Three wise men? You must be joking!
Anon.

—Now, children, can anyone tell me the names of the three gifts that the Three Kings gave to baby Jesus?
—Gold, Frankenstein and myrrh.   **Teacher and kindergarten child**

—What do we know about the Magi?
—They taught Luke Skywalker everything he knows.
                              Stephen Fry and Phill Jupitus, QI (*Quite Interesting*)

And so during these holiday seasons, we thank our blessings …
                                                        George W. Bush

We are quite lucky this year because Christmas falls on Christmas Day.
                                                        Bobby Gould

Innit a coincidence that Jesus was born on Christmas Day?
                                                Ali G, *Da Ali G Show*

I think they should move Christmas to July when the stores aren't so crowded.
                                        Goldie Hawn, *Rowan & Martin's Laugh-in*

In my family, when I was growing up, we always called the decorations you hang on Christmas trees "tinkle-tonkles." I only realized we were the only ones to do so when, as a grown-up, I went into a department store and asked for them by name.   **Listener, BBC Radio**

Aren't we forgetting the true meaning of Christmas? You know, the birth of
Santa.
                                                    Bart Simpson, *The Simpsons*

I remember when I was about six, a friend of mine said, "There's no Father
Christmas, you know." And I said, "Yes, there is, because last year he brought
me lots of presents." And my friend said, "No, Father Christmas doesn't exist …
it's your dad." And I didn't know whether to be really upset or really excited—
the fact that my dad, every Christmas, got into a sleigh and went round the
whole world delivering presents to all the boys and girls.
                                                    Rory McGrath

For his holiday gift, my husband asked for a huge TV. So I just moved his chair
closer to the one we already have.
                                                    Wendy Liebman

This Christmas, I'm giving mostly ethical gifts. I've bought a goat for an African
family. They're not very pleased. They live in the flat above me.
                                                    Steve Punt, *The Now Show*

We were poor as children. One Christmas I asked Santa for a yo-yo and all I got
was a piece of string. My father told me it was a yo.
                                                    Brendan O'Carroll

My parents didn't have very much money. Every year, Mum would give us each
a Christmas haircut, then we'd sit down to turkey with all the trimmings.
                                                    Milton Jones

What a beautiful day for taking your clothes off, strapping your legs round the
back of your neck and saying, "How's this for an oven-ready turkey?"
                                                    Ken Dodd

Turkey carcasses make fantastic stock. It's good enough to drink on its own.
                                                    Simon Hopkinson, chef

My ten favorite things about Christmas: 1. It only comes once a year. 2. It only
lasts a day. 3. I can't think of anything else.
                                                    Neil Pye, *The Young Ones*

Finlay's very excited. He informed me he's the postman in the school nativity
play. I'm told it's a very important role.
                                                    Andrea McLean, *Loose Women*

So, what's this year's nativity play about?
                                                    Carolyn Flynn

At this year's nativity play the Angel Gabriel announced his presence to the Virgin Mary with the words, "Hail! Thou art highly flavored ..."

Angela Hoyle

Nobody does Christmas like the Jews.

Tracey Ullman

Oy to the world.

Frasier Crane, *Frasier*

Do we have to keep talking about religion? It's Christmas!

Danielle Chase, *My So-Called Life*

An American guy who works with me in a London bank said, "You guys are working on July 4th? I don't believe it! Don't you celebrate it?" Er, American Independence Day ...

Grace Cooper

PARTY

Party at Joe's house! Be there or be stupid! ...
Lowell, you can be both.
Roy Biggins, Wings

—Bob and I are giving a 4th of July party. Would you like to come?
—Oh, great! When is it?

Emily Hartley and Howard Borden, *The Bob Newhart Show*

—This Elton John party, was that a pre- or post-Oscar party?
—Yes.

Interviewer and Paris Hilton

She talked the entire time about colonic irrigation and matters of that sort. Rabbiting on about rock stars and colonic irrigation. And hairdressers.

Professor Norman Stone, on Princess Diana

I'm fascinated about anything. I'll talk for seven hours about splinters.

Marlon Brando

The 16th Duke of Norfolk was heard to turn to a lady guest on his right and say, "I have only two topics of conversation—cricket and drains. Choose."

Brian Masters, *The Dukes*

If conversation is flagging, I ask the gentleman on my right, "Are you a bed-wetter?"

Vivien Murphy

In a final desperate attempt to evoke a response from my lethargic dinner partner I found myself asking, "Do you like string?"

Jerry Wadsworth

Actor and wit Gilbert Gottfried met Jackie Onassis at a party but found the conversation hard going. By way of small talk, he unthinkingly found himself saying, "And where were you when Kennedy was shot?"

Williams College Trivia

My best party trick, which I used to play with my elder brother, was for both of us to go into a room, each with a bottle of whiskey, and when we had finished our beverages, one of us went out and knocked on the door and the other had to guess who it was.

Sir Clement Freud, *Just a Minute*

—You know what I hate most after a big party?
—Trying to find your underwear in the big pile?

Blanche Devereaux and Rose Nylund, *The Golden Girls*

—We never have parties.
—What about that huge one, you know, with champagne, a band, a lot of holy men or something?
—That was our wedding.

Marge and Homer Simpson, *The Simpsons*

GIFTS

So, if you've got a birthday coming up within the next 12 months
or so ...
Lynda Berry

Those presents the Three Wise Men brought Jesus—were they for his birthday or Christmas?

Karl Pilkington

I like fruit baskets because it gives you the ability to mail someone a piece of fruit without appearing insane. Like, if someone just mailed you an apple you'd be like, "Huh? What the hell is this?" But if it's in a fruit basket you're like, "This is nice."

Demetri Martin

—You said you loved Pagliacci!
—Yes, the opera, not the little porcelain crying clown figurine!

Roz Doyle and Frasier Crane, *Frasier*

Put candles on a cake, it's a birthday cake. Put candles on a pie, and somebody's drunk in the kitchen. Go check on Grandma.

Jim Gaffigan

My auntie sent me a birthday card that said, "I was going to enclose some money, but I'd already sealed the envelope."

Rick Moore

—Okay, now remember, whatever's in this box, we split it in two.
—What if it's a puppy?

Joe and Brian Hackett, *Wings*

A chess set ... cool! It's one of those checker sets for smart people and gays.

Randy Hickey, *My Name Is Earl*

I once persuaded my tiny son to write his laborious thanks in a thank-you note and gave him a minimal formula: "Thank you very much for the (blank). I like it very much." His aunt reported back that his card to her read, "Thank you very much for the £10. I like it very much."

Valerie Grove

A Belated Birthday Wish ... From Your Conjoined Twin

Chris Doyle, greeting card message

Happy Birthday. I have adopted a child in your name. He arrives shortly.

Greeting card, cyranet.com

I'm a fairly modern man—I've got no problem buying tampons. But apparently they're not a "proper present."

Jimmy Carr

—You said you gave Mary Jane a pearl necklace!
—Obviously you missed the whole point of that story.

Scarface and Thurgood Jenkins, *Half Baked*

THE NATURAL WORLD

ANIMALS—GENERAL

Nature makes only dumb animals. We owe the fools to society.
Honoré de Balzac

D'you ever cut your fingernails with pinking shears and pretend you're a fox?
Harry Hill

—I don't see a single cow.
—I don't even see a married one.
Larry and Curly (The Three Stooges), *The Yoke's on Me*

I like dolphins. If dolphins were human, I'd be a dolphin.

Jason Donovan

—Dad, what's the whale's blowhole for?
—I'll tell you what it's not for, son. And when I do, you'll understand why I can never go back to Sea World. **Chris and Peter Griffin,** *Family Guy*

Two fish are in a tank. One says to the other, "How do you drive this thing?"
Anon.

—How do elephants make love under water?
—They first remove their trunks. **Anon.**

—Can you get an elephant drunk?
—Yes, but he still won't go up to your apartment.
Peter Marshall and Paul Lynde, *Hollywood Squares*

—What do you get when you cross a camel with a leopard?
—Is it a fireside rug you can have a good hump on?
Stephen Fry and Jo Brand, QI (*Quite Interesting***)**

The great roe is a mythological beast with the head of a lion and the body of a lion, though not the same lion. **Woody Allen**

Is a ferret a bird? **Jade Goody, British TV personality**

My two favorite animals are pork chops and bacon.
Homer Simpson, *The Simpsons*

—Did you ever have a pet?
—You mean, like, an animal?

Diane Chambers and "Coach" Ernie Pantusso, *Cheers*

—Why are you walking a lobster on a lead in the parks of Paris?
—Why should a lobster be any more ridiculous than a dog or any other animal that one chooses to take for a walk? I have a liking for lobsters. They are peaceful, serious creatures. They know the secrets of the sea, they don't bark and they don't gnaw upon one's monadic privacy like dogs do.

Passerby and Gérard de Nerval

Overfeed a black Labrador, put flippers on his feet, grease him down and balance a ball on his nose, then pretend to your neighbors you have a pet seal.

Viz **magazine**

The little boy's puppy was sick and his mother said, "We must take him to the vet—that's an animal doctor." The little boy thought for some time, then said, "Mummy, will the animal doctor be a dog or a cat?"

James Gavin

I was riding a horse, and its leg was broken, so I had to shoot it. Everybody on the carousel freaked out.

Tom Cotter

In all the years of shoeing horses, there's never been a "Cuban heel period."

Mark Radcliffe, *Radcliffe and Maconie,* **BBC Radio**

How would you know if your goldfish was incontinent?

Ray Fitzgerald

Due to the shape of the North American elk's esophagus, even if it could speak, it could not pronounce the word "lasagne."

Cliff Clavin, *Cheers*

Two kangaroos were talking to each other, and one said, "I hope it doesn't rain today. I hate it when the children play inside."

Anon.

—What happened to the hyena who fell into a pot of gravy?
—He made a laughing stock of himself.

Anon.

An asp is a small snake that once bit Cleo ... Cleo Laine.

Young child, *Small Talk*

—What do you call a sheep with no legs?
—A cloud.

Anon.

It's a known fact that the sheep that give us steel wool have no natural enemies.

Gary Larson

I enjoy the company of cattle. I really enjoy knowing them, running my hand over them.

Russell Crowe

One disadvantage of being a hog is that at any moment some blundering fool may try to make a silk purse out of your wife's ear.

J. B. Morton

CAT

Cats are smarter than dogs. You can't get eight cats to pull a sled through snow.

Jeff Valdez

People see the litter tray in my kitchen and say, "Oh, do you have a cat?"
I say, "No, that's for guests."

Valerie Cook

In China, a healthy cat has been born with three heads. Here, kitty, kitty, kitty.

Craig Kilborn

If I die before my cat, I want a little of my ashes put in his food so I can live inside him.

Drew Barrymore

I found out why cats drink out of the toilet. My mother told me it's because the water is cold in there. And I'm like, how does my mother know that?

Wendy Liebman

If you're sick of being covered in cat hair, get some sticky tape and wrap it around your cat.

Adam Bloom

—I just spent four hours burying the cat.
—Four hours to bury a cat?
—Yes. It wouldn't keep still ...

Monty Python's Flying Circus

I ain't a pussy-person. When people look at me, they don't think "cat," they think "dog."

Lynda La Hughes, *Gimme, Gimme, Gimme*

DOG

Millions of Americans own dogs because they are good-natured, simple, and easily amused. I am referring here to the Americans.
Dave Barry

—Oh, what a charming little animal.
—Do you know dogs, Mr. Melonchek?
—Know dogs? I used to be a chef in a Korean restaurant!

Rocco Melonchek and Lillian Oglethorpe, *Brain Donors*

Some dog I got. We call him Egypt because in every room he leaves a pyramid.

Rodney Dangerfield

—What's your dog's name?
—I don't know. He never told me.

Caroline and Adam, *Untamed Heart*

—I call my dog Eddie Spaghetti.
—Oh, he likes pasta?
—No, he has worms.

Martin Crane and Daphne Moon, *Frasier*

—Does your dog bite?
—No.
—Nice doggie ... ouch! I thought you said your dog didn't bite!
—That's not my dog.

Inspector Clouseau and hotel clerk, *The Pink Panther Strikes Again*

In an American Animal Hospital Association poll, 33 percent of dog owners admitted that they talked to their dogs on the phone or left messages on an answering machine when they were away.

Sunday Express

Better not take a dog on the space shuttle, because if he sticks his head out when you're coming home his face might burn up.

Jack Handey, *Deep Thoughts*

A dog is not intelligent. Never trust an animal that's surprised by its own farts.
Frank Skinner

Too bad Lassie didn't know how to ice skate, because then if she was in Holland on vacation in winter and someone said, "Lassie, go skate for help," she could do it.
Jack Handey

—How many times have I told you not to take the dog out without a muzzle?
—I put a muzzle on, but I couldn't breathe.
Abbott and Costello, *Rio Rita*

My dog ... can lick anyone.
Anon.

Help control the pet population: Teach your dog abstinence.
Stephen Colbert

I'm a mog: half-man, half-dog. I'm my own best friend.
Barf, *Spaceballs*

Dog owners! Don't waste money on a lead! Simply walk your dog backward holding its tail.
Viz **magazine**

It is said that over time, owners come to resemble their dogs. But does that excuse Auntie Hilda from shitting in the garden?
Simon Munnery

The other day I saw two dogs walk over to a parking meter. One of them says to the other, "How do you like that? Pay toilets."
Dave Starr

Dogs have no money. They're broke their entire lives. You know why dogs have no money? No pockets.
Jerry Seinfeld

WANTED: Good home for year-old basset hound. Understands every word owner says, but ignores it.
Notice in store window Portsmouth, U.K.

I poured some spot remover on my dog. Now he's gone.
Steven Wright

A man loses his dog, so he puts an ad in the paper that says, "Here, boy!"
Spike Milligan

Well, crying isn't going to bring the dog back—unless your tears smell like dog food.
Homer Simpson, *The Simpsons*

BIRDS

A bird does not sing because it has an answer. It sings because it
has a song.
Chinese proverb

Two guys are walking down the street when one guy exclaims, "How sad—a dead bird." The other guy looks up and says, "Where?"
Anon.

Imagine if birds were tickled by feathers.
Steven Wright

I wonder what kind of bird Humpty Dumpty would have hatched out to had he lived?
Harry Hill

Do pigeons walk man-toed?
George Carlin

How do the birds know it is a sanctuary?
Sir Keith Joseph, being shown around a bird sanctuary

Little Mary was visiting her grandmother in the country. Walking in the garden, Mary chanced to see a peacock, a bird she had never seen before. After gazing in silent admiration, she ran into the house and cried, "Come quickly, Granny, one of your chickens is in bloom!"
Christian Herald

Them things that look like eyes, are they their real eyes?
Jade Goody, looking at peacock feathers, *Big Brother 3* (U.K.)

Ford, you're turning into a penguin. Stop it.
Douglas Adams, *The Hitchhiker's Guide to the Galaxy*

INSECTS

Aerodynamically the bumble bee shouldn't be able to fly, but the bumble bee doesn't know it, so it goes on flying anyway.
Mary Kay Ash

Look at that ugly little bee. Makes honey. I'm a nice-looking person and all I can do is make a little wax with my ears.
Milt Kamen

"Like bees around honey"—why are bees so attracted to honey since they make it? It can only be vanity.
Simon Munnery

Bees make honey—how do they do that? Do earwigs make chutney? Do spiders make gravy?
Eddie Izzard

A myth is a moth's sister.
Anon.

It's only when you look at an ant through a magnifying glass on a sunny day that you realize how often they burst into flames.
Harry Hill

Ants can carry 20 times their own body weight, which is useful information if you're moving out and you need help getting a potato chip across town.
Ron Darian

Bought an ant farm. I don't know where I'm gonna get tractors that small.
Steven Wright

NATURE

Look deep into nature, and then you will understand everything better.
Albert Einstein

Look up there! That's the sky!
Murray Walker

Today I saw a red and yellow sunset and thought, How insignificant I am! Of course, I thought that yesterday, too, and it rained.

> Woody Allen

How I detest the dawn. The grass always looks like it's been left out all night.

> Hardy Cathcart, *The Dark Corner*

My neighbor asked if he could use my lawnmower and I told him of course he could, so long as he didn't take it out of my garden.

> Eric Morecambe

There's a sight to take your breath away—the smell of hyacinths.

> Peter Seabrook

—These flowers are completely out of water, Vicar.
—They're silk, Alice.

> Alice Tinker and Rev. Geraldine Grainger, *The Vicar of Dibley*

Why would you water a rubber plant?

> DJ, BBC Radio

My fake plants died because I did not pretend to water them.

> Mitch Hedberg

I have a very aristocratic gardenia, who wasn't doing too well, so my boyfriend gave it a shot of cocaine, and that really perked it up.

> Bette Midler

Of all the wonders of nature, a tree in summer is perhaps the most remarkable; with the possible exception of a moose singing "Embraceable You" in spats.

> Woody Allen

—I was watching an interesting tree-cutting ritual last night on TV.
—I saw that. It was a bonsai tree special.
—Who cares about the trees! Those people were HUGE!

> Lowell Mather and Roy Biggins, *Wings*

I went to a petrified forest and all the animals were afraid of me.

> Buzz Nutley

We went out on the streets and asked people, "How was Mount Rushmore formed?" The most popular answer was, "Erosion."

> Jay Leno

WEATHER

We will never be an advanced civilization as long as rain showers
can delay the launching of a space rocket.
George Carlin

It's warm and wet in London this morning, let's find out how Isobel Lang is—
warm and wet as well?

Newsreader, to weather girl, *BBC Breakfast* **(YT)**

There is a trough of low pleasure over Europe.

Weather reporter, BBC

And there's fog on the M25 in both directions.

John Humphreys, BBC newscaster

Blue Skies Unless It's Cloudy

Weather headline, *San Francisco Chronicle*

—It was over a hundred in the shade.
—You shouldn't have stayed in the shade.

P. G. Wodehouse, *If I Were You*

When it gets hot like this, you know what I do? I put my undies in the icebox.

The Girl, *The Seven Year Itch*

If you saw a heat wave, would you wave back?

Steven Wright

It's been one of the warmest 1994s this century.

Richard Allinson, Capital Radio

The wind is absolutely still.

David Coleman

I can see the strong wind blowing the sun toward us.

Brian Johnston

—What a nice summer evening—typically English.
—Mmm, yes, the rain's lovely and warm.

The Goon Show

It rained hard enough to fill a wire basket.   Proverb

—Did you notice the heavy fog last night?
—No, nothing wakes me.   Morecambe and Wise

Two snowmen in a field. One says to the other, "Can you smell carrots?"
                    Anon.

—Danny, I hope you're giving your little brother a turn on the sledge.
—Of course, Mummy. I have it downhill and he has it up.
                    Jane and Danny Graham

It gets late early out there.   Yogi Berra

There will be a rain dance Friday night, weather permitting.
                    George Carlin

THE ENVIRONMENT

Putting humans in charge of the Earth is the cosmic equivalent of
letting Eddie Murphy direct.
Alf, ALF

George Bush says he's committed to tackling global warming: He's sending
20,000 troops to the sun.   David Letterman

Don't postpone that visit to the wax museum, the planet is getting warmer.
                    Pierre Légaré

If everyone on Earth just stopped breathing for an hour, the greenhouse effect
would no longer be a problem.   Jerry Adler, *Newsweek*

I think the end of the cold war is what started global warming.
                    Steven Wright

If trees could scream, would we be so cavalier about cutting them down? We
might, if they screamed all the time, for no good reason.
                    Jack Handey, *Deep Thoughts*

Made from recycled plastic bottles
> **Statement on a badge worn around the neck of the U.K. Deputy Prime Minister, John Prescott, at the Earth Summit**

When they put up a whole farm of windmills off the northeast coast of Norfolk, which is on the main migratory route to Scandinavia, are we going to get sliced-up ducks coming across?
> **Prince Philip**

These wind farms are ridiculous. As if this country doesn't have enough wind of its own without wasting electricity making more of it by running these big fans.
> **Ben Cormack, *Viz* magazine**

But will wind farms ever produce enough electricity to make the turbines go round?
> **Prince Philip**

—Dad, we're trying to save electricity.
—But, Lisa, if we start conserving, the environmentalists win!
> **Lisa and Homer Simpson, *The Simpsons***

We've got to pause and ask ourselves: How much clean air do we need?
> **Lee Iacocca**

I've always thought that underpopulated countries in Africa are vastly underpolluted.
> **Lawrence Summers, Chief Economist of the World Bank, explaining in a memo why toxic waste should be exported to the Third World**

I propose a limitation be put on how many squares of toilet paper can be used in any one sitting.
> **Sheryl Crow**

How Green Were the Nazis?
> **Book title, Franz-Josef Bruggemeier, Mark Cioc and Thomas Zeller**

I hug trees so hard there's been a bit of talk in the neighborhood.
> **Joseph O'Connor**

Nuke the Unborn Gay Whales
> **Bumper sticker**

I know that the human being and the fish can coexist peacefully.
> **George W. Bush**

Soon there will be no more whales left: My wife and I will just have to do without them.
Joseph Heller, *Something Happened*

Red squirrels—you don't see many of them since they became extinct.
Michael Aspel

As president of Commercial Rubbish Company, I mounted a poster on my garbage collection trucks: "Satisfaction Guaranteed or Double Your Garbage Back."
Sid Blumberg

She ran after the garbage truck, yelling, "Am I too late for the garbage?" "No, jump in!
Henny Youngman

ARTS & ENTERTAINMENT

CULTURE

You can lead a whore to culture, but you can't make her think.
Dorothy Parker

Britain, Britain, Britain, cultural capital of the world. The Sistine Chapel: British. Mozart's Requiem: British. The Great Wall of China: British.

Tom Baker, *Little Britain*

What did you go into the museum for? It wasn't raining.   **Old Mother Riley**

To you, Baldrick, the Renaissance was just something that happened to other people, wasn't it?   **Edmund Blackadder,** *Blackadder II*

My hunch is the gays started the Renaissance. Two gay guys at a party go, "Say, wouldn't it be fun to make religious paintings of hot naked guys, and sell them to churches?"   **Bob Smith**

—There's a lot of culture in this city …
—I took you to the zoo, what more d'you want?

Cheryl and Jim, *According to Jim*

I went to the museum where they had all the heads and arms from the statues that are in all the other museums.

Steven Wright

Shouldn't the Air and Space Museum be empty?   **Dennis Miller**

ART

Hello Dali!
Anon.

Dada wouldn't buy me a Bauhaus.

Anon.

Come to my house and I'll show you my Toujours Lautrec.

Sam Goldwyn

I thought the guy who painted the Mona Lisa was called Pistachio.

Jade Goody, British TV personality

I don't recall exactly where I bought my Picasso. It was in Paris—in the left wing, I think.

Sam Goldwyn

Picasso had his pink period and his blue period. I am in my blonde period right now.

Hugh Hefner

—What art do you have on your bedroom wall?
—I paint myself actually.
—Do you get into bed before you're dry?

Janet Street-Porter, Boris Johnson and Paul Merton, *Have I Got News for You*

I want to thank you for taking time out of your day to come and witness my hanging.

George W. Bush, at the dedication of his portrait

On [Tony Blair's] first visit [to Tate Modern Art Museum] he made his famous gaffe after being introduced to novelist Ian McEwan … According to McEwan, "Blair took my hand in that political way and said, "I really love your work. I've got two of your paintings." McEwan corrected him, but Blair still insisted that he had McEwans on his walls rather than on his bookshelves.

Evening Standard

I call this painting, "A Maid On Her Night Out Winding a Grandfather Clock with Her Left Hand."

Curly (The Three Stooges),
Wee Wee Monsieur

Sign of an incompetent abstract expressionist painter: Inspires comments from gallery patrons that "My four-year-old nephew couldn't do that."

Elden Carnahan

—I'm one of the impressionists.
—Well, it don't impress me.

Anthony Hancock and Mrs. Crevatte, *The Rebel*

You know, I'm no art critic, but I know what I hate.

Mr. Burns, *The Simpsons*

I don't know that much about art. I don't even know what I like.

Dr. Hill, *Wire in the Blood*

As the lady said, "Well, if isn't art, then I like it."   **John Cage**

Her artistic sense was exquisitely refined, like someone who can tell butter from "I Can't Believe It's Not Butter."   **Barbara Collier**

If the eyes follow you round the room, it's a good painting. If they don't, it isn't.

Pete, *Dud and Pete*

When my daughter was about seven-years-old, she asked me one day what I did at work. I told her I worked at the college—that my job was to teach people how to draw. She stared back at me, incredulous, and said, "You mean they forget?"   **Howard Ikemoto**

Damien Hirst tends to use everyday objects such as a shark in formaldehyde.

Arts commentator, BBC Radio

—Have you never seen a woman naked?
—It's just like in the paintings.
—But without one of them cherubs in just the wrong place.

Betty Bagwell and Samuel Pepys,
The Private Life of Samuel Pepys

—A painter once asked me to pose for him—with no clothes on!
—Really? Did you do it?
—Yeah! It was quite exciting. He was painting our kitchen at the time.
Alice Tinker and Rev. Geraldine Grainger, *The Vicar of Dibley*

—How many surrealists does it take to change a light bulb?
—A vibrating Norwegian horse box full of sea cucumbers.   **Anon.**

—It's a self-portrait.
—Who of?   **Anthony Hancock and Mrs. Crevatte,** *The Rebel*

Every so often, I like to go to the window, look up and smile for a satellite picture.   **Steven Wright**

I don't have a photograph, but you can have my footprints. They are upstairs in my socks.   **Groucho Marx**

I call it performance art, but my friend calls it a waste of time. History will decide.   **Harris K. Telemacher,** *L.A. Story*

POPULAR MUSIC

I don't know anything about music.
In my line you don't have to.
Elvis Presley

—Ladies and gentlemen, here is Miss Lena Horne doing one of her great numbers ...
—[*the band strikes up*] Eighty-three!
Dick Martin and Lena Horne, *Rowan & Martin's Laugh-in*

Now, John Paul Young with his greatest and only hit. **Charles Nove**

—How is a hit song like Jack the Ripper?
—One is a chart topper, the other is a tart chopper. **Steven Papier**

1983—that was the year we lost Sir Ralph Richardson, and gained this from Kajagoogoo ... **Simon Bates, radio host**

My second hit was a flop. **Shakin' Stevens**

I want to do records for my peace of mind. So when I do kick the bucket, I can say, "I did that." **Rod Stewart**

I always wanted to be a Muppet. So when *Sesame Street* approached me to guest star, I thought, I'm going to be on this! **James Blunt**

Rock stars, is there anything they don't know?
Homer Simpson, *The Simpsons*

In Take That, we didn't talk about anything of substance. We were like the People's Popular Front of Judea in *The Life of Brian*.
Robbie Williams

I thought Kanye West was a tube station near Uxbridge.
Jonathan Ross

Detroit—or "Motor Town" as they call it for short. **Linda Lewis**

I now know it's rap music ... I thought it was called rat music.
Jonathan Aitken, former conservative member of Parliament (U.K.)

Three cheers for rap music—hip-hop...

Tim Vine

Eric Clapton, as everyone knows, is the Clark Gable of rock music.

Simon Bates

I like to think of us as Clearasil on the face of the nation. Jim Morrison would have said that if he was smart, but he's dead.

Lou Reed

I used to levitate on stage but a lot of that was chemical, I think.

Julian Cope, of The Teardrop Explodes

We want to be the band to dance to when the bomb drops.

Simon Le Bon, of Duran Duran

I'd rather be dead than singing "Satisfaction" when I'm 45.

Mick Jagger

The Stones would keep going even if they all died.

Mick Jagger

Chuck Berry penned the words "My ding-a-ling, my ding-a-ling, I want you to play with my ding-a-ling." If only he'd given a thought to how these lyrics could be construed by lewd-minded folk.

Mrs. Merton

We lit candles and sat around listening to John Lennon sing with genuine passion in his voice about how he was the egg man, and they were the egg men, and he was also the walrus, and, by God we knew exactly what he meant.

Dave Barry

"Something" is the greatest love song ever written—it shows what great songwriters Lennon and McCartney were.

Frank Sinatra, on a song written by George Harrison

Wow! Paul McCartney! I read about you in history class.

Lisa Simpson, *The Simpsons*

The band never actually split up—we just stopped speaking to each other and went our own separate ways.

Boy George

—You've got a "Greatest Hits" record coming out. Will there be any new songs on it?

—Yeah, I've written a couple of new ones, which will be on it.

Jackie Brambles and Sophie Ellis-Bexter, *Loose Women*

Singing is a gift from God, and when people say I can't sing, it's kind of like insulting God.

Fergie

I never sing in the shower 'cause I never shower. But we do have a bath that vibrates at G-flat. So I do a lot of vocal mantras in the style of Sly Stone on "There's A Riot Goin' On."

Julian Cope, of The Teardrop Explodes

Save money on expensive tickets to "open-air festivals" next summer. Simply put up a tent in your own back garden, piss up the side of it, and steal your own shoes.

Simone Glover, *Viz* **magazine**

All music is folk music. I ain't heard no horse sing a song.

Louis Armstrong

You don't understand country and western music. It's about the real things in life—murder, train wrecks, amputations, faucets leaking in the night—all stuff like that.

Tom Hartman, *Mary Hartman, Mary Hartman*

Apparently, if you play country and western music backward, your lover returns, your dog comes back and you cease to be an alcoholic.

Linda Smith

Sign of an incompetent folk-singing family: Flees the Nazis by escaping to the Sudetenland.

Russell Beland

I cry when I listen to it.

Paris Hilton, on her debut album, *Paris*

As long as there is, you know, sex and drugs, I can do without the rock 'n' roll.

Mick Shrimpton, *This Is Spinal Tap*

All the good music has already been written by people with wigs and stuff.

Frank Zappa

CLASSICAL MUSIC

Beethoven can write music, thank God—
but he can do nothing else on Earth.
Ludwig van Beethoven

I don't know much about classical music. For years I thought the "Goldberg
Variations" were something Mr. and Mrs. Goldberg tried on their wedding
night.
Woody Allen

And now we have "The Bum of the Flightlebee" by that well-known Russian
composer, Ripmekorsetzov ...
Radio announcer

Play some Picasso.
Chris Morris, ex NBA forward, to a pianist while on a date.

Isn't it amazing how music can conjure up a whole era of the past which you'd
thought you'd forgotten about ... ? Like with me, whenever I hear Ravel's
"Bolero" I think of Eileen Latimer. I can't think why I keep thinking of her
whenever I hear that tune. I think it may be due to the fact that she came round
to tea one day and smashed the record over my head.
Pete, *Dud and Pete*

Now, here's some Swedish music seen through German ears ...
Presenter, BBC Radio

That was played by the Lindsay String Quartet—or, at least, two-thirds of them.
Sean Rafferty, BBC Radio

—I didn't know you could play the piano. Do you play by ear?
—Oh, no. I use my hands like everybody else.
Marsha Manning and Weeji, *Hit the Ice*

I only know two tunes. One is "Clair de Lune," the other one isn't.
Victor Borge

—You're playing all the wrong notes!
—I'm playing all the right notes ... but not necessarily in the right order.
André Previn and Eric Morecambe, *The Morecambe & Wise Show*

You handle Handel like nobody handles Handel. And your Delius—delirious!

Detective Sweeney, *Unfaithfully Yours*

If there's any time left over, I fill in with a lot of runs up and down the scale.

Wladziu Valentino Liberace

I'd have given my right arm to be a pianist. Bobby Robson

—How long have you been studying music?
—Fifteen years.
—You know, two more years and you could have been a plumber.

Chico Marx and Leon Belasco

I don't know anything about classical music. I don't know Beethoven from ... Beethoven's the only one I know. Todd, *Frasier*

I like Beethoven, especially the poems.

Ringo Starr

Disappointing news for Beethoven as his 9th Symphony drops nine places in our Hall of Fame. Jamie Crick, Classic FM (U.K.)

Debussy is so brilliant at conjuring up a whole scene with the use of his instruments ... "La Mer" ... there she is—Debussy's mother, comes into the room, a silver tray covered with a silver teapot, silver cups, silver hair. D'you hear the tea being poured? Pete, *Dud and Pete*

I adore young people. I try and stay young myself. Do you know I even entered the Young Musician of the Year the other day? He was furious!

Sir Bernard Chumley, played by Matt Lucas

As Mr. Hywel Morgan is indisposed and at present in hospital, all his singing engagements will be cancelled for the present. We are pleased to say that he is progressing slowly. *Welsh Press*

The concerto was written in four flats because Rachmaninoff had to move four times when he wrote it. Victor Borge

Mozart is celebrating the 200th anniversary of his death.

Derek Jameson

ERIK SATIE, COMPOSER:
EXAMPLES OF MUSICAL DIRECTIONS TO
PERFORMERS OF HIS PIANO WORKS

Modestly, I beg you
Superstitiously
Very Turkish
Open the head
In a very particular way
Very lost
Alone, for one moment
A little bit warm
Light like an egg
Like a nightingale who would have toothaches
To be played with both hands in the pocket

OPERA

Anything that is too stupid to be spoken is sung.
Voltaire

—Leonard and I are going to the opening of *La Traviata* tonight.
—You wouldn't catch me eating that foreign muck.

Cissie and Ada, aka Roy Barraclough and Les Dawson

—Why does Pavarotti always hold a hankie?
—Because he's got a sandwich in it.

Jeremy Hardy and Linda Smith, *The News Quiz*, BBC Radio

I went to watch Pavarotti once. He doesn't like it when you join in.

Mick Miller

I really liked *Tosca*. Even the music was good.   **Yogi Berra**

The Hairstylist of Seville.   **John Benitez, near-miss opera title**

MUSICAL INSTRUMENT

Play the music, not the instrument.
Anon.

Are you doing what I told you? Are you thinking of that reed as a woman's nipple?
Joey Fagan to Dean Fay practicing the saxophone, *The Commitments*

—What do you get if you cross a drummer with a gorilla?
—A stupid gorilla.
Anon.

My advice to amateurs wanting to get into playing the drums is to play the guitar.
Keith Moon, drummer for The Who

To get your playing more forceful, hit the drums harder.
Keith Moon, drummer for The Who

I don't understand why people think it's so difficult to learn to play guitar. I found it incredibly easy. You just pick a chord, go twang and you've got music.
Sid Vicious, of The Sex Pistols

His cello playing is just terrible. He had no conception of the instrument. He was blowing into it.
Cello teacher, *Take the Money and Run*

No one should be allowed to play the violin until he has mastered it.
Jim Fiebig

DANCE

We're fools whether we dance or not,
so we might as well dance.
Japanese proverb

I grew up with six brothers. That's how I learned to dance—waiting for the bathroom.

Bob Hope

When you're dancing and you put your hands way above your head, that's very non-guy. There's a kind of homosexual line that exists right at your shoulders.

Quentin Tarantino

The ballerina rose gracefully *en pointe* and extended one slender leg behind her, like a dog at a fire hydrant.

Jennifer Hart

Mummy, why don't they get taller dancers?

Little girl, on seeing ballet dancers *en pointe*

Imagine how awesome *The Nutcracker* would be if they actually did what the title promised.

Joel Stein

I would imagine if you understood Morse code, a tap dancer would drive you crazy.

Mitch Hedberg

I could dance with you till the cows come home. On second thoughts, I'd rather dance with the cows till you come home.

Groucho Marx

FILM & HOLLYWOOD

Nobody knows anything.
William Goldman

—Hey, you wanna go see a movie?
—No thanks, I've already seen one.

Rachel Green and Phoebe Buffay, *Friends*

—I took Tim to see *Doctor Zhivago*.
—What the hell's wrong with him now?

Carmen and Yogi Berra

My favorite film is the French film, *And*. It was released here as *ET*.

Milton Jones

I saw a poster for *Mission: Impossible III* the other day. I thought to myself: It's not really impossible if he's already done it twice.

Mark Watson

—No, no, I don't want to see an Australian film. I hate subtitles.
—This one is no problem. It's dubbed.

Brandee and Diane Chambers, *Cheers*

Sorry, son. Your mom got us tickets to a snooty movie directed by some Swedish meatball.

Homer Simpson, *The Simpsons*

I took my girlfriend to the cinema. At the end of the film, when the credits were running, she asked, "Where's Panavision?" It says "Filmed in Panavision."

Listener, *The Ken Bruce Show*, BBC Radio

—Did you ever see that film where your man has his head transplanted onto a fly, and the fly's head was transplanted onto the man?
—Oh, yes ... what was it called?
—*Out of Africa*, I think.

Father Dougal and Father Ted,
Father Ted

I saw the movie *Crouching Tiger, Hidden Dragon*, and I didn't see any tigers or dragons. Then I realized, it's because they're crouching and hidden.

Steve Martin

—Why did you name the movie *Bananas*?
—Because there are no bananas in it.

Reporter and Woody Allen

I think that *Clueless* was very deep. I think it was deep in the way that it was very light. I think lightness has to come from a very deep place if it's true lightness.

Alicia Silverstone

—Did the movie *Fatal Attraction* scare you?
—Only the scary parts.

Reporter and Yogi Berra

One is no longer safe in one's own home ... It's like that really scary movie, that really violent one. Damn, what's it called? *Chocolate Orange*.

Linda La Hughes, *Gimme, Gimme, Gimme*

I went to the movie theater and the sign said, "Adults: $5, Children: $2.50." I told them I wanted two boys and a girl.

Steven Wright

[in a movie theater] Ooh, floor popcorn!

Homer Simpson, *The Simpsons*

I got kicked out of a movie theater the other day for bringing my own food in. I argued that the concession stand prices were outrageous. Besides, I hadn't had a barbecue in a long time.

Steven Wright

Hey, wouldn't it be terrible if we ended up having to eat each other? Like those sailors did in that film, um … *We Ended Up Having to Eat Each Other*.

Vyvyan Basterd, *The Young Ones*

Steve McQueen looks good in this movie. He must have made it before he died.

Yogi Berra

A friend was watching the film *Titanic* with us and said, "Why are you all crying? It's not as if it's a true story."

Listener, BBC Radio

I think maybe one day I'd like to do a singing-boxer film.

Elvis Presley

Go see that movie for yourself, and see for yourself why you shouldn't see it.

Sam Goldwyn

They stayed away in droves.

Sam Goldwyn

I'm working on a screenplay. It's called *Schindler's List 2: Let's Get This Party Started*.

Zach Galifianakis

It's too cerebral. We're trying to make a movie here, not a film!

Kit Ramsey, *Bowfinger*

Working in film is like making love to a gorilla. You don't stop when you want to stop; you stop when the gorilla wants to stop.

David Janssen

You Hollywood people! If Van Gogh could see what you did to his life story, there goes the other ear. And if old Tootles LeTrec could see what you did to his life story, he'd punch you all in the knee.

Hieronymus Merkin, *Can Hieronymus Merkin Ever Forget Mercy Humppe and Find True Happiness?*

I know someone who wrote a World War II movie set in Germany. The studio executives said, "Could you make the Nazis nicer?"

Patricia Marx

—Are you attending the Cannes film festival this year?
—I hope so. Where is it being held this year?

Reporter and Christina Aguilera

Sundance is weird. The movies are weird. You actually have to think about them when you watch them.

Britney Spears, after walking out of a screening of
The Singing Detective at the Sundance Film Festival

There's an awful lot of Greeks in it.

Harry Cohn, producer, turning down an adaptation of *The Iliad*

I suggested to the producer that the story would work better if it was set in 1820. "1820?" he said, "When was that?"

Ed Hartman

This will make Beethoven.

Walt Disney, on *Fantasia*

You can hardly tell where the computer models finish and the real dinosaurs begin.

Laura Dern on computer-generated effects in *Jurassic Park*

NEAR-MISS MOVIE TITLES

Rosencrantz and Guildenstern Are Unconscious   Joan Wurtzel

Lawrence of the United Arab Emirates   Anne Kouts

Fiddler on the Porch   Sue Powell

The Agony and the Fun   Mark S. Goodman

Lady Chatterley's Very Good Friend   Anne Kouts

Good Ole Gatsby   Nicholas Suder

SHAKESPEARE

In America it is considered a lot more important to be a great
Batman than a great Hamlet.
Kevin Kline

I thought I'd begin by reading a poem by Shakespeare but then I thought, Why
should I? He never reads any of mine.

Spike Milligan

I went to see a play once. There was this king and he had the ghost of his dead
father hanging over him. And it really did 'is 'ead in.

Shelley Unwin, *Coronation Street*

[*prompter, to actor center stage*] ... or *not* to be!   **Peter Adler**

—I think there's something rotten in the
state of Denmark.
—It's all that cheese.

Diane Chambers and "Coach" Ernie Pantusso, *Cheers*

—Which of these is not a play by Shakespeare: a) *Romeo and Juliet*
b) *The Taming of the Shrew* c) *Babe: Pig in the City*.
—I don't know who this geezer is, who's meant to have written or directed these
things. I think it's Babe—they talk normal in that.

Big Brother and Brian Belo, *Big Brother 8* (U.K.)

Romeo and Tracey   **Dave Oglesby, near-miss play title**

—When Juliet asks, "O Romeo, Romeo, wherefore art thou, Romeo?" she is not
wondering where he is; rather, she is commenting on the fact of his being named
Romeo.
—Now that I know that, what do I do?

Linus and Lucy Van Pelt, *Peanuts*

You can't go by what a girl says, when she's giving you the devil for making a
chump of yourself. It's like Shakespeare. Sounds well but doesn't mean anything.

P. G. Wodehouse, *Joy in the Morning*

—Paul, here's your question: In the play *King* Lear, King Lear had three of them—Goneril, Cordelia and Regan. Who were they?
—King Lear had *Goneril*?

Peter Marshall and Paul Lynde, *Hollywood Squares*

He thought Coriolanus was something you went to the doctor's with.

Sally Webster, *Coronation Street*

A theater review about the Roundabout Theater Company's production of Shakespeare's *The Tempest* misinterpreted a gesture. The actors' intent was to portray eighteenth-century gentlemen taking snuff, not cocaine.

Correction, *The New York Times*

A new book says that Shakespeare was gay. In fact, his boyfriend was the first guy to do Shakespeare in the park.

David Corrado

Eric Andronicus

Alan Curtis, near-miss play title

The Taming of the Vole

Serena Johnson, near-miss play title

Shakespeare is fantastic. And to think he wrote it all with a feather!

Sam Goldwyn

—They've offered me the part of Shylock in *The Merchant of Venice*.
—Screw 'em! Tell 'em you'll only play the merchant.

Edward G. Robinson and Sam Goldwyn

Playing Shakespeare in *Shakespeare in Love*, I was covered in ink. Shakespeare must have been. Jesus! You have to resharpen your quill after a page of writing. Shakespeare must've gone through so many geese.

Joseph Fiennes

Shakespeare's plays are absolutely packed with filth. I've found more than a hundred terms for vagina alone.

Héloïse Sénéchal, academic

Did you see my Bottom at Stratford-upon-Avon? Many consider it my best part.

Eric Morecambe

—I don't know why you bother. People don't want to see that rubbish. That last one you dragged me along to—*Richard the Hundred and Eleventh*—
—*Richard the Third*.
—Yeah. Terrible.

Albert and Harold Steptoe, *Steptoe and Son*

What if Barbara Cartland wrote the plays of William Shakespeare?

Jonathan Paul

Well, ahmmm, you know, something's neither good nor bad but thinking makes it so, I suppose, as Shakespeare said.

Donald Rumsfeld, Secretary of Defense (YT)

ACTORS & ACTING

Dear Ingrid—speaks five languages
and can't act in any of them.
Sir John Gielgud, on Ingrid Bergman

I was lousy in school. Real screwed up. A moron. I was antisocial and didn't bother with the other kids. I didn't have any brains. I didn't know what I was doing there. That's why I became an actor.

Sir Anthony Hopkins

—As a child, I was bitten by the acting bug. Then it burrowed under my skin and laid eggs in my heart. Now those eggs are hatching and I … the feeling is indescribable.
—I know what you mean. Our dog had that.

Moe Syzslak and Homer Simpson, *The Simpsons*

Many actors want to play Hamlet and Macbeth, and ever since I became an actor, from the very beginning, I just wanted to play a Shetland pony. I can't explain why.   Dustin Hoffman

Acting is easier and smoother than singing—it's less drama.

Beyoncé Knowles

I realized I should try harder as an actress because I'd never make it as a waitress.
Jane Krakowski

I would rather start out somewhere small, like London or England.

Britney Spears on the possibility of starring on Broadway

I had to go and see this guy, very important man, and everyone said, "Watch out, Shelley, the second you get into his office, he'll tear your dress off!" "I'll remember," I said. "I'll wear an old dress."

Shelley Winters

Did you hear about the starlet so dumb that she slept with the writer?

Producer's joke

I failed my audition as Romeo through a misunderstanding over a simple stage direction. My copy of the script clearly said, "Enter Juliet from the rear."

Lester Stevens

—I've been studying Stanislavski.
—Stan who?

Hugh Laurie and Stephen Fry, *A Bit of Fry and Laurie*

I knew Doris Day before she was a virgin.

Oscar Levant

When you improvise, do you actually have to make it up?

Paula Yates

I can do anything you want me to do as long as I don't have to speak.

Linda Evangelista

I'm ready for my close-up, Mr. DeVille!

Angelica, *Rugrats*

The director and actress did not get on well, although Björk denies reports that she was so upset during filming that she ate her dress (a rumor that few people other than Björk would need to deny).

Holden Frith, on the making of Lars von Trier's *Dancer in the Dark*

Butler in Dudley Moore Film Dies

Daily Sport, reporting the death of Shakespearean actor, Sir John Gielgud

FAME & CELEBRITY

With fame I become more and more stupid, which, of course, is a
very common phenomenon.
Albert Einstein

I won't be happy until I'm as famous as God.   **Madonna**

The most famous football player in the world ... Michael Beckham!
                                                                Commentator, ABC

I love being famous. It's almost like being white.   **Chris Rock**

Of course, I don't have breasts. If I did have, I'd be in the number one spot over
Madonna.   **Spike Lee**

Not many people realize just how well-known he is.   **Lord Gowrie**

He's very, very well-known. I'd say he's world-famous in Melbourne.

Dame Edna Everage, on her alter ego, Barry Humphries

He rose without a trace.

Kitty Muggeridge, on David Frost, British TV presenter

I was on a bus and I heard someone say, "I saw one of those Two Fat Ladies the
other day—not the dead one."   **Kevin Ashman**

I hate name-dropping, and I told the Duke of Edinburgh as much recently.
                                                                         Frank Carson

There's a cord sticking out of the back of my DVD machine. Might you tell me
where it goes?
        **Prince Philip on meeting the Oscar-winning actress Cate Blanchett
                         and being told she worked "in the film industry"**

I was on the street. This guy waved to me, and he came up to me and said, "I'm
sorry, I thought you were someone else." And I said, "I am."
                                                                       Demetri Martin

When people find out that I'm just a human being, I guess I disappoint them.

Beyoncé Knowles

Few of us have any idea what it's like living in a goldfish bowl, except, of
course, for those of us who are goldfish.   **Graham Taylor**

There are moments, like in a bathroom stall at O'Hare Airport, you hear, "Is that her?" "Did she gain the weight back?" "She's shorter than I thought." Once I walked out and three women applauded. That is when I knew: I am famous.

Oprah Winfrey

My private life is so private, even I'm not sure who I'm sleeping with.

Chrissie Hynde

—Somebody came in and asked for my autograph while I was in labor.
—Did you give it to them?
—Yeah. With a scalpel.

Jo Brand and Mark Radcliffe,
Radcliffe and Maconie, BBC Radio

—I have the autograph of Horatio Nelson.
—And what does it say?
—It says "Horatio Nelson."

Caller and expert, LBC Radio (U.K.)

—Why do you think you get more fan mail than anyone else in the group?
—I dunno. I suppose it's because more people write to me.

Reporter and Ringo Starr

I once had a large gay following, but I ducked into an alleyway and lost him.

Emo Philips

He once called me at 5 a.m. from his hotel in Mayfair to say he couldn't find the room service menu. He was such a drama queen.

Shelley Short, former personal assistant to Pete Burns

Me and Bonehead would just walk into a hotel room and empty it out the window.

Noel Gallagher, of Oasis

I trashed my hotel room. Totally and utterly. Paintings on the floor, everything. Then I thought that I'd get into trouble, so I tidied it all up again.

Liz McClarnon, of Atomic Kitten

I'm not into throwing plasma TVs out of the window. Besides, plasma screens are really heavy and most windows are reinforced these days.

Ronan Keating, of Boyzone

I once jumped off a hotel balcony in Manchester and swung from a chandelier in the foyer. A security man had to get a ladder to get me down.

Toyah Willcox

—When was the last time you used public transport?
—The day before yesterday. I went in a taxi.

Interviewer and George Weah, soccer player

When Mariah wanted to get rid of her chewing gum, somebody put their hand out to take it and that appeared to be their only job.

Lorraine Kelly, GMTV (U.K.) presenter,
on Mariah Carey's appearance on her show

I open my own can of soda, just like a regular person.

Mariah Carey

"Do you have any idea just who I am?" "Someone who thinks he's important?"

Russell Beland

My grandfather built this town!

Paris Hilton, after being threatened with being thrown out
of a Las Vegas club for having no proof of ID

There are so many people with so little talent making so much money.

Mel C, Spice Girl

TELEVISION

Don't you wish there was a knob on the TV to turn up the intelligence?
There's one marked "brightness" but it doesn't work.
Gallagher

My grandfather and the whole family used to sit for hours in front of the television watching it intently. Eventually he would say, "Will we switch it on?"

Kevin McAleer

How did you guys run so slowly in the show's opening scene? You know, where you're running down the beach?

Jessica Simpson to Pamela Anderson, regarding the
slow-motion opening shot in *Baywatch*

Today we look at virginity, and losing it for the first time.

Richard Madeley, *Richard & Judy*

Coming up. John Leslie speaks about Ulrika's rape claims, and we taste the food loved by Marie Antoinette—cockerels' testicles and marzipan vagina cakes.

Richard Madeley, *Richard & Judy*

After the break: Are we all descended from a Scottish millipede?

Mark Austin, *News at Ten* (U.K.)

You know the really great thing about television? If something important happens, anywhere in the world, night or day ... you can change the channel.

Rev. Jim Ignatowski, *Taxi*

RADIO

Radio is the theater of the mind;
television is the theater of the mindless.
Steve Allen

Okay, let's straight away get to our first dedication: "Dear Chris, please say a big hello to Connie Lingus who's 69 on Tuesday. She'll be enjoying my meat and two veg on Sunday at 12:00. Wish her all the very best, tell her I look forward to seeing her when she comes. Thanks ever so much," says Ivan R. Don ...

Presenter, BBC Radio, Radio Bloopers U.K. 2008 #1 (YT)

—What inspired you to embark on a career in the media?
—It was accidental, after I met the head of BBC Northern Ireland at a conference on dry rot.

Reporter and Sean Rafferty, BBC Radio presenter

Georgie Worsley is Master of the Old Surrey and Burstow and West Cunt—Kent Hunt, is out hunting this morning in Lingfield in Surrey. Good morning!

Nicky Campbell, BBC Radio, Radio Bloopers U.K. 2007 #1 (YT)

Thank God for the time delay!

John Inverdale, BBC Radio, after a rugby fan said, "I couldn't fucking stand the Poms winning." There was no time delay.

[*during a radio call-in*]
—Can you just do us a favor? Give your phone a bang or something or give it a clean ...

—Or take the sock off that you're talking through.
—I've got a harelip and cleft palate, so it might sound strange.
—Sorry about that. We just thought it was a really bad line.
DJs and caller, unidentified radio station, Radio Bloopers U.K. 2007 #1 (YT)

We would like to welcome back long-wave listeners and apologize for the 20-minute break in transmission. We hope it didn't spoil your enjoyment of *30-Minute Theater*.
Announcer, BBC Radio

—That show, *In Our Time*, that you do on Radio 4 on a Wednesday ...
—Thursday ...
—I knew that ... Have you any idea what you're really talking about on it? Be honest: Is it in code?
Steven Wright and Melvyn Bragg, *Steven Wright in the Afternoon*, BBC Radio

The joy of *Desert Island Discs* is hearing the great and the good of society pretending to love Beethoven's "Ode To Joy" and Debussy's Second Symphony when we all know, the minute they're through the front door, they're dancing in their pants to "It's Raining Men" by the Weather Girls.
Stephen Fry, BBC Radio, *This Is Your Life*

COMEDY

The inability to get a joke is the first sign of ignorance. Like when you tell a joke about a guy and he gets mad at you? That's a dumb guy.
Chris Rock

—Some people call me a wit.
—And they're half right.
Robert Woolsey and Bert Wheeler

Before I got into comedy, I was a plumber for 150 years—although that's just an estimate.
Gordon Southern

To me, clowns aren't funny. In fact, they're kind of scary. I've wondered where this started and I think it goes back to the time I went to the circus and a clown killed my dad.
Jack Handey, *Deep Thoughts*

I don't laugh out loud, hardly ever—maybe once every five years.

Rowan Atkinson

She has no sense of humor. She's American. **Boy George, on Madonna**

Tonight we're trying a little experiment. Half of the audience will get the real jokes, and half of you will get placebos.

David Letterman

I love telling jokes. I think they're the closest thing to poetry—and I understand them better. **Dustin Hoffman**

If you go parachuting, and your parachute doesn't open, and your friends are all watching you fall, I think a funny gag would be to pretend you were swimming.

Jack Handey, *Deep Thoughts*

If you know any jokes, send them in. They don't have to be good, just funny.

DJ, Classic FM (U.K.)

If you tell a joke in the forest, but nobody laughs, is it a joke? Steven Wright

My six-year-old has a pretty good idea [what I do for a living]. I went down to her school and did a talk about being a stand-up. There were 90 of these five-year-old girls, who just looked at me like I was talking bollocks. This little kid said, "Do you change color when you go on stage?" And I replied, "Well, no, not unless I've had a few vodkas too many." And she said, "Oh, I thought you were a stand-up chameleon."

Jo Brand

People always ask me, "Were you funny as a child?" Well, no. I was an accountant. **Ellen DeGeneres**

Two nuns walk into a bar. One says, "I think we're in the wrong joke."

Anon.

A man enters a bar. It was an iron bar. No, *goes* into a bar. Walks into a bar, that's it. A man walks into a bar, that's it. A man walks into a pub, it was an iron pub. Henry Cooper used to do that one. Tommy. Tommy Bar used to walk into that one. Oh no, that can't be right.

Hugh Laurie, *A Bit of Fry and Laurie*

That was so funny I almost forgot to laugh.   Gilda Radner

—What's green, hangs on a wall and whistles?
—A herring—because you can paint it green and nail it to the wall.
The whistling part is added just to make the riddle hard.
                                                              Leo Rosten

Is it possible for a comedian to be too Irish?
                                        Bruce Dessau, on Kevin McAleer

I started my act with "Impressions of People You've Never Heard Of," and
finished with some "Impersonations with an Inner Tube."
                                                         Michael Bentine

At the theater I worked at last week, the act before me was so bad that they
were still booing while I was on.   Ken Dodd

That is the saving grace of humor: If you fail, no one is laughing at you.
                                                       A. Whitney Brown

SCIENCE & TECHNOLOGY

SCIENCE

The years passed, mankind became stupider at a frightening rate.
Some had high hopes that genetic engineering would correct this
trend in evolution, but sadly the greatest minds and resources were
focused on conquering hair loss and prolonging erections.
Narrator, Idiocracy

A neutron walks into a bar. "I'd like a beer," he says. The bartender serves up a beer. "How much will that be?" asks the neutron. "For you?" replies the bartender. "No charge."
Anon.

Who is Heinzstein?
Jade Goody, *Big Brother 3* (U.K.)

Does the name Pavlov ring a bell?
Anon.

As an adolescent I aspired to lasting fame, I craved factual certainty and I thirsted for a meaningful vision of human life—so I became a scientist. This is like becoming an archbishop so you can meet girls.
Matt Cartmill

—What did the nuclear physicist have for lunch?
—Fission chips.
Anon.

—Dad, why is there wind?
—Trees sneezing.
Calvin and his dad, *Calvin and Hobbes*

And how does gravity work? And if it were to cease suddenly, would certain restaurants still require a jacket?
Woody Allen

I've been noticing gravity since I was very young.
Cameron Diaz

I'm really into quantum physics. Some of my friends are into it, some of them aren't, so I'm trying to get them excited about discovering all these interesting things about thoughts and the power of thoughts. It gives me chills thinking about it.
Carmen Electra

Electricity is really just organized lightning.
George Carlin

I'm fascinated by air. If you took the air out of the sky, all the birds would fall on the ground. And the planes, too.
Jean-Claude Van Damme

Gravity is seriousness. If it were to cease, we should all die of laughing.
Hugh Mason

The speed of light is very fast.
Carl Sagan

What I do know about physics is that to a man standing on the shore, time passes quicker than to a man on a boat—especially if the man on the boat is with his wife.
Woody Allen

It takes more hot water to make cold water hot than it takes to make hot water cold.
Larry Dowd

That's all right, but you still haven't found out what makes the bath water gargle when you pull the plug out.
Prince Philip, to a scientist at England's National Physical Laboratory

After working on the equation for 30 years, Professor Stevens made a remarkable discovery: His wife had left him and he'd wasted his life.
Frankie Boyle, *Mock the Week*

If I have seen further it's because I have stood on the shoulders of giant ants.
Jonathan Paul

If I have not seen as far as the others, it is because giants were standing on my shoulders.

Jeff Goll

ASTRONOMY

Sometimes I think the surest sign that intelligent life
exists elsewhere in the universe is that none of it has tried
to contact us.
Calvin, Calvin and Hobbes

Did you ever wonder if there were any other planets besides Earth?
Father Dougal, *Father Ted*

Mars must be one of the most inhospitable places on Earth.

Reporter, BBC Radio

Is that sun up there the same one my mum sees in Essex?

Brian Belo, in the garden of the Big Brother House
in Elstree, *Big Brother 8* (U.K.)

There are two suns, aren't there? One here and one abroad?

Jonathan Greening, soccer player

[It's] time for the human race to enter the solar system.

Dan Quayle

I wish outer space guys would conquer the Earth and make people their pets, because I'd like to have one of those little beds with my name on it.

Jack Handey, *Deep Thoughts*

—You guys—I just saw a UFO!
—What a coincidence! Fez and I were just talking about how stupid you are.

Michael Kelso and Stephen Hyde, *That '70s Show*

[*an "alien" appears out of a "flying saucer" in her back yard*] Do you want a cup of tea?

Janet Elford, *Beadle's About* (YT)

Ahhh, aliens! Don't eat me. I have a wife and kids … eat them!

Homer Simpson, *The Simpsons*

A few nights ago, my wife and I were startled by a strange flashing light 200 feet above our heads. Only when my daughter reminded us that we lived in a lighthouse was the mystery solved.

R. M. Doyle, *Viz* magazine

I have spotted a UFO. I was in my observatory one night, looking at the moon. Then I saw dozens of flying saucers swirling around. I thought, "The Martians have arrived!" But then I realized I was looking at pollen slightly out of focus.

Patrick Moore, astronomer

I've never owned a telescope, but it's something I'm thinking of looking into.

George Carlin

The Chinese just put a man in space. They didn't use a rocket. They stood on each other's shoulders and passed him up.

Al Murray, as The Pub Landlord

For centuries, people thought the moon was made of green cheese.
Then the astronauts went there and found that the moon is really a big hard rock. That's what happens to cheese when you leave it out.

Ted Roberts

You know Neil Armstrong? How long do you think you could talk to him for before mentioning the moon? **Joe, *Early Doors***

When you arrived on the moon, was the people who lived there very friendly, or was they scared of you?

Ali G, interviewing Buzz Aldrin, *Da Ali G Show*

Making toast on the moon would be tricky. It's all about timing. If you're not there when it pops it's "Goodbye toast!"

John Maclain

I got a bit of moon rock once. When I broke it open it had "moon" written all through it. **Ken Dodd**

We Americans spent millions of dollars developing a pen that could write in space. You know what the Russians did? Used a pencil.

Leo McGarry, *The West Wing*

—Do you ever think man will walk on the sun?
—No. The sun is too hot. It is not a good place to go to.
—What happens if they went in winter when the sun is cold?
—The sun is not cold in the winter.

Ali G and Buzz Aldrin, *Da Ali G Show*

I have no quarrel with Einstein.

Simon Jenkins

Einstein got most of the things right about black holes. I'm not an expert, I must admit. **Brian May, of Queen**

—I saw the Earth from the clouds.
—Did it look round?
—Yes, but I don't think it saw me. ***The Goons***

MATHEMATICS

You have to be able to count if only so that at 50
you don't marry a girl of 20.
Maxim Gorky

—Let's try this again, shall we? I have two beans, and I add two more beans.
What does that make?
—Umm ... a very small casserole?

Edmund Blackadder and Baldrick, *Blackadder II*

I once dated a guy who was so dumb he couldn't count to 21 unless he was
naked.   **Joan Rivers**

I double-checked it six times.   **Maria Berra**

In my day we didn't have hand-held calculators. We had to do addition on our
fingers. To subtract, we had to have some fingers amputated.

Jon Patrick Smith

Cut the pizza into four slices, not eight. I'm not hungry enough to eat eight.

Yogi Berra

How long did it take six men to build a wall if three of them took a week? I
recall that we spent almost as much time on this problem as the men spent on
the wall.   **Gerald Durrell**

I could never make out what those damned dots meant.

Lord Randolph Churchill, U.K. Chancellor of the Exchequer,
on decimal points

He couldn't count his balls and get the same number twice.   **Anon.**

Mind you, 39 is a nice round number.   **Cliff Morgan**

I'm a big Bono fan, but the man can't count. On "Vertigo," he begins with
"*Uno, dos, tres, catorce,*" which is "1, 2, 3, 14" in Spanish. So maybe there
isn't a crisis in Africa. Bono's just miscounted.

Al Pitcher

—What do you get if you divide the circumference of a pumpkin by its diameter?
—Pumpkin pi.

Anon.

—What is an isosceles triangle?
—Somewhere in Bermuda?

Interviewer and Tommy Lee

She doesn't understand the concept of Roman numerals. She thought we fought World War Eleven.

Joan Rivers

It was a game of three halves.

Steve Davis

—A man has five children. Half of them are boys. Is that possible?
—No.
—Yes, it is. The other half are also boys.

The Benny Hill Show

STATISTICS

Fifty percent of the public don't actually know what the term "50 percent" means.

Patricia Hewitt, U.K. Trade Secretary

At least 50 percent of the population are women, and the rest are men.

Harriet Harman, Member of Parliament

—Don't sit on the fence, Terry, what chance do you think Germany have of getting through?
—I think it's 50/50.

Jimmy Hill and Terry Venables

Never go for a 50/50 ball unless you are 80/20 sure.

Ian Darke

Shearer could be at 100 percent fitness, but not peak fitness.

Graham Taylor

He was giving 101 percent in effort, which is the least you can ask for.

Tony Allcock

Nichol never gives more than 120 percent.

Kevin Keegan

Did you know that 175 percent of all drive-by shootings happen near French windows?
Linda La Hughes, *Gimme, Gimme, Gimme*

Oh, Ron, there are literally thousands of other men that I should be with instead, but I am 72 percent sure that I love you.
Veronica Corningstone, *Anchorman*

The average male has sex 2,580 times during their life. Statistically, that means I'm gonna live until I'm 197.
Jimmy Carr, *8 Out of 10 Cats*

She's 80 percent nuts, 20 percent normal, 95 percent talented.
Simon Cowell, on an *X Factor* contestant

Ten years ago, only a third of schoolchildren went on to higher education. Now it is 33 percent.
Teachers' spokesman

I always find that statistics are hard to swallow and impossible to digest. The only one I can ever remember is that if all the people who go to sleep in church were laid end to end, they would be a lot more comfortable.
Mrs. Robert A. Taft

TECHNOLOGY

New technology is common, new thinking is rare.
Sir Peter Blake

You know when you step on a mat in the supermarket and the door opens? For years I thought that was a coincidence.
Richard Jeni

I'm such a Luddite. I can't even load a CD onto an iPod.
Uma Thurman

For those interested in detailed specifications, I can say it weighs about the same as a medium-sized banana.
Andrew Marr, trying out an electronic book

The big advantage of a book is it's very easy to rewind. Close it and you're right back at the beginning.
Jerry Seinfeld

Who ever thought a nuclear reactor could be so complicated?
Homer Simpson, *The Simpsons*

I'm a bit of a technophobe—I love technology.

Steve Allen

A robotic dog? Is he housebroken or is he going to leave batteries all over the floor?

Miles Monroe, *Sleeper*

101 Uses for the Old VCR: No. 102—Plug it in each New Year's Eve to celebrate with the blinking 12:00.

Robin D. Grove

COMPUTER

If you put tomfoolery into a computer, nothing comes out
but tomfoolery. But this tomfoolery, having passed through
a very expensive machine, is somehow ennobled
and no one dares criticize it.

Pierre Gallois

I have just paid an enormous amount of money for a Dell laptop and it's like giving somebody a 747. I can barely get on the Internet to get my mail.

Larry Hagman

Great, isn't it? I've got a $2,000 computer and all I know how to do is play the golf game on it.

Mark Hardy

I don't know anything about computers. I don't even know how often to change the oil.

Buzz Nutley

Don't worry, head. The computer will do all the thinking from now on.

Homer Simpson, *The Simpsons*

I am Holly, the ship's computer, with an IQ of 6,000—the same as 6,000 PE teachers.

Holly, *Red Dwarf*

—I've booted up, I've patched in, I'm online, offline, downloaded and EXTREMELY CHEESED OFF!
—You need to integrate your power supply at its source, Sir.
—What?
—Plug it in.   **D. C. Robert Kray and D. I. Derek Grim, *The Thin Blue Line***

To start press any key. Where's the "any" key?

Homer Simpson, *The Simpsons*

A Dell technician received a call from a customer who was enraged because his computer had told him he was "bad and an invalid." The tech explained that the computer's "bad command" and "invalid" responses shouldn't be taken personally.   *Wall Street Journal*

A Dell technician advised his customer to put his troubled floppy back in the drive and close the door. The customer asked the tech to hold on, and was heard putting the phone down, getting up and crossing the room to close the door to his room.   *Wall Street Journal*

Another Dell customer called to say he couldn't get his computer to fax anything. After 40 minutes of troubleshooting, the technician discovered the man was trying to fax a piece of paper by holding it in front of the monitor screen and hitting the "send" key.

Wall Street Journal

I think I bought a bad computer. The mouse bit me.   David Letterman

I get such an attitude with spellcheck. "No! That's a person's name, spellcheck! You are so dumb, spellcheck! I was right, you were wrong! Oh. That is how you spell Wednesday. Thanks, spellcheck."   Jim Gaffigan

I asked my speech recognition program, "Can you recognize speech?" Its response was, "No, I can't wreck a nice beach."

Jeff Goris

—What's your password? I want to sign in and test the new system we set up.
—"Detonate." ... I like typing "Detonate" and hitting "Enter." It's extremely satisfying.   Boss and office girl, www.overheardintheoffice.com

A printer consists of three parts: the case, the jammed paper tray and the blinking red light.

Dave Barry

If you really want to impress people with your computer literacy, add the words "dot com" to the end of everything you say dot com.

Dave Curtis

You're right, ma'am. Yes, that is entirely our fault. We should have explained that you'll need to have a computer to teach a course online.

IT manager, on the phone

MICROSOFT WINDOWS ERROR MESSAGES

Are you sure you want to send "Recycle Bin" to the Recycle Bin?

Cannot delete file, not enough free space. Please delete one or more files and try again.

An error has occurred while creating an error report.

Catastrophic failure. Tip: To check if additional information is available at the Microsoft website, click More Help.

Error: No error occurred.

INTERNET

Usenet is like a herd of performing elephants with diarrhea—massive, difficult to redirect, awe-inspiring, entertaining and a source of mind-boggling amounts of excrement when you least expect it.
Gene Spafford

During my service in the United States Congress, I took the initiative in creating the Internet.
Al Gore

The Internet is a great way to get on the net.
Bob Dole

Information is moving, you know, nightly news is one way, of course, but it's also moving through the blogosphere and through the Internets.
George W. Bush

Will the highways on the Internet become more few?
George W. Bush

Can you copy the Internet onto this disk for me?　　**Customer in a computer store**

INVENTIONS

I sometimes wonder if the manufacturers of foolproof items keep a
fool or two on their payroll to test things.
Alan Coren

It's only a toy.

**Gardiner Green Hubbard, on seeing his son-in-law
Alexander Graham Bell's telephone, 1876**

Here we are at the twenty-first century, but where's the world of the future we
were always told about? Where are the flying cars? Where are the robots doing
our housework? Where are the people zipping around in jetpacks? I'm sorry, but
clapping my lights on and off doesn't cut it.

Radio advertisement

The greatest aid to love this century. It could be a more significant advance for
lovers than Viagra.

A spokesman for British megastore Tesco, on its new odorless garlic bread

My husband, Norm, has invented a revolutionary heat-seeking bedpan.

Dame Edna Everage

I'd like to get four people who do cartwheels very good, and make a cart.

Mitch Hedberg

[*after Bart turned himself green in a science accident*] Don't be discouraged,
son. I bet Einstein turned himself all sorts of colors before he invented the light
bulb.

Homer Simpson, *The Simpsons*

Scientists have come up with a fantastic invention for looking through solid
walls. It's called a window.

Richard Feynman

Probably the earliest fly swatters were nothing more than some sort of striking
surface attached to the end of a long stick.

Jack Handey, *Deep Thoughts*

I like digital cameras because they enable you to reminisce immediately. It's like,
click, look at us, we're so young, standing right there, where does the time go?

Demetri Martin

I still have a hard time believing that toilets don't need electricity to work. I put the order: fire, wheel, then toilet, then Xbox.

John Maclain

It is impossible to transmit speech electrically. The "telephone" is as mythical as the unicorn.   Professor Johann Poggendorff, 1860

The guy who invented the first wheel was an idiot. The guy who invented the other three, he was a genius.   Sid Caesar

Everything that can be invented has been invented.

Charles H. Duell, Commissioner
of the U.S. Office of Patents, 1899

LETTERS & E-MAILS

Why do you sit there looking like an envelope without an address
on it?
Mark Twain

I was taking a bath in a Leningrad hotel when the floor concierge yelled that she had a cable for me. "Put it under the door," I cried. "I can't," she shouted. "It's on a tray!"   Anthony Burgess

—You're sending your mother an empty envelope?
—I wanted to cheer her up. You know, no news is good news.

George Burns and Gracie Allen

—This letter feels kind of heavy. I'd better put another stamp on it.
—What for? It'll only make it heavier.

George Burns and Gracie Allen

[*writing a letter*] As usual, I'm writing slowly because I know you can't read fast.

Corporal Walter "Radar" O'Reilly, *M*A*S*H*

I would have answered your letter sooner, but you didn't send one.

Goodman Ace

The man who would stoop so low as to write an anonymous letter, the least he might do is to sign his name to it.

Sir Boyle Roach

Never answer an anonymous letter.

Yogi Berra

Nowadays, when you get a handwritten letter in the mail you're like, "What? Has someone been kidnapped? Well, I'm not opening it, it's probably filled with anthrax."

Jim Gaffigan

E-mail has made sending regular mail such a chore. "Wait, I stick it in an envelope and now I gotta go outside? What am I, a triathlete?"

Jim Gaffigan

Before man reaches the moon, your mail will be delivered within hours from New York to Australia by guided missiles. We stand on the threshold of rocket mail.

Arthur Summerfield, U.S. Postmaster General, 1959

Whatever I write in an e-mail, it doesn't mean anything. It is just words I write.

Paris Hilton

TELEPHONE

I have always wished that my computer would be as easy to use as
my telephone. My wish has come true. I no longer know how to
use my telephone.
Bjarne Stroustrup

Ask me anything, a telephone number, what time it is in Adelaide.
Tell you what, I can tell you exactly what I'll be doing on August 3rd, say. Hang on. [*presses a few buttons*] Nothing's happening—oh, yes, see, it says, "Nothing."

Hugh Laurie, *A Bit of Fry and Laurie*

[*on a cell phone*] How did the market close? Uh-huh. Well, roll over my amalgamated, split my utilities, and double my capital venture overlays. Now call me in an hour, and tell me what the hell I'm talking about!

Roland T. Flakfizer, *Brain Donors*

—Hello, Yogi. Sorry to call so late. I hope I didn't wake you.
—Nah, I had to get up to answer the phone anyway.

Max Nicholas and Yogi Berra

Are you eating breakfast cereal or is it just a bad line?

Corporal Maxwell Q. Klinger, *M*A*S*H*

[*jumping out of the bath to answer the phone*] You'll have to speak up, I'm wearing a towel.

Homer Simpson, *The Simpsons*

—If Brett calls, I'm incommunicado.
—Where?

Kim Craig and Kath Day Knight, *Kath & Kim* (U.K.)

—Tell him I'm not in.
—[*on the phone*] He's not here. I tell you he's not here. If you don't believe me, you can ask him yourself. [*shouting off the phone*] George, will you tell him yourself you're not here! He doesn't believe me!

George Burns and Gracie Allen

—[*on the phone*] I know ... I know ... I know ... Oh, I know!
—Then why is she telling you?

Sybil and Basil Fawlty, *Fawlty Towers*

Call me, Ishmael.

Peter De Vries

So I got home and the phone was ringing. I picked it up and said, "Who's speaking, please?" And a voice said, "You are."

Tim Vine

Imagine how weird phones would look if your mouth was nowhere near your ears.

Steven Wright

This bloke I met texted me, and I texted him back, but then he didn't text me again till the next day. "Sorry I didn't text you back earlier," he said, "but my bat died." I said, "Really? I didn't know you had a bat." He said, "I don't. I was talking about my battery."

Chantelle Houghton, *Celebrity Big Brother 4* (U.K.)

My date was late, so I called her cellphone to see if she'd left yet. She was still in her apartment, getting her keys and her purse and things. Then she got really emotional and said, "I can't leave until I find my phone!" I was like, "It's pressed to your ear!"

Matt G.

Old telephone books make ideal personal address books. Simply cross out the names and addresses of people you don't know.

Viz magazine

I know a woman who programmed all the phones in her house to speed-dial 911. So to dial it now, you have to hit Memory-1-6.

Marc Leibert

All our operators are either drunk or fornicating right now, but if you care to leave a message when you hear the tone ...

Hugh Leonard

Press 1 for medical emergency, press 2 for fire ... For an electrical fire, press 1; for burning wood, press 2 ...

Art Grinath

—Do I have to pay for that over the phone?
—Yes, ma'am.
—Do you take cash?

Customer and customer service agent

When you delete a phone number from your phone, where does it go?

Emma Greenwood, *Big Brother 5* (U.K.)

Sir William Harcourt, when telephoned by a bore, would pour ink into the receiver, secure in the belief that it would trickle into the ear or the mouth of his inquisitor.

Kenneth Rose, *Curzon: A Most Superior Person*

For people who like peace and quiet: a phoneless cord.

Anon.

YOU CAN'T ARGUE WITH THAT!

Next contestant, Mrs. Sybil Fawlty from Torquay. Specialist subject:
The Bleeding Obvious.
Basil Fawlty, Fawlty Towers

China is a big country, inhabited by many Chinese.
General Charles de Gaulle, president of France

—What do you expect to find here in Australia?
—Australians, I should think.
Reporter and John Lennon

London isn't the largest city, but it's definitely larger than the next largest.
Brian Hayes

—What's the White House like?
—It's white.
Child and George W. Bush, during a visit to the U.K.

Our nation must come together to unite.
George W. Bush

A church spire nestling among the trees ... there's probably a church there too.
Richie Benaud

Graveyards have a morbid reputation. Many people associate them with death.
The Bishop of Bath and Wells

—What does a Venus flytrap catch?
—Flies?
Ed Doolan and caller, BBC Radio

The difference between Sly Stallone and me is I am me and he is him.
Arnold Schwarzenegger

The next rise in mortgage rates will probably be an increase.
Spokesman for CBI, a British lobbying company

Deals work best when each side gets something it wants from the other.
Donald Trump

—What's the difference between stock-car racing on Saturday night and on Sunday afternoon?
—It's basically the same, only darker.

Reporter and Alan Kulwicki

In an action film you act in the action. If it's a dramatic film you act in the drama.

Jean-Claude Van Damme

For NASA, space is still a high priority.

Dan Quayle

When this table was first made it was brand new.

Arthur Negus

We were unanimous—in fact, everybody was unanimous.

Eric Heffer, Member of Parliament

When I have been asked during these last weeks who caused the riots and the killing in Los Angeles, my answer has been direct and simple: Who is to blame for the riots? The rioters are to blame. Who is to blame for the killings? The killers are to blame.

Dan Quayle

Therapy can be a good thing; it can be therapeutic.

Alex Rodriguez

A man who stayed awake for more than 11 days and nights put his marathon feat down to his diet. Tony Wilson, 43, ate a diet of raw food. Asked how he felt after more than 260 hours without sleep, he replied, "Pretty tired."

Newsreader, BBC Radio

The answer to darkness is to turn on the light.

Lord Hailsham

Carcinogens Cause Cancer Says Book

Headline, *Contra Costa Independent*

You're a great traveler. Every day of the year, you're somewhere in the world!

Gary Richardson

You can observe a lot just by watching.

Yogi Berra

We're either going to do what we said we're going to do with the UN, or we're going to do something else.

Bill Clinton, on the UN operation in Bosnia

It just shows that shocks can happen when you least expect them.

Willo Flood

Things are more like they are now than they ever were before.

Dwight D. Eisenhower

For readers who have been wondering about the Jim Fiebig column, he has stopped writing it—Ed.

Indianapolis Star

It ain't over till it's over.

Yogi Berra

SOCIETY & POLITICS

POLITICS

What luck for rulers that men do not think.
Adolf Hitler

Politics would be a helluva good business if it weren't for the goddamned people.
Richard Nixon

A lot of times in politics you have people look you in the eye and tell you what's not on their mind.
George W. Bush (YT)

Democracy used to be a good thing but now it has gotten into the wrong hands.
North Carolina senator Jesse Helms

I can't believe that we are going to let a majority of the people decide what is best for this state.
Louisiana congressman John Travis

We've got a strong candidate. I'm trying to think of his name.
Senator Christopher Dodd

I can promise you that when I go to Sacramento, I will pump up Sacramento.
Arnold Schwarzenegger, on running for governor of California

My chances of becoming prime minister are about as good as the chances of finding Elvis on Mars, or my being reincarnated as an olive.
Boris Johnson, mayor of London

I want to wrong that right.
John Prescott

I'd make all crime illegal.
Danny Wallace

I don't even know what politicians do. I'd make all stuff for women—Tampax and sanitary towels—free for women. We shouldn't have to pay for that. It's ridiculous.
Jade Goody, British TV personality

Politics gives guys so much power that they tend to behave badly around women. And I hope I never get into that.
Bill Clinton

And everybody wants to be loved—not everybody, but—you run for office, I guess you do. You never heard of anybody say, "I want to be despised, I'm running for office."
George W. Bush (YT)

If you're sick and tired of the politics of cynicism and polls and principles, come and join this campaign.

George W. Bush

Signs your presidential campaign is in trouble:
You're often described as "John Kerry without the charisma."
You've been running negative ads about yourself.
In times of trouble, you ask yourself, "What would George W. Bush do?"

David Letterman

Sign you're watching a bad election: The exit poll question is, "Did you have trouble finding the exit?"
\

David Letterman

It's no exaggeration to say that the undecideds could go one way or another.

George Bush Sr.

They wanted me to get up at the absolute crack of dawn to go milking. In retrospect, I probably should have done it. I do know which end of a cow to pull, roughly speaking—if you see what I mean.

Boris Johnson, on being a candidate for the British House of Commons

It's a pleasant change to be in a country that isn't ruled by its people.

Prince Philip, visiting Paraguay, 1962

When I was in third grade, there was a kid running for office. His slogan was, "Vote for me and I'll show you my wee-wee." He won by a landslide.

Dorothy Zbornak, *The Golden Girls*

When I was in first grade, my teacher told us the President was married to the First Lady, and all I could think was, "Wow, I wonder if she ever saw any dinosaurs?"

Steven Wright

I have learned the difference between a cactus and a caucus. On a cactus, the pricks are on the outside.

Morris K. Udall

I am not a politician, but as far as I understand, the left and right are the same thing. It doesn't matter who is in power, it's the same and everyone has a long list of complaints.

Frankie Dettori

How do you tell a Communist? Well, it's someone who reads Marx and Lenin. And how do you tell an anti-Communist? It's someone who understands Marx and Lenin.

Ronald Reagan

—But I'm telling you, I'm an anti-Communist!
—I don't care what kind of Communist you are, get outta here!

**Warner Brothers executive and Harry Warner,
during the McCarthy witch-hunts**

Sign of an incompetent Liberal: Has a bleeding pancreas.   **Tom Witte**

As I rose to my feet I was conscious of all thought draining from my brain, as when a colander is lifted from a sink of water.

**Boris Johnson, mayor of London, on being asked a difficult question
at a debate on the theme of "The Tory Way to Cut Taxes"**

Those who say that I am not in agreement with the policy are, rightly or wrongly, quite wrong.

British Conservative politician William Whitelaw

"In what circumstances should a businessman be able to roll over tax losses from one year to the next?" one poor man asked; and I whiffled away, with that ghastly feeling one used to get in an exam when asked to write an essay about the Venerable Bede, and all one can remember is that he was a monk who lived in Jarrow, and you find yourself discussing what Jarrow "must have been like" back then, and the contours of his beard.

**Boris Johnson, mayor of London, during a debate
on the theme of "The Tory Way to Cut Taxes"**

Is Disneyland a member of the UN?

**Ali G, interviewing Boutros Boutros-Ghali,
former United Nations Secretary General, *Da Ali G Show***

In 1973, a Conservative party official visiting Liverpool to sound out opinion on the Common Market stopped a woman in the street and asked her views. "Where are they building it, love?" she asked.

Daily Telegraph

Join the EU Because There Are Better-Looking Men There

**Estonian poster campaign encouraging women to
vote for European Union membership**

—Because I am independent of any party, I will write "To Let" on my forehead.
—And under that, Tom, write, "unfurnished."

Tom and Richard Sheridan

I am not quite certain what my right honorable friend said, but we hold precisely the same view.

Margaret Thatcher

I went up the greasy pole of politics step by step.

Michael Heseltine

A week is a long time in politics, and three weeks is twice as long.

Rosie Barnes

—I think this policy should be considered carefully.
—Your colleague has said the policy should be screwed up and thrown into a rubbish bin.
—Quite right. I think it should be screwed up and thrown into a rubbish bin, then taken out and considered very carefully.

British Conservative politician William Whitelaw and questioner,
during a special election

I am mindful of the difference between the executive branch and the legislative branch. I assured all four of these leaders that I know the difference, and that difference is they pass the laws and I execute them.

George W. Bush

This strategy represents our policy for all time. Until it's changed.

Marlin Fitzwater, White House press secretary

And truth of the matter is, a lot of reports in Washington are never read by anybody.

George W. Bush

If I know the answer I'll tell you the answer, and if I don't, I'll just respond—cleverly.

Donald Rumsfeld, Secretary of Defense (YT)

I think if you know what you believe, it makes it a lot easier to answer questions. I can't answer your question.

George W. Bush

Neither in French nor in English nor in Mexican.

George W. Bush, declining to answer reporters' questions in Canada

To link me to George Bush is like linking me to an Oscar. It's ridiculous.

Arnold Schwarzenegger

All I can tell you is when the governor calls, I answer his phone.

George W. Bush, on Arnold Schwarzenegger

This foreign policy stuff is a little frustrating.

George W. Bush

We'll be sending a person on the ground there pretty soon to help implement the malaria initiative, and that initiative will mean spreading nets and insecticides throughout the country so that we can see a reduction in death of young children that—a death that we can cure.

George W. Bush, pledging aid to Liberia (YT)

I'm going to try to see if I can remember as much to make it sound like I'm smart on the subject.

George W. Bush, when asked about a possible flu pandemic

I'm not into this detail stuff. I'm more concepty.
Donald Rumsfeld, Secretary of Defense

I can assure you that, even though I won't be sitting through every single moment of the seminars, nor will the Vice President, we will look at the summaries.

George W. Bush

It's clearly a budget. It's got a lot of numbers in it.
George W. Bush

None of us really understands what's going on with all these numbers.

David Stockman, Director of the Office of Management and Budget during the Reagan administration, on the budget

I'm not worried about the deficit. It is big enough to take care of itself.

Ronald Reagan

This president is going to lead us out of this recovery. It will happen.

Dan Quayle

We'll be heading for deepening heights of recession.

Liberal Member of Parliament

The President has kept all of the promises he intended to keep.

George Stephanopoulos, Clinton White House aide

Needless to say, the President is correct. Whatever it was he said.

Donald Rumsfeld, Secretary of Defense, on George W. Bush

The President doesn't want any yes-men and yes-women around him. When he says no, we all say no.

Elizabeth Dole, aide to Ronald Reagan

That's a good question. Let me try to evade you.   Paul Tsongas

Solutions are not the answer.   Richard Nixon

We are not without accomplishment. We have managed to distribute poverty
equally.   **Nguyen Co Thatch, Vietnamese Foreign Minister**

We hoped for the best, but things turned out as usual.
                             Viktor Chernomyrdin, Russian Prime Minister

POLITICIANS

The only man who had a proper understanding of
Parliament was old Guy Fawkes.
George Bernard Shaw

There's a lot of blowhards in the political process, you know, a lot of hot-air
artists, people who have got something fancy to say.
                                                        George W. Bush

Gordon Brown is your chancellor of the ex-checker, right? I have two questions:
a) what is the chancellor of the ex-checker? and, b) why isn't he checking any
more?   **Richard Schiff**

I was chancellor of the exchequer ... for five years and ... I never understood it.
                                                        Winston Churchill

—Who was Winston Churchill: a rapper; U.S. president; the prime minister; or
king?
—Wasn't he the first black president of America? There's a statue of him near
me—that's black.   **Questioner and Danielle Lloyd, model**

The essence of being a prime minister is to have large ears.
                                                        Michael Heseltine

Who? Oh yeah... he's, like, your president? I don't know what he looks like.
                             Paris Hilton on Tony Blair, then British Prime Minister,
                                                    to British *GQ* magazine

—If you could be anyone for the day, who would it be?

—I'd be the president of the U.S. ... just to get a ride in Air Force One.

Questioner and Richard Bacon, BBC Radio

You've done a nice job decorating the White House.

Jessica Simpson, upon being introduced to U.S. Secretary
of the Interior, Gale Norton, while touring the White House

Anyway, this is the Oval Office. It's a shrine to democracy. And we treat it that way. When people walk in here, they—they don't come in here in bathing suits and flip-flops.

George W. Bush, showing German reporter
Kai Diekmann around the White House

That's George Washington, the first president, of course. The interesting thing about him is that I read three—three or four books about him last year. Isn't that interesting?

George W. Bush, showing German reporter
Kai Diekmann around the White House

—What was the most wonderful moment in your terms of being president so far?
— The best moment was—you know, I've had a lot of great moments ... I would say the best moment was when I caught a seven-and-a-half pound large-mouth bass on my lake.

George W. Bush and Kai Diekmann, 2006

DIMWIT POLITICIANS
WHAT THEY SAY ABOUT THEM

If God had intended politicians to think, he would have given them brains.

Sir Humphrey Appleby, *Yes, Minister*

In politics stupidity is not a handicap.

Napoleon Bonaparte

I've heard he's been called Bush's poodle. He's bigger than that.
George W. Bush, on Tony Blair

There was so little English in that answer that President Chirac would have been happy with it.
William Hague, to John Prescott

Why, this fellow doesn't know any more about politics than a pig knows about Sunday.
Harry Truman, on Dwight D. Eisenhower

Gerald Ford looks like the guy in a science-fiction movie who is first to see the creature.
David Frye

So dumb he can't fart and chew gum at the same time.
Lyndon B. Johnson, on Gerald Ford

Gerald Ford is a nice guy, but he played too much football with his helmet off.
Lyndon B. Johnson

I know for a fact that Mr. Reagan is not clear about the difference between the Medici and the Gucci. He knows that Nancy wears one.
Gore Vidal

He thinks arms control is some form of deodorant.
Pat Schroeder, on Ronald Reagan

In a disastrous fire in Ronald Reagan's library, both books were destroyed. And the real tragedy is that he hadn't finished coloring one.
Jonathan Hunt

The fox ... knows many small things, whereas the hedgehog knows one big thing. Ronald Reagan was neither a fox nor a hedgehog. He was as dumb as a stump.
Christopher Hitchens

Dan Quayle is more stupid than Ronald Reagan put together.
Matt Groening

Dan Quayle is so dumb he thinks Cheerios are donut seeds.
Jim Hightower

Bill Clinton is a man who thinks international affairs means dating a girl from out of town.
Tom Clancy

GEORGE W. BUSH

IN HIS OWN WORDS

Bushism: a magnificent pratfall of the cerebral cortex, in which a lifetime of experience and learning and intuition comes hurtling out upside down and backward, wearing its underpants on its head.
Washington Post

I think anybody who doesn't think I'm smart enough to handle the job is underestimating.

I want everyone to hear loud and clear that I'm going to be the president of everybody.

My job is a job to make decisions. I'm a decision—if the job description were, what do you do—it's decision maker.

I'm the decider, and I decide what is best.

And as you know, my position is clear—I'm a commander guy.

If this were a dictatorship, it would be a heck of a lot easier, just so long as I'm the dictator.

I'm the master of low expectations.

My job is to, like, think beyond the immediate.

I will have a foreign-handed foreign policy.

More and more of our imports come from overseas.

Presidents, whether things are good or bad, get the blame. I understand that.

There's a huge trust. I see it all the time when people come up to me and say, "I don't want you to let me down again."

Well, I think if you say you're going to do something and don't do it, that's trustworthiness.

And there is distrust in Washington. I am surprised, frankly, at the amount of distrust that exists in this town. And I'm sorry it's the case, and I'll work hard to try to elevate it.

I'm a patient man. And when I say I'm a patient man, I mean I'm a patient man.

When I was young and irresponsible, I was young and irresponsible.

You never know what your history is going to be, like, until long after you're gone.

I'll be long gone before some smart person ever figures out what happened inside this Oval Office.

They have miscalculated me as a leader.

They misunderestimated me.

GEORGE W. BUSH

WHAT THEY SAY ABOUT HIM

Sheridan dreamt up Mrs. Malaprop, Shakespeare conceived of
Falstaff, but only God could have created George W. Bush.
Karan Thapar

George W. Bush surrounds himself with smart people the way a hole surrounds itself with a donut.   **Dennis Miller**

In the Clinton administration, we worried the President would open his zipper. In the Bush administration, they worry the President will open his mouth.
James Carville

Speech Presents Challenge for Bush
Headline, *Atlanta Journal-Constitution*

President Bush gave his first-ever presidential radio address in both English and Spanish. Reaction was mixed, however, as people were trying to figure out which was which.   **Dennis Miller**

I went to a dinner with former President Carter. He is a rather good egg and made me nostalgic for those heady days when world leaders had a brain. Today, of course, the free world is run by a man who can't eat a pretzel unaccompanied.

Sandi Toksvig

Nuclear testing in North Korea, war in Iraq, earthquake in Japan ... Bush keeps asking, "Where is Superman?"

David Letterman

The President is a cross-eyed Texan warmonger, unelected, inarticulate, who epitomises the arrogance of American foreign policy.

Boris Johnson, then Member of Parliament,
unsigned editorial in the *Spectator*, 2003

The White House is giving George W. Bush intelligence briefings. You know, some of these jokes just write themselves.

David Letterman

George Bush overcame an incredible lack of obstacles to achieve his success.

Jon Stewart

George W. Bush says he reads the Bible every day. He's 56 years old—finish the book! I've polished off three Tom Clancy novels since he's been elected. I'd tell him what happens to Jesus, but I don't wanna ruin it for him.

Gregg Rogell

George Bush says, "Al Gore's book needs a lot of explaining." Of course, Bush says that about every book.

Bill Maher

Recently, members of Hillary Clinton's presidential campaign accused John Edwards of acting like President Bush. The accusation came after Edwards answered "yes" at a debate to the question, "Have you ever stuck a fork in an electrical socket?"

Gary Vider

Bush said today he is being stalked. He said wherever he goes, people are following him. Finally, someone told him, "Psst, that's the Secret Service."

Jay Leno

When you take George Bush out of his own environment, when you take him out of his own culture, like in Israel, for example, he makes mistakes. And anybody would. Earlier today, he was speaking to a group of people in Jerusalem and he finished up by saying, "*Ich bin ein* Jewish guy."

David Letterman

Russia has started a territorial dispute with the United States by claiming that it owns the North Pole. President Bush was furious and said, "That's ridiculous, everyone knows that the North Pole is owned by Santa."

Conan O'Brien

At his father's state banquet for the Queen in 1991 ... he boasted to her that he had embroidered his new cowboy boots with the phrase "God Save the Queen," before confessing he had been his family's black sheep. "Who's yours?" he then asked the sovereign, to the horror of his mother.

Rupert Cornwell

George W. Bush just got a lovely birthday present from Laura—a gold-plated vacuum flask. He put it proudly on his desk and waited for an aide to ask about it. At last, "What is it?" asks one. "Laura says it keeps hot things hot and cold things cold." "So what have you put in it?" asks the aide. "Soup and ice cream."

Anon.

Do you do this with Christmas lights? You have a string of them and one bulb is dead, and you flick the bulb with your finger to get it to light up? Same thing they do with George Bush before a debate.

Jay Leno

I'm proud of George. He's learned a lot about ranching since that first year when he tried to milk the horse. What's worse, it was a male horse.

Laura Bush

"Is he dumb?" Barbara Bush, the former First Lady, once mused about her son. "Dumb, yes, he's dumb as a fox."

Rupert Cornwell

The Corleones of American politics.

Michael Ignatieff, on the Bush family

Will Hanging Help Bush?

Headline, *York Daily Record*

ROYALTY

When you look at Prince Charles, don't you think someone in the
Royal Family knew someone in the Royal Family?
Robin Williams

What a beautiful day for running into Buckingham Palace, finding the smallest
room in the house and saying, "How about that for a royal flush?!"

Ken Dodd

They could do with a pub here; a nice pint of lager would be nice.

Rod Stewart, at a Buckingham Palace garden party

Will you have to sing "God Save My Gracious Me"?

Princess Margaret, on being told by her father that he would be king

I rise very early and have a cold shower and sing an aria. It really gets the blood
rushing to the brain.

Princess Michael of Kent, on her morning routine

—Are you of royal stock?
—No, my father was a grocer. I'm of vegetable stock.

Morecambe and Wise

We've all got a bit of noble blood in our veins. Do you know that we're all in
line for succession to the throne? Well, if 48,200,701 people died, I'd be queen.

Pete, *Dud and Pete*

—According to a survey by Coinstar in 2006, if the Queen's head were to be
removed from coins, who would the public want to replace her: Ricky Gervais,
Wallace and Gromit, or Wayne Rooney?
—Wallace and Gromit.

The Independent

CRIME

I prefer the wicked rather than the foolish.
The wicked sometimes rest.
Alexandre Dumas

Freeze, mother-stickers, this is a fuck-up!
Would-be robber, waving a gun in a Florida bank. The staff dissolved into hysterics and the humiliated robber fled, empty-handed.

—Who do you think may have perpetrated this awful crime?
—Well, we believe this to be the work of thieves.
Alan Bennett and Peter Cook, *The Great Train Robbery*

Eyewitnesses were on the scene in minutes.

Adam Boulton

WANTED: For Assault, Armed Robbery, and Committing a Lewd and Immoral Dance With a Chocolate Pudding.
Tagline, *Take the Money and Run*

Burglars—when fleeing from the police, run with your right arm sticking out at 90 degrees, wrapped in a baby mattress in case they set one of their dogs on you.
***Viz* magazine**

If you're being chased by a police dog, try not to go through a tunnel, then onto a little seesaw, then jump through a hoop of fire. They're trained for that.
Milton Jones

If you're a police dog, where's your badge?

James Thurber, to an Alsatian

Two men who stole six sheep from a farm at Mundford found they could only get five of them in the back of their van. So the other one had to sit in the cab between the two men. But the men had to pass through a town on their way home. They feared the sheep sitting in the cab would be conspicuous, so they disguised it by putting a hat on its head.

Eastern Evening News

My favorite chair is a wicker chair. It's my favorite chair because I stole it. I was at a party, a very crowded party, and when no one was looking I went over to it and I unravelled it and stuck it through the keyhole in the door. The girl who was in it was almost killed.

Steven Wright

Ah, if only I could steal enough to be an honest man!

Aldo Vanucci, After the Fox

Once somebody stole our car. I asked my wife if she saw who it was. She said, "No, but I did get the license number."

Rodney Dangerfield

—I can't drive a stolen car!
—It's the same principle—four gears forward, one reverse.

Nicole Bonnet and Simon Dermott, How to Steal a Million

Two pretzels are walking down the street. One is assaulted.

Anon.

My old man was so dumb he picked a guy's pocket on an airplane and tried to make a run for it.

Rodney Dangerfield

Overdue book? This is the biggest frame-up since OJ!

Homer Simpson, The Simpsons

I came out with my hands up, kicking the book ahead of me. They took me down to the main branch on Fifth Avenue in New York, and they took away my glasses for a year.

Woody Allen

A robber armed with a gun demanded cash at a Burger King restaurant in Ypsilanti, Michigan ... But the assistant said he couldn't open the cash register without a food order. "All right, give me some onion rings," said the robber. "Sorry," said the assistant, "they're off." The robber fled empty-handed.

The Sunday Times

His latest venture on to the roads took him only yards from his house before a community policeman stopped him for not riding a motorcycle while wearing a helmet, York magistrates heard.

York Evening Press

Asked why he had taken the weathervane, Maudseley told the court that he had climbed onto the church roof looking for lead, but there wasn't any. He continued, "If I came home empty-handed in the middle of the night, the wife would have thought I was up to no good."

Lancashire Evening Post

Murderers—need to dispose of a body? Simply parcel it up and post it to yourself via DHL. You will never see it again.

Viz magazine

My director said I should try it out. I should have notified the store and said I was going to come and shoplift. I'm sorry.

Winona Ryder, claiming she was researching for a movie part when she was caught shoplifting from Saks Fifth Avenue in Beverly Hills

This woman goes into a gun shop and says, "I want to buy a gun for my husband." The clerk says, "Did he tell you what kind of gun?" "No," she replied, "he doesn't even know I'm going to shoot him."

Phyllis Diller

I gotta finish him off while I'm still temporarily insane!

Groundskeeper Willy, *The Simpsons*

—You can't just go around killing people.
—Why not?　　　　　　　　**John Connor and The Terminator, *Terminator***

—How could you do something so vicious?
—It was easy, my dear. You forget I spent two years as a building contractor.

Jane and Ludwig, *Police Squad!*

The black-bearded criminal must have got in through the door or the windows. Everything else was locked.　　　　　　　　　**The Goon Show**

—I heard noise. I thought it was robbers, so I hid my jewels. Now I can't remember where.
—Ma, you don't have any jewels.
—Thank God, because I can't find them.

Sophia Petrillo and Dorothy Zbornak, *The Golden Girls*

—How do you explain this huge rise in crime?
—There's so much more to nick.

Interviewer and Douglas Hurd, Member of Parliament

Outside of the killings, Washington has one of the lowest crime rates in the country.　　　　　　　　　　　　　　　　**Marion Barry, mayor of Washington D.C.**

If crime went down 100 percent, it would still be 50 times higher than it should be.　　　　　　　　　　**John Bowman, Washington D.C. Council member**

The streets are safe in Philadelphia, it's only the people who make them unsafe.

**Frank Rizzo, ex-Police Chief
and Mayor of Philadelphia**

We've got a rule in the band—no matter what trouble you're going to get into, never get arrested in a country that doesn't use your own alphabet ... If you get arrested in a country that uses squiggles or a box or a line instead of proper letters, you're fucked, mate, you're never coming home.

Noel Gallagher, of Oasis

I'd just like to say to the old man who was wearing camouflage gear and using crutches, who stole my wallet earlier, "You can hide, but you can't run."

Milton Jones

—What did this attacker look like?
—I dunno, I didn't see him, mate.
—I see. And would you recognize him if you didn't see him again?
—Straight away!　　　　　　　　　　　　　　　　　　*The Goon Show*

One witness told the commissioners that she had seen sexual intercourse taking place between two parked cars in front of her house.

Atlantic City Press

She said the man sat on the benches in only his boxer shorts for about five minutes, and exposed himself. "It wasn't long, but it was long enough," Mrs. Mankin said.　　　　　　　　　　　　　　　　　　*The Star-Democrat*

A flasher has denied exposing himself on Guernsey, saying he was merely holding a hot dog. Eric De Jersey, 61, produced a similar hot dog in court as his lawyer insisted, "He had ... in his right hand, a jumbo sausage in a roll." But De Jersey was found guilty of indecent exposure.

The Sunday Times

I know this serial flasher. He was thinking of retiring, but he's decided to stick it out for another year.

Anon.

Should rapists be castrated at birth?

Twiggy Rathbone, Hot Metal

Let's talk about conspiracy things. Let's go back to the grassy knoll. Who actually shot JR?

Ali G, Da Ali G Show

POLICE

Did you ever stop to think why cops are always famous for being dumb? Simple. Because they don't have to be anything else.

The Professor, Mr. Arkadin

Look, lady, I am what I am and I do what I do. A few guys make shoelaces, others lay sod, some make a good living neutering animals. I'm a cop.

Lieutenant Frank Drebin, Naked Gun 33⅓

Director of Knowledge Architecture; Head of Protective Services; Head of Citizen Focus; Director of Criminal Justice Change.

Assorted job titles, Suffolk Police Department

The police are not here to create disorder. They're here to preserve disorder.

Richard Daley, mayor of Chicago

—I heard police work is dangerous.
—It is. That's why I carry a big gun.
—Aren't you afraid it might go off accidentally?
—I used to have that problem.
—What did you do about it?
—I just think about baseball.

Jane Spencer and Detective Frank Drebin, Police Squad!

—Now, Detective Drebin, I don't want any trouble like you had on the South Side last year, that's my policy.

—Well, when I see five weirdos dressed in togas, stabbing a man in the middle of the park in full view of a hundred people, I shoot the bastards, that's my policy.

—That was a Shakespeare in the Park production of *Julius Caesar*, you moron! You killed five actors! Good ones!

New York Mayor and Detective Frank Drebin, *Police Squad!*

My husband and I were very concerned when our son arrived home last night in a police car. Then I remembered, he is a policeman, and his partner always drops him off home after work.

Avern, *Viz* magazine

[*on the phone*] Hello? Police? I've apprehended a burglar. Forty-five minutes?! But I'm sitting on him—is that legal?

Mark Corrigan, *Peep Show*

Attention, attention! This is Papa Bear. Put out an APB for a male suspect, driving a … car of some sort, heading in the direction of, uh, you know, that place that sells chili. Suspect is … hatless! Repeat, hatless!

Chief Wiggum, *The Simpsons*

Somewhere in the naked city lurks a one-armed, one-legged, one-eyed man responsible for the murder for which Ryan Harrison has been wrongfully accused. To find him, all Ryan needs is a clue.

Tagline, *Wrongfully Accused*

You know, fingerprints are just like snowflakes: They're both very pretty.

Chief Wiggum, *The Simpsons*

[*on a two-way radio*]
—Husband on murderous rampage. Send help. Over.
—Phew, thank God it's over! I was worried for a little bit.

Marge Simpson and Chief Wiggum, *The Simpsons*

—Do you know why I'm here?
—You got all Cs in school?

Police officer and Sarah Silverman,
The Sarah Silverman Program

Policemen are numbered in case they get lost.

Spike Milligan

You can't touch me, my cousin is Scotland Yard.

Naomi Campbell

—Is this some kind of bust?
—Yes, ma'am, it's very impressive, but we need to ask you a few questions.
Woman and Detective Frank Drebin, *Police Squad!*

What a detective! Once, a burglar robbed a safe wearing calfskin gloves. He took the fingerprints and five days later he arrested a cow in Surrey.

Eric Morecambe

—Who are you and how did you get in here?
—I'm a locksmith and I'm a locksmith.
Detective Frank Drebin and Dutch, *Police Squad!*

Mrs. Twice? I'm Detective Drebin. We're sorry to bother you at a time like this. We would have come earlier but your husband wasn't dead then.
Detective Frank Drebin, *Police Squad!*

—Your husband was found DOA.
—Oh, my God! He's dead?
—Oh, I'm sorry. He was DUI. I get those two confused.
Chief Wiggum and Marge Simpson, *The Simpsons*

—Your daughter has been kidnapped.
—What do I do?!
—I believe you work in the textile industry.
Detective Frank Drebin and Warner, *Police Squad!*

When I was young, if I heard on the news that someone was "helping police with their enquiries," I thought they must be a really nice person to lend a hand.
Listener, *Saturday Live*, BBC Radio

Help the local police by popping into the mortuary each day to see if you can identify any of the bodies.

J. Lewis Maitland, *Viz* magazine

LAW & LAWYERS

If law school is so hard to get through,
how come there are so many lawyers?
Calvin Trillin

—Have you ever had your deposition taken before?
—No.
—Well, it's just like we're sitting in a living room talking, except that you're
nervous and I'm not.   **Lawyer and defendant**

Sign of an incompetent lawyer: Won't confer with you without his lawyer present.

M. Lilly Welsh

—Who is going to defend you?
—I need no man to defend me. The Lord is my defender.
—You would be well advised to employ someone better known locally.

Lawyer and defendant

Magistrates on the Carlisle Bench were determined to suppress hooliganism at
country dances, the chairman said. A doorkeeper at the hall declared that two
rotten eggs were thrown at the dancers, but defending counsel asserted that the
eggs were fresh.

Manchester Guardian

Sign your lawyer is incompetent: As he is questioning you on the witness
stand, he keeps asking you whether you realize you are under oath.

Daniel Gray

IN COURT

ACTUAL TRANSCRIPTS FROM OFFICIAL
COURT RECORDS

—Now, you realize you have been placed under oath this afternoon.
—Yes, I do.
—And what does that mean to you?
—Tell the truth.
—If you don't tell the truth, what could happen to you?
—Go to hell.
—Or something worse: go to the Marinette County Jail.

—What is your occupation?
—I'm a thief.
—Thief. I see. How's business?
—It's a little slow right now.
—And how do you get along when you are not working at your usual occupation?
—I'm usually in prison.

—Were you ever in the service?
—Yes.
—What branch?
—Navy.
—Did you get an honorable discharge?
—No.
—Was it dishonorable?
—No.
—What was it?
—I don't know.
—What did it say on the discharge?
—Unable to mop.

—What is your marital status?
—Right now it's not too good.

—How old is your son, the one living with you?
—Thirty-eight or thirty-five, I can't remember which.
—How long has he lived with you?
—Forty-five years.

—And who else lives in the house besides you and Sam Allbright?
—No one but my dog Jasper.
—Is he married?
—Jasper?
—Mr. Allbright.
—No, he is divorced.

—Do you know Mr. John Smith?
—Yes.
—Do you know how I can get in touch with him?
—Yes, I have his number at home.
—Do you know Jane Johnson?
—Yes.
—Do you know how I can get in touch with her?
—I think I have her number at home.
—Do you know David Smith?
—Yes, he's dead.
—Do you know how I can get in touch with him—well, no, I guess you wouldn't.
—No, I don't have those kinds of connections.

—What happened to your right eye?
—Got shot.
—What was that all about?
—It was my ex-wife.
—She shot you in the face?
—Right.
—I assume you got a divorce from her after that?
—No.
—How long did you stay married?
—About six months. We hadn't been married when this happened.
—Oh, you weren't married? She shot you and you got married afterward?
—Yes.
—What were you expecting from your marriage that never occurred?

—Well, somebody to help shoulder the burden of being married.
—And who owned the car?
—My mom and dad.
—And they're your parents?
—Yeah.

—And do you see your dad in court?
—Not often.

—You said he threatened to kill you?
—Yes. And he threatened to sue me.
—Oh, worse yet.

—What was the first thing your husband said to you when he woke up that morning?
—He said, "Where am I, Cathy?"
—And why did that upset you?
—Because my name is Susan.

—Did you ever stay all night with this man in New York?
—I refuse to answer that question.
—Did you ever stay all night with this man in Chicago?
—I refuse to answer that question.
—Did you ever stay all night with this man in Miami?
—No.

—Is it true what the petitioner says, that you're living with another man?
—It's true.
—Do you know that that's adultery, a crime in New York state?
—But I'm moving to New Jersey.

—Do you remember when Sunday was that week?
—Well, yes, I assume it followed Saturday.

—And when was that?
—I guess it was sometime before noon or after noon.

—Are you married, sir?
—Yes.
—And to whom are you married?
—My wife.

—Do you know how far pregnant you are right now?
—I'll be three months on November 8.
—Apparently, then, the date of conception was August 8?
—Yes.
—What were you and your husband doing at that time?

—James stood back and shot Tommy Lee?
—Yes.
—And then Tommy Lee pulled out the gun and shot James in the fracas.
—No sir, just above.

—Are you restricted in some way by having your third finger shot off?
—Yeah, a little.
—What could you do before the accident that you couldn't do now?
—Wear a ring on it.

—Since that time—well, let me put it this way. Nowadays, do you ever have trouble getting an erection?
—It's—it's harder than before.
—You mean harder to get one?
—No—right, it's hard to get.

—I want to know what you recall feeling physically.
—I can't remember what I recall.

—What's your first recollection at the Royal Columbian Hospital?
—Waking up and seeing my girlfriend there and then throwing up.

—The hospital is to the right?
—It was on this side.
—When you say this side, can you say right or left?
—Yeah, right or left.

—So you don't recall the exact distance?
—That he was from me? Or I was from him?

—What did he say?
—About that? All the way back he—I've never been called so many names.
—You're not married, I take it.

—Can you tell the court what that man looked like?
—He's kind of an Oriental guy, Puerto Rican, sort of Oriental.
—When you mentioned Oriental, you mean like Chinese or Japanese?
—No, Arab. Something like that.
—What does an Arab look like?
—To me?
—Yes.
—Like a Mexican.

—So, there were two supervisors?
—Yes, White and Black.
—Are those the names or the ethnic groups?
—Well, both.
—OK. So it's Mr. White and Mr. Black and they are black and white?
—Yeah. One's black and one's white.
—Who's black and who's white?
—Mr. Black and Mr. White.
—No, no. I'm sorry. For example, is Mr. Black black and Mr. White white?
—Oh, OK. No, Mr. White is black and Mr. Black is white.

—Do you know the defendant?
—Yes.
—Did you see the defendant shoot these people?
—No. I seen it was Jimmy Jones.
—Do you know Jimmy Jones?
—Yes, I know Jimmy Jones very well.
—And this man who you saw shoot these people, could you tell me if he was black or white?
—I don't know if he was white or black, but I know it was Jimmy Jones because I know Jimmy Jones.

—When did he scratch his initials into the watch?
—I couldn't tell you, but it was previous to his death.

—Where were you when you fell two years ago?
—In a hurry.

—Please put an "X" where you fell.
—On my behind?
—No, I meant on the exhibit.

—Please review this document. Do you know what a fax is?
—Yeah, I do, man. It's when you tell the truth, man, tell it like it is. That is what the facts is.

—Do you wear a two-piece bathing suit now that you have a scar?
—I don't wear a bathing suit at all now.
—That can be taken two ways.

—Do you know whether he put his seat belt on, or are you just surmising he didn't?
—I know that he didn't put his seat belt on.
—What is your personal observation of that?
—Because when we were driving down the street he was mooning people through the back window.

—When one of you rides with the other, I suppose you are in the same vehicle at the same time?
—Yes.

—Where were you on the bike at that time?
—On the seat.
—I mean where in the street?

—To the charge of driving while intoxicated, how do you plead?
—Drunk.

—Did they ever serve you more than one drink at a time?
—No. I can't drink more than one drink at a time.

—Were you present when specimens were taken from you in the conduct of this examination?
—Yes.

—Are you still going to Alcoholics Anonymous?
—No, sir, that's been about five years ago. I hadn't had no problem with it since. I hadn't drank nothing in two years. I wasn't no alcoholic to start with. Just a plain drunk.

—Where was the security officer in relation to you when you were struck by a car?
—To my left.
—How far to your left?
—I don't really remember. I was getting run over at the time.

—Are you sexually active?
—No, I just lie there.

—You went on a rather elaborate honeymoon, didn't you?
—I went to Europe, sir.
—And you took your new wife?

—When was the next occasion that you had difficulty with your wife?
—April 27, I believe it was, when she backed over me with the automobile.

—How was your first marriage terminated?
—By death.
—And by whose death was it terminated?

—Now, did you have any children with Richard?
—Yes, three boys.
—Do you remember their names?

—Have you ever tried to commit suicide?
—Yes, sir.
—Were you ever successful?
—No, sir.

—I have never been at that apartment complex, so I will ask you if you can describe it for me. When you came out of your apartment on the second floor, where was the elevator in relation to your apartment?
—Where was the elevator? I don't know where the elevator was. It would be up or down.

—Were you acquainted with the deceased?
—Yes, sir.
—Before or after he died?

—Can you describe the individual?
—He was about medium height and had a beard.
—Was this a male, or a female?

—What happened then?
—He told me, he says, "I have to kill you because you can identify me."
—Did he kill you?
—No.

He told me he'd played the gigolo in Belgium. I thought it was a musical instrument.

It was not me who killed those two men, because that night I was shooting two other men.

—When he went, had you gone and had she, if she wanted to and were able, for the time being excluding all the restraints on her not to go, gone also, would he have brought you, meaning you and she, with him to the station?
—Objection. That question should be taken out and shot.

—And then you went to which doctor?
—Not a witch doctor.
—Pardon?
—Did you say a witch doctor?
—No. Which doctor, which one?

DOCTORS' EXPERT WITNESS STATEMENTS

ACTUAL TRANSCRIPTS FROM OFFICIAL COURT RECORDS

—Doctor, will you take a look at those x-rays and tell us something about the injury?
—Let's see, which side am I testifying for?

—What was the diagnosis of the report?
—Headaches and acute subluxation complex of the cervical spine associated with radiculitis, myositis and spasm of the cervical para vertebral musculature.
—In layman's terms, would you explain that for us, Doctor?
—It was neck strain.

—And you are assuming that she's going to live beyond the year 62, until under some actuarial tables that statistically she would die. Is that right?
—Yes, I'm assuming she would live until she dies.

—Would you enlighten the court what a "positive chandelier" sign is?
—Well, that's when you manipulate the uterus with the patient lying on the table, and it causes such discomfort that they want to grab the chandelier if you have one in your office.

He was probably going to lose the leg, but at least maybe we could get lucky and save the toes.

Now, Doctor, isn't it true that when a person dies in his sleep, in most cases he just passes quietly away and doesn't know anything about it until the next morning?

—Doctor, how many autopsies have you performed on dead people?
—All my autopsies have been on dead people.

—Do you recall the time that you examined the body?
—The autopsy started around 8:30 p.m.
—And Mr. Edgington was dead at the time?
—No, he was sitting there on the table wondering why I was doing an autopsy.

—Doctor, before you performed the autopsy, did you check for a pulse?
—No.
—Did you check for blood pressure?
—No.
—Did you check for breathing?
—No.
—So then, is it possible that the patient was alive when you began the autopsy?
—No.
—How can you be so sure, Doctor?
—Because his brain was sitting on my desk in a jar.
—But could the patient still have been alive, nevertheless?
—It is possible that he could have been alive and practicing law somewhere.

LAWYERS' QUESTIONS & STATEMENTS

ACTUAL TRANSCRIPTS FROM OFFICIAL COURT RECORDS

Were you just visiting Grand Junction, Tennessee, at the time you were born?

You were there until the time you left, is that true?

So, you were gone until you returned?

Were you present when your picture was being taken?

Without relating the conversation, tell us what was said.

Can you recall how fast your vehicle was going when you parked?

Did you feel the second impact before the first one?

How far apart were the vehicles at the time of the collision?

You say that you cannot remember the accident, but can you say that the accident has in any way affected your memory, or don't you remember?

You have testified that you can bend forward with your head, but can you touch your toes with your chin?

Where are your hemorrhoids located?

Do you suffer any pain other than when you breathe?

Well, if it wasn't your right leg, and it wasn't your left leg, which leg was it?

Do you have any other complaint about your teeth besides the fact that you haven't got them?

SENTENCING

If this is justice, I'm a banana.
Ian Hislop, editor, Private Eye

—Order! Order!
—Yeah, I'll have a hot dog and a bottle of pop.
Judge and "Muggs" McGinnis, *Block Busters*

He is tried on 52 counts of robbery and is sentenced to 800 years in federal prison. At the trial, he tells his lawyer confidentially that with good behavior he can cut the sentence in half.
Narrator, *Take the Money and Run*

We find the defendants *incredibly* guilty.
Foreman of the jury, *The Producers*

—I sentence you to 125 years.
—One-hundred-twenty-five years? Oh God! I'll be 169 when I get out.
Judge and Harry Donahue, *Stir Crazy*

—Defendant is remanded to the custody of the sheriff, who is ordered to carry into execution the order of the court.
—Judge, can I say something?
—Sure.
—Did you say "executed"?
—No, you got 30 years, Mr. Ashford.
Judge and defendant, actual transcript from official court records

I accept responsibility for the murder. If I lose my life, I can live with that.
William "Cody" Neal, convicted murderer

—I have no fear of the gallows.
—No?
—No. Why should I? They're going to shoot me.
Boris Grushenko and father, *Love and Death*

—Shot at sunrise?
—I hope it's cloudy tomorrow.

Oliver Hardy and Stan Laurel, *The Flying Deuces*

CAPITAL PUNISHMENT

I am against using death as a punishment.
I am also against using it as a reward.
Stanislaw J. Lec

Life is indeed precious. And I believe the death penalty helps to affirm the fact.

Ed Koch, mayor of New York

I am for the death penalty. Who commits terrible acts must get a fitting punishment. That way he learns the lesson for the next time.

Britney Spears

It's a proven fact that capital punishment is a known detergent for crime.

Archie Bunker, *All in the Family*

I don't see why there should be any question about capital punishment. I think everyone in the capital should be punished.

Goldie Hawn, *Rowan & Martin's Laugh-in*

PRISON

A man will be imprisoned in a room with a door that's unlocked and opens inward; as long as it does not occur to him to pull rather than push it.
Ludwig Wittgenstein

Paris Hilton is going to prison. She was stopped for driving while banned. Paris will be going down for 45 days. That's longer than she did in her video.

Graham Norton, *The Graham Norton Show*

I like my mug shot. I think I have a really great mug shot. It looks like a magazine shoot.   **Paris Hilton**

Being a thief is a terrific life, but the trouble is they do put you in the nick for it.   **John McVicar**

How nice to see you all here.   **Roy Jenkins, British politician, visiting a jail**

—And what are you in prison for, my man?
—Murder, Home Secretary.
—Splendid, splendid!
          William Whitelaw, British politician, and prisoner, on a prison visit

I'm only in prison because of my beliefs: I believed the nightwatchman was asleep.   **Norman Stanley Fletcher, *Porridge***

—When they put me in prison I'll be brave. I can handle it.
—But, Blanche, you don't understand. They put you in a *women's* prison.
              Blanche Devereaux and Rose Nylund, *The Golden Girls*

Woman Off to Jail for Sex with Boys   **Headline, *Ontario Record***

A recreation yard with the sun beating down on you is prematurely ageing. Take skin cream.
                Heidi Fleiss, "Hollywood madam," advice to Paris Hilton

—Ladies, I am going to turn this place into *Midnight Express*.
—In that case, I think I should tell you now, I'm no good on roller skates.
              Prison governor and prisoner, *The Dutch Elm Conservatoire*

—This place is like Guantanamo Bay.
—Keep off, it's nothing like Spain.
              **Detective Chief Inspector Sam Tyler and Detective
              Chief Inspector Gene Hunt, *Life on Mars* (U.K.)**

Wow! Look at these toilets! And just inches from your bed—talk about luxury!
              Bart Simpson, looking at cells in a penitentiary, *The Simpsons*

Terrific companionship. Education. No taxes, no traffic jams, no mobiles.
                                   Jonathan King, sex offender

So what's the plan now? You go back to your cell? For the rest of the day?
              **Louis Theroux, to the head of a white supremacist gang
              serving life in San Quentin, *Louis Theroux: Behind Bars***

JUDGE

The penalty for laughing in a courtroom is six months in jail;
if it were not for this penalty, the jury would never hear
the evidence.

H. L. Mencken

Gibberish.

New York Judge Robert Patterson, after beginning to read a Harry Potter
book. He was hearing a copyright case involving J. K. Rowling.

The trouble is, I don't understand the language. I don't really understand what a
website is.

Judge Peter Openshaw presiding over a trial of three men
accused of Internet terror offences, 2007

How can a bed be turned into a sofa?

Judge Seddon Cripps, unfamiliar with a futon

What is this Teletub?

Judge Francis Aglionby, about a Teletubby jigsaw puzzle

What is "shredded wheat"? Is it a television presenter?

French Judge, during the trial of Geoffrey Boycott in Grasse, France, 1998

WAR & PEACE

War is God's way of teaching Americans geography.

Ambrose Bierce

I just want you to know that, when we talk about war, we're really talking
about peace.   George W. Bush

Our enemies are innovative and resourceful, and so are we. They never stop
thinking about new ways to harm our country and our people, and neither
do we.   George W. Bush

The vast majority of Iraqis want to live in a peaceful, free world. And we will find these people and bring them to justice.

George W. Bush

I think war is a dangerous place.

George W. Bush

And a year from now, I'll be very surprised if there is not some grand square in Baghdad that is named after President Bush.

Richard N. Perle, U.S. political adviser,
September 22, 2003

I think we are welcomed. But it was not a peaceful welcome.

George W. Bush, on the reception of American forces in Iraq, 2005

—Would you have gone to war against Saddam Hussein if he refused to disarm?
—You bet we might have.

Reporter and Senator John Kerry

You took an oath to defend our flag and our freedom, and you kept that oath underseas and under fire.

George W. Bush, addressing war veterans

I want to remind you all that in order to fight and win the war, it requires an expenditure of money that is commiserate with keeping a promise to our troops to make sure that they're well paid, well trained, well equipped.

George W. Bush

I went to the Congress last September and proposed fundamental supplemental funding, which is money for armor and body parts and ammunition and fuel.

George W. Bush

Call me old-school, but I miss the Cold War.

Garry Shandling

My fellow Americans, I'm pleased to tell you today that I've signed legislation that will outlaw Russia forever. We begin bombing in five minutes.

Ronald Reagan, doing a soundcheck prior to an address
on National Public Radio (YT)

We are not at war with Egypt. We are in an armed conflict.

Sir Anthony Eden, 1956

The war situation has developed, not necessarily to Japan's advantage.
Emperor Hirohito, announcing Japan's surrender, 1945

The Jews and Arabs should sit down and settle their differences like good
Christians.
Warren Austin, U.S. diplomat

Port Stanley Airport is surrounded by howitzers pointing skyward—which is the
direction from which an air attack would most likely come.
News reporter, BBC

Security is the essential roadblock to achieving the road map to peace.
George W. Bush

The only way we can win is to leave before the job is done.
George W. Bush

U.S. planes have the capability to penetrate deep into Soviet soil.
General Rogers

How did I know the B-1 bomber was an airplane? I thought it was vitamins for
the troops.
Ronald Reagan

—My Great Uncle Percy was in the trenches of the First World War. You know
what he used to say?
—What?
—"Aahh! Bloody Hell! Germans! Thousands of 'em! Ahhhh!"
Eddie and Richie, *Bottom*

Why do old people insist on referring to World War I as "The Great War"?
Surely World War II with its higher death toll and use of atomic weapons was
loads better.
G. Delaney, *Viz* magazine

Now tell me, was it you or your brother that was killed in the war?
Headmaster of Shrewsbury School, to an old boy, 1919

I have already lost two cousins to the war, and I stand ready to sacrifice my
wife's brother.
Artemus Ward

Britain is littered with war memorials dedicated to "those who have fallen"
during the two world wars. Has anybody considered building a monument to
the poor sods who weren't bone idle or too clumsy to keep their footing and
who actually got shot?
W. Donachie, *Viz* magazine

We would not be here but for those people who gave their lives and very often gave their futures.   **Simon Bates**

I was classified "4P" by the draft board. In the event of war, I'm a hostage.
                                                                  Woody Allen

What on earth was Adolf Hitler thinking of?   **Mrs. Merton**

When I enlisted, Sam Goldwyn said, "I'll cable Hitler and tell him to shoot around you."   **David Niven**

I read a book called *The Secret Life of Adolf Hitler*. It told me things that I never knew. For instance, when Hitler was having sex, he liked to pee on people. That put me right off him.   **Martin Mor**

What if Hitler had been accepted into art school in 1906 and given up politics? Mussolini later has to go it alone. When *Casablanca* is filmed, the actors in the bar scene try to compete against "La Marseillaise" with "That's Amore." The movie bombs.   **Elden Carnahan**

I wouldn't believe Hitler was dead even if he told me so himself.   Hjalmar Schacht

Poor visibility in the blackout is the cause of many accidents, so ladies are recommended to carry a white Pekinese.
                           Handy Hint in a women's magazine, 1940

—Fire at will!
—Which one's Will?   **Moe and Curly (The Three Stooges), *Back to the Woods***

— Looks like enemy aircraft at 12 o'clock.
—Really? Twelve o'clock? Well, that gives us about … [*checks his watch*] … 25 minutes. Think I'll step out for a burger.
                    Jim Pfaffenbach and Admiral Benson, *Hot Shots*

What if Germany had not attacked Russia during World War II? The expression would be, "As American as apple strudel."
                                                                  Chuck Smith

The best advice against the atom bomb is not to be there when it goes off.
                                   ***British Army Journal*, February 1949**

If we could just get everyone to close their eyes and visualize world peace for an hour, imagine how serene and quiet it would be—until the looting started.

Joseph Romm

World peace could be a possibility—if it weren't for those damned foreigners!

Spike Milligan

VIOLENCE

The most intelligent bit of spectator violence I ever heard of happened at a football match in Brazil. An enraged spectator drew his gun and shot the ball.

John Cohen

No question that the enemy has tried to spread sectarian violence. They use violence as a tool to do that.

George W. Bush

—Is it not dangerous to sell people knives called Rambo Knives?
—I wouldn't say so. A lot of them can't spell.

Reporter and store owner

Man Slashes Friend in Argument Over Who Had The Hairiest Buttocks

Headline, *New Jersey News*

—Let's step outside and settle this like men!
—We are outside.
—OK, let's step inside and settle it like women.

Roland T. Flakfizer and Lazlo, *Brain Donors*

I wish we lived in the day where you could challenge a person to a duel.

Zell Miller, senator

I can't fight a duel to the death. I can't do anything to the death. Doctor's orders. I have this ulcer condition, and death is the worst thing for it.

Boris Grushenko, *Love and Death*

They wouldn't be running in gangs if they were my children. I'd be out with a baseball bat looking for them.

Frank Rizzo, mayor of Philadelphia, on youth problems

In a dangerous neighborhood, always walk backward so no one can sneak up on you.
                                                                    Barry Blyveis

I was going to thrash them within an inch of their lives, but I didn't have a tape measure.
                                                                    Groucho Marx

—Carla, don't do it! I'm telling you to turn the other cheek.
—Oh, Sammy, moonin' her isn't enough—I want to hurt her!
                                        Sam Malone and Carla Tortelli, *Cheers*

"Nagging" Wife Critical After Hammer Attack
                                                    Headline, *Trenton Times*

I'll take this candelabrum and beat that walnut you use for a head into a nutburger.
                                        Alfred de Carter, *Unfaithfully Yours*

That's one of the tragedies of this life—that the men who are most in need of a beating up are always enormous.
                                John D. Hackensacker, *The Palm Beach Story*

I got in a fight one time with a really big guy, and he said, "I'm going to mop the floor with your face." I said, "You'll be sorry." He said, "Oh, yeah? Why?" I said, "Well, you won't be able to get into the corners very well."
                                                                    Emo Philips

If you don't shut up, I'm going to stuff your head up your bum, and you'll spend the rest of your life wandering around on all fours looking for the light switch.
                                                                    Eddie, *Bottom*

—[*whacking Rick in the crotch with a cricket bat*] Shut yer face, traitor!
—Ha! Missed both my legs!
                                    Vyvyan Basterd and Rick, *The Young Ones*

I'd horsewhip you if I had a horse.
                                                                    Groucho Marx

Take your face out of my foot!
                                                                    Chico Marx

Honey, I forgot to duck.
                                                    Ronald Reagan, after being shot

Getting shot hurts.
                                                    Ronald Reagan, after being shot

We have only one person to blame, and that's each other.
                                                    Barry Beck, after a brawl

—Look, I'm a sportsman. I'll let you choose the way you want to die.
—All right, how about old age?

KAOS Agent and Maxwell Smart, *Get Smart*

A good way to threaten someone is to light a stick of dynamite. Then you call up the guy and hold the burning fuse to the phone. "Hear that?" you say. "That's dynamite, baby."

Jack Handey, *Deep Thoughts*

Willie saw some dynamite,
Couldn't understand it quite.
Curiosity never pays;
It rained Willie seven days.

Anon.

TERRORISM

One of the cardinal maxims of guerrilla war: The guerrilla wins if he does not lose. The conventional army loses if it does not win.
Henry Kissinger

I was surprised how British Muslims reacted to the Danish cartoons. I thought, How can you get this worked up about a cartoon? But then I remembered how angry I was when they gave Scooby-Doo a cousin.

Paul Sinha

In the old days you knew a bomb hoax was a hoax. The trouble is now that you have to take them so damn seriously.

British House of Commons official

—Did they ever catch the people that sent Tampax through the post?
—No, they did not. It wasn't Tampax, it was Anthrax.
Ali G and Brent Scowcroft, former U.S. National Security Advisor, *Da Ali G Show*

We cannot let terrorists and rogue nations hold this nation hostile or hold our allies hostile.

George W. Bush

Free societies will be allies against these hateful few who have no conscience, who kill at the whim of a hat.

George W. Bush

We'll continue to enhance protection at our borders and coastlines and airports and bridges and nuclear power pants.
George W. Bush (YT)

[*addressing an American audience*] We support your war of terror.
Borat Sagdiyev, *Borat*

I think al-Qaeda is a lethally dangerous man ... I think Qaeda needs to be found and buried forever ...
Radio interviewee, Radio Bloopers U.K. 2008 #1 (YT)

We do know, of certain knowledge, that he [Osama bin Laden] is either in Afghanistan, or in some other country or dead. And we know of certain knowledge that we don't know which of those happens to be the case.
Donald Rumsfeld, Secretary of Defense (YT)

The longer this goes on, the clearer it will be that Saddam's weapons of mass destruction did not present a direct threat to this country, or about as much threat as a tub of superannuated taramasalata.
Boris Johnson, mayor of London

Zacarias Moussaoui was arrested on August 16, 2001, after officials at a flight school in Minneapolis became suspicious that he wanted to learn how to fly and to turn a jumbo jet, but not how to land or take off.   ***The Times***

Sign of an incompetent al-Qaeda terrorist: Hijacks a flight simulator.
Brian Broadus

The fact is that when a suicide bomber strikes once, he or she may strike again.
John Simpson

Why would they do that? Wouldn't they think it was kind of painful?
Anna Nicole Smith, on suicide bombers

They say being a hostage is difficult. But I could do that with my hands tied behind my back.   **Phil Nichol**

There was a time when driving an SUV meant you had a tiny penis. Now, according to some new commercials, it also means you support terrorists, who also have tiny penises. Of course, all cars use gasoline and thus support terrorists, only less so. The answer is the hybrid gas-electric car, which only supports terrorists when going uphill.
Jon Stewart, *The Daily Show*

Rebel Threats Keep Traffic Light in El Salvador

Headline, *Atlanta Journal*

British Army bomb-disposal squads who attempt to defuse car bombs early, and before areas are properly evacuated, will be responsible for endangering civilian lives. **Irish Republican Army statement, 1988**

Do you think David Trimble will stick to his guns on decommissioning?

Interviewer

When I was young, "the troubles" were what women called their periods, so when "the troubles" started in Northern Ireland and they kept talking about "the troubles" on the news, you can imagine my confusion.

Alan Coren

I believe in making the world safe for our children, but not for our children's children, because children should not be having sex.

Jack Handey

THE ARMED FORCES

If there's one thing I can't stand, it's an intellectual admiral.
Henry Kissinger

I said I was the greatest, not the smartest.
Muhammad Ali, after failing the U.S. Army IQ test

At the army medical, the doctor said, "Take all your clothes off." I said, "Shouldn't you take me out to dinner first?"

Spike Milligan

This is Captain Pak, R.O.K. And this is Lieutenant Mulcahy, G.O.D.
Lieutenant Colonel Henry Blake, *M*A*S*H*

Excuse me, sir. Is green the only color these uniforms come in?
Private Judy Benjamin, *Private Benjamin*

In my army uniform I looked like the loser in a sack race.

Peter Ustinov

[*looking around the barracks*] I can't sleep in a room with 20 strangers. And I mean, look at this place! The army couldn't afford drapes? I'll be up at the crack of dawn here!   **Private Judy Benjamin**, *Private Benjamin*

—One, two; one, two; one, two ...
—Three is next, if you're having trouble.

Drill sergeant and Boris Grushenko, *Love and Death*

Forwarddd ... *DRINK*!   **Captain Benjamin "Hawkeye" Pierce**, *M*A*S*H*

—Sorry, baby.
—That's Major to you!
—Sorry, Major baby.   **Captain Benjamin "Hawkeye" Pierce and**
Major Margaret "Hot Lips" Houlihan, *M*A*S*H*

How long was I in the army? Five foot eleven.   **Spike Milligan**

My only qualification for being put at the head of the Navy is that I am very much at sea.   **Edward Carson**

He's the sort of admiral I would follow up any hill, anywhere.
Lieutenant Colonel Oliver North

Men will follow this officer—if only out of sheer curiosity.
Officer's annual confidential appraisal report

I resigned from the army after two weeks' service in the field, explaining I was "incapacitated by fatigue" through persistent retreating.
Mark Twain

WEAPONS

Don't press any buttons!
Camilla, Duchess of Cornwall, to Prince Charles after he
was handed a Taser gun during a police station visit

—Sorry, you can't buy that gun today. The law requires a five-day waiting period. We've got to run a background check.

—Five days? But I'm mad now!
Gun-store owner and Homer Simpson, *The Simpsons*

I think anyone who doesn't vote for a stronger gun control law ought to be shot.
Dave Madden, *Rowan & Martin's Laugh-in*

For every fatal shooting, there were roughly three nonfatal shootings. And, folks, this is unacceptable in America. It's just unacceptable. And we're going to do something about it.
George W. Bush

Don't move. I've got a gun. Not here, but I got one.
Ryan Harrison, *Wrongfully Accused*

It had all the earmarks of a CIA operation; the bomb killed everybody in the room except the intended target.
William F. Buckley Jr.

We understand the fright that can come when you're worried about a rocket landing on top of your home.
George W. Bush

Our bombs are smarter than the average high-school student. At least they can find Kuwait.
A. Whitney Brown

Instead of trying to build newer and bigger weapons of destruction, mankind should be thinking about getting more use out of the ones we already have.
Jack Handey

CBS News reports that the Pentagon once considered building a bomb filled with hormones that would turn enemy soldiers gay ... Experts say the gay bomb would have meant battlefield victories for the U.S. and higher ratings for the Tony Awards.
Conan O'Brien

I do not like this word "bomb." It is not a bomb. It is a device which is exploding.
Jacques Le Blanc, French Ambassador to New Zealand, on France's nuclear testing

Fireworky thingys.

**Unnamed British Secret Intelligence Service agent, describing
part of the SIS arsenal, at the Princess Diana inquest**

If I went to war, instead of throwing a grenade, I'd throw one of those small pumpkins. Then maybe my enemy would pick up the pumpkin and think about the futility of war. And that would give me the time I need to hit him with a real grenade.   **Jack Handey,** *Deep Thoughts*

A slipping gear could let your M-grenade launcher fire when you least expect it. That would make you quite unpopular in what's left of your unit.

Army Magazine of Preventive Maintenance

Everyone in the Swiss Army owns a Swiss Army knife. That's why no one messes with Switzerland.   **Cliff Clavin,** *Cheers*

It's hard to conceal a water balloon.   **Calvin,** *Calvin and Hobbes*

—Hey, don't point that thing at me!
—It's only my baby.
—I dare say. But point it the other way.   **P. G. Wodehouse,** *A Few Quick Ones*

They couldn't hit an elephant at this dist—

General John Sedgwick

BUSINESS

Jesus saves! But wouldn't it better if he invested?
Anon.

I understand small business growth. I was one.   **George W. Bush**

Under New Mismanagement.   **Brendan Beary**

—I's got some business ideas that I just want to tell you … What is the most popular thing in the world?
—Music.
—No. Ice cream! Everyone has it. And what is the problem with ice cream?
—I have no idea.

—It drips. So, me idea is what?
—To make a drip-proof ice cream?
—No. But that's a fuckin' brilliant idea! All right, whatever. You ain't gonna come out with that, though, are you?
—No, I promise you I won't.   **Ali G and Donald Trump,** *Da Ali G Show*

Over a long weekend, I could teach my dog to be an investment banker.
Herbert Allen, President of Allen & Company Inc.,
an investment banking firm

I have a few business ideas. For a nominal fee, I provide a service where I will eat and describe pork to kosher people.   **David Cross**

A stupid practice that a business might perpetrate: Pay toilets also have coin slots inside for pay toilet paper.   **Chuck Smith**

What we are doing is in the interest of everybody, bar possibly the consumer.

Aer Lingus spokesman

We also do this nice sherry decanter. It's cut glass and it comes complete with six glasses on a silver-plated tray that your butler could bring you in and serve you drinks on. And it only costs £4.95. People say to me, "How can you sell this for such a low price?" I say, "Because it's total crap."
Gerald Ratner, on Ratners, a British jewelry chain store

We own a lot of Gillette, and you can sleep pretty well at night if you think of a couple billion men with their hair growing on their faces. It is growing all night while you sleep. Women have two legs, it is even better. So it beats counting sheep.   **Warren Buffett**

Socks Lower in Tokyo   **Misprint,** *The New York Times*

To those critics who are so pessimistic about our economy, I say, "Don't be economic girlie men!"   **Arnold Schwarzenegger**

Let's make sure that there is certainty during uncertain times in our economy.
George W. Bush (YT)

ADVERTISING

Advertising may be described as the science of arresting the human
intelligence long enough to get money from it.
Stephen Leacock

I'm proud to see his penis 25 feet tall. It's huge. It's enormous. Massive.
Victoria Beckham, on her husband David's Armani
underwear billboard advertisement

Product not actual size   **Disclaimer on a Burger King ad showing a**
"King Kong–sized" Whopper crushing a car

Elvis never drank wine, but if he did, this is the wine he would have ordered.
Colonel Tom Parker, manager of Elvis Presley,
on "Always Elvis" white wine

I'll perform any operation for $129.95! Come in for brain surgery and receive a
free Chinese finger trap! You've tried the best, now try the rest!
Dr. Nick Riviera, ad, *The Simpsons*

[*at the end of a commercial for a combination hair restorer / penis enlarger*]
Possible side effects include loss of scalp and penis.
TV announcer, *The Simpsons*

—You've played so many things … a sheepdog, a penguin, a chimp, a glow-
worm …
—I've played a menstrual period. It's one of my favorite little voices.
I thought, How on earth do you play a menstrual period? And then I thought, I
know, she's a naughty little schoolgirl, and she goes "Hee-hee-hee, you didn't
expect to find me on your holiday, did you?!"
Andrew Denton and Miriam Margolyes,
Enough Rope with Andrew Denton

I've turned down commercials that will undermine, never mind the dignity of
office, but my own dignity. There was one glorious one where they wanted me
to pretend to be in marital bliss with Alice Cooper. My reply to my agent was,
"Just remind me—who is she?"
Ann Widdecombe, British member of
Parliament and TV personality

Well, I'm the prince and I'm sort of slaying a dragon, which is something I've never done before, obviously.

David Beckham, on appearing in a publicity portrait for Disney

I'm trying to sell advertising space on my bottom. As I am a woman and wear a skintight catsuit, I thought it might be quite popular.

Carina Willoughby, bobsledder

—Excuse me, can you tell me why you're going around with a blank sandwich board?
—It's my day off.

Peter Vincent

MONEY

There was a time when a fool and his money were soon parted, but now it happens to everybody.
Adlai Stevenson

I saw a bank that said "24 Hour Banking," but I don't have that much time.

Steven Wright

My wife went into a bank and asked if she could open a joint account. When a clerk asked her with whom, she replied, "Someone with lots of money, of course."

Don Foreman

—Okay, we need $40,000. How much do we have in the check book?
—Seventy dollars.
—Have we deposited any $40,000 checks that haven't cleared yet?
—No.

Homer and Marge Simpson, *The Simpsons*

I don't have a bank account because I don't know my mother's maiden name.

Paula Poundstone

—Does the high cost of living bother you?
—No, I live in the ground-floor apartment.

**Alan Sues and Goldie Hawn,
*Rowan & Martin's Laugh-in***

I know how hard it is for you to put food on your family.

George W. Bush

I do not borrow on credit cards, it's too expensive. I have four children.
I give them advice not to pile up debt on their cards.

Matt Barrett, Chief Executive of Barclays Bank (U.K.)

—Do you have any money?
—No.
—How can we get some? Who do you know that we could sue?

Calvin and Hobbes, *Calvin and Hobbes*

—What would you do if you found a million dollars?
—I'd see if I could find the guy who lost it, and if he was poor, I'd give it back.

Reporter and Yogi Berra

—This pound note you lost. What color was it?
—Green.
—It's mine! Mine was green!

The Goon Show

I'm so naive about finances. Once when my mother mentioned an amount and I
realized that I didn't understand, she had to explain, "That's like three
Mercedes." Then I understood.

Brooke Shields

I'm paying you nothing, and I won't pay you a cent more!

Sam Goldwyn

He's got a wonderful head for money. There's this long slit on the top.

Sir David Frost

If there's anyone listening to whom I owe money, I'm prepared to forget it if
you are.

Errol Flynn

Mr. Laurel and Mr. Hardy have cast off all financial worries. Total assets: one
Ford—model 1911, one tent—model 1861, one union suit, two shirts and three
socks.

Tagline, *One Good Turn*

They lived on money borrowed from each other.

George Moore

Save money on expensive personalized car number plates by simply changing your name to match your existing plate.

Mr. KVL 741, *Viz* magazine

I got tired listening to one million dollars here, one million dollars there. It's so petty.   **Imelda Marcos, First Lady of the Philippines**

Like most supermodels, I won't get out of bed for less than £3,000. Unlike most supermodels, I don't get out of bed very often.

Simon Munnery

Son, if you really want something in this life, you have to work for it. Now quiet, they're about to announce the lottery numbers.

Homer Simpson, *The Simpsons*

Save money on batteries by taking them out of your doorbell, then going to the door every two minutes to see if there's anyone there.

***Viz* magazine**

Beat the credit-card companies at their own game by running up massive bills on your credit cards and then killing yourself before your statements arrive, thus avoiding repayment.   **D. Payne, *Viz* magazine**

Money can't buy poverty.   **Marty Feldman**

Money can't buy you love, but it can get you some really good chocolate ginger biscuits.   **Dylan Moran**

TAX

The hardest thing in the world to understand is the income tax.
Albert Einstein

Let me tell you my thoughts about tax relief. When your economy is kind of ooching along, it's important to let people have more of their own money.

George W. Bush

You bet I cut the taxes at the top. That encourages entrepreneurship ... We ought to make the pie higher!   **George W. Bush**

RICH

The foolish sayings of a rich man pass for wise ones.
Spanish proverb

Money is the key to financial success.   David Kleinbard

I'd rather be rich than stupid.   Jack Handey, *Deep Thoughts*

I'd pay anything to be rich.   Michael A. Genz

I don't want to be rich. I want to be effluent!
Kim Craig, *Kath & Kim* (U.K.)

It's a bit like being poor, but having a hell of a lot of money.
Griff Rhys Jones, on being a millionaire

When I was a kid I had no idea I lived in a mansion. Then I went to a friend's house and I was like, "Oh ..."   **Paris Hilton**

It is easier for a rich man to get through the eye of a needle than for a camel to get into heaven.   **Andy Mulligan**

I had to get rich in order to sing like I'm poor again.   **Dolly Parton**

If the rich could hire other people to die for them, the poor could make a wonderful living.   **Yiddish proverb**

POOR

I've known what it is to be hungry, but I always went right
to a restaurant.
Ring Lardner

First, let me make it very clear, poor people aren't necessarily killers. Just because you happen to be not rich doesn't mean you're willing to kill.
George W. Bush

We'll never win the war on poverty till all those poor people surrender.

Jo Anne Worley, *Rowan & Martin's Laugh-in*

—We've spent over a million dollars on the space program, and some people say that we should have given it to the poor.
—Now, what do the poor people know about how to run a space program?

Rowan & Martin's Laugh-in

I can't forget the poverty-stricken days of my youth. I never had any shoes. My father used to black my feet and lace my toes up.

Les Dawson

I'm as poor as a church mouse that's just had an enormous tax bill on the very day his wife ran off with another mouse, taking all the cheese.

Edmund Blackadder, *Blackadder the Third*

Poor? I couldn't afford the doctor's bill. You're looking at the only man in the world who's had his appendix taken out and put back in again.

Eric Morecambe

CHARITY

When it comes to giving, some people stop at nothing.
Yiddish proverb

Jesus cured me. I was hopping along, minding my own business. All of a sudden, up here he comes. Cures me. One minute I'm a leper with a trade, next minute my livelihood's gone. Not so much as a by-your-leave. "You're cured, mate." Bloody do-gooder.

Ex-leper, *Monty Python's Life of Brian*

Volunteering is for suckers. Did you know that volunteers don't even get paid for the stuff they do?   **Homer Simpson,** *The Simpsons*

A woman came from the parish council and asked me if I wanted to run a half marathon. And I said, "Oh, no, I couldn't do a half marathon." And she said,

"You really should think about it. It's for partially sighted and blind children." So I thought, "Well, fuck it, I could win that."
                                                                    Dave Spikey

—Would you like to buy a raffle ticket for the church for 50 cents?
—Now what would I do with a church if I won one?
                        Little Boy and Jack Griffith, *Papa's Delicate Condition*

I want to go to Egypt and Japan and open orphanages—a chain of them.
                                                                    Lindsay Lohan

Right, let's go and look at some more piccaninnies.
                        Boris Johnson, mayor of London, to Swedish UNICEF
                              workers and their black driver, in Uganda

Cardinal Basil Hume brought sweets for the children. Even the good were getting it wrong.

                              Michael Buerk, on the Ethiopian famine,
                        Ethiopia: A Journey with Michael Buerk, BBC TV

Maris is the soul of generosity. Just last week she donated all her cocktail dresses to a homeless shelter.
                                                          Niles Crane, *Frasier*

—Why anyone would choose to be homeless is beyond me.
—Honey, nobody chooses to be homeless. It's because they did something bad.
                        Karen Walker and Jack McFarland, *Will & Grace*

Homelessness is homelessness no matter where you live.
                              Glenda Jackson, Member of Parliament

Do you come here often?
                  Edward Kennedy, senator, to a patron of a Brooklyn soup kitchen

What's a soup kitchen?
                                                                    Paris Hilton

Chef Throws His Heart into Helping Feed Needy   Headline, *Louisville Courier*

The girls and I feel so terrible when we see all those unfortunate people in the poor part of town. So we've decided to do something about it. From now on, we're not going to drive through the poor part of town.
                              Lily Tomlin, *Rowan & Martin's Laugh-in*

—How large a donation do you want from me?
—Fifty dollars will keep my nursery babies in milk for a month.
—Get awfully mildewed, won't they?

Stanley Slade and Elizabeth Cartwright, *The Doughgirls*

I'd like to help you out. Which way did you come in?

Henny Youngman

TRAVEL & COUNTRIES

GEOGRAPHY

He had brought a large map representing the sea,
Without the least vestige of land:
And the crew was much pleased when they found it to be
A map they could all understand.

Lewis Carroll, "The Hunting of the Snark"

Wow! Brazil is big!

**George W. Bush, on seeing a map of Brazil at a meeting with the
Brazilian President, Luiz Inácio Lula da Silva**

How long does it take you to get home? Eight hours! Me too! Russia's a big
country and you're a big country!

**George W. Bush, to President Hu Jintao of China
at the G8 Summit in Russia, 2006 (YT)**

He [George W. Bush] said, "So what state is Wales in?" I said, "Erm, it's a
separate country next to England." And he went, "Oh, Okay." I didn't know
what to say.   **Charlotte Church**

It's an enormous country—you know, it's bigger than Texas. Or as big, I guess—
I haven't looked lately.

Donald Rumsfeld, Secretary of Defense, on Iraq (YT)

I didn't go down there with any plan for the Americas or anything. I went
down to find out from them and [learn] their views. You'd be surprised.
They're all individual countries.

Ronald Reagan, after a tour of South America

One day, we hiked up to the top of the highest mountain in Wales and Jade said,
"Can you see Canada from here?"

Kelly Bryant, on Jade Goody, British TV personality

Rio de Janeiro—ain't that a person?

Jade Goody, British TV personality

She thinks Bosnia Herzegovina's the Wonderbra model.

Isabel Wolff

—Hairy Scots! Tonight we march north on England!
—But England's south!
—Aye ... we're gonna march right round the world and sneak up on them from behind!
The Goon Show

I stopped a man from Wigan in the street on the way to the football and I asked him, "How do you get to the JJB Stadium?" And he said, "Me brother takes me."
Dave Spikey

Hoping to improve my son's knowledge of geography, I bought him an atlas for Christmas. A few days later I asked him, "Where's Portugal?" Without hesitating, he answered, "Three pages after France."
Laura Greene

I have the world's oldest globe. It's flat.
Buzz Nutley

The cool thing about being famous is traveling. I have always wanted to travel across seas, like to Canada and stuff.
Britney Spears

—It took the class 40 minutes to locate Canada on a map.
—Oh, honey, anyone could miss Canada. All tucked way down there.
Marge and Homer Simpson, *The Simpsons*

I love Africa in general—South Africa and West Africa, they are both great countries.
Paris Hilton

I like most of the places I've been to, but I've never really wanted to go to Japan, simply because I don't like eating fish. And I know that's very popular out there in Africa.
Britney Spears

I have an existential map. It has "You are here" written all over it. People ask me where I live, and I like to say E5.
Steven Wright

Remember, you can always find east by staring directly at the sun.
Bart Simpson, *The Simpsons*

—But you don't even know where Australia is!
—Most people don't know where Australia is. The difference between knowing and caring are two different things—and I don't care.
Gerry Stergiopoulos and Charley Uchea, *Big Brother 8* (U.K.)

—Carla, what do you know about geography?
—I know what creek you're up.

Sam Malone and Carla Tortelli, *Cheers*

TRAVEL & TOURISM

The greatest unexplored territory in the world
is the space between the ears.
Bill O'Brien

I want to hang a map of the world in my house. Then I'm gonna put pins into all the locations that I've traveled to. But first, I'm going to have to travel to the top two corners of the map so it won't fall off the wall.   Mitch Hedberg

—I've been planning this vacation for years. I'm finally going to see Easter Island.
—Easter Island, the place with the giant heads?
—With the giant WHAT-now?

Moe Syzslak and Homer Simpson, *The Simpsons*

I can't wait to see Japan—all those Geisha boys and girls!

Freddie Mercury

I enjoyed the Luge.   Michael Jordan, on his trip to Paris

The holy land of Israel is a Mecca for tourists.

Anon.

—Where am I? Am I in Kansas City?
—No. You're in Wu Hu, China.
—What is Wu Hu doing in Kansas City?
—Maybe you're lost.
—Kansas City is lost! I am here!

Henry R. Quail and hotel manager, *International House*

If you don't know where you're going, you might not get there.

Yogi Berra

According to the map, we've only gone four inches.

Harry Dunne, *Dumb & Dumber*

We're lost, but we're making good time.

Yogi Berra

How can the French expect to attract our tourist trade? This year, at five different hotels, the tap marked "C" turned out to be "H."

Letter, *Evening Chronicle*

After college I wanted to go to Europe, but I couldn't afford it, so I went backpacking round Epcot.

Wendy Liebman

What time do they turn on the Northern Lights?

Tourist in Alaska

Do they turn the Falls off at night?

Tourist at Niagara Falls

STREETS FULL OF WATER. PLEASE ADVISE.

Robert Benchley, in a cable sent on arriving in Venice

What time does the volcano erupt?

Tourist, on Mount Etna

I went to Naples to see Vesuvius and do you know what? The bloody fools had let it go out.

Spike Milligan

I don't want any more culture. It makes my feet hurt.

Gwendolyn Dilley, *I Dream Too Much*

—Have you had a chance to visit the Parthenon during your trip to Greece?
—I haven't been to that club yet.

Reporter and Shaquille O'Neal

You'd think, with all these tourists about, they'd build an elevator to the top.

Tourist, climbing up to the Parthenon

The problem with London is the tourists. They cause the congestion.
If we could just stop tourism we could stop the congestion.

Prince Philip

—Gee, I just love this Westminster Cathedral. Tell me, is it prewar?
—Madam, it is pre-America.

American tourist and London tour guide

My wife and I were thinking of going to Ireland personally, to see what all the fuss is about. But we couldn't face having all the injections.

Hugh Laurie, *A Bit of Fry and Laurie*

[*American tourist in front of the Sphinx in Egypt*] Is there anything interesting to see around here?

Gregory Webster, overheard, *The Graham Norton Show*

The pyramids? That's that range of mountains between France and Spain, isn't it?

Annie McClintock

Does the sun set in the west here too?

American tourist in Australia

Room service? Send up a larger room!

Groucho Marx, *A Night at the Opera*

Why doesn't my room have a sea view?

Tourist at hotel in London

—I expect to be able to see the sea.
—You can see the sea. It's over there between the land and the sky.
—I'd need a telescope to see that.
—Well, might I suggest you move to a hotel closer to the sea. [*under his breath*] Or preferably in it.

Mrs. Richards and Basil Fawlty, *Fawlty Towers*

How long is the Royal Mile?   **Tourist in Edinburgh**

Can you give us directions to Brigadoon?   **Tourist in Scottish tourist office**

I don't want matured whiskey, I want fresh!

Tourist in an Edinburgh, Scotland, pub

We'd like directions to Loch Lomond and the Trollops.

Tourist in Edinburgh, Scotland, tourist office

Is there anyone here who speaks Australian?

Tourist in Edinburgh, Scotland tourist office

Where's the French Embassy?   **Tourist in Paris**

—So there actually is a Paris Hilton? Is it hard to get into the Paris Hilton?
—Actually, it's a very exclusive hotel, no matter what you've heard ...
—Do they allow double occupancy at the Paris Hilton? Is the Paris Hilton roomy?
—It might be for you, but most people find it very comfortable.
—Well, I'm a VIP. I might need to use the back entrance.

Jimmy Fallon and Paris Hilton, *Saturday Night Live* **(YT)**

Our hotel's called the Hotel Eingang.

Tourist in Austria (*eingang* **means "entrance")**

Mallorca—an island completely surrounded by sea ...   **Glyn Haydn**

If we go snorkeling, will we get wet?   **Tourist in the Maldives**

Where are Rhett and Scarlett buried?   **Tourist in Atlanta, Georgia**

Where do they grow totem poles?   **Tourist in British Columbia**

How long did it take to dig this?   **Tourist at the Grand Canyon**

Where are the faces of the presidents?   **Tourist at the Grand Canyon**

How far above sea level are we?   **Tourist on cruise ship**

Does the crew sleep on board?   **Tourist on cruise ship**

What time is the midnight buffet?   **Tourist on cruise ship**

Did you hear about that tourist boat on a cruise in the Atlantic—it ran into an iceberg. And what were they doing at the time? They were looking for icebergs!

Graham Norton, *The Graham Norton Show*

COUNTRIES—GENERAL

A country is a piece of land surrounded on all sides by boundaries, usually unnatural.
Joseph Heller, Catch-22

I love the Australian flag: Britain at night.   **Jerry Seinfeld**

I asked my little granddaughter, Carrie, if she'd enjoyed her visit to Australia. "Oh, yes!" she said. "We saw kangaroos and wombats, but my favorite was the Coca-Cola bears."

Lilian Curtis

I have lived 78 years without hearing of bloody places like Cambodia.

Winston Churchill

I guess Canada's not that bad. Their beer has twice the amount of alcohol as ours does and they've got a pot leaf on their flag.

Joy Turner, *My Name Is Earl*

Keep good relations with the Grecians.

George W. Bush

I have never felt any ethnic connection between the Greeks and me, other than how hairy I am.

George Michael

What Iran needs now is a more modern leader—a *mullah* lite.

Shappi Khorsandi, Iranian-born comedian

There's nothing more deep than recognizing Israel's right to exist. That's the most deep thought of all ... I can't think of anything more deep than that.

George W. Bush

Is Jerusalem a real place? I thought it was just in the Bible.

Jade Goody, British TV personality

To the Italians I say this: "Rome wasn't built in a day. Perhaps it could have been if you spoke less with your arms."

Simon Munnery

What do you call it when an Italian has one arm shorter than the other? A speech impediment.

Anon.

—What do Japanese men do when they have erections?
—Vote.

Anon.

After telling my mum that a mate was on holiday in Kuala Lumpur, she said, "Aren't they the little people in *Charlie and the Chocolate Factory*?"

Anon.

The Mexicans—these tiny little men from South America ...

Harry Carpenter

What a beautiful day for knocking on the door of the Kremlin and shouting, "Is Len in?"

Ken Dodd

Do you need a passport to get to Scotland?

Jade Goody, British TV personality

—You think I'm finished?
—No, Swedish.

Ingrid Svenson and Jessica Tate, *Soap*

Venezuela, that's the Italian city with the guys in the boats, right?

Murad Muhammad, boxing agent

GREAT BRITAIN

Only in Britain could it be thought a defect to be "too clever by half." The probability is that too many people are too stupid by three-quarters.
John Major

Britain, Britain, Britain. We've had running water for over ten years, we have a tunnel connecting us to Peru and we invented the cat.

Tom Baker, *Little Britain*

The sage of Knotty Ash, Ken Dodd, once said, "We British have an advantage over other people because we're not foreign."

Stephen Garnett

We have all got to be as British as *Carry On* films and Scotch eggs and falling over on the beach while trying to change into your swimming trunks with a towel on.

Boris Johnson, mayor of London

I left England at the age of four—when I found out I couldn't be king.

Bob Hope

My folks were English. They were too poor to be British. I still have a bit of British in me. In fact, my blood type is solid marmalade.

Bob Hope

I love England, especially the food. There's nothing I like more than a lovely bowl of pasta.

Naomi Campbell

England? England is in London, right?

Eminem

IRELAND

I never met anyone in Ireland who understood the Irish question, except one Englishman who had been there only a week.

Kenneth Fraser

—How do you confuse a Kerryman?
—Place three shovels against a wall and ask him to take his pick.

Anon.

Dublin is a city with a very dense population.

Dusty Young

In Ireland, schizophrenics are treated not by one psychiatrist but two.

Barry Took

Two out of every one people in Ireland are schizophrenic.

Jimeoin

Ireland is officially bilingual, a fact which is reflected in the road signs. This allows you to get lost in both Irish and English.

Frank McNally

I once saw a road sign in Ireland which read, "Warning! This is a one-way cul-de-sac at both ends."

Spike Milligan

The Irish don't know what they want and are prepared to fight to the death to get it.

Sidney Littlewood

Experts have discovered there was no potato famine in Ireland. We just forgot where we'd planted them.

Dylan Moran

You couldn't have a famine in Ireland now; people would just eat out.

Kevin McAleer

AMERICA

Even stupid people in Britain are smarter than Americans.
Madonna

You know one thing that's wrong with this country? Everybody gets a chance to have their fair say.

Bill Clinton

People think everyone from the South is married to their sister and has seen a UFO. I tell 'em, "Hell, I'm just *dating* my sister, and I could swear it wasn't a weather balloon."

Jeff Foxworthy

New York is my Lourdes, where I go for spiritual refreshment ... a place where you're least likely to be bitten by a wild goat.

Brendan Behan

You can walk down the street [in New York] and end up ... in a shop that sells, I don't know, staplers from all over the world ... You don't get that in LA—that kind of, I don't know, specialty.

Cameron Diaz

It's as American as a burrito.   Lieutenant Fergus Falls, *Wrongfully Accused*

I don't feel we did anything wrong in taking this great country away from [the Indians]. There were great numbers of people who needed new land, and the Indians were selfishly trying to keep it for themselves.

John Wayne

I love California. I practically grew up in Phoenix.

Dan Quayle

I once spent a year in Philadelphia. I think it was on a Sunday.

W. C. Fields

TRANSPORTATION— GENERAL

Our Lady of Blessed Acceleration, don't fail us now!
Elwood Blues, The Blues Brothers

A Polish man in a helicopter goes up to 800 feet. Down it comes! What happened? "It got chilly up there, so I turned off the fan."

Henny Youngman

[*hearing a police siren whiz by*] He's not going to sell much ice cream going at that speed!

Eric Morecambe

Calling a lift is easy. Simply press the button and wait. And then press the button again. Many lifts work on the pressure you exert on the call button, so hitting it a hundred times will make it arrive a lot faster.

Guy Browning, *Never Push When It Says Pull*

Leaving a classy New York hotel, Robert Benchley instructed the uniformed man standing by the door to hail a taxicab for him. "Sir," said the man indignantly, "I am NOT a doorman. I am a rear admiral in the United States Navy." "In that case," said Benchley, "call me a battleship!"

Paul Mills

Venetian water taxis are the best things in the world. If Sophia Loren were a boat, she'd be one.

Laurence Llewelyn-Bowen

Take most people, they're crazy about cars ... I'd rather have a goddam horse. A horse is at least human, for God's sake.

J. D. Salinger, *The Catcher in the Rye*

I've never driven a horse before.

Tara Reid

Horses? I don't ride anything I can't put gas into.

Fonzie, *Happy Days*

What a con these so-called radio-controlled taxis are! I got in one the other day and there was a man inside driving it.

Jay Beneaux, *Viz* magazine

—So, do you enjoy being a cab driver?
—Nah. As soon as I get my driver's licence, I'm quitting.

Roland T. Flakfizer and Rocco Melonchek, *Brain Donors*

—[*the amount on a taxi meter is rising quickly*] Aren't those numbers going by a little fast?
—You're probably just a speed reader.

Roland T. Flakfizer and Rocco Melonchek, *Brain Donors*

You can leave in a taxi. If you can't get a taxi you can leave in a huff. If that's too soon, you can leave in a minute and a huff.

Groucho Marx

This is a customer announcement: Would the nutter who just jumped onto the track please get back onto the platform, as the rats get jealous when someone invades their territory.

London Underground announcement

BUS

—Is it far to Finsbury Park?
—Oh, it's quite a distance. If you're going to walk you'd have to catch a bus.

Anon.

Using the Stagecoach bus could not be easier … First of all, decide on what bus you need … As the bus approaches, you will be able to see the route number and destination on the front. If this is your bus, then simply signal for the driver to stop, wait until the bus is stopped and the doors are fully opened and step on board. Tell the driver where you are going and what type of ticket you require ... When you want to get off, press the bell once. For your safety we recommend you remain seated until the bus has arrived at the stop.

"Using The Bus" manual, Stagecoach Buses (U.K.)

We always take the bus to the terminus so you don't have to think.

George, of "Gilbert and George"

I miss bus conductors—my chosen profession until I discovered that they did not get to keep the money they collected.

Sir Clement Freud

CAR

Wouldn't it be nice if the wattage of a car stereo could not exceed the IQ of the driver?
Robert Maine

I get around as nature intended: in a car. Kate, *French Kiss*

I know a lot about cars. I can look at a car's headlights and tell you exactly which way it's coming. **Mitch Hedberg**

—Homer, I don't want you driving around in a car you built yourself.
—Marge, you can sit there complaining, or you can knit me some seat belts.

Marge and Homer Simpson, *The Simpsons*

I installed my own air bags in my car: I got an old beanbag chair, some helium and a compressor, and if I hit the accident just right, I should be floating up in the sky laughing hysterically. **Steven Wright**

We'll be talking to a car designer who crossed a Toyota with Quasimodo and came up with the Hatchback of Notre Dame.

Ronnie Barker

My four-year-old son said, "That's not a toy ota, it's a big ota!"

Trina Bouvet

I suppose if I'm absolutely honest, I use my penis as a sort of car substitute.

Stephen Fry, *A Bit of Fry and Laurie*

Conditions on the road are bad, so if you are just setting off for work, leave a little earlier.

Kelvin O'Shea

My nan got in the car with my brother-in-law. As he adjusted the wing mirrors, she said, "Ooh, do you use those?" She's been driving for years.

Matthew Morgan, *The Russell Brand Show*

A friend of mine is a pilot, and we were going somewhere in his car, and for no reason at all he waited 45 minutes before pulling out of his driveway.

Steven Wright

—You drive everywhere, do you?
—Everywhere.
—Even to your car?

Bill and Hannah Warren, *California Suite*

When you're ten-years-old and a car drives by and splashes a puddle of water all over you, it's hard to decide if you should go to school like that or try to go home and change and probably be late. So while he was trying to decide, I drove by and splashed him again.

Jack Handey, *What I'd Say to the Martians*

These so-called speed humps are a joke. If anything they slow you down.

Tim Wakefield, *Viz* magazine

I was stopped once for going 53 in a 35-mile zone, but I told 'em I had dyslexia.

Spanky

Speed has never killed anybody. Suddenly becoming stationary. That's what gets you.

Jeremy Clarkson

—[*crashing the car*] She ran right in front of the car!
—It's a statue, you idiot!

Harold Bisonette and Amelia Bisonette, *It's a Gift*

Motorists—avoid getting prosecuted for using your phone while driving. Simply pop your mobile inside a large shell and the police will think you are listening to the sea.

Viz magazine

I'll tell you what seems to cause a lot of accidents ... people leaving flowers by the side of the road.

Milton Jones

Is it just me, or does anyone else get the amount you're allowed to drink when you're driving mixed up with the amount you're allowed to take through customs?

Harry Hill

The answer to this last question will determine whether you are drunk or not: "Was Mickey Mouse a cat or a dog?"

Actual traffic cop, question to motorist

You didn't think we give pretty women tickets? You're right, we don't. Sign here.

Actual traffic cop

The funny thing about driving your car off a cliff, I bet you're still hitting those brakes.

Jack Handey, *Deep Thoughts*

A woman was so nervous about her driving test that she drove through a wall and ran over the examiner as she arrived at the test center in Calgary, Canada, reports Auto Express. The magazine didn't say whether she passed.

The Sunday Times

I remember learning to drive on my dad's lap. He'd work the brakes.
I'd work the wheel. Then I went to take the driver's test and sat on the examiner's lap. I failed the exam. But he still writes to me.

Garry Shandling

I was driving around the other day and my oil light came on. But that little symbol looks nothing like an oil can. When it first came on I thought, Well, apparently my car is low on gravy.

Tom Ryan

A red light came on the dashboard and he said, "What's that?" I said, "Don't worry about that, that's just to tell whether that bulb is working."

Steven Wright

I have a rented car, which is a flat-rate 12 cents a mile. In an effort to cut down on the mileage charge, I back up every place.

Woody Allen

Kilometers are shorter than miles. Save gas, take your next trip in kilometers.

George Carlin

On some nights I still believe that a car with the gas needle on empty can still run for about 50 miles more if you have the right music very loud on the radio.

Hunter S. Thompson

It puzzles me how they know what corners are good for filling stations. Just how did these fellows know there was gas and oil under there?

Dizzy Dean

Never get anyone trained in tai chi to back you into a parking space. You'll be there all day. **Harry Hill**

You know those balls that they put on car antennas so you can find them in the parking lot? Those should be on every car.

Homer Simpson, *The Simpsons*

I thought that sign you see when parking, "Maximum Stay: 2 hrs. No return within 2 hrs," meant you could not return to your car for two hours and had to stay away for that exact amount of time.

Gail Powell

Stupidity is not a handicap. Park elsewhere! **Anon.**

—I don't start no trouble. I mind my own business.
—Going up to a traffic cop who's writing out a ticket for your van and eating the citation right in front of his face absolutely falls under "starting trouble."

Mr. T and Amy, *The A-Team*

[Americans driving in England]
— Clark, you're on the wrong side of the road!
—Yes I know, honey, I'm also on the wrong side of the car.

Ellen and Clark Griswold, *European Vacation*

Sorry we're so slow, we're from Canada

Handwritten sign seen in the rear window of a rented car in the U.K.

I had to stop driving my car for a while ... the tires got dizzy.

Kevin McAleer

One time a cop pulled me over for running a stop sign. He said, "Didn't you see the stop sign?" I said, "Yeah, but I don't believe everything I read."

Steven Wright

—You know, this is a one-way street.
—I was only going one way.

Officer Anderson and Jeannie, *I Dream of Jeannie*

Don't drive standing up through the sunroof while you are closing it.

Advice in car owner's manual

Most cars on our roads have only one occupant—usually the driver.

Carol Malia, BBC

Inside every car there's a pedestrian waiting to get out.

Bumper sticker

Ban Bumper Stickers

Bumper sticker

—Are we there yet?
—No.
—Are we there yet?
—No.
—Are we there yet?
—No.
—Where are we going?

Grampa and Homer Simpson, *The Simpsons*

TRAIN

As it went on, the little engine kept bravely puffing faster and faster,
"I think I can, I think I can, I think I can."
The Little Engine That Could

So I said to this train driver, "I want to go to Paris." He said, "Eurostar?" I said, "I've been on telly, but I'm not Dean Martin." Mind you, at least Eurostar's comfortable; it's murder on the Orient Express.

Tim Vine

Can we have a window seat? We want a good view of the fish.

American tourist, to Eurostar booking agent

The whistle shrilled, and in a moment I was chugging out of Grand Central Station. I had chugged only a few feet when I realized I had left without the train, so I had to run back and wait for it to start.

S. J. Perelman

Next train's gone!

Jeremiah Harbottle, *Oh, Mr. Porter!*

I knew I was going to take the wrong train so I left early.

Anon.

We apologize for the late running of the train. This is due to us following a train that is in front of us.
British Rail announcement

We apologize for the delay. This is due to passengers getting on and off.
British Rail announcement

If you want to alight at Durham, we apologize. The driver forgot to stop.
Great North Eastern Railway announcement (U.K.)

I heard this announcement at the station last week: "We apologize for the late arrival of this train. This is due to inefficiency."
Alan Titchmarsh

We apologize for the delay—it is due to the fact that we are ten minutes early.
Platform announcement, Thurles train station, Ireland

Why is it that people never seem to fight on top of trains these days?
Justin D. Cobram, *Viz* magazine

—So, did you see which train crashed into which train first?
—No, they both ran into each other at the same time.
Interviewer and teenager, BBC Radio

There will be no last train tonight.
Sign at train station

Thank you for traveling with South West Trains. Please make sure you take all your belongings when leaving the train. This is particularly important if you work for Her Majesty's Government.
South West Trains announcement (U.K.)

AIR TRAVEL

How difficult can it be to fly a plane? I mean,
John Travolta learned how.
Graham Chapman

I booked a flight the other day and the clerk asked, "How many people will be traveling with you?" I said, "I don't know. It's your plane."

Steven Wright

When people ask me how I'm getting to the airport I say, "Well, I'm flying to one of them."

Steven Wright

I went to the airport information desk. I said, "How many airports are there in the world?" She said, "I don't know."

Jimmy Carr

Attention: If a stranger has put something in your bag without your knowledge, please report it to us immediately.

Michelle Stupak

I've always thought of starting my own airline—if I could get a bunch of investors together—called Air Smoke. We'd make smoking mandatory.

Johnny Depp

Avoid airlines that have anyone's first name in their titles, like "Bob's International" or "Air Fred."

Miss Piggy

I was told I was traveling "Virgin Upper" and I misheard it.

Russell Brand, after reportedly having sex with a
Virgin Airlines flight attendant during a flight

I am here to make an announcement that this Thursday, ticket counters and airplanes will fly out of Ronald Reagan Airport.

George W. Bush (YT)

My six-year-old son enjoys watching planes fly over our house. Boarding a plane for the first time this summer, he said, "Mummy, when do we get smaller?"

Anne Wilkinson

—Daddy, how do airplanes fly?
—When you do good things, magic pixie dust keeps the planes in the air. But every time you do something bad—like disturb me while I'm watching the game—a plane crashes and hundreds of people die.

Ben Lee

—We have clearance, Clarence.
—Roger, Roger. What's our vector, Victor?

Roger Murdock and Captain Oveur, *Airplane!*

[as the plane is about to take off]
—Nervous?
—Yes.
—First time?
—No, I've been nervous lots of times.

Ann Nelson and Ted Striker, *Airplane!*

I've got no confidence in the pilot. When he makes a left turn he puts his hand out.

Rodney Dangerfield

Flying a plane is no different to riding a bicycle. It's just a lot harder to put baseball cards in the spokes.

Captain Rex Kramer, *Airplane!*

Pilot's number one rule: Always try to keep the number of landings you make equal to the number of takeoffs you've made.

Paul Andrews

Fun thing for a pilot to do in a jet: Annoy your fellow pilots by leaving the indicator on.

David Letterman

In the words of a stewardess on the London to Manchester flight, "In the unlikely eventuality of a landing on water…" It would take a damned good pilot to pull that one off; or one with absolutely no sense of direction.

Peter Ustinov

You know you're in trouble when, at the control tower, there's a note taped to the door that says "Back in 5 minutes."

Jeff Foxworthy

—Control tower to pilot, control tower to pilot, what is your height and position?
—Pilot to control tower, pilot to control tower, I'm 5 feet 10 inches and I'm sitting down.

Anon.

Would the owner of a red-and-tan Boeing 737 please report to the tarmac? Your lights are on.

Eric Murphy

I had a job as an airline pilot. I was fired because I kept locking the keys in the plane. They caught me on an 80-foot stepladder with a coat hanger.

Steven Wright

—Strangely enough, this air traffic control room has no windows.
—Well, actually it's the radar room.
—So how do you manage to see the planes?
—By radar.

Simon Bates and Royal Air Force officer, BBC Radio

If you travel as much as we do, you appreciate how much more comfortable aircraft have become. Unless you travel in something called economy class, which sounds ghastly.

Prince Philip

On a flight to Belfast, I was upgraded to business class. I was a bit scared. I thought, will I have to play golf?

Jeremy Hardy

I've heard of some creative cost measures before, but getting rid of the life jackets is *inspired*. Sure, tell them they're under the seats, but nobody ever checks, so why have them?

Brian Hackett, *Wings*

—Assume flight crash positions!
—What's that?
—It's the position you want to be found dead in.

Joe Hackett and Antonio Scarpacci, *Wings*

Your seat cushions can be used as flotation devices. In the event of an emergency water landing, please take them with our compliments.

Flight Attendant

I am not afraid of crashing. My secret is, just before we hit the ground, I jump as high as I can.

Bill Cosby

I'm always amazed to hear of air-crash victims so badly mutilated that they have to be identified by their dental records. What I can't understand is, if they don't know who you are, how do they know who your dentist is?

Paul Merton

I bet the main reason the police keep people away from a plane crash is they don't want anybody walking in and lying down in the crash stuff, then when somebody comes up, act like they just woke up and go, "What was that?!"

Jack Handey, *Deep Thoughts*

Ladies and gentlemen, there's no reason to become alarmed, and we hope you'll enjoy the rest of your flight. By the way, is there anyone on board who knows how to fly a plane?
                                                    Elaine Dickinson, *Airplane!*

The knack of flying is learning how to throw yourself at the ground and miss.
                                                    Douglas Adams

—How was your flight, your Royal Highness?
—Have you ever flown in a plane?
—Oh, yes, your Royal Highness, often.
—Well, it was like that.   **Official and Prince Philip**

That was the worst flight I've ever had, and I was once in a midair collision.
                                                    Davis Lynch, *Wings*

It's great to be back on terra cotta.   **John Prescott**

The last time I was in Dublin Airport, I spent hours waiting for two bags. My wife and my mother.
                                                    Brendan Grace

Houses will be able to fly by 2000 ... The time may come when whole communities may migrate south in the winter, or move to new lands whenever they feel the need for a change of scenery.
                                                    Arthur C. Clarke, 1966

BOAT

A whale-ship was my Yale College and my Harvard.
Herman Melville

In the transatlantic single-handed yacht race, Mr. Owen Smithers has been disqualified for using both hands.
                                                    Ronnie Barker

Is the poop deck really what I think it is?   **Homer Simpson, *The Simpsons***

The captain was on the bridge, pretty sure that he knew the way to New York but, just to be on the safe side, murmuring to himself, "Turn right at Cherbourg and then straight on."

                                                    P. G. Wodehouse, *Life with Freddie*

—Please divert your course 15 degrees to the north to avoid a collision.
—Recommend you divert your course 15 degrees to south to avoid collision.
—This is the captain of a U.S. Navy ship. I say again, divert your course.
—No. I say again, you divert YOUR course.
—This is the USS *Lincoln*, the second largest ship in the U.S. Atlantic Fleet. DIVERT YOUR COURSE NOW!
—This is Harbor Lighthouse. Your call.   **Anon.**

The ship is sinking. We must try and save it. Help me get it into the lifeboat.
                                                                Spike Milligan

—How do you sink an Irish submarine?
—Knock on the hatch.   **Anon.**

THE UNIVERSE

THE WORLD

The universe never did make sense. I suspect that it was built on a government contract.
Robert A. Heinlein

In the beginning, the world was without form, and void. And God said, "Let there be light!" And God separated the light from the dark. And did two loads of laundry.   **Kevin Krisciunas**

And on the eighth day God said, "Okay, Murphy, you can take over now."
Michael Redmond

We shouldn't fear a world that is more interacted.   **George W. Bush**

It's a small world. But I wouldn't want to have to paint it.
Steven Wright

A man who was attempting to walk around the world drowned today.
George Carlin

Your theory of a donut-shaped universe is intriguing, Homer. I may have to steal it.
Dr. Stephen Hawking, to Homer Simpson, *The Simpsons*

This is still a dangerous world. It's a world of madmen and uncertainty and potential mental losses.   **George W. Bush**

I used to have sleepless nights worrying the earth could be destroyed by an asteroid. The funny thing is, I now know for certain that the planet will be hit by an asteroid, but I don't have problems sleeping.
Lembit Opik, Member of Parliament

He is known for talking about steroids hitting the earth. We don't sit every day and talk about steroids.
Gabriela Irimia, of British pop duo The Cheeky Girls, on Lembit Opik

LIFE

In the book of life, the answers aren't in the back.
Charlie Brown, Peanuts

As the light changed from red to green to amber and back to red again, I sat there thinking about life. Was it nothing more than a lot of honking and yelling? Sometimes it seemed that way.
Jack Handey, *Deep Thoughts*

It's important for us to explain to our nation that life is important. It's not only life of babies, but it's life of children living in, you know, the dark dungeons of the Internet.
George W. Bush

There's more to life than getting drunk, being naked and having sex.
Alex Sibley, *Big Brother 3* (U.K.)

Life is like arriving late for a movie, having to figure out what was going on without bothering everybody with a lot of questions and then being unexpectedly called away before you find out how it ends.
Joseph Campbell

I was wondering how my life would have been different if I'd been born one day earlier, and I thought maybe it wouldn't be different at all, except that I'd have asked that question yesterday.
Steven Wright

—Life is like a deckchair on a cruise ship. Passengers open up these canvas deckchairs so they can sit in the sun. Some people place their chairs facing the rear of the ship so they can see where they've been. Other people face their chairs forward—they want to see where they're going. On the cruise ship of life, Charlie Brown, which way is your deckchair facing?
—I've never been able to get one unfolded.
Charlie Brown and Lucy Van Pelt, *Peanuts*

Sometimes life seems like a dream, especially when I look down and see that I forgot to put on my pants.
Jack Handey

Life is like a grapefruit. It's sort of orangey-yellow and dimpled on the outside, wet and squidgy in the middle. It's got pips inside, too. Oh, and some people have half a one for breakfast.
Douglas Adams, *So Long, and Thanks for All the Fish*

If life gives you a lemon, make lemonade. However—if life gives you a pickle, you might as well give up because pickleade is disgusting.

Clifton J. Gray

When life gives you lemons, make apple sauce.

Angelica, *Rugrats*

—Life is a wonderful thing ...
—When you've seen as much of life as I have, you'd rather have a cup of tea.

P. G. Wodehouse, *Sam the Sudden*

—Life is like a cup of tea.
—Why?
—Why not?

Interviewer and Walter Matthau

BELIEFS

Beliefs: those things we hold to be true,
despite evidence to the contrary.
Joseph O'Connor

I know what I believe. I will continue to articulate what I believe and what I believe—I believe what I believe is right.

George W. Bush

Well, who you gonna believe—me or your own eyes?

Chico Marx

I'll have to see him before I believe he's invisible.

Policeman, *The Invisible Man Returns*

You never believe nuttin'. You're one o' them septics.

Archie Bunker, *All in the Family*

I believe what I said yesterday. I don't know what I said, but I know what I think, and, er, I assume it's what I said.

Donald Rumsfeld, Secretary of Defense (YT)

He just can't believe what's not happening to him.

David Coleman

—If you believe in angels, then why not unicorns or leprechauns?
—Oh, Lisa, everyone knows leprechauns are extinct.

Lisa Simpson and Kent Brockman, *The Simpsons*

In real life, Diane Keaton believes in God. But she also believes that the radio works because there are tiny people inside it.

Woody Allen

AMERICAN CREDO

Americans believe ...

That a man will do anything for the woman he loves.

That all criminals get caught sooner or later.

That all girls educated in convents turn out in later life to be hell-raisers.

That all great men have illegible signatures.

That an Italian puts garlic in everything he eats, including coffee.

That something mysterious goes in the rooms back of chop suey restaurants.

That what draws men to horseraces is love of the sport.

That a brass band always makes one feel like marching.

That because a married woman stays loyal to her husband she loves him.

That all one has to do to gather a large crowd in New York is to stand on the curb a few moments and gaze intently at the sky.

That a working man always eats what is in his dinner pail with great relish.

That it is dangerous to drink out of a garden hose, since if one does one is likely to swallow a snake.

That when they drop anything on the floor in a canning factory they put it into the can without washing it, no matter how dirty the floor is.

That cows have very sad eyes.

That when one stands close to the edge of a dizzy altitude, one is seized peculiarly with an impulse to jump off.

That all nuns have entered convents because of unfortunate love affairs.

That a person's sensations while drowning are rather agreeable and that on the whole it is a very pleasant death.

H. L. Mencken and George Jean Nathan, extracts from *American Credo*

ASTROLOGY & SUPERSTITION

When you go to a mindreader, do you get half price?
David Letterman

I went to the tarot card reader and I said, "It's my birthday today, can you tell me what the cards say?" She said, "Sure: To Tim, Happy Birthday, love from Granny."
Tim Vine

—[*gazing into a crystal ball*] Do you know what I see when I look into this?
—Goldfish?
Edgar Bergen and Charlie McCarthy, *Stage Door Canteen*

Once a psychic said, "God bless you." I said, "I didn't sneeze." She looked deep into my eyes and said, "You will, eventually." And damn it if she wasn't right. Two days later I sneezed.
Ellen DeGeneres

I read in the paper that a clairvoyant in Chorley has set her house on fire. She'd left her crystal ball on the window ledge, the sun shone through, set fire to the curtains and that was that. I'm thinking she should have seen that coming.
Dave Spikey

One of the most astounding cases of clairvoyance is that of the noted Greek psychic, Achilles Loudos. Loudos realized that he had unusual powers by the age of ten, when he could lie in bed and, by concentrating, make his father's false teeth jump out of his mouth.
Woody Allen

We're psychopathic!   Amanda Marchant, after winning the telepathic task
                                 with her twin sister, *Big Brother 8* (U.K.)

I'm a peripheral visionary. I can see into the future but just way off to the side.
                                                          Steven Wright

Quasimodo predicted all of this.   Bobby Bacala, *The Sopranos*

That said, the inevitable failed to happen.
                                                          John Pulman

A black cat crossing your path signifies that the animal is going somewhere.
                                                          Groucho Marx

I'm not superstitious or anything like that, but I'll just hope we'll play our best
and put it in the lap of the Gods.
                                                          Terry Neill

I always used to put my right boot on first, and then obviously my right sock.
                                                          Barry Venison

It is bad luck to be superstitious.
                                                          Andrew W. Mathis

I'm a Leo. Leos don't believe in that astrology stuff.
                                                          Tom Neff

Scorpio (Oct. 24–Nov. 21): There will soon come a time when your happiness
depends on where and whether an enormous man catches a ball.
                                                          Horoscope, *The Onion*

A friend of mine said his girlfriend could never understand why people tap their
heads when they say, "Touch wood!"
                                                          Nick Wallis, BBC Radio

The only thing I'm superstitious about is 13 in a bed.
                                                          Joey Evans, *Pal Joey*

THE SUPERNATURAL

The supernatural is the natural not yet understood.
Elbert Hubbard

A wizard walks down a street and turns into a shop.

Anon.

Abra-ca-pocus!

Bugs Bunny

Pardon me, boy, is this the Transylvania station?

Dr. Frankenstein, *Young Frankenstein*

—Mummy, Mummy, what's a vampire?
—Shut up and eat your soup before it clots.

Anon.

I know there's no such thing as Dracula. You know there's no such thing as Dracula. But does Dracula know it?

Lou Costello, *Abbott and Costello Meet Frankenstein*

—But, Dracula, I thought you were having fun!
—Fun? How would you like to go around looking like a head waiter for 700 years?

Mr. Renfield and Count Dracula, *Love at First Bite*

Sometimes I have the devil of a job convincing ghosts they are actually dead.

Canon John Pearce-Higgins, on exorcism

—How much do you charge for haunting rooms?
—How many rooms?

Chic Johnson and Harry Selby, *Hellzapoppin'*

When I was younger, there was a house on my street that I thought was haunted. At night, you'd hear screams coming from all over the house ... plus, anyone who went in never came out. Later I found out it was just a murderer's house.

Jack Handey, *Deep Thoughts*

—Don't big empty houses scare you?
—Not me, I used to be in vaudeville.

Cicily and Wally Campbell, *The Cat and the Canary*

Doltergeist: a spirit that decides to haunt someplace stupid, such as your septic tank.

David Genser

I was walking down the street and I saw a dead baby ghost in the road. On reflection, it might have been a handkerchief.

Milton Jones

I went with an exorcist for a bit. I just want to know really practical things, like how do you hold someone possessed by the devil.

Keanu Reeves

—Have you any concrete evidence of ghosts?
—No. Very few ghosts are made of concrete.

Michael Bentine

Samuel Taylor Coleridge was asked, "Do you believe in ghosts?" "No, ma'am," he replied, "I've seen too many."

Lucy Finn

Not only did he not believe in ghosts, he wasn't even afraid of them.

Georg Christoph Lichtenberg

—There are spirits all around you.
—Well, could you put some in a glass with a little ice? I need it badly.

Miss Lu and Wally Campbell, *The Cat and the Canary*

GOD

A Russian astronaut and a Russian brain surgeon were once discussing religion. The brain surgeon was a Christian but the astronaut was not. The astronaut said, "I've been out in space many times but I've never seen God or angels." And the brain surgeon said, "And I've operated on many clever brains but I've never seen a single thought."

Jostein Gaarder, Sophie's World

I suppose God is a bit like the Loch Ness monster. Not a lot of people have seen him, but there's the odd photograph ... He doesn't look like a load of tires though.

Father Dougal, *Father Ted*

It's God—I'd have known Him by Blake's picture anywhere.

Robert Frost

My dear child, you must believe in God in spite of what the clergy tell you.

Benjamin Jowett

—I think God is everywhere.
—Even in liver?

Gabe Kotter and Arnold Horshack, *Welcome Back, Kotter*

Fortunately, God suffers fools gladly, I think. It's part of His job, and it's the only explanation I can think of for my own survival.

Mary Fairchild

I wish God were alive to see this.

Homer Simpson, *The Simpsons*

RELIGION—GENERAL

O senseless man, who wouldn't know how to make a maggot and yet will make gods by the dozen.

Michel de Montaigne

I definitely want Brooklyn to be christened, but I don't know into what religion.

David Beckham

—What's your religion?
—I pretty much just do whatever Oprah tells me to.

Tracy Jordan and Liz Lemon, *30 Rock*

She's one of those Seven Day Adventuresses ...

Constance Darg

Being a scientologist, when you drive past an accident it's not like anyone else. As you drive past you know you have to do something about it because you know you're the only one that can really help.

Tom Cruise (YT)

I did not marry the first girl I fell in love with because there was a tremendous religious conflict at the time. She was an atheist and I was an agnostic. We didn't know which religion not to bring the children up in.

Woody Allen

The one thing Father always gave up in Lent was going to church.

Clarence Day

I'm not Catholic, but I gave up picking my belly button for lint.

Emo Philips

I was much cheered, on my arrival [in prison], by the warder at the gate, who had to take particulars about me. He asked my religion and I replied, "Agnostic." He asked how to spell it, and remarked with a sigh, "Well, there are many religions, but I suppose they all worship the same God." This remark kept me cheerful for about a week.

Bertrand Russell, jailed in 1918 for antiwar activities

CHRISTIANITY

Born again? No, I'm not.
Excuse me for getting it right the first time.
Dennis Miller

—Now, Tommy, tell me what we must do before we can expect forgiveness of our sins.
—We gotta sin!   **Sunday school teacher and child**

My young daughter came home from Sunday school and asked, "Mummy, what did Moses do with the pills?" "Pills?" I puzzled. "What pills are you talking about?" She explained, "Teacher said that Moses brought the tablets down from Mount Sinai."   **Annabelle Kirby-Lee**

[*teaching Brian how to cross himself*] Spectacles, testicles, wallet and watch.
Charlie McManus, *Nuns on the Run*

—Is Jesus a man or is he a woman?
—He's neither a man nor woman.
—Wot? You mean he's a ladyman?

Ali G and the Bishop of Corsham, *The 11 O'Clock Show*

Jesus is the same as God, isn't he? A bit younger.

Neville, *Men Behaving Badly*

THE BIBLE

So far as I remember, there is not one word in the Gospels in praise
of intelligence.
Bertrand Russell

I know my gospels—Matthew, Mark, Luke and Jim.

Harvey Baines, *Waiting for God*

The Bible is an Irish book because it says that it all began at the beginning.

Dave Allen

If you drop a Bible on a field mouse, it'll kill it. So maybe the Bible's not all good.

Harry Hill

I like the Bible as a book. Just like I like *The Cat in the Hat*.

Marilyn Manson

At church the other Sunday, my four-year-old grandson watched a parishioner
go up to the lectern to read the lesson, and when he saw the huge Bible he
looked at his mother and exclaimed, "He's not going to read *all* of it, is he?"

Lord Carrington

Seeking a christening gift for my grandson in a well-known bookshop, I came
across a handsomely bound presentation Bible—highly suitable, except that the
print was too small. However, the assistant assured me that the book was ideal
for my purpose, since "it was not designed to be read."

David Hunt

I peeked at the end: The Devil did it.

Captain John "Trapper" McIntyre, *M*A*S*H*

What if Adam and Eve don't eat the apple? Worms eat the apple, obtain knowledge, and rule the planet. The Macarena and the high five are never invented.

Ned Bent

—My favorite Bible story is the rich man and the poor man.
—Is that the one where Jesus drives the moneylenders from the temple?
—There was no *cars* for Jesus. Cars wasn't invented in the olden days.

Seven-year-old girl and Bill Cosby, *Kids Say the Darndest Things*

—My favorite Bible story is the trick Jesus did at the wedding and turned water into wine.
—So tell me, what does that trick at the wedding teach us?
—The more wine you get, the better the wedding.

Sam, age eight, and Bill Cosby, *Kids Say the Darndest Things*

—And what's *your* favorite Bible story?
—The Three Little Pigs.

Bill Cosby and Jill, age six, *Kids Say the Darndest Things*

BIBLICAL BLOOPERS

The Jews were a proud people and throughout history they had trouble with unsympathetic Genitals.

When Mary heard she was the mother of Jesus, she sang the Magna Carta.

Lot's wife looked back at the city and was turned into a pillow of salt.

Moses went up to Mount Cyanide to get the Ten Commandments.

David was a Hebrew king who was skilled at playing the liar.

Solomon, one of David's sons, had 300 wives and 700 porcupines.

CATHOLIC

Why should we take advice on sex from the Pope?
If he knows anything about it, he shouldn't.
George Bernard Shaw

Like most Irish people, I was born a Catholic. This came as a big shock to my parents, who were Jewish. **Michael Redmond**

For a long time I thought I wanted to be a nun. Then I realized that what I really wanted to be was a lesbian. **Mabel Maney**

Crucifixes are sexy because there's a naked man on them. **Madonna**

I think it's rather unfair on priests that they're not allowed to get married. I think that if a priest meets another priest and they like one another they should be allowed to marry. **Dave Allen**

—It used to be common enough. The favorite son would become a doctor, and the idiot brother would be sent off to the priesthood.
—Your brother's a doctor, isn't he, Ted?
Father Ted and Father Dougal, *Father Ted*

—What was that sermon about?
—Sorry, Ted, I was concentrating too hard on looking holy.
Father Ted and Father Dougal, *Father Ted*

We were discussing the possibility of making one of our cats Pope recently and we decided that the fact that she was not Italian and was female made the third point, that she was a cat, quite irrelevant.
Katharine Whitehorn

I'd love a Chinese Pope to be elected. Can you imagine receiving Holy Communion from a Chinese Pope? You'd kneel down and he'd go, "Ah, you going to have this here, or take away?"
Dave Allen

The Vatican announcement carried no explanation for the resignation, which in Vatican terms means the decision was prompted from above.
Journal Star

JEW

With all the Jewish comics in the world, how come Israel doesn't
have a Laughing Wall?
Lotus Weinstock

We Jews believe it was Santa Claus who killed Jesus Christ.

Kinky Friedman

—Are you Jewish?
—No. I'm half-Irish, half-Italian, half-Mexican.

Dave Buznick and Chuck, *Anger Management*

—I've always wanted to be Jewish.
—Really, how come?
—Well, I just think that Jewish women have got really nice clothes, you know,
like Chanel suits and expensive things.

Shanessa Reilly and Jonty Stern, *Big Brother 8* (U.K.)

Jews are like everyone else, only more so.

Jewish saying

—How come so many doctors are Jewish?
—Because their mothers are.

Sophia Petrillo and Doctor Harris, *The Golden Girls*

On Easter Sunday, when my pious neighbors were on their way to church, I put
a large sign in my store window: "Christ Has Risen—But Our Prices Remain the
Same."

Herschel Bloom

You elect me the first Jewish governor of Texas, I'll reduce the speed limit to
54.95.

Kinky Friedman, running for election

Who is Yom Kippur? Is that the name of the new Japanese designer?

Kathy Ireland, model

[Kabbalah] helps you confront your fears. Like, if a girl borrowed my clothes
and never gave them back, and I saw her wearing them months later, I would
confront her.

Paris Hilton

I think that Kabbalah is very punk rock.

Madonna

—Wicca's a Hollywood fad.
—That's Kabbalah, you jerk.

Bart and Lisa Simpson, *The Simpsons*

—Are you religious?
—I guess ... I guess I'm a nonpracticing Jew.
—Hey, I'm a nonpracticing virgin!

Lelaina and Michael, *Reality Bites*

Everybody blames the Jews for killing Christ. And then the Jews try to pass it off on the Romans. I'm one of the few people who believe it was the blacks.

Sarah Silverman

And I reflected on how "Torah" and "Koran" are spelled, realizing that the two religions differ not one bit in the middle, only at the fringes.

Leonard Greenberg

My God! It's enough to drive a girl into a convent! Do they have Jewish nuns?

Sally Bowles, *Cabaret*

ATHEIST

Atheism: a nonprophet organization.
Anon.

Being an atheist is tough. It makes it really hard to be polite, especially after someone next to you sneezes.

John Maclain

When I told the people of Northern Ireland that I was an atheist, a woman in the audience stood up and asked if the God I didn't believe in was Catholic or Protestant.

Quentin Crisp

An Irish atheist is one who wishes to God he could believe in God.

John P. Mahaffy

IMMORTALITY

If Shaw and Einstein couldn't beat death, what chance have I got?
Mel Brooks

—If you could live forever, would you and why?
—I would not live forever, because we should not live forever, because if we were supposed to live forever, then we would live forever, but we cannot live forever, which is why I would not live forever.
Miss Alabama, during the 1994 Miss USA contest

I plan to live forever, or die trying.
Vila Restal, *Blake's 7*

AFTERLIFE

An intelligent hell would be better than a stupid paradise.
Victor Hugo

"Where will you go after you die?" said a samurai to Zen master Hakuin. "How am I supposed to know?" replied Hakuin. "But you're a Zen master!" cried the samurai. "Yes," said Hakuin, "but not a dead one." **Anon.**

Is there an afterlife? Well, there's an afterbirth, so why shouldn't there be an afterlife?
Kevin McAleer

What do we know about the beyond? Do we know what's behind the beyond? I'm afraid some of us hardly know what's beyond the behind.
"Brother" Theodore Gottlieb

When I die, I hope to go to heaven, wherever the hell that is.
Ayn Rand

My young son asked me what happens after we die. I told him we get buried under a bunch of dirt and worms eat our bodies. I guess I should have told him the truth—that most of us go to Hell and burn eternally—but I didn't want to upset him.

Art Grinath

Bigots say that all gay people are going to hell. If that's true, I'd like to see how everyone in heaven's going to get their hair done.

Judy Carter

REINCARNATION

Well, this was fun. Let's do it again sometime.
Quniaron Bellthing, epitaph

—Do you believe people come back from the dead?
—You mean like Republicans?

Cicily and Wally Campbell, *The Cat and the Canary*

Reincarnation: born again as a tin of condensed milk.

I'm Sorry I Haven't a Clue

Reintarnation: coming back to life as a hillbilly.

Barry Blyveis

You know me as a performer, but in truer life I would have been a bee. It's a lovely lifestyle. I like honey, flowers, the fur coat and all the colors. And the hours are good, too.

Alistair McGowan

I always had a thought that I might have been Shakespeare in another life.

Quentin Tarantino

In one of history's more absurd acts of totalitarianism, China has banned Buddhist monks in Tibet from reincarnating without government permission.

Newsweek

I don't believe in reincarnation, and I didn't believe in it when I was a hamster.

Shane Richie

HISTORY

If it wasn't for the Enlightenment, you wouldn't be reading this
right now. You'd be standing in a smock,
throwing turnips at a witch.
Charlie Brooker

As Henry VIII said to each of his three wives, "I won't keep you long."
Ronald Reagan

—July 19th ... any idea why that should be important?
—Would it be the day the Ice Age ended?
Father Ted and Father Dougal, *Father Ted*

After supper she got out her book and learned me about Moses and the
Bulrushers; and I was in a sweat to find out all about him; but by and by she let
it out that Moses had been dead a considerable long time; so then I didn't care
no more about him; because I don't take no stock in dead people.
Mark Twain, *Huckleberry Finn*

I really dig Hannibal. Hannibal had real guts. He rode elephants into Cartilage.

Mike Tyson

For ten years Caesar ruled with an iron hand. Then with a wooden foot, and
finally with a piece of string.

Spike Milligan

—Wow, an apothecary table! What period is it from?
—Uh, it's from ... yore. Like, the days of yore, you know.
Phoebe Buffay and Rachel Green, *Friends*

What if Martin Luther were alive today? The Wittenberg door might be covered
with 95 little yellow sticky notes. **Michael Jahr**

I have a theory that hieroglyphics are just an ancient comic strip about a
character named Sphinxy. **Harry Burns,** *When Harry Met Sally*

What would alien anthropologists conclude about us if they arrived on Earth a million years from now and found only plastic bubble wrap? "Wow, near the end they must have sold air by the cubic inch! Poor wretches."

Dave Curtis

It was to one of my ancestors that King Harold, at the Battle of Hastings, spoke his very last words. He said, "Watch where you're pointing that bow and arrow, you'll have somebody's eye out in a minute."

Ronnie Corbett

If history is going to repeat itself, I should think we can expect the same thing again.

Terry Venables

The Ottoman Empire, what was this? A whole empire based on putting your feet up?

Jerry Seinfeld

It's a little-known fact that the tan became popular in what is known as the Bronze Age.

Cliff Clavin, *Cheers*

Many people think that Joan of Arc was immortal but she did in fact exist.

Douggie Brown

They all laughed at Joan of Arc, but she went right ahead and built it.

Gracie Allen

Joan of Arc was a maid of New Orleans who was burnt to a steak.

Schoolboy's blooper

He thought Richard the Lionheart was the first transplant.

Sara Mills

My wife was a very ignorant woman. For years she thought the Charge of the Light Brigade was the electricity bill.

Les Dawson

I think we all agree, the past is over.

George W. Bush

I never even knew where Rome was. That's how good I was at history.

Rick Parfitt

The 1970s and 80s—you're not missing anything. There's a gas shortage and A Flock of Seagulls. That's about it.

Austin Powers, *Austin Powers:
The Spy Who Shagged Me*

What does Grace know about Cambodia? She thinks Khmer Rouge is make-up.

Will Truman, *Will & Grace*

And today will go down in history as January 17, 1991.

DJ, Classic Gold Radio (U.K.)

You have a real feel for the history of the past, don't you?

Derek Jameson

The American people are proud to welcome Your Majesty back to the United States—a nation you've come to know very well. You dined with *ten* U.S. presidents. You helped our nation celebrate its bicentennial in 176– in 1976. [*Realizing he has just added 200 years to the Queen's age, the President halts and looks sheepishly across at Her Majesty who, in true royal style, had politely been pretending not to have heard his gaffe. But when he does not resume his speech, she does look over at him.*] She gave me a look that only a mother could give a child.

George W. Bush, to Queen Elizabeth II (YT)

Whenever I reflect upon the events of the summer of 1776, I feel thankful that I wasn't one of the Founding Fathers. Mainly because I'd be dead now.

David Gunter

My wife's great grandfather was actually killed at Custer's Last Stand. He didn't actually take part in the fighting; he was camping nearby and went over to complain about the noise.

Ronnie Corbett

The Holocaust was an obscene period in our nation's history. I mean in this century's history. But we all lived in this century. I didn't live in this century.

Dan Quayle

People always ask me, "Where were you when Kennedy was shot?" Well, I don't actually have an alibi.

Emo Philips

Am I the only one to think that John F. Kennedy was killed by a peanut allergy? You may laugh, but there was an empty packet of KP Dry Roasted found on the grassy knoll.

Harry Hill

I can remember exactly what I was doing when I heard the news. I was listening to the news.

Hugh Laurie, *A Bit of Fry and Laurie*

When I asked her where she was when Kennedy was shot she said, "Ted Kennedy was shot?!"

Harry Burns, *When Harry Met Sally*

THE FUTURE

Neither a wise man nor a brave man lies down on the tracks of history to wait for the train of the future to run over him.
Dwight D. Eisenhower

You know what I'm really looking forward to? The future.

Doc Hibbert, *The Simpsons*

The future isn't what it used to be.

Yogi Berra

Don't tell me about the future … It's the same as anywhere else … Just the same old stuff in faster cars and smellier air.

Douglas Adams, *Mostly Harmless*

I'm going to make a prediction: It could go either way.

Ron Atkinson

I would not say that the future is necessarily less predictable than the past—I think the past was not predictable when it started.

Donald Rumsfeld, Secretary of Defense (YT)

The most surprising thing that happened to me was when I had a plane crash. I didn't expect that—no one warned me.

Frankie Dettori

The future will be better tomorrow.

Dan Quayle

THE BODY

APPEARANCE— GENERAL

A face unclouded by thought.
Lillian Hellman, on Norma Shearer

For one dollar, I'll guess your weight, your height or your sex.
Navin R. Johnson, *The Jerk*

[*introducing two entirely normal men of average build*] Ladies and gentlemen ... this is the world's greatest novelty: the Pronkwonk twins—Redwood and Brentwood! Redwood is the smallest giant in the world, while his brother, Brentwood, is the largest midget in the world. They baffle science.
Larson E. Whipsnade, *You Can't Cheat an Honest Man*

How long have you had that birthmark?
W. C. Fields

Are you eating a tomato, or is that your nose?
Charlie McCarthy, to W. C. Fields, *You Can't Cheat an Honest Man*

Thanks, you don't look so hot yourself.
Yogi Berra, after being told that he looked cool

My cousin's built like Sophia Loren. Boy, is he embarrassed about it.
Larry Hovis, *Rowan & Martin's Laugh-in*

I have the brain of an eagle, the heart of a lion, the engorged member of a rampant hippopotamus: All I need now is some glue.
Simon Munnery

—Just look straight into the camera.
—I can't do that. That's my bad side.
Photographer and unnamed celebrity

How can someone with glasses so thick be so stupid?
Bart Simpson, *The Simpsons*

—Must you wear glasses?
—Oh, no, sir. Only when I want to see.
"Coach" Wheeler and "Junior" Jackson, *That's My Boy*

If only faces could talk!   Pat Summerall

Men's legs have a terribly lonely life—standing in the dark in your trousers all day.   Ken Dodd

No amount of junk food or Coca-Cola can change your skin. And if, God forbid, it does, have a great makeup artist standing by.
Paris Hilton, *Confessions of an Heiress*

She was a red head. No hair, just a red head.   Les Dawson

HAIR

I'm not offended by dumb-blonde jokes because I know I'm not dumb. I also know I'm not blonde.
Dolly Parton

—What's the difference between a blonde and a shopping trolley?
—A shopping trolley has a mind of its own.   **Anon.**

Blondes are not dumb. If you want to make me angry, try telling me I'm stupid … I know for a fact that I have a higher IQ than 99 percent of brunettes.
Hayden Panettiere

Did you hear about the blonde who got a pair of water skis? She's still looking for a lake with a slope.   **Anon.**

The only way you can tell a woman's true hair color is by her vagina.
I caught a glimpse of Pamela Anderson's backstage while she was changing, and I can tell you, her true hair color is: bald, totally bald.
Sarah Silverman

I'm waxed clean—hairless as the day I was born. But don't say, "Tia has no pubic hair." That's so clinical. Use a nice euphemism. Say, "She mowed her secret garden," or, "She's cleared the way to the Promised Land."
Tia Carrere

Earlier this year I had my hair feng shuied.   **Jerry Hall**

Sometimes you like to let the hair do the talking.

James Brown, The Godfather of Soul

There are times when I flick through magazines and think I'm in danger of becoming a prisoner of my own hair.

Brian May, of Queen

—Frank, with your long hair, from where I'm sitting, you could be a woman.
—With your wooden leg, from where I'm sitting, you could be a table.

Disabled interviewer and Frank Zappa

Yeah, there was a mouse living in my hair for a brief time. Elvis was his name— not innately—I gave that name to him.

Russell Brand

Change your hairstyle all the time … Tell everyone you're wearing hair extensions even if you aren't, because they don't expect you to tell them.

Paris Hilton, *Confessions of an Heiress*

I recorded my hair this morning. Tonight, I'm watching the highlights.

Jay London

—I went to your dad's barbershop today. I didn't know that haircuts hurt.
—Haircuts don't hurt.
—I fell out of the chair.

Charlie Brown and Rerun Van Pelt, *Peanuts*

—Did you ever make any mistakes cutting people's hair?
—When I was training, I cut someone's necklace off.

Brian Dowling and Helen Adams, *Big Brother 2* (U.K.)

A competition hairdresser is a completely different breed. He looks in five dimensions.

Hairdresser, *Hair Wars*

A follically challenged superstar who shall be nameless was staying at a hotel when a hairdresser turned up. The superstar's PR said, "I'm sorry, he's checked out." "But he can't have!" cried the hairdresser. "I've come to do his hair!" "Oh, don't worry," said the PR, "he's left his hair."

Stuart Maconie

He doesn't dye his hair; he bleaches his face.

Johnny Carson, on Ronald Reagan

—Are you losing your hair?
—No, I'm growing my forehead.

Luke Currano

The worst thing a man can do is to go bald. Never let yourself go bald.

Donald Trump

I'm not actually bald. It's just that I'm taller than my hair.

Clive Anderson

I'm fascinated that hair grows after death. I'm looking forward to that.

Clive Anderson

I was going to buy a book on hair loss, but the pages kept falling out.

Jay London

—Do you like my new toupee?
—Oh, my God, I thought it was a yachting cap!

Cyril Ritchard and Noël Coward

The hair is real, it's the head that's a fake.   **Steve Allen**

Better a bald head than no head at all.

Seumas MacManus

Don't point that beard at me, it might go off.

Groucho Marx

It's not a beard. It's an animal I've trained to sit very still.

Bill Bailey

—D'you think I should keep the beard?
—I think you should keep the beard and lose the rest of you.
Mel Cooley and Buddy Sorrell, *The Dick Van Dyke Show*

HEIGHT

Never trust a man with short legs.
Brains too near their bottoms.
Noël Coward

He's even smaller in real life than he is on the track.

David Coleman

Have you always been small?

Derek Thompson

In the rear, the small diminutive figure of Shoaib Mohammed who can't be much taller or shorter than he is.

Henry Blofeld

I don't think that there's anyone bigger or smaller than Maradona.

Kevin Keegan

Not just jockeys, I think all small people should have to wear a number.

Harry Hill

The Pope was smaller than expected, but only in size.

Jack Charlton

A lot of people have asked me how short I am. Since my last divorce, I think I'm about $100,000 short.

Mickey Rooney

BEAUTY

Any girl can be glamorous. All you have to do is stand still
and look stupid.
Hedy Lamarr

Oh, my God, if I cover my good eye you look just like Courteney Cox!

Jack Donaghy, *30 Rock*

—I haven't been this excited since I got the card saying I'd won a beauty contest, do you remember?
—We were playing Monopoly at the time, weren't we?

Alice Tinker and Rev. Geraldine Grainger, *The Vicar of Dibley*

As Miss America, my goal is to bring peace to the entire world and then get my own apartment.

Jay Leno

Sign of an incompetent Miss America contestant: Asked which person she admires most, she says, "My plastic surgeon."

Sue Lin Chong

I can't believe we still have the Miss America pageant. This is America! Where we're not supposed to judge people based on how they look; we're supposed to judge people based on how much money they make.

Heidi Joyce

Miss World is still a popular contest even though it's had its fair share of knockers.

Julia Morley

—Do you think I could be Miss World?
—Depends on whose world we're talking about.

Anne Robinson and contestant, *The Weakest Link*

She used to be Miss World—Miss Carpet World.

Mrs. Merton

Why is it that the winner of the Miss Universe contest always comes from Earth?

Rich Hall

I've always been a big fan of beauty. Sure, you can't judge a book by its cover, but who wants to have sex with a book?

Stephen Colbert

It was God who made me so beautiful. If I weren't, then I'd be a teacher.

Linda Evangelista

I'm more handsome than I act.

Garry Shandling

UGLY

Plain women know more about men than beautiful ones do.
Katharine Hepburn

We used to play Spin the Bottle when I was a kid. A girl would spin the bottle and if it pointed to you when it stopped, the girl could either kiss you or give you a dime. By the time I was 14, I owned my own home.

Gene Perret

Shary Bobbins and I were engaged to be wed back in the old country. Then she got her eyesight back.

Groundskeeper Willie, *The Simpsons*

Darling, let me cover your face in kisses! On second thoughts, just let me cover your face.

Groucho Marx

When I called my gynecologist for an appointment, he said, "How about you just describe yourself over the phone."

Judith E. Cottrill

I've been called ugly, pug ugly, fugly, pug fugly, but never ugly ugly.

Moe Syzslak, *The Simpsons*

God, what gorgeous staff I have. I just can't understand those who have ugly people working for them.

Jade Jagger

COSMETIC SURGERY

A woman went to a plastic surgeon and asked him to make her like Bo Derek. He gave her a lobotomy.
Joan Rivers

—What's new, Norm?
—Most of my wife.

Sam Malone and Norm Peterson, *Cheers*

—I paid four grand a breast for my wife's boob job.
—How much did that cost you, then?

Boycie and Trigger, *Only Fools and Horses*

Our breasts are bigger than before—we've gone from a 34A to a 34C. We are proud of our breasts like a man would be with a new Ferrari.

Gabriela Irimia, of British pop duo The Cheeky Girls

How do you not just topple over?

John Lydon, to British model Jordan

Years ago, I asked my dad for a boob job and he said it would cheapen my image.

Paris Hilton

She's had her face lifted. It's not safe to leave anything lying about these days, is it?

Jimmy Fallon

I think that the longer I look good, the better gay men feel.

Cher

—I've had five reconstructive surgeries.
—I knew you made love like an ugly woman.

Celeste Cunningham and Jack Donaghy, *30 Rock*

After a period of years, the new skin gets older and older.

Unnamed Doctor

His forehead was so wrinkled, he had to screw his hat on.

Carlton Alsop

—I wouldn't want to have plastic surgery. I pad my bra with chicken fillets.
—Ugh. Don't they smell?

Cindy Ferguson and Tracey Blake

I did get my balls done … I got them unwrinkled. It's the new thing in Hollywood—ball ironing.

George Clooney, *Esquire* magazine

The only way to look younger is not to be born so soon.

Charles M. Schulz

FASHION

You can't think with your clothes on.
Florence Allen

I bet living in a nudist colony takes all the fun out of Halloween.
Jason Steinhorn

Red is the new green!
Slogan, British Red Cross

Green is the new red!
Peter Tatchell

Does fashion matter? Always—though not quite as much after death.
Joan Rivers

I never follow fashion just because it's fashionable.
Coleen McLoughlin, wife of Wayne Rooney

I shop in secondhand shops ... I had this little black straw boater, fingerless gloves and Doc Marten shoes spray-painted silver with glitter ... Maybe the final straw came when I decided to use a kettle for a handbag.
Ashley Jensen

My grandma was like, "Oh, Christina, you look like a whore!" I explained that's the idea.
Christina Aguilera

Those hot pants of hers were so damned tight, I could hardly breathe.
Benny Hill

I dress sexily—but not in an obvious way. Sexy in a virginal way. Victoria Beckham

I'm surprised there aren't more celebrities in burqas. You wouldn't have to work out. You could let yourself go. We should design a nonreligious celebrity burqa with a floral print.
Kate Beckinsale

I always thought a yashmak was a bloody silly idea. If a woman's got a pretty face she should show it. The only thing I *would* advocate is a gag if she talked too much.
Gerald Durrell, *Fillets of Plaice*

If it becomes illegal to wear the veil at work, beekeepers will be furious.

Milton Jones

By Jove, missus! What a beautiful day for turning a Scotsman upside down and saying, "How's that for a lampshade!"

Ken Dodd

Is there anything worn under the kilt? No, it's all in perfect working order.

Spike Milligan

—Why did the blonde take her new scarf back to the store?
—Because it was too tight.   Anon.

My girlfriend has crabs. I bought her fishnet stockings.   **Jay London**

She has so many clothes, she never wears the same outfit once.

Gretchen Berra

Real diamonds! They must be worth their weight in gold!

Sugar Kane Kowalczyk, *Some Like It Hot*

You couldn't tell if she was dressed for an opera or an operation.

Irvin S. Cobb

An article about Ivana Trump and her spending habits misstated the number of bras she buys. It is two dozen black, two dozen beige and two dozen white, not two thousand of each.

Correction, *The New York Times*

If I'm wearing a bra that doesn't match the knickers, I feel like I'm walking with a limp.   **Elle Macpherson**

I don't know my hat size. I'm not in shape yet.   **Yogi Berra**

Some of you may be wondering why I'm wearing this shirt. It's because, if I didn't, I'd be naked from the waist up.

Demetri Martin

Monks are the acceptable face of hoodies.
Mark Radcliffe, *Radcliffe and Maconie*, BBC Radio

—Have you got a hoodie?
—Actually, I've been circumcised.   **Sue White and Dr. Dear, *Green Wing***

I just got some new pajamas with pockets in them. Which is great, because before that I used to have to hold stuff when I slept.   Demetri Martin

There were nine buttons on her nightgown, but she could only fascinate.
Homer Haynes

I lost a buttonhole.   **Steven Wright**

I wonder why everyone dressed old-fashioned in those days. They don't do it now.   **Kathy Anderson, *Father Knows Best***

I went into this bar and sat down next to a pretty girl. She looked at me and said, "Hey, you have two different colored socks on." I said, "Yeah, I know, but to me they're the same because I go by thickness."
Steven Wright

Everyone notices nice shoes. They are like windows to the soul.
Natasha Hamilton, of British pop group Atomic Kitten

My shoes are size 2½—the same size as my feet.   **Elaine Paige**

—What made you think I was gay?
—Your shoes ... Those shoes are definitely bi-curious.
Liz Lemon and Jack Donaghy, *30 Rock*

At the end of the day, you've got to have the balls to be feminine.
Susannah Constantine, *What Not to Wear* (U.K.)

HEALTH & MEDICINE

It's too bad that stupidity isn't painful.
Anton Szandor LaVey

—Mr. Brown, I'm going to sneeze.
—At who?
—At-choo!

Jim Copp and Ed Brown

—It's probably rhinovirus.
— OH, MY GOD! What's *that*?
—A cold.

Dr. Gregory House and patient, *House*

I look out for any slightest symptoms of bird flu in my family. I'm watching like a hawk.

Nguyen Thanh Hung

You might get bird flu if you ate ground-up turkey droppings on your cornflakes for a week, or there again you might not.

Boris Johnson, mayor of London

Oh, love, can you get me some of that cunnilinctus for my cough?

Edna Steele

My son complains about headaches. I tell him all the time: When you get out of bed, it's feet first.

Henny Youngman

My whole family's lactose-intolerant; when we take pictures we can't say "cheese."

Jay London

I tell ya, life is tough. For years I was getting a ringing in my ears. It's getting worse. Now I'm getting busy signals.

Rodney Dangerfield

Sir Freddie Laker said, "You should have regular checkups. You need to go to the doctor and ask him to stick his finger up your bum. He'll be able to tell you what's what ... When you're bent over and the doctor's got his finger up your bum, make sure that he hasn't got both his hands on your shoulders."

Sir Richard Branson

I feel like I lost my virginity that day in so many ways.

Ben Affleck, on trying colonic irrigation

Next to gold and jewelry, health is the most important thing you can have.

Phyllis Diller

I'm very healthy. When you clean toilets for ten years, it's like one big vaccine for everything.

Lewis Kiniski, *The Drew Carey Show*

This guy is so fit, he'll be in good health two years after he's dead.

Captain Benjamin "Hawkeye" Pierce, *M*A*S*H*

You know she's got a cyst on her aviary.

Dorothy Mair

When my grandfather fell ill, my grandmother covered his back with lard. After that, he went downhill very quickly.

Milton Jones

My Auntie Marge has been ill for so long now that we've changed her name to "I Can't Believe She's Not Better."

Jeff Green

After her accident, my nan had a plastic hip put in, but I thought they should have replaced it with a slinky, coz if she did fall down the stairs again …

Steve Williams

Blood?! That should be on the inside!

Fielding Mellish, *Bananas*

It hurt the way your tongue hurts after you accidentally staple it to the wall.

Brian Broadus

I can stand anything but pain!   **Lester Marton, *The Band Wagon***

—I thought chicken soup was the universal cure-all.

—Not for flesh wounds.

Rick and A. J. Simon, *Simon & Simon*

The trouble with heart disease is that the first symptom is often sudden death, and that's a very hard symptom to deal with.

Unnamed doctor

Don't worry about your heart; it will last as long as you live.

W. C. Fields

She's in perfect condition except for one thing: She's dead.

Dr. Quincy, *Quincy*

I tried to give blood the other day. But the blood bank wouldn't take it. They wanted to know where I got it from.   Wally Wang

—What kind of blood do proofreaders have?
—Type O.   Rosemarie Jarski

—Where's the alimentary canal?
—I think it's somewhere in Africa.   Melissa and Susan Clough

The President has painful hemorrhoids and is being treated by his physician, Rear Admiral ... er, Rear Admiral William Lookass ... Lukash?

Newscaster

—He's in hospital for an operation on his piles.
—Poor man, he has had a rough passage this year.

Parishioner and Rev. Evans

Little Lucy had a cough and wanted some medicine. She tried in vain to take the lid off the cough syrup bottle. I explained to her that it was a childproof cap and I'd have to do it for her. She stared at me, wide-eyed, and said, "Mummy, how does it know it's me?"   Alison Coates

My little lad, Leo, twisted his leg badly playing football. I took him to casualty and they strapped it up. Arriving home, his mum asked him how he'd got on at the hospital. "I had to sit on a table and then they x-rated me," he explained.

Carl Firth

The doctors x-rayed my head and found nothing.

Dizzy Dean, after being hit on the head by a baseball

—What other health problems do you have?
—My heart doesn't beat.   Lawyer and witness,
actual transcript from official court records

—I've got high blood pressure and water retention. You know what that gives you?

—Boiling water?

Sheila and Bren Furlong, *Dinnerladies*

Getting an angina attack 300 meters from the top of Everest was a pain in the neck.

Sir Ranulph Fiennes

—He's got a nosebleed?

—Where?

Chris New, overheard, *The Graham Norton Show*

We're concerned about AIDS inside our White House—make no mistake about it.

George W. Bush

When God gives you AIDS—and God does give you AIDS—make lemon-AIDS!

Sarah Silverman

They're saying you can catch AIDS from a mosquito. I say if your dick is small enough to screw a mosquito, why the hell would you wanna live?

Anon.

NURSE

ACTUAL EXTRACTS FROM NURSES' EXAM PAPERS

The heart is an organ the shape of a heart.

Blood is a red vicious liquid containing solids and salts.

Blood is returned from the head by the juggler vein.

From the kidneys lead two ducks, these find their way into the bladder.

The human body is covered with mussels, some of which we can move when we want to, others we can't.

The large intestine terminates at the anus where it is guarded by a spinster.

The medulla oblong garter is an important structure and is gray or white in color.

The ear is the organ of earing.

Wax glands in the ear protect the organ from foreigners.

The large intestines are in the elementary track.

As most men cannot have babies their pelvises are somewhat rigid compared with childbearing females.

The male organ of degeneration is called a penis.

If a patient is found to be suffering from poison an anecdote should be found as soon as possible.

The patient was admitted with a sebaceous sister in his scrotal sac.

The fits she had been having regularly were thought to be historical and not epileptic.

Junior nurses were warned to give nothing sugared, the patient being a diabolic.

In coronary thrombosis the severity of the attack depends on the sight of the clot.

The nurse must never be instructed to apply the tourniquet over the patient's bear skin.

Olive oil is injected into the rectum using a tube and funnel, nurse will follow this later along with a soap and water enema.

The genteel organ is washed next, making sure it is thoroughly dried.

—What can be done to ease a patient's sore throat?
—The soreness of a patient's throat can be eased with a gargoyle.

Two bronchos entered the lungs via a depression.

Owing to coughing, the patient may become a little horse.

The patient was given an expectorant for his coffin.

The patient had a crop of blockheads all over his face.

The patient did not look well, and said she felt offal.

Food should not be picked up by hand but with tongues.

A specimen of urine is taken, tested and then placed in the patient's notes.

—What can be done to aid the patient's recovery?
—Artificial restoration may help the patient to recover.

Respiration is when the patient breathes in and then expires.

The patient recovered in spite of the treatment.

DENTIST

Never go to a dentist with blood in his hair.
Willy Rushton

—Ron, rush upstairs and fetch me your mother's toothbrush.
—What do you want with Mother's toothbrush?
—I've got my new suede shoes on and I've trodden in something.
Pa and Ron Glum, *The Glums*

In life, a person has three sets of teeth: a) Temporary; b) Permanent; c) False.
Nurse's examination paper

Now, have you ever had this tooth pulled before? **W. C. Fields**

Dentist's favorite hymn: "Crown Him With Many Crowns" **William R. Long**

DOCTOR

What do doctors know? They practice medicine for
15 years and they still don't know to warm their hands
before a breast examination.
Sophia Petrillo, The Golden Girls

—Doctor, doctor! I keep thinking that I'm a lady who delivers babies!
—It's all right, you're just going through a midwife crisis.   **Anon.**

To avoid delay, please have all your symptoms ready.
                                              Sign in a doctor's waiting room

Avoid waiting for a doctor's appointment by making one for nine o'clock every morning. If you wake up feeling well, simply phone up and cancel it.
                                                              Viz **magazine**

My doctor once said to me, "Do you think I'm here for the good of your health?"
                                                              Bob Monkhouse

How are you? You should have two of everything down the sides and one of everything down the middle.   **Ken Dodd**

—You know why I wanted to become a doctor?
—Flattering drawstring pants?
                                              Ben and Jinx, *Buffy the Vampire Slayer*

I told my doctor, "It hurts when I do this." He said, "Don't do that."
                                                              Henny Youngman

You're pushing your stethoscope too far in your ears, Doctor. I think it scratched your brain.   **Lieutenant Colonel Henry Blake,** *M*A*S*H*

—Doctor, doctor, I keep thinking I'm a teepee and a wigwam.
—Calm down, you're two tents.   **Anon.**

I went to my doctor with a sore foot. He said, "I'll have you walking in an hour." He did. He stole my car.   **Henny Youngman**

—What happened when you took the medicine the doctor had prescribed for you?
—Well, sir, it gave me vomiting and gonorrhea.
                                              Lawyer and witness, actual transcript
                                              from official court records

So I went to the doctor's. He said, "You've got hypochondria." I said, "Not that as well!"   **Tim Vine**

—What you've got is a classic case of insomnia.
—Oh, no. I knew it was something terrible! Okay, give it to me straight. How long have I got?

—Fifty, maybe sixty, years.
—Fifty or sixty years? Oh, my God, a slow death!
Larry and Balki, *Perfect Strangers*

Hey, this man is not breathing! Don't people usually breathe?
Homer Simpson, *The Simpsons*

Oh, my God, I think he's had a heart attack! Does anyone know how to give artificial insemination?
Martin Peel

—Could you go for a doctor?
—Sure, send him in!
Vicomte Gilbert de Vareze and Countess Valentine, *Love Me Tonight*

—I'll give him artificial respiration.
—Artificial? For what you charge, you should give him the real thing.
Moe and Larry (The Three Stooges), *Sweet and Hot*

I visited my local GP last week complaining of a sore throat and stiff neck. Imagine my surprise on being told I had absent mindedly swallowed a flute.
Danny Keough, *Viz* **magazine**

[*treating a patient with frostbite*] Look, writing your name in the snow with your pee is good, drunken fun when your name is something like Joe Smith, but when your name is Stanislav Kasacinski and it's ten below out, you're just frostbite waiting to happen.
Dr. John Becker, *Becker*

—The doctor had to remove a bottle from the man's back passage.
—How did he swallow that, then?
Carl Johnson and Ellen Birch

I went to my doctor and told him, "My penis is burning." He said, "That means somebody's talking about it."
Garry Shandling

My love is like a red, red ... well, see for yourself, Doctor.
I'm Sorry I Haven't a Clue

Stroke Patients: Don't Feel Alone.
Notice in doctor's waiting room

Sign of an incompetent doctor: Asks if you have an allergy to placebos.
Daniel Dunn

The trouble with being a hypochondriac these days is that antibiotics have cured all the good diseases.
Caskie Stinnett

Is glandular fever a good disease or a bad disease?

Presenter, BBC Radio

My father invented a cure for which there was no known disease—unfortunately my mother caught the cure and died of it.

Victor Borge

Women are more prone to premenstrual tension.   **Dr. J. McCormack**

I never had PMS. I had a BMW.   **Rose Nylund, *The Golden Girls***

Fibroids? Isn't that a breakfast cereal?   **Victoria Wood**

Volunteers are being given fake placebos.

Derek Jameson

I went to the doctor last week. I said, "Can I have some sleeping pills for the wife?" He said, "Why?" I said, "She's woke up."

Les Dawson

A blonde goes to the doctor's and says, "Doctor, you have to help me, I hurt all over!" "Can you be more specific?" he says. So she touches her right knee with her finger. "Ouch!" she cries. Then she touches her forehead. "Ouch!" And then she touches her neck. "Ouch!" "I think I know what's wrong with you," says the doctor. "You've broken your finger."   **Anon.**

What's great about aspirin is that no matter how long you suck on it, it never loses its flavor.   **Gregg Rogell**

—Doctor, doctor, there's a strawberry growing out the top of my head.
—I'll give you some cream to put on that.   **Anon.**

—What if I die during the operation?
—You're not going to die!
—You know, I'd settle for even one more day. God knows why. Tomorrow I'm cleaning out the closets.

Sophia Petrillo and Dorothy Zbornak, *The Golden Girls*

—The treatment comes in three stages.
—Let's get this right: that is stage one, then stage two, then stage three.

Nurse and Robbie Vincent, BBC Radio

My doctor is wonderful. Once, when I couldn't afford an operation, he touched up the x-rays.

Joey Bishop

—Are you sure you're a doctor?
—The Internet University of Science Stuff seems to think so.

Gary Andrews and doctor, *Gary the Rat*

My dear old friend King George V always told me he would never have died but for that vile doctor, Lord Dawson of Penn.

Margot Asquith

Too many good docs are getting out of the business. Too many OB/GYNs aren't able to practice their love with women all across their country.

George W. Bush (YT)

—I'm a kinesiologist. Kinesiology is a holistic therapy that uses muscle-testing to identify stress and find appropriate ways of dealing with it.
—And how long have you been doing this mumbo-jumbo?

Contestant and Anne Robinson, *The Weakest Link*

Can you cure the fear of needles with acupuncture?

Pierre Légaré

He's got to go in for a hernia operation, but when he gets over that he'll be back in harness again.

Peter Alliss

They were able to get him to hospital. He's in the intensive-care ward at Our Lady of the Worthless Miracle.

Detective Frank Drebin, *Police Squad!*

HOSPITAL

One of the most difficult things to contend with in a hospital is the assumption on the part of the staff that because you have lost your gall bladder you have also lost your mind.

Jean Kerr

Guard Dogs Operating

Sign outside a hospital

—Who are the most decent people in the hospital?
—The ultrasound people.   David O'Doherty

Welsh hospitals are worried because Mrs. A is out of control. No, sorry, MRSA.
                                                           John Sparkes

WET FLOOR—This is Not an Instruction
                                    Notice in the hospital's men's bathroom

A hospital is no place to be sick.   Sam Goldwyn

—Come, come, Matron, surely you've seen a temperature taken like this before?
—Yes, Colonel, but never with a daffodil.
                                    The Colonel and Matron, *Carry On, Nurse*

I've never had major knee surgery on any other part of my body.
                                                           Winston Bennett

He just wanted to get that knife into me. He'd cut you if you had dandruff.
                                                           Fanny Brice

[*singing, while operating on Homer*] The kneebone's connected to the ...
something, the something's connected to the ... red thing, the red thing's
connected to my wrist watch ... Uh-oh.
                                    Dr. Nick Riviera, *The Simpsons*

[*during surgery*] Nurse, get that cat outta here!
                                    Dr. Michael Hfuhruhurr, *The Man with Two Brains*

—Can you save him?
—Can't be sure. I'm not a very good doctor.
                                    Topper Harley and Doctor, *Hot Shots*

An old age pensioner is to sue a hospital after she went in for a leg op—and got
a new anus.   *The Sun*

Can you hear me? Squeeze my hand once for "yes" and twice for "no."

                                    Relative to patient in a coma

—You were in that coma for quite some time.
—Have they invented the hover-car yet?
—No.
—Damn.

Dr. Todd and Dr. McCartney, *Green Wing*

You probably don't remember, but you were in a serious accident …You're going to be fine. Lots of drink and plenty of hot sleep.

Hugh Laurie, *A Bit of Fry and Laurie*

—Who would have thought that being hit by lightning would land you in hospital? I was hit by lightning and I never had to go to hospital.
—You're different from most people, Dougal. All that happened to you was balloons kept sticking to you.

Father Dougal and Father Ted, *Father Ted*

The illness has given me time to think—which is always dangerous.

David Blunkett, Member of Parliament, undergoing surgery in 2003

Of course, an accident like this makes you think … it forces you to take a closer look at your own life … it makes you want to ask questions … like WHY ME?

Snoopy, *Peanuts*

People say to me, "You were close to death five times. This must have been an extraordinary experience. What did you learn from it?" And I say, "Yes, I did learn something, and I'd like to pass it on: Illness is a nuisance, and extreme illness is a FUCKING nuisance."

Michael Winner

HOSPITAL NOTES

The patient is an 84-year-old widow who no longer lives with her husband.

The patient had never been fatally ill before.

The emergency doctor suspected suicide, but the patient later denied this.

The patient has no past history of suicides.

The patient denies shaking and tremors, but her husband states that she was very hot in bed last night.

The patient stated that she had been constipated for most of her life until 2004 when she got divorced.

She is numb from the toes down.

The patient was unresponsive in bed.

The patient went to bed feeling perfectly well but woke up dead.

ADDICTION & DRUGS

In the U.K., cocaine goes hand in hand with champagne, yoga and organic vegetables. It has an exclusive, upmarket cachet.
Alex James, of Blur

I was walking down the road the other day, and I couldn't help but notice how beautiful the world is. And I thought to myself, "Why would anyone in their right mind bother to take drugs?" Then I remembered I was on drugs, and that was the reason.
Simon Munnery

When I arrived, in my capacity as the girlfriend, to sort things out, Shane calmed down enough to explain to me that he had taken 15 to 20 tabs of acid earlier in the evening, and had become convinced that the Third World War was taking place and that he, as the leader of the Irish Republic, was holding a summit meeting in his kitchen between the heads of state of the world superpowers: Russia, China, America and Ireland. In order to demonstrate the cultural inferiority of the United States, he was eating a Beach Boys album. The unusual thing about all of this is that I reacted to it as calmly as I would have if Shane had told me that he was upset because his telly was on the blink. To me, it was a perfectly normal occurrence.
Victoria Clarke, on Shane MacGowan of The Pogues

If God dropped acid, would he see people?
Steven Wright

He didn't know anything about drugs. He thought uppers were dentures.
Archie Griffin

I say no to drugs. But they won't listen.
Anon.

It was a sobering experience.

Lindsay Lohan, on rehab

I think I was once given cocaine, but I sneezed, and so it did not go up my nose. In fact, I may have been doing icing sugar.

Boris Johnson, mayor of London

I brought party mix, complete with uppers, downers and candy corn. Just don't tell my doctor; he's trying to get me off sugar.

Karen Walker, *Will & Grace*

I'm grateful for doing those drugs, because they kept me from getting laid and I would have gotten AIDS.

Steven Tyler, of Aerosmith

Posh boys can't take drugs, man. They're lightweights.

Liam Gallagher, of Oasis,
on Pete Doherty and Tom Chaplin

I don't do drugs. If I want a rush I get out of a chair when I'm not expecting it.

Dylan Moran

—I had a hard life. My mother was killed by a drug dealer.
—Phoebe, your mom killed herself.
—She was a drug dealer.   **Phoebe Buffay and Monica Geller, *Friends***

Why are there no recreational drugs taken in suppository form?

George Carlin

When I pictured heroin, I pictured some crazy crackhead with no shoes under a bridge. You never think that is going to be you. And it never was me. I was never under a bridge, and I always had shoes.

Nicole Richie

I tried heroin once, but it didn't have any effect. Mind you, I was high on coke at the time.   **Tom Baker, *Little Britain***

I tried sniffing coke once, but the ice cubes got stuck in my nose.

Anon.

The strangest thing I've tried to snort? My father. He was cremated and I couldn't resist grinding him up with a little bit of blow.

Keith Richards, of The Rolling Stones

One time when me was high, me sold me car for, like, 24 Chicken McNuggets.

Ali G, *Da Ali G Show*

Cocaine? Habit-forming? Of course not. I ought to know. I've been using it for years.

Tallulah Bankhead

—I thought they didn't let people with drug convictions into America.
—It's not so much a conviction, darling, it's more a strong belief.

Saffy Monsoon and Patsy Stone, *Absolutely Fabulous*

Does Class A guarantee quality?

Ali G, *Da Ali G Show*

The main problem with heroin is it's very moreish!

Harry Hill

—What should you do if your children want to talk about solvent abuse?
—Take a deep breath.

Brian Mawhinny, reporter and conservative British politician

Hooked on the Internet? Help is just a click away.

Anon.

ALCOHOL—GENERAL

Drinking makes such fools of people, and people are such fools to begin with that it's compounding a felony.

Robert Benchley

If You Drink to Forget, Please Pay in Advance

Sign in a bar in Indiana

I'm sorry, sir, the bar won't be open for half an hour; would you like a drink while you're waiting?

Irish barmaid

How about a martini? You know what they say about martinis: A martini is like a woman's breast—one ain't enough and three is too many.

Bar Girl, *The Parallax View*

My body will not tolerate spirits. I drank two martinis on New Year's Eve and tried to hijack the elevator and fly to Cuba.

Woody Allen

When I say I would like a little whiskey I mean I would like a large little whiskey. **William Whitelaw, Member of Parliament**

Drinkers got a shock when they flocked to a Norfolk pub advertising topless bar staff. The staff were all men. *Sunday Mirror*

Death Doesn't Deter Students From Drinking
Headline, *Roanoke Times*

—Will you join me in a glass of wine?
—You get in first, and if there's room enough, I'll join you.
Peggy Hopkins Joyce and Henry R. Quail, *International House*

—Can I interest you in a nightcap?
—No, thanks, I don't wear them.
Jane Spencer and Lieutenant Frank Drebin, *The Naked Gun*

—Brandy, please.
—Armagnac?
—Yeah, that'll do fine if you're out of brandy.
Del Boy Trotter and barmaid, *Only Fools and Horses*

[*pouring champagne*] What you want is some more of this imprisoned laughter of pleasant maids of France ...
Egbert Floud, *Ruggles of Red Gap*

—Ooh, what big bubbles!
—Yes, they had big grapes that year. **Jack Benny and Fred Allen**

The quality of a champagne is judged by the amount of noise the cork makes when it is popped.

Mencken and Nathan's Ninth Law of the Average American

—Try this very expensive pink champagne and tell us what you think.
—[*taking a sip*] I'm getting Febreze ...
Richard Madeley and Alan Carr, *Richard & Judy*

I like that pink champagne—Don Perrier.
Jade Goody, *Big Brother 3* (U.K.)

—Can I pour you a draft, Mr. Peterson?
—A little early, isn't it?
—For a beer?
—No, for stupid questions.

Woody Boyd and Norm Peterson, *Cheers*

Ah, no, Father Jack! Not Toilet Duck! You know what that does to you! You'll be seeing the pink elephants again!

Father Ted, *Father Ted*

—I was drinking to forget.
—Forget what?
—I don't know. I've forgotten.

Peter Barlow and Shelley Unwin, *Coronation Street*

WINE

Quickly, bring me a beaker of wine, so that I may whet my mind
and say something clever.
Aristophanes

—Are you interested in wine?
—Only the drinking part.

Barbara Covett and Richard Hart, *Notes on a Scandal*

—I thought a little spot of this might refresh you ... It's Châteauneuf 1924.
—Gee, that's pretty old. Haven't you got anything new?

Elvira Hawkley and Stan Laurel, *Nothing but Trouble*

I saw a wino. He was eating grapes. I was like, "Dude, you have to wait."

Mitch Hedberg

You can almost smell the cedar wood from the oak barrels.

Oz Clarke

[*wine tasting*] Um ... the first one was dog, the second cat. No? They were both cat?

Stephen Fry, *A Bit of Fry and Laurie*

"It is a little, shy wine like a gazelle." "Like a leprechaun." "Dappled, in a tapestry meadow." "Like a flute by still water."

Evelyn Waugh, *Brideshead Revisited*

As a school kid, I fermented anything I could: fruit, vegetables, rice, anything but grapes. It was all pretty undrinkable, but it went down well at school parties. Then I moved on to distilling it. It was still hard to drink, but some carrot whiskey did briefly manage to run the lawnmower.

Alan Limmer, winemaker

Six years and you haven't learned *any-thing*—it's white wine with Hershey bars.

Harry Barnes, *Making the Grade*

Pissed into an empty wine bottle so I could continue watching Monty Python, and suddenly thought, "I've never tasted my own piss," so I drank a little. It looked just like Orvieto Classico and tasted of nearly nothing.

Brian Eno, *A Year with Swollen Appendices: The Diary of Brian Eno*

If you spill red wine you can neutralize it with white wine. Does the same principle apply when you drink a glass of red wine?

Anon.

DRUNK

The hard part about being a bartender is figuring out who is drunk and who is just stupid.

Richard Braunstein

—How many gin and tonics have you had?
—Three gins, one tonic.

Sidney Cochran and Diane Barrie, *California Suite*

He once had his toes amputated so he could stand closer to the bar.

Mike Harding

—I don't know if I am standing on my head or my heels.
—Sift the evidence. At which end of you is the ceiling?

P. G. Wodehouse, *Cocktail Time*

—I'm feeling pretty drunk.
—Well, it's business drunk. It's like rich drunk. Either way it's legal to drive.

Liz Lemon and Jack Donaghy, *30 Rock*

—I know a good way to decide if we're too drunk to drive—if I can drive that remote-control car, I'm okay.
—Randy, that's not a remote-control car. That's a cat.

Randy and Earl Hickey, *My Name Is Earl*

I saw things and had peculiar quasi-religious experiences. I thought I was John the Baptist, and I would talk to the sea at Malibu and the sea would talk back to me.

Sir Anthony Hopkins

Three highballs, and I think I'm St. Francis of Assisi.

Dorothy Parker

Remember that time you drank three margaritas and thought you were the dancing broom from *Fantasia*?

Dorothy Zbornak, *The Golden Girls*

When I played drunks, I had to remain sober because I didn't know how to play them when I was drunk.

Richard Burton, actor

At Joan Collins's wedding … we all got drunk on champagne while waiting for the food. I think Shirley Bassey had definitely had a bit too much to drink because she sang without a band and when Helen Worth from *Coronation Street* said how good she was, Shirley replied, "The band wasn't too loud, was it?"

Christopher Biggins

Here's a tip: Never get drunk while wearing a hooded sweatshirt. You will eventually think there's someone right behind you.

Dave Attell

I poured bourbon over my cornflakes for breakfast.

Larry Hagman, *Hello Darlin'*

—What do you call a man who puts bourbon on his cornflakes?
—A cereal adulterer.

I'm Sorry I Haven't a Clue

Artists are renowned for being binge drinkers. Have you ever had a bottle of binge?

Paul Merton, to Tracey Emin, *Room 101*

HANGOVER

An American monkey, an Ateles, after getting drunk on brandy,
would never touch it again, and
thus was wiser than many men.
Charles Darwin

—My head hurts.
—That's your brain trying to comprehend its own stupidity.

Eric and Red Forman, *That '70s Show*

—Was I in this bar last night and did I spend a $20 bill?
—Yeah.
—Oh, boy, that's a load off my mind! I thought I'd lost it.

Egbert Sousé and Bartender, *The Bank Dick*

—I once got drunk and woke up in a mixture of my own urine and vomit.
—You say that like it's a negative thing.

Frank Skinner and Robert Downey Jr., *The Frank Skinner Show*

After a night out with Johnny Vegas, he was sick in a teapot.

Jeremy Clarkson

I once saw Michael Scott taking alternate sips of Scotch and Alka-Seltzer, thereby acquiring and curing a hangover simultaneously.

Hugh Leonard

SMOKING

I ponder things. Smokers do.
David Hockney

—[*offering a cigarette*] Cigarette?
—Yes, I know. **Detective Frank Drebin and Sally,** *Police Squad!*

He smokes like a fish. **Simon Bates**

Tobacco is my favorite vegetable. **Frank Zappa**

Hi, I'm Troy McClure. You may remember me from such self-help videos as "Smoke Yourself Thin" and "Get Confident, Stupid."
Troy McClure, *The Simpsons*

Smoking kills. If you're killed, you've lost a very important part of your life.
Brooke Shields

But when I don't smoke I scarcely feel as if I'm living. I don't feel as if I'm living unless I'm killing myself. **Russell Hoban,** *Turtle Diary*

A friend of mine a couple of weeks ago went to Aspen. He had a cigar going up in the ski lift. He couldn't find his matches and asked, "Have you got a lighter?" and the ski guy said, "I'm sorry, sir, this is a nonsmoking mountain."
Sir David Frost

We all know smoking is bad. I know I'm going to quit some day. If I thought I wasn't, I'd quit now. **Dylan Moran**

Quitting smoking is kinda like going to prison. If you can get through the first three days, you got a fighting chance. First we tried the tapes, then we tried the patches. Someone told us to try carrot sticks as a substitute, but we couldn't get the damn things to light.
Earl Hickey, *My Name Is Earl*

101 ways to quit smoking. Idea number 102: After purchase, dip each cigarette in kerosene. Let dry and replace in pack.
Katherine Hooper

Save money on expensive nicotine gum by chewing ordinary gum and smoking a cigarette at the same time. *Viz* **magazine**

I keep a lighter in my pocket at all times. I'm not a smoker, I just really love certain songs. **Demetri Martin**

FOOD & DRINK

A gourmet is just a glutton with brains.
Philip W. Haberman Jr.

I love food! I eat nothing else!   **Anon.**

Two cannibals eating a clown. One says to the other, "Does this taste funny to you?"   **Tommy Cooper**

I'm so hungry I could eat a vegetable!

Al Bundy, *Married … with Children*

—Do you like codfish balls?
—I don't know. I've never attended any.

Peter De Vries

Sorry, I don't eat buffalo.   **Jessica Simpson, when offered Buffalo wings**

—Look, mummy, suede apples!
—No, dear, those are peaches.   **Mother and young son**

It has nothing to do with frogs' legs. No amphibian is harmed in the making of this dish.

Nigella Lawson, celebrity chef, explaining the British recipe for toad-in-the-hole to Americans

—What's my speciality? What does Mommy make all the time? What does Mommy make a lot of?
—Money!
—Mommy's tacos!

Kate Hudson and son, Ryder, age four, interview, *Vogue* magazine

Whole hearts and kidneys? Ugh! Why've you given us people's hearts and kidneys to eat, Big Brother?

Samantha Marchant, *Big Brother 8* (U.K.)

Is porridge the new sushi?   *The Times*

When you're in Korea, you have to eat as the Romans do.

                                                              Tony Francis

—Here, try some of these. I call them "Angel Wings."
—They're Pringles.

Kate O'Brien and Drew Carey, *The Drew Carey Show*

Every morning I get up and I make instant coffee and I drink it so I'll have
enough energy to make the regular coffee.

                                                              Steven Wright

—For breakfast this morning I had Smarties cereal.
—Oh, my God, I didn't even know Smarties made a cereal.
—They don't. It's just Smarties in a bowl with milk.

                                    Moss and Jen, *The IT Crowd*

I am teetotal and vegetarian, so I do live on tea. I don't like Earl Grey tea, but it
may be class prejudice against earls, as I don't believe in all that, rather than the
tea itself.   **Tony Benn, Member of Parliament**

Put the kettle on, Mother. It suits you!   **Ken Dodd**

I used this product called "I Can't Believe It's Not Butter" 'cause, sometimes,
when I'm eating toast, I like to be incredulous. "How was breakfast?"
"Unbelievable!"   **Demetri Martin**

I've Never Wronged an Onion So Why Does It Make Me Cry?
                                    Title, British music hall song

—Mr. Simpson, you have clearly taken items from the candy rack and placed
them on this donut.
—Um ... what do you mean?
—A Mars bar is not a sprinkle, sir.   **Apu Nahasapeemapetilon and**
                                             Homer Simpson, *The Simpsons*

—[*seeing a sign on a box: SUGAR FREE DONUTS*] Ooh, sugar-free donuts!
—No, that is sugar—with free donuts.

                                             Marge Simpson and
                                    Apu Nahasapeemapetilon, *The Simpsons*

I fancy having a bit of rabbit for my tea tonight. Could anyone tell me if it's cheaper from a butcher's or a pet shop?

J. Picklay, *Viz* magazine

If it has got four legs and it's not a chair, if it has got two wings and it flies but is not an airplane, and if it swims and it's not a submarine, the Cantonese will eat it.

Prince Philip

Whether one eats a cat or not is a personal choice, and I don't want to sway anyone one way or another. But if you do, there is one obvious cooking tip: Always remember to remove the bell from the cat's collar before cooking. You don't want to make a tinkling sound every time you burp.

Mike Royko, *For the Love of Mike*

I knew a chef who, when he'd forgotten to defrost the prawns, put them in his mouth to thaw them.
Frank Gill

Finish your vegetables! There are children in Beverly Hills with eating disorders.

John Callahan, cartoonist

I don't mind eating if it's possible to make a martini sandwich.

Captain Benjamin "Hawkeye" Pierce, *M*A*S*H*

Brains need careful handling, or they are apt to disintegrate.

Jocasta Innes, *The Pauper's Cookbook*

So I went down the local supermarket. I said, "I want to make a complaint. This vinegar's got lumps in it." He said, "Those are pickled onions."

Tim Vine

When will greengrocers stop referring to "new potatoes"? They've been out for years now, so isn't it about time they just called them "potatoes"?

T. Doyle, *Viz* magazine

FOR SALE: Golden, ripe, boneless bananas. 39 cents a pound.

Ad in *The Missoulian*

—I could go for a dish of ice cream.
—We haven't got any ice cream.

—Well, you could go and get some ice cream.
—Get me my new hat, and I'll go and get some ice cream.
—You're going to get it in your hat?

Stan Laurel and Oliver Hardy, Come Clean

What a con this so-called evaporated milk is. I opened a tin of it the other day and it was still completely full.

Jules, Viz magazine

A jar of mincemeat I bought carried the following message: The contents are sufficient for a pie for six persons or twelve small tarts.

David Morris-Marsham

—Hey, my oyster stew doesn't have any oyster in it.
—If that bothers you, better skip dessert. It's angel cake.

Robert L. Rodgers

—Name two vegetables beginning with the letter *s*.
—Strawberries and spinach.
—Strawberries are not a vegetable.
—Spinach and ... spuds!

Big Brother and Jade Goody, Big Brother 3 (U.K.)

What's a sparagus?

Jade Goody, Big Brother 3 (U.K.)

Is an egg a vegetable?

Jodie Marsh, Celebrity Big Brother 4 (U.K.)

If you don't cook the yellow bits of eggs you get semolina.

Jade Goody

How does a hen know the size of an eggcup when it lays an egg?

Ken Dodd

What if chickens laid pineapples instead of eggs? Henhouses would need more than just subdued lighting and music to keep the chickens calm.

Chuck Smith

Is there chicken in chickpeas?

Helen Adams, Big Brother 2 (U.K.)

We have some shepherd's pie peppered with actual shepherd on top.

Mrs. Lovett, Sweeney Todd: The Demon Barber of Fleet Street

What's in kidney beans?

Helen Adams, Big Brother 2

—What's hummus?
—Ooh, there was shock from the audience at that: He's never shocked me before but now he has.

Marilyn Manson and Graham Norton, *The Graham Norton Show*

Piccalilli? I don't know what it is. Piccalilli's off Monopoly.

Amanda Marchant, *Big Brother 8* (U.K.)

When I was small, I would refuse to drink water when I ate fish because I thought the fish would reconstitute itself in my stomach.

Peter Ustinov

He never touches water; it goes to his head at once.

Oscar Wilde

—Gracie, isn't that boiling water you're putting in the refrigerator?
—Yes. I'm freezing it, so whenever I want boiling water, all I have to do is defrost it.

Harry von Zell and Gracie Allen

He heard we were running short of water, so he wants us to dilute it.

Fozzie, *The Muppet Show*

People aren't happy with the one plain drink—they want all sorts of combinations. We crave new tastes. I can't wait for alcoholic sausages.

Kevin Gildea

The other day as I was trying to piece together a meal from the meager remains I had left in my fridge and I thought, Wow, this is probably what happened when they made the platypus.

John Maclain

I tried boiling pig's feet once, but I couldn't get the pig to stand still.

Anon.

If only I had some eggs, I'd make eggs and bacon—if I had the bacon.

British Army catchphrase, World War I

This recipe is certainly silly. It says to separate two eggs, but it doesn't say how far to separate them.

Gracie Allen

—I shall prepare my turnip surprise.
—And the surprise is?
—There's nothing else in it but turnip.

Baldrick and Edmund Blackadder, *Blackadder II*

The first time my husband asked me for an aspirin and a glass of water I knew exactly what to do—I phoned my mother for the recipe.

Gracie Allen

I can't see the point in making tons of food if people are just going to sit there and eat it.

Jenny Eclair

Is jelly cooked?

Helen Adams, *Big Brother 2* (U.K.)

Son, go easy on the orange juice. That stuff doesn't grow on trees—wait, it does! So why is it so damned expensive?

Hal, *Malcolm in the Middle*

My mate's got a microwave in his kitchen. It says "Enjoy your meal" when you get something out. But I won't since I was drying my pants in it.

James May, *Top Gear*

VEGETARIAN

I won't eat anything that has intelligent life, but I'd gladly eat a
network executive or a politician.
Marty Feldman

I've gone vegetarian now, I mean, I know I had a sausage roll yesterday, but it's not really meat, is it? I mean, there's no animal called a "sausage."

Janine, *The Fast Show*

—Don't you have anything at this barbecue that wasn't slaughtered?
—I think the veal died of loneliness.

Lisa and Homer Simpson, *The Simpsons*

What is the meat in chili con carne? ... I thought it was like, dunno, vegetarian. I didn't think there was real meat in chili con carne.

Brian Belo, *Big Brother 8* (U.K.)

I'm a Volvo-vegetarian. I'll eat an animal only if it was accidentally killed by a speeding car.
Ron Smith

I'm moving toward being vegan. When I crack an egg now, I look and think, Could that have become a baby?

Heather Mills, *Viva!* magazine

It was symbolic of 12 years of being bloody hungry.
Paul Weller, on why he stopped being a vegetarian

I'm actually a reverse vegetarian. I don't wear leather, but when I go out, I wear corned beef shoes.
Tim Vine

RESTAURANTS

A lot of chefs stick a banana up a duck and
call themselves geniuses.
Sanche de Gramont

—Do you serve lobster?
—Yes, sir, we serve anyone.
Punch magazine

—Would you like a prawn cocktail?
—No, thanks, I don't drink.
Waiter and Jeff Stone

—How would you like your egg?
—Medium rare, please.
Waitress and American tourist

[*sniffing the air in a restaurant*] Is that parmesan, or babies? I can never tell the difference.
Stephen Merchant

Is this chicken, what I have, or is this fish? I know it's tuna, but it … it says "Chicken of the Sea."

Jessica Simpson, eating Chicken of the Sea canned tuna

I told you the food here should not be taken internally.

Captain Benjamin "Hawkeye" Pierce, *M*A*S*H*

I'm kicking off my diet with a cheeseburger—whatever Jamie Oliver says, McDonald's are incredibly nutritious and, as far as I can tell, crammed full of vital nutrients and rigid with goodness.

Boris Johnson, mayor of London

Sign of an incompetent fast-food employee: You order fries and he asks if you want fries with that.

Garrett Thomson

Courteous and efficient self-service.

Notice outside a New York restaurant

You go to a steakhouse, guess what folks—no cow tank.

Richard Jeni

—I'll have chocolate flavor ice cream.
—I'm sorry, but we're out of chocolate.
—Have you any mustachio?
—No, we're out of mustachio.
—You're out of mustachio?
—[*angrily*] Yes!
—Out of mustachio ... What other flavors are you out of?
—Strawberry ... We're also out of orange, gooseberry and chocolate.
—All right, I'll have it without chocolate.

Stan Laurel and ice cream vendor, *Come Clean*

—There's a fly in my ice cream.
—The flies here go in for winter sports.

Bebe McGuire and Clarence Brewster,
Sing Your Troubles Away

—Monsieur Henri's cuisine is really quite adventurous. Did you know there's snails on the menu tonight?
—Well, that doesn't surprise me. He never washes the cabbage.

Cissie and Ada, aka Roy Barraclough
and Les Dawson

—He took me to a really nice restaurant.
—Oh, did you go Dutch?
—Nah, Chinese.

Linda Robson and Pauline Quirke, *Pauline's Quirkes*

—Oh, *garçon*! Bring me a small demitasse.
—Bring me one, too—in a big cup.

> Oliver Hardy and Stan Laurel, *Below Zero*

Nobody goes to that restaurant any more. It's too crowded.

> Yogi Berra

I never go to all-you-can-eat places. I just can't eat that much.

> Jerrold M. Witcher

I love rosé wine—but I prefer the cheap stuff. When we go to posh restaurants, I always want to ask, "You got any Blossom Hill?"

> Coleen McLoughlin, wife of soccer player Wayne Rooney

Sign of an incompetent sommelier: "Do you want a glass with that?"

> Kyle Bonney

—She had the soup of the day.
—What was it?
—Friday.

> Nana and Barbara Royle, *The Royle Family*

Oh, I see they've got the soup *du jour* today, that's one of my favorites.

> Peter De Vries

Never order soup in an open-air restaurant, because if it starts to rain, you'll never finish it.

> Victor Lewis-Smith

Hey, waiter, I'm in my soup!

> Fly, *A Bug's Life*

—What's the difference between roast beef and pea soup?
—Anyone can roast beef.

> Anon.

Garçon! Another glass of milk—and two fresh straws.

> Oliver Hardy, *Below Zero*

—You drank it all! We were supposed to share it.
—I couldn't help it. My half was on the bottom.

> Oliver Hardy and Stan Laurel, *Men o' War*

—Have you got anything without Spam in it?
—Well, there's Spam, egg, sausage and Spam. That's not got much Spam in it.

> *Monty Python's Flying Circus*

I finally figured out what Spam stands for: Stuff Posing As Meat.

Bill Engvall

Can I have the same please, but with different-shaped pasta? What do you call those pasta in bows? Like a bow tie, but miniature. Like an Action Man bow tie.   **Alan Partridge**, *I'm Alan Partridge*

Forget it. I've had enough. I'm going out for an honest British kebab.

Hugh Laurie, *A Bit of Fry and Laurie*

WEIGHT

The waist is a terrible thing to mind. The mind is a terrible thing to waste.

Anon.

Maybe kings would slim down if they started eating regular-sized candy bars.

Jason Love

A stupid practice that a restaurant might perpetrate: A large scale in a restaurant with an arrow pointing to a mark that says, "You must weigh less than this to order the Triple Death by Chocolate dessert."

Art Grinath

You're as light as a heifer—uh, feather.

Trixie Lorraine, *Gold Diggers of 1933*

If I had my way, fat people would be strangled at birth.

Tom Baker, *Little Britain*

We all get heavier as we get older because there's a lot more information in our heads.   **Vlade Divac, basketball player**

Behind every great man is a great woman, and thank heaven I have Lillian because, quite frankly, I enjoy the shade.

Roland T. Flakfizer, *Brain Donors*

WeightWatchers will meet at 7 p.m. in the hall. Please use the large double door at the side entrance.   **Church newsletter**

DIET

No diet will remove all the fat from your body because the brain is
entirely fat. Without a brain you might look good, but all you could
do is run for office.
Covert Bailey

I once drove with friends from Cannes to Nice. It took about an hour, and we
dieted all the way.
Elsa Maxwell

I'm so hungry my spare tire's deflated.

Josh Mallon, *The Road to Singapore*

—My doctor says I need more iron in my diet. What do you suggest?
—Eat your car keys.
**Customer in a health food store and Mork,
*Mork & Mindy***

I'm on a grapefruit diet. I eat everything except grapefruit.

Chi Chi Rodriguez

If you have a pear-shaped body, you should not wear pear-colored clothes or act
juicy.
Demetri Martin

There's a new Chinese diet. Order all the food you want but use only one
chopstick.
Bob Monkhouse

I am on two diets at the moment because you don't get enough to eat on one.
Peter Sissons

I eat only white foods: eggs, sugar, grated bones, the fat of dead animals, veal,
salt, coconut, chicken cooked in white water, fruit mold, rice, turnips,
camphorated sausage, dough, cheese (white), cotton salad, and certain fish
(skinless).
**Erik Satie, to get him in the mood for composing "Socrate,"
which he wanted to be "white and pure like Antiquity"**

What's the two things they say are healthiest to eat? Chicken and fish. You
know what you should do? Combine them: Eat a penguin.
Dave Attell

A fast has no real nutritional value.

Unidentified dietician

I gave up coffee and *The New York Times* on the same day.

Malachy McCourt

I don't diet. I just don't eat as much as I'd like to.

Linda Evangelista

—Oh, no, no, I can't eat 15 gallons of yogurt!
—Oh, it's not going in that end, Mr. Lightbody.

William Lightbody and Dr. Kellogg,
The Road to Wellville

My wife's on a new diet: coconuts and bananas. She hasn't lost any weight, but can she climb a tree!

Henny Youngman

To lose weight I started eating saccharine. Now I've got artificial diabetes.

Jackie Vernon

That's enough health. I need a fag.

Charles Kennedy, Member of Parliament, after launching
a campaign to promote healthy food

EXERCISE

I'm against the New York City marathon because it just gets my
hopes up: At first it seems like 20,000 idiots are leaving the city, but
then they just make a big loop and come right back.

Dr. John Becker, Becker

OK, everyone, now inhale … and dehale!

Maury Wills, baseball player, taking
his teammates through warm-up exercises

He's breathing pretty hard, but I suppose that's his own way of getting air into his lungs.

Jim Neilly

What do you wear on a running machine? I can't bring myself to wear flat shoes.

Victoria Beckham

I don't really understand miles. I didn't actually know how far it was going to be.

> Jade Goody, British TV personality, who collapsed and was taken to
> the hospital after 21 miles of the 26.2-mile London marathon

I try to go for longer runs, but it's tough around here at the White House on the outdoor track … It's sad that I can't run longer. It's one of the saddest things about the presidency.

> George W. Bush

The trouble with jogging is that the ice falls out of your glass.

> Martin Mull

Signs you won't win the New York City marathon:
You pulled a hamstring filling out the application.
Every couple of miles, you stop and ask for directions.
You're frequently mistaken for the fat guy from *Lost*.

> David Letterman

My mother-in-law had to stop skipping for exercise. It measured seven on the Richter scale.

> Les Dawson

My wife is doing Pilates. I think that's his name.

> Peter Sasso

So I went down my local gym. I said, "Mr. Nasium, can you teach me how to do the splits?" He said, "How flexible are you?" I said, "I can't make Tuesdays."

> Tim Vine

—Can you touch your toes?
—No, sir.
—Then how do you wash your feet, you dirty little man?

> Doctor and patient, *I'm Sorry, I'll Read That Again*, BBC Radio

My doctor told me I should get out of breath three times a week, so I took up smoking.

> Jo Brand

I went to a massage parlor. It was self-service.

> Rodney Dangerfield

I tried exercise as a means of burning fat, but it didn't work for me. When the fat started burning, it smelled like bacon and made me hungry.

> Planojo

DISABILITY

You pity a man who is lame or blind, but you never pity him for
being a fool, which is often a much greater misfortune.
Rev. Sydney Smith

—How does a blind parachutist know when to open his chute?
—When the lead on his guide dog goes slack.   **Anon.**

I met a guy this morning with a glass eye. He didn't tell me—it just came out in
conversation.   **Jerry Dennis**

Well, my brother says "Hello!" So, hurray for speech therapy.

Emo Philips

Dyslexic man walks into a bra.   **Anon.**

In this enlightened age, we don't do jokes about dyslexia because it's not clever
and it's not furry.
Humphrey Lyttelton, *I'm Sorry I Haven't a Clue*, BBC Radio

I had dyslexia as a child. I used to write about it in my dairy.   Zach Galifianakis

Sign of an incompetent Tourette's Syndrome sufferer: "You gosh-darned
danged noodlehead! What the H-E-double-hockey-sticks are you ..."
Meg Sullivan

The 5,000 or so volunteers are breaking their backs to make sure these
Paralympics are a success.   **Commentator, BBC Radio**

Our walking encyclopedia on disablement problems, Ann Davies, is waiting in
her wheelchair to hear from you.

Robbie Vincent, radio presenter

Are you a stand-up comedian or a sit-down comedian?
**Cherie Blair, to Laurence Clark,
comedian and wheelchair user**

I learned that people in wheelchairs are allowed to have marathons ... which, to me, seems like cheating—but what are ya gonna say?

Sarah Silverman

As you can possibly see, I have an injury myself—not here at the hospital, but in combat with a cedar. I eventually won. The cedar gave me a little scratch.

George W. Bush, after visiting wounded war veterans
from an amputee care center in Texas

If you are deaf, press 1 ...

Maja Keech

Do you know they have telephones for the deaf now? They don't ring. They just light up. So the deaf person can see that there's somebody on the phone. They pick it up and say, "Hello ... Hello ... Hello?"

Dave Allen

Deaf people: Wearing oven-gloves outdoors is an ideal way to stop strangers from eavesdropping on your conversation.

Viz magazine

My grandfather is hard of hearing. He needs to read lips. I don't mind him reading lips, but he uses one of those yellow highlighters.

Brian Kiley

Say what you want about the deaf ...

Jimmy Carr

I give money to a company that makes hearing aids on a regular basis. More people should hear me sing.

Christina Aguilera

—Peter, are you going to ask that question with shades on?
—I can take them off.
—I'm interested in the shade look, seriously.
—All right, I'll keep it, then.
—For the viewers, there's no sun.
—I guess it depends on your perspective.
—Touché.

George W. Bush and Peter Wallsten,
LA Times journalist, who is legally blind (YT)

I wonder what the word for "dots" looks like in Braille?

Demetri Martin

They've got Braille now in the toilets on the train. As if a blind person couldn't smell that was a fucking toilet. They're hardly gonna go, "Mmm ... buffet car?"

Alan Carr

Let's see if we can find someone who speaks Braille.

Anneka Rice

I asked this woman why she had two Seeing Eye dogs, and she said one was for reading.

Jonathan Katz

Do you know, they now do eating dogs for the anorexic?

Prince Philip, to Susan Edwards, who is visually impaired and was with her guide dog

I'm honored to shake the hand of a brave Iraqi citizen who had his hand cut off by Saddam Hussein.

George W. Bush

—Your niece has three feet?
—Yes, my sister said so in her letter. Listen: "You wouldn't know little Jean. Since you last saw her, she's grown another foot."

George Burns and Gracie Allen

I saw a man with a wooden leg, and a real foot.

Steven Wright

—My most embarrassing moment was when my artificial leg fell off at the altar on my wedding day.
—How awful! Do you still have an artificial leg?

Caller and Simon Fanshawe, Talk Radio (U.K.)

New Law Has California Highway Patrol Officer Jumping for Joy: Lieutenant who lost his legs is exempted from physical agility test.

Headline, *The Los Angeles Times*, first edition

New Law Is Leap Forward for California Highway Patrol Officer: Lieutenant who lost his legs wins exemption from physical agility test.

Headline, *The Los Angeles Times*, second edition

One always overcompensates for disabilities. I'm thinking of having my entire body surgically removed.

Douglas Adams

RETIREMENT

They look upon retirement as something between euthanasia and castration.

Leon A. Danco

What will you do when you leave football, Jack—will you stay in football?

Stuart Hall, BBC Radio

I guess I'm gonna just fade into Bolivian.

Mike Tyson

I'm retired—but in order to keep myself in retirement in the manner to which I am accustomed, I have to work. It's an Irish retirement.

Dave Allen

AGE

About 60 years ago, I said to my father, "Old Mr. Senex is showing his age; he sometimes talks quite stupidly." My father replied, "That isn't age. He's always been stupid. He is just losing his ability to conceal it."

Robertson Davies

—What's a geriatric?
—A German footballer scoring three goals.

Bob Monkhouse

At a church social, a little boy came up and asked me how old I was. I said, "I'm 76." "And you're still alive?" he said.

Jack Wilson

I'm 72. A lot of people my age are dead at the present time.

Casey Stengel

He certainly looks older than he did last year.

Mark Cox

—What fantastic genes you have!
—I don't have any.
—I don't mean trousers.

Anita Anand and Arthur Billington, age 88, BBC Radio

I have reached an age when I look as good standing on my head as I do right side up.

Frank Sullivan

George Burns is a man old enough to be his own father.

Red Buttons

A sexagenarian? At *his* age? That's disgusting.

Gracie Allen

It takes a long time to become young.

Pablo Picasso

My seven-year-old, who is now ten …

Lady Olga Maitland

I'm ten in England and I'm ten in Scotland, 'cause there's no time difference.

Scottish boy, *Small Talk*

Moses Kiptanui, the 19-year-old, turned 20 a few weeks ago.

David Coleman

Ronnie O'Sullivan, 20 years of age, but his shoulders are much older.

"Whispering" Ted Lowe

The Germans only have one player under 22 and he's 23.

Kevin Keegan, former international soccer player

I'm 28 now and they say you peak at 28—so my best years are still ahead of me.

Kieron Dyer, soccer player

When a player gets to 30, so does his body.

Glenn Hoddle, British soccer team manager

He's 31 this year. Last year he was 30.

David Coleman, former sports commentator

And then there's Johan Cruyff, who at 35 has added a whole new meaning to the word anno Domini.

Archie Macpherson, soccer commentator

When I was 40, my doctor advised me that a man in his forties shouldn't play tennis. I heeded his advice carefully and could hardly wait until I reached 50 to start again.

Hugo L. Black

John Lennon would have had his 56th birthday today. How old would he be if he was still alive?

Paula White

I'm too old to be a rent boy and too young to be a wino. I'm at that difficult age.

Wayne Slob, *Harry Enfield and Chums*

After Sunday school, my granddaughter asked thoughtfully, "Grandad, were you in the ark?" "Of course not!" I replied. "Then why weren't you drowned?" she said.

James Potter

My daughter once asked me if I was alive when the world was black and white, because everything she saw that was old on TV was black and white.

Chuck Close

When I was your age, television was called "books."

Grandpa, *The Princess Bride*

Not only are they getting older, they're living longer.

Tim Smith

Most of us will live to be centurions.

Dover Reporter

If I'd known I was gonna live this long, I'd have taken better care of myself.

Eubie Blake, who died at age 100

To become 100 years old, you have to start young.

Maurice Roche

When I found a dead body, they said I was 39. I'm 36. I was more traumatized by the fact they got my age wrong than the fact I'd found a stiff.

Amanda Holden, actress

I've always been a bit more maturer than what I am.

Samantha Fox

The older I get the more passionate I become about ageism.

Robin Cook, Member of Parliament

Ageing seems to be the only available way to live a long time.

Daniel Auber

The older you get, the prouder you get of your age. I tell people I'm 73½.

Dame Eileen Atkins

90 is the new 70.

Katharine Whitehorn

If I had known what fun it is to be 83, I would have done it long ago.

Tony Benn, former Member of Parliament

You look great for your age and I have no idea how old you are.

Steven Wright

The great thing about Alzheimer's is that you keep on making new friends.

George Melly

Like many women my age, I am 28 years old.

Mary Schmich

DEATH & DYING

If a man has learnt to think, no matter what he may think about, he
is always thinking of his own death.

Leo Tolstoy

I never thought I'd live to see the day of my death.

Sam Goldwyn

I don't want to die. I think death is a greatly overrated experience.

Rita Mae Brown

Death can do no more than kill you.

W. N. P. Barbellion

Those who survived the San Francisco earthquake said, "Thank God, I'm still alive." But, of course, those who died—their lives will never be the same again.

Barbara Boxer, senator from California

It's a time of sorrow and sadness when we lose a loss of life.

George W. Bush

One dies only once, and it's for such a long time!   Molière

Glenn Miller became a legend in his own lifetime due to his early death.
Nicholas Parsons

Once you're dead, you're made for life.
Jimi Hendrix

After riding a gallop on my horse, one of the trainer's grooms came in on foot and stated, "I am terribly sorry, he fell dead. He has never done that before."
Lord Grenfell

It was still a shock when George died. It was the last thing I thought he'd do.
Angie Best

He had had enough of being dead.
**Anne Darwin, on her husband, John, who faked his own death
in a canoe only to return from the "dead" five years later**

I thought I was dead. But it turned out I was just in Nebraska.
Little Bill Daggett, *Unforgiven*

I am so busy I have had to put off the date of my death.
Bertrand Russell

Last month, my aunt passed away. She was cremated. We think that's what did it.
Jonathan Katz

—There shouldn't be heart attacks, or cancer or anything like that. There should just be a certain age where you have to turn your life in, like a library book. You pack your bag, you go and that's that.
—I wouldn't know what to pack.
Rose Nylund and Blanche Devereaux, *The Golden Girls*

Perhaps the cruellest tragedy in the death of James E. Dever is that had it happened a few minutes later, he might still be alive.
Chester Daily News

A passing policeman was unable to revive him despite using the kiss of death.
Reporter, BBC Radio

Once he'd died, his life was over.   Lulu

He never even lived to be a vegetable.

Homer Simpson, *The Simpsons*

I intend to live forever. So far, so good.

Steven Wright

[*two women meeting on a bus*]
—Buried my mother last week.
—Oh ... She dead, then?

John Windsor, overheard, *The Graham Norton Show*

Yogi Berra called his former New York Yankees battery-mate Whitey Ford, who has skin cancer, and asked him, "You dead yet?"

Tom Fitzgerald

—I'm still alive.
—How do you know that?
—I can tell when I get up in the morning. If I don't get up, that means I'm dead.

Groucho Marx and Woody Allen

When I die, I'm going to leave my body to science fiction.

Steven Wright

My cousin just died. He was only nineteen. He was stung by a bee—the natural enemy of the tightrope walker.

Emo Philips

—The drink killed him.
—Was he an alcoholic?
—No, he was run over by a Guinness truck.

Miranda and Mrs. Doubtfire, *Mrs. Doubtfire*

A verdict of accidental death was recorded by Surrey coroner Michael Burgess following the demise in Haselmere of a 26-year-old maintenance worked who suffocated in his sleep. The man, who had taken sleeping tablets, was found dead with two tampons in his nostrils. His girlfriend had helped him put them there "in a bizarre bid to stop him snoring."

Midhurst and Petworth Observer

How did Captain Hook die? He wiped with the wrong hand.

Tommy Sledge

When I die I want my friends to eat me. I want to be fed through a wood chipper, then be spread over a wheat field, then have a cake baked from the crop for all my pals to lunch on.

Larry Hagman

My dad's dying wish was to have his family around him. I can't help thinking he would have been better off with more oxygen.

Jimmy Carr

If I die from [being hit by] airplane frozen bathroom waste, my friends and family would have trouble stifling a laugh. And who could blame them, really? "How did he die?" someone might ask. "I guess you could say he got pissed off."

Scott Adams, *The Dilbert Blog*

She drowned at the end of her life.

Alan Frank

My brother-in-law died. He was a karate expert, then joined the army. The first time he saluted, he killed himself.

Henny Youngman

And then my bereavement counsellor died. I didn't know who to turn to.

Hugh Laurie, *A Bit of Fry and Laurie*

They say you shouldn't say nothing about the dead unless you can say something good. He's dead. Good.

Moms Mabley

—How was Robert Maxwell feeling in the last few days?
—He was in a very buoyant mood.

Sir Trevor McDonald and Richard Stott

If I could drop dead right now, I'd be the happiest man alive.

Sam Goldwyn

If you die in an elevator, be sure to push the up button.

Sam Levenson

For most people, death comes at the end of their lives.

Expert, Greater London Radio

—My uncle fell through a trapdoor and broke his neck.
—Was he building a house?
—No, they were hanging him.

Stan Laurel and Oliver Hardy, *The Laurel and Hardy Murder Case*

Ernest Gallo, the winemaker, has died. He was 97. But most wine experts agree that 97 is a good year to die.

Craig Ferguson

The founder of Holiday Inn has died, aged 90. Unfortunately, he checked out after 3 p.m., so they charged him for an extra day.

Conan O'Brien

Arthur the human chameleon crawled across a tartan rug and died of exhaustion.

Ronnie Barker

SUICIDE

—He's dead. They say he blew his brains out.
—I'm amazed he was such a good shot.

Friend and Noël Coward

Suicide is a real threat to health in a modern society.

Virginia Bottomley, Member of Parliament

The suicide rate is so high in Sweden that tall buildings are banned.

Vic Reeves and Bob Mortimer, *Shooting Stars*

—Were you suicidal?
— Nah ... I'm not that clever to do a suicide. I wouldn't know how to tie a rope in the first place, you know what I mean?

Emma Brockes, journalist, and Frank Bruno, boxer

I couldn't commit suicide if my life depended on it.

Jennifer Hart

Without the possibility of suicide, I would have killed myself long ago.

E. M. Cioran

You'll kill yourself if it's the last thing you do!

Swami Talpur, *Abbott and Costello Meet the Killer, Boris Karloff*

I was going to commit suicide the other day, but I must not have been serious because I bought a beach towel.

Steven Wright

Indecisive about committing suicide? Then hang yourself with a bungee rope.

Viz magazine

It's against Roman law to take one's own life. The penalty is death.

Miles Gloriosus,
A Funny Thing Happened on the Way to the Forum

A 23-year-old man in Hartland, Maine, was hospitalized after an attempted suicide by crucifixion. He had built a wooden cross, placed it on the floor and nailed one hand to it. According to the arresting officer, "When he realized that he was unable to nail his other hand to the board, he called 911."

Bangor Daily News

—You know, women do this right. Bottle of pills, head in the oven. Never make a mess.
—Yeah, that's because we women always have to clean everything up.

Jelly Grimaldi and Faith Yokas, *Third Watch*

A coroner in Kendal has returned an open verdict on a joiner who's thought to have shot himself in the head with a nail gun. Michael Holden was described by the coroner, Ian Smith, as a troubled young man, but said no one could know what was going through his mind at the time.

Newsreader, BBC Radio Cumbria,
Radio Bloopers U.K. 2007 #1 (YT)

—I tried to kill myself yesterday by taking 1,000 aspirin.
—What happened?
—Oh, after the first two I felt better.

Anon.

FUNERAL

Why is it that we rejoice at a birth and grieve at a funeral? Is it because we are not the person involved?
Mark Twain

Cremation Service: $895—plus $35 one-time membership.

Newspaper ad, Pennsylvania

Dying is to cost more at King's Lynn, Norfolk. Higher burial charges are being introduced. Increased cost of living is blamed.

Daily Telegraph

My father lived in a Berkshire village where people did not use the expression, D.V.—*Deo volente* ("God willing"), but said, "If spared." One day a new widow went to see the rector and said, "I'm sorry to tell you, Rector, that my husband has just passed away and wishes to be buried Thursday, if spared."

John Hedges

I walked by a funeral parlor the other day. It had a sign in the window: "Closed because of a birth in the family."

Jackie Vernon

You should not leave someone's ashes on a doorstep whether they are deceased or not.

Tom Bull, funeral director

Members of the family kindly request mourners to omit floral tributes. The deceased was allergic to flowers.

Obituary notice, *The New York News*

I was standing beside the coffin at the funeral home, thinking about my flashlight and its batteries. Then I thought, maybe he's not dead, maybe he's just in wrong.

Steven Wright

I have one last request. Don't use embalming fluid on me. I want to be stuffed with crabmeat.

Woody Allen

Sign of an incompetent embalmer: Emphasises cleavage.

Mark Updike

No one would go to Hitler's funeral if he was alive today.

Ron Brown, Member of Parliament

Always go to other people's funerals, otherwise they won't go to yours.

Yogi Berra

I want Bach's Toccata and Fugue in D played at my funeral. If it isn't, I shall jolly well want to know why.

Sybil Thorndike

If anyone at my funeral has a long face, I'll never speak to him again.

Stan Laurel

I watched a funeral go by once and asked who was dead. A local man said, "It's the fella in the coffin."

Dave Allen

I was prostate with grief.

Tony Soprano, *The Sopranos*

After being an awed witness of the funeral of King Edward VII, the little daughter of Lord Kinnoull refused to say her prayers that night. "God will be too busy unpacking King Edward," she said.

Lord Riddell

A recent survey called "Funeral Rights" revealed that many people admitted to "secret disappointment" with their funeral service.

Crosby Herald

This is a great day for France!

Richard Nixon, attending the funeral of President Georges Pompidou

A wake is an amazing tradition. They throw a great party for you on the one day they know you can't come.

Michael Gold, *The Big Chill*

It was a catered funeral. It was held in a big hall with accordion players, and on the buffet table was a replica of the deceased in potato salad.

Woody Allen

During the funeral procession of Mr. William Johnson, who died at the age of 79, his boyhood friend John Jamieson, aged 77, dropped dead at the graveside. Naturally, this threw a gloom over the entire proceedings.

Shetland Times

He was such a hypochondriac that they buried him next to a doctor.

Steve Lawrence

An Irishman's last wish was to be buried at sea, which was most unfortunate for his three friends who died digging the grave.

Anon.

EPITAPH

Surrounded by fucking idiots.
Lindsay Anderson

I asked my nine-year-old grandson, Trevor, what he would like on his tombstone. He said, "Pepperoni, cheese and mushrooms."

E. Gene Davis

Here lies Mick Jagger ... gathering moss.

Ellen Maltz

Al Gore: Biodegrade in peace.

John Verba

Dolly Parton: Did not drown.

Richard N. Crenshaw

Bernard Lacoste: See you later, alligator.

Michael Levy

THE
BRAIN

EDUCATION

I'm all for school busing. I've learned so much more in a school bus
than I'll ever learn in a school.
Jo Anne Worley, Rowan & Martin's Laugh-in

Rarely is the question asked, "Is our children learning?"   **George W. Bush**

When I was young, my mother used to say to me, "To pay for your education,
your father and I had to make a lot of sacrifices." And it was true, because they
were both druids.   **Milton Jones**

It's important to pay close attention in school—for years I thought that bears
masturbated all winter.   **Damon R. Milhem**

My topic today is the purpose of theology ... There is nothing better than being
in a class where no one knows the answer.

Sally Brown, *Peanuts*

The illiteracy level of our children are appalling.   **George W. Bush**

—[*singing*] We don't need no education.
—Yes, you do. You just used a double negative.

Roy and Moss, *The IT Crowd*

—How is education going to make me smarter? Besides, every time I learn
something new, it pushes some old stuff out of my brain. Remember when I
took that home winemaking course, and I forgot how to drive?
—You were drunk!   **Homer and Marge Simpson,** *The Simpsons*

If I didn't have some kind of education, then I wouldn't be able to count my
money.   **Missy Elliott**

Education isn't everything. For a start, it isn't an elephant.

Spike Milligan

Me having no education, I had to use my brains.

Bill Shankly, soccer coach

SCHOOL

"You don't know anything about anything," he pointed out gently.
"It is the effect of your English public school education."
P. G. Wodehouse, Sam the Sudden

I was teacher's pet. She kept me in a cage at the back of the class.

Ken Dodd

I went to a girls' school, and it made me so stupid that I could barely remember how to breathe.   **India Knight**

—Do you remember your school motto?
—[*unsure if Angus Deayton is asking her or Paul Merton*] Who are you looking at?
—That must have been a tough school.

Angus Deayton, Glenda Jackson and Paul Merton,
Have I Got News for You

I went to a convent in New York and was finally fired for my insistence that the Immaculate Conception was spontaneous combustion.

Dorothy Parker

If they ever come up with a Swashbuckling School, I think one of the courses should be Laughing, Then Jumping Off Something.

Jack Handey, *Deep Thoughts*

Chemistry is a class you take in high school or college, where you figure out two plus two is 10, or something.   **Dennis Rodman**

—When you were young, what did you like best about school?
—When it's closed.   **Reporter and Yogi Berra**

I was bullied at school, called all kinds of different names. But one day I turned on my bullies and said, "Sticks and stones may break my bones but names will never hurt me." And it worked! From then on, it was sticks and stones all the way.

Harry Hill

—So, what did you do in school today?
—Well, I broke in my purple clogs.

Mel and Cher Horowitz, Clueless

Their homework is so hard these days … It's totally done differently to what I was teached when I was at school.

David Beckham, on why he gave up trying to help
his six-year-old son, Brooklyn, with his homework

TEACHERS

Those who can't do, teach. And those who can't teach, teach gym.
And of course, those who couldn't do anything, I think, were
assigned to our school.
Woody Allen

—Good grief! I'm doomed! I didn't make the honor roll this month! This will be a shock to my mom and dad … They want me to be the smartest kid in the world.
—What do you think will happen?
—Well, obviously the first step will be to put in a complaint about the teacher.

Linus Van Pelt and Charlie Brown, Peanuts

Parent–Teacher Night: Let's Share the Blame

Banner hung above the entrance of Springfield Elementary School, The Simpsons

I would like to teach you something. I would like to be Michelle Pfeiffer to your angry black kid who learns that poetry is just another way to rap.

Jack Donaghy, 30 Rock

—I'm going to teach that kid everything I know.
—What's he going to do the second half of the day?

Roy Biggins and Helen Chapel, Wings

—Now, children, take out your red crayons.
—Mrs. Hoover, I don't have a red crayon …
—Why not?
—I ate it.

Ralph Wiggum and Mrs. Hoover, *The Simpsons*

EXAMS & TESTS

Laura and I really don't realize how bright our children is sometimes
until we get an objective analysis.
George W. Bush

I asked my son, "How did the English test go?" He replied, "Oh, I done great."
Chris Banks

Me fail English? That's unpossible!
Ralph Wiggum, *The Simpsons*

The beginners' Sunday school teacher used gold stars at the top of pupils' test
papers to reward excellent work. One boy who received a large zero on his took
the test paper home and explained to his mother, "Teacher ran out of stars, so
she gave me a moon."
Florence Nagle

I can't understand why I flunked American history. When I was a kid, there was
so little of it.
George Burns

Finding the examination room, which was tucked away in a fifth-floor alcove of
London's Birkbeck College, was itself a challenge, and one a couple of the
examinees failed to meet. Perplexed by the building's layout, they arrived too
late to take the first test.
Andrew Anthony, taking a Mensa IQ test

And the shocker is, I lost out on the intelligence test. They asked me to name the
seven dwarfs, but apparently I didn't name the seven they had in mind.
Rose Nylund, *The Golden Girls*

I understand my tests are popular reading in the teachers' lounge.
Calvin, *Calvin and Hobbes*

I took an IQ test and the result was negative.
Anon.

I got my IQ tested when I was about seven years old ... On the test, I was supposed to draw a line from the table to the sink but I misheard the teacher and drew a *lion* from the desk to the sink, which took rather longer than the test allowed for because of the tail and ears etc.

Rhod Sharp, BBC Radio

[*faking illness to avoid a school test*] Ohhh, my ovaries.

Bart Simpson, *The Simpsons*

Now I lay me down to rest,
I pray I pass tomorrow's test.
If I should die before I wake,
That's one less test I'll have to take.   *A Student's Prayer*, Anon.

[*taking a test*] A gas mask, a smoke grenade and a helicopter, that's all I ask!

Calvin, *Calvin and Hobbes*

—What did you get on your SATs test?
—Nail polish.   **Interviewer and Jennifer Lopez**

My son Raymond crept back into school one night and had a prior peek at the exam papers ... And he still didn't bleedin' pass!

Norman Stanley Fletcher, *Porridge*

I even flunked gym.   **Keanu Reeves**

—I only failed my engineer's exam by the narrowest of narrow margins.
—You what? You walked in there, wrote "I am a fish" 400 times, did a funny little dance and fainted.

Arnold Rimmer and Dave Lister, *Red Dwarf*

Next week I have to take my college aptitude test. In my high school, they didn't even teach aptitude.   **Tony Banta, *Taxi***

Exam question that was rejected: Spell Mississippi without looking at how we've spelt it in the question.

Frankie Boyle, *Mock the Week*

This isn't right. This isn't even wrong.

**Wolfgang Pauli, Nobel Laureate in Physics,
on a fellow physicist's paper**

Failed quite brilliantly.

Lord Snowdon, on leaving college without a degree

You sign all your official letters "Arnold Rimmer BSc." The BSc stands for "Bronze Swimming Certificate."
Dave Lister, *Red Dwarf*

I have a BA in dope, but a PhD in soul.
Lou Reed

To those of you who received honors, awards and distinctions, I say, well done. And to the C students, I say, you too can be President of the United States.
George W. Bush, commencement address to graduates of Yale University, 2001

REPORT CARDS

This boy listens in class with the flawless dignity of the dead.

The dawn of legibility in this boy's handwriting discloses his utter inability to spell.

The boy is every inch a fool, but luckily for him he's not very tall.

This boy will make a good foreman, judging by the way he watches other people work.

His mind is like unto a muddy pond in which occasionally gleams a goldfish.

COLLEGE

A fool's brain digests philosophy into folly, science into superstition and art into pedantry. Hence university education.
George Bernard Shaw

If you're like me, you won't remember everything you did here. That can be a good thing.
George W. Bush, commencement address to graduates of Yale University, 2001

Dublin University contains the cream of Ireland: rich and thick.

Samuel Beckett

College is breaking my spirit. Every single day, they're telling me things I don't know. It's making me feel stupid.

Marty, *Gilmore Girls*

Unwise first line of a college application: While the government might consider me an enemy combatant, I prefer to think of myself as a freedom fighter.

Chuck Smith

INTELLIGENCE

It is not clear that intelligence has any long-term survival value.
Professor Stephen Hawking

—What are we gonna do?
—Well, we're just gonna have to use our brains.
—Damn it.

Lucky Day and Dusty Bottoms, *Three Amigos!*

—Daddy, isn't it obvious to you?
—Nothing is ever obvious to me.

Lisa and "Coach" Ernie Pantusso, *Cheers*

Some of it is over my head, and I'm six feet ten inches.

Marty Conlon, basketball player

It has been well said of Sigsbee H. Waddington that, if men were dominoes, he would be the double-blank.

P. G. Wodehouse, *The Small Bachelor*

He doesn't know, but if anyone knows, he would.

Murray Walker

I would dance and be merry, life would be a ding-a-berry, if I only had a brain.

The Scarecrow, *The Wizard of Oz*

He had just about enough intelligence to open his mouth when he wanted to eat, but certainly no more.

P. G. Wodehouse, *Barmy in Wonderland*

He has not so much brain as earwax.

William Shakespeare, *Troilus and Cressida*

His ignorance covers the world like a blanket, and there's scarcely a hole in it anywhere.

Mark Twain

—I am not as stupid as you think.
—No, you're not. You couldn't be.

Alan Davies and Stephen Fry, *QI* (*Quite Interesting*)

You think I know fuck nothing ... well, let me tell you, I know fuck all!

Michael Curtiz, director

He's very smart. He has an IQ.

Leo Rosten

It takes a smart man to know he's stupid.

Barney Rubble, *The Flintstones*

—How stupid can you get?
—How stupid do you want me?

Peter Patterson and Freddie Franklin, *Abbott and Costello Meet the Mummy*

I'm as thick as a whale omelet.

Prince George, *Blackadder the Third*

I'm alone in space with a man who'd lose a battle of wits with a stuffed iguana.

Arnold Rimmer, *Red Dwarf*

Beneath the elaborately constructed veneer of the bumbling buffoon, there may well be a bumbling buffoon.

Boris Johnson, mayor of London, on himself

You know, I'm not as dumb as you look.

Stan Laurel, to Oliver Hardy, *Their First Mistake*

I make Jessica Simpson look like a rock scientist.

Tara Reid

—What if she [Helen] has got an IQ of 25?
—Actually, I'm only 23.

Brian Dowling and Helen Adams, *Big Brother 2* (U.K.)

Your head is just something you keep your hat on, isn't it?
                    Inspector Raymond Fowler, *The Thin Blue Line*

—A common misperception of [you] is ...
—Can you give me an example? That I'm thick? Cos I ain't.
                    Elisa Bray and Jade Goody, British TV personality

I'm so smart now. Everyone is always like, "Take your top off." Sorry, no. They always want to get that money shot. I'm not stupid.
                    Paris Hilton

I am so smart, I am so smart, S-M-R-T, I mean S-M-A-R-T.
                    Homer Simpson, *The Simpsons*

I am so clever that sometimes I don't understand a single word of what I am saying.   **Oscar Wilde**

If *I* can't understand it, what chance has the general public got?
                    Derek Jameson, DJ

Don't try to understand, try to overstand.   Kieron "Science" Harvey, *Big Brother 6* (U.K.)

—You know, Gracie, I'm beginning to think that there's nothing up there.
[*points to his own head*]
—Oh, George, you're so self-conscious.
                    George Burns and Gracie Allen

I know a lot of people think I'm dumb. Well, at least I ain't no educated fool.
                    Leon Spinks, former boxer

You've got the brain of a four-year-old boy, and I bet he was glad to get rid of it.
                    Groucho Marx

Eh, you, don't call my daughter stupid! No one calls my daughter stupid—except me.   **Bianca Jackson,** *EastEnders*

I may be dumb, but I'm not stupid.   **Donald Regan**

If he's so smart, how come he's dead?

                    Homer Simpson, *The Simpsons*

THINKING

Brain: an apparatus with which we think we think.
Ambrose Bierce

—OK, brain. You don't like me and I don't like you. So let's hurry up and solve this one so I can go back to killing you with beer.
—Deal.   **Homer Simpson and Homer's brain,** *The Simpsons*

It's not that I'm stupid. I just don't think sometimes.   **Colin Farrell**

—You know what I think?
—That reindeer really know how to fly?
Rose Nylund and Dorothy Zbornak, *The Golden Girls*

—It's so quiet up here you can hear yourself think.
—I don't hear anything.   **Alex Reiger and Reverend Jim,** *Taxi*

—I just had an idea!
—The first time's always exciting, isn't it?
Bob and Dr. John Becker, *Becker*

I'm an ocean, because I'm really deep. If you search deep enough you can find rare exotic treasures.   **Christina Aguilera**

—What are your immediate thoughts, Walter?
—I don't have any immediate thoughts at the moment.
Brough Scott, horseracing commentator,
and Walter Swinburn, jockey

I know what you're thinking; you're thinking, What's the best way to transport an owl?   **Harry Hill**

Do you mind if I have another idea?
Stan Laurel, to Oliver Hardy, *Way Out West*

—I have a hunch
—So did Quasimodo.

Dr. Wayne Fiscus and Dr. Mark Craig, *St. Elsewhere*

In the studio, I do try to have a thought in my head, so that it's not like a blank stare.

Cindy Crawford

If I think too much, it kind of freaks me out.

Pamela Anderson

I don't really think, I just walk.

Paris Hilton

If you'll excuse me, I need to be alone with my thought.

Jack McFarland, *Will & Grace*

I thought it would be great, you know, to have some time alone with my thoughts. Turns out I don't have as many thoughts as you'd think.

Joey Tribbiani, *Friends*

GENIUS

When a true genius appears in the world, you may know him by
this sign, that the dunces are all in confederacy
against him.
Jonathan Swift

—What do you get when you cross a genius with a hooker?
—A fucking know-it-all.

Gilbert Gottfried

Nobody in football should be called a genius. A genius is a guy like Norman Einstein.

Joe Theismann

Don't geniuses live in lamps?

Patrick Star, *SpongeBob SquarePants*

He is like a lighthouse in the middle of a bog—brilliant but useless.

John Kelly

Stephen Hawking's not a genius. He's pretentious. Born in Kent and talks with an American accent.

Ricky Gervais

—People think it must be fun to be a super genius, but they don't realize how hard it is to put up with all the idiots in the world.

—Isn't your pants' zipper supposed to be in the front?
Calvin and Hobbes, *Calvin and Hobbes*

ILLOGICAL LOGIC

I never came upon any of my discoveries through the process of
rational thinking.
Albert Einstein

Welcome to our morning soiree.

Danny Baker, BBC Radio personality

I'll tell you one fact—it may be rather boring, but it's interesting …

Barbara Cartland, novelist

I went to the pictures tomorrow
I took a front seat at the back.
I bought a plain cake with currants in
I ate it and gave it them back.

Children's rhyme

Absolutely right, but just a fraction wrong.

David Coleman

Nothing difficult is ever easy.

Anon.

I stand here, neither partial nor impartial.

Sir Boyle Roach

I drank some boiling water because I wanted to whistle.

Mitch Hedberg

—Did you see that?
—No.
—Neither did I.

Sidney and Willy Wang, *Murder by Death*

I ain't been nowhere, but I'm back.

Rocky Lockridge

Only one man ever understood me. And he didn't understand me.

Georg Wilhelm Friedrich Hegel

The only thing which isn't up for grabs is no change, and I think it's fair to say,
it's all to play for, except for no change.

Rhodri Morgan, the First Minister for Wales

It's a partial sellout.

Skip Caray

I'm here 13 days and I haven't been to the same restaurant once.

Sir Terry Wogan

Can I just say, that's a true urban myth.

Adele Roberts, *Big Brother 3* (U.K.)

Everybody hates me because I'm so universally liked.

Peter De Vries

The reason I put the salt in the pepper shaker and the pepper in the salt shaker is that people are always getting them mixed up. Now when they get mixed up, they'll be right.

Gracie Allen

I reckon I know why they got two sets of steps. One's for going up and the other's for going down.

Jethro Bodine, *The Beverly Hillbillies*

—Sit down, please, Miss West.
—I'll sit when I've finished standing.

Film producer and Mae West

Tell them to stand closer apart.

Sam Goldwyn

They were standing there like sitting ducks.

Richard Thompson

He was standing there making a sitting target of himself.

Terry Lawless

We've got to sit down and have a think about where we stand. Roy McFarland

I used to sit in your seat, so I know exactly where you stand.

Harry Malone, *CI5: The New Professionals*

We can't sit here and stand for it.

Peter Temple-Morris

[They] should stand or fall on their own two feet.

Edwina Currie

I don't want to look further than as far as I can see.

Frank Bruno

Our consistency's been all over the place.

Andy Hinchliffe

We have self-belief in each other.   Gavin Hastings

Perhaps I know to what extent I can go too far.   Jean Cocteau

We're all in this together—by ourselves.   Lily Tomlin

I have already not made that point.   David Frost

And my concern, David, is several.   George W. Bush

My mother and I were on a completely different wavelength. We were like chalk and cheese. But that's where the similarity ends.

Kevin McAleer

—She told me not to tell you that she's got a surprise for you.
—Well, don't tell me.
—I won't. I can keep a secret.

Stan Laurel and Oliver Hardy, *Twice Two*

We are never prepared for what we expect.   James A. Michener

Exceeded expectations? I'd say he's done more than that.

Yogi Berra

I'd miss you even if we never met.   Nick Mercer, *The Wedding Date*

Golly, Mr. Wabbit, I hope I didn't hurt ya too much when I killed ya.
Elmer Fudd to Bugs Bunny, *Duck! Rabbit, Duck!*

I answered in the affirmative with an emphatic "No!"

Sir Boyle Roach

Sometimes you have to get to know someone really well to realize you're really strangers.   Mary Richards, *Mary Tyler Moore*

I'm *not* a minority. I'm an outnumbered majority.
Ed Brown, *Chico and the Man*

Individuality is fine. As long as we do it together.

Major Frank Burns, *M*A*S*H*

The only way of preventing what is past is to put a stop to it before it happens.
Sir Boyle Roach

Finally, but by no means last ...   Andy Peebles

I concluded from the beginning that this would be the end, and I am right, for it is not half over.
Sir Boyle Roach

A sad ending, albeit a happy one.   Murray Walker

PHILOSOPHY

Every great thinker is someone else's moron.
Umberto Eco

A philosophy professor and a sociologist are holidaying at a nudist camp. The philosopher turns to his colleague and asks, "I assume you've read Marx?" "Yes," replies the sociologist, "I think it's these wicker chairs."
Anon.

I wonder if chairs go, "Oh no! Here comes another asshole!"
Robin Williams

I am sitting with a philosopher in the garden; he says again and again, "I know that that's a tree," pointing to a tree that is near us. Someone else arrives and hears this, and I tell them, "This fellow isn't insane. We are only doing philosophy."
Ludwig Wittgenstein

All I know is, I'm not a Marxist.   Karl Marx

Apart from the known and the unknown, what else is there?
Harold Pinter

There are a few unknowns that we don't know about it.
Glenn Hoddle

The message is that there are known knowns—there are things we know that we know. There are known unknowns—that is to say, there are things that we now know we don't know. But there are also unknown unknowns—there are things we do not know we don't know. And each year we discover a few more of those unknown unknowns.

Donald Rumsfeld, Secretary of Defense (YT)

I think there could be a category of unknown knowns ... Actually, Rumsfeld didn't exhaust all the possibilities.

Boris Johnson, commenting on
Donald Rumsfeld's statement above

You're beginning with an illogical premise, and proceeding perfectly logically to an illogical conclusion, which is a dangerous thing to do.

Donald Rumsfeld, Secretary of Defense

I know. You know I know. I know you know I know. We know Henry knows and Henry knows we know. We're a knowledgeable family.

Eleanor of Aquitaine, *The Lion in Winter*

You can expect Bobby to be Bobby. If Bobby ain't Bobby, Bobby just can't be Bobby.

Bobby Brown

I'm an optometrist. I always believe in good—well, you know what I mean. I believe in good stuff.

Mychal Thompson, former NBA player

—Do we really exist?
—Bert, can you feel your underwear?
—Yeah.
—Then we really exist.

Herbert Viola and David Addison, *Moonlighting*

If something's neither here nor there, where the hell is it?

Chic Murray

One man's ceiling is another man's floor.

Mork, *Mork & Mindy*

In a nutshell, my philosophy is: Don't panic when you're trapped inside a nutshell—someone's bound to want a nut sooner or later.

Peter Kay

—What do you get if you cross *The Godfather* with a philosopher?
—An offer you can't understand.

Anon.

Descartes is sitting in a bar having a drink. The bartender asks him if he would like another. "I think not," he says, and vanishes in a puff of logic.

Anon.

TRUTH

It is dangerous to be sincere unless you are also stupid.
George Bernard Shaw

See, in my line of work you got to keep repeating things over and over and over again for the truth to sink in, to kind of catapult the propaganda.

George W. Bush

I never know how much of what I say is true.
Bette Midler

I told 'em the truth and they fell for it.

Judge Harry Stone, *Night Court*

I swear on my mother's life—my late mother's life ...
Alex "Hurricane" Higgins

The reality could not be further from the truth.
Presenter, BBC TV

The truth hurts, doesn't it? Oh, sure, maybe not as much as jumping on a bicycle with the seat missing, but it still hurts.
Lieutenant Frank Drebin, *The Naked Gun*

Cross my heart and hope to eat my weight in goslings.
W. C. Fields

LIES

It takes a wise man to handle a lie;
a fool had better remain honest.
Norman Douglas

I ran out of gas! I got a flat tire! I didn't have change for cab fare! I lost my tux at the cleaners! I locked my keys in the car! An old friend came in from out of town! Someone stole my car! There was an earthquake! A terrible flood! Locusts! IT WASN'T MY FAULT, I SWEAR TO GOD!

Jake Blues, *The Blues Brothers*

That's our story, and we're stuck with it.

Stan Laurel, *A Chump at Oxford*

—You're lying!
—Of course I am, but hear me out!

Rocco Melonchek and Roland T. Flakfizer, *Brain Donors*

I misspoke.

Hillary Clinton, on claiming that she was under sniper fire in Bosnia

I trusted you. You wear glasses.

Angie Jordan, *30 Rock*

I wasn't lying. I was writing fiction with my mouth.

Homer Simpson, *The Simpsons*

I was not lying. I said things that later on seemed to be untrue.

Richard Nixon

I was provided with additional input that was radically different from the truth. I assisted in furthering that version.

Colonel Oliver North, from his Iran-Contra testimony

I don't want to tell you any half-truths unless they're completely accurate.

Dennis Rappaport

Sometimes in politics you've got to lie, and I think we should be honest about that.

Charles Kennedy, Member of Parliament

THE
MIND

FEAR & PARANOIA

Tell me your phobias and I will tell you what you are afraid of.
Robert Benchley

They say cheese gives you nightmares. Ridiculous! I'm not scared of cheese.

Ross Noble

—That bull wouldn't hurt a fly!
—Yeah, but I'm not a fly.

Oliver Hardy and Stan Laurel, *The Bullfighters*

When I was on holiday, when I was about eight, I found a snake's skin and I was teasing my sister with it. She said, "Put it down! There's diseases on it." Ten years later, I'm 18 and had some mates round and I'm telling them how my sister's afraid of snakes and she chose then to tell me the truth: I'd been running around with a used condom.

Ricky Gervais, *Room 101*

Even snakes are afraid of snakes.

Steven Wright

—It was not a moth, it was a bat! I could tell from that eerie high-pitched screech.
—That was you!

Niles and Frasier Crane, *Frasier*

I've coughed up scarier stuff than that

Grampa Simpson, *The Simpsons*

I discovered I scream the same way whether I'm about to be devoured by a Great White or if a piece of seaweed touches my foot.

Kevin James

I'm afraid of sharks, but only in a water situation.

Demetri Martin

—There's nothing to it. All you have to do is look the lion straight in the eyes. Lions are afraid of that. I read that in a book.
—But did the lion read the book?

Oliver Hardy and Stan Laurel, *Nothing but Trouble*

—There's no reason to be afraid of oatmeal.
—It's not really the oatmeal I'm afraid of. It's the guy on the box with the scary hat.

Dean and Chuckie, *Rugrats*

Fear nothing—except insects. And sweaty guys who insist on kissing you when they come up to say hello.

Paris Hilton, *Confessions of an Heiress*

—Daddy, I'm scared. Too scared to even wet my pants.
—Just relax and it'll come, son.

Ralph and Chief Wiggum, *The Simpsons*

I'd like to buy a new kite—red, blue, yellow ... I don't care ... the color doesn't matter. Do you have one that isn't afraid of heights?

Charlie Brown, *Peanuts*

Some people are afraid of heights. Not me, I'm afraid of widths.

Steven Wright

I have a claustrophobia for heights.

Lady Elizabeth Dale

[*on a rollercoaster*] I'd never voluntarily do something like this... but the tip is to keep your eyes open and just go with the flow, feel it, enjoy it, look at the sunny day, look at the beach ... I really don't like this ... nooooooooooooooooooo .... aaghhhhhhhhh .... shutting my eyes ... ooohhhhhhhh .... don't like it ... aghhhhhhhh ... I'm so glad I didn't have breakfast ... noooooooohhhhh ... I think it's nearly over ... ughhh ... I'm definitely, definitely a horse-carousel girl. I'm really sorry, I'm an absolute wuss.

Rachel Harrison, television reporter, riding the "Infusion"
rollercoaster in Blackpool, England (YT)

I don't like being afraid. It scares me.

Margaret "Hot Lips" Houlihan, *M*A*S*H*

I get goose pimples. Even my goose pimples get goose pimples.

Wally Campbell, *The Cat and the Canary*

And then it came to me that today is nothing more than tomorrow's yesterday, and I was no longer afraid.

David Ronka

Well, that takes care of the heebies, but I still got the jeebies.

Kate O'Brien, *The Drew Carey Show*

MADNESS & THERAPY

Stupidity often saves a man from going mad.
Oliver Wendell Holmes

I was walking down the street and I heard this voice saying, "Good evening, Mr. Dowd." Well, I turned around and here was this big six-foot rabbit leaning up against a lamppost. Well, I thought nothing of that because when you've lived in a town as long as I have, you get used to the fact that everybody knows your name.
Elwood P. Dowd, *Harvey*

I didn't expect him to be that mad in real life.
Jenny Frost, of pop group Atomic Kitten, meeting Ozzy Osbourne

They're watching me. I know when people are looking at me. I can tell by their eyes. And that's why I wear the crash helmet—well, for two reasons: a) It makes it harder for them to read your thoughts; and g) it makes them think that you've got a motorbike.
Kevin McAleer

—Frank, don't be paranoid.
—I'm only paranoid because everyone's against me.
Hawkeye and Major Frank Burns, *M*A*S*H*

Am I schizophrenic? One side of me probably is, but the other side is right down the middle, solid as a rock.
David Bowie

It's psychosomatic. You need a lobotomy. I'll get a saw.
Calvin, *Calvin and Hobbes*

I'm one of the few males who suffers from penis envy.
Alvy Singer, *Annie Hall*

If you lose your job, your marriage and your mind all in one week, try to lose your mind first, because then the other stuff won't matter that much.
Jack Handey, *Deep Thoughts*

—How did ADD affect you while in jail?
—Well, it's attention deficit disorder, so it's hard to pay attention to things. And I don't know, I just ...
Larry King and Paris Hilton, *Larry King Live*

—Your complaint alleges that you have had problems with concentration since the accident. Does that condition continue today?
—No, not really. I take a stool softener now.

Lawyer and witness, actual transcript from official court records

—I would say it's a nervous breakdown. What do you think, Doctor?
—It appears to be an acute epileptoid manifestation and a pan phobic melancholiac with indication of a neurasthenia cordus.
—Is that more expensive than a nervous breakdown?

Pepi Katona and doctor, *The Shop Around the Corner*

It was really sad when I went to visit my friend Jim at the state mental institution. He was convinced he was on a tropical island with no cares and no worries. It took me a long time to convince him that no, he was in a room with bare walls and a bare bed and he was wearing a straitjacket.

Jack Handey, *What I'd Say to the Martians*

He's in hospital suffering from a nervous breakdown, but no doubt he will soon be better and running around like a maniac.

Simon Bates

Anyone who goes to a psychiatrist needs his head examined.

Sam Goldwyn

There's no stigmata connected to going to a shrink.

Carmine Lupertazzi, *The Sopranos*

—Why did you quit analysis?
—I went sane.

Hannah and Bill Warren, *California Suite*

MEMORY

Everyone has a photographic memory. Some just don't have film.
Steven Wright

— [*answering the phone*] Hello, Cheers bar. [*to the people in the bar*] Is there an Ernie Pantusso here?
—That's you, Coach.
—Speaking.

"Coach" Ernie Pantusso and Sam Malone, *Cheers*

Why is it that I can recall a cigarette ad jingle from 25 years ago, but I can't remember what I just got up to do?

Calvin's dad, *Calvin and Hobbes*

Canon. Sawyer's splendid absent-mindedness once led him, while welcoming a visitor at the railway station, to board the departing train and disappear.

New Statesman

Am in Market Harborough. Where ought I to be?

G. K. Chesterton, telegram to his wife

Insufficient Memory

Slogan on T-shirt

I'm blessed with total recall, except about where I left my umbrella.

Hubert Gregg

I knew exactly where it was, I just couldn't find it.

Tim Berra

Are you telling me you have a photogenic memory?

College secretary, to William R. Long

Miss Evans, the accomplished sister of the Provost of Eton, was at a friend's dinner party. She forgot she was not in her own house, and was heard apologizing to a lady near her, "I can't tell you, my dear, how sorry I am that the dinner is a failure—I can never rely on my cook."

E. M. Ward

Ted Heath came and talked to me at a party. A little later, in another part of the room, he did so again. When I gently reminded him that we had just had the same conversation, he ticked me off for having moved.

Robin Bryer

Mr. George Harvest, minister of Thames Ditton, was one of the most absent-minded men of his time... One day Lady Onslow, being desirous of knowing something of the most remarkable planets and constellations, requested Mr. Harvest, on a fine starlight night, to point them out to her, which he undertook to do; but in the midst of his lecture, having occasion to make water, thought this need not interrupt it, and accordingly directed that operation with one hand, and went on in his explanation, pointing out the constellations with the other.

Francis Grose, 1796

Aunt Dosia, who married a parson, retained a faint beauty in her old age, but her wits wilted. Once at the Easter Communion, when her husband handed her the full chalice, she drained it to the last drop, murmuring, "Perfectly delicious," and handed it back in the presence of the whole congregation.

Shane Leslie, *Long Shadows*

My old friend Maltby, the brother of the bishop, was a very absent-minded man. One day at Paris, in the Louvre, we were looking at the pictures, when a lady entered who spoke to me, and kept me some minutes in conversation. On rejoining Maltby, I said, "That was Mrs—. It has been so long since we met, she had almost forgotten me and asked me if my name was Rogers." Maltby, still looking at the pictures: "And was it?"

Clive Rogers

A well-known conductor was taking the orchestra through a symphony when the first violin managed to indicate with his bow that the conductor's fly buttons were undone. Hastily, he turned his back on the orchestra, and buttoned himself up—in front of an audience of 5,000 people.

Michael Bateman

Hertfordshire firefighters were called to a small blaze at a kitchen in Cherry Way, Hatfield, after an elderly lady put her handbag in the oven thinking it was her dinner. The handbag was badly burned and largely inedible, but the money inside the purse was saved.

Welwyn and Hatfield Herald and Post

I'll always remember 1995 as the year I found out *Star Trek* wasn't real.

Daniel Johns, of Silverchair

I find that the further back I go, the better I remember things, whether they happened or not. **Mark Twain**

—Oh, by the way, I want to thank you for having us over for dinner the other night. Cheryl and I thought the stroganoff was marvelous.
—But, sir, we didn't have dinner the other night.
—Really? Then where the hell was I? And who's this Cheryl?

Admiral Benson and Lieutenant Commander Block, *Hot Shots*

I remember your name perfectly, but I just can't think of your face.

Rev. William Archibald Spooner

I never forget a face—especially if I've sat on it.

P. J. Decker, *All-American Murder*

Don't forget to kill Tim.

Al Swearengen, *Deadwood*

TIME

Time is a great teacher; unfortunately it kills all its pupils.
Hector Berlioz

—What time is it?
—You mean now?

Tom Seaver and Yogi Berra

It's just gone 17 minutes past four. That's the time, by the way.

Paul Jordan

I'm hopeless at telling the time. I need a digital watch with capital letters.

Richard Littlejohn

The sands of time are chiming toward the 21st century.

Sally Jessy Raphael

The time is twenty-half and a five minutes past eight.

BBC radio presenter

And the hourglass ticking off the seconds.

Waldemar Januszczak

Everyone, circumcise your watches!

Jim, *According to Jim*

It's now five past twelve, sometime on Sunday night.

Tom Boswell

As usual it's three minutes past eight o'clock.

David Jensen

Senate office hours are from twelve to one with an hour off for lunch.

George S. Kaufman

—Do you know the phrase "carpe diem"?
—It's fish bait, right?

C. D. Bales and Chris McConnell, *Roxanne*

It's not only a race against the clock but a race against time itself.

BBC presenter

The clock is going to tick one way or the other.   **James Naughtie**

It's exactly half past seven—more or less.   **BBC radio presenter**

The time at 8:20 just coming up to 8:20.   **Don Mosley**

It's exactly nine minutes past nine—and that doesn't happen very often.

Douglas Moffat

A stitch in time would have confused Einstein.   **Anon.**

It's actually tomorrow in Tokyo. Do you realize that there are people alive here in Minneapolis who are already dead in Tokyo?

Ted Baxter, *Mary Tyler Moore*

The ability of dandelions to tell the time is somewhat exaggerated, owing to the fact that there is always one seed that refuses to be blown off; the time usually turns out to be 37 o'clock.   **Miles Kington**

Time flies like an arrow. Fruit flies like a banana.

Groucho Marx

How long will this 24-hour rail strike last?

Eamonn O'Neal, BBC Radio host

It's later than it's ever been.   **Lotus Weinstock**

The spring and autumn time changes should happen at noon so we don't have to get up in the middle of the night to adjust all our clocks.

Russell Beland

When you're riding in a time machine way far into the future, don't stick your elbow out the window, or it'll turn into a fossil.

Jack Handey, *Deep Thoughts*

Gosh, that takes me back ... or is it forward? That's the trouble with time travel, you never can tell.   **Dr. Who**

At the end of the day, isn't it time we called it a day?

John Morris

We'll be back at the same time next week at the slightly later time of ten past eleven.

Michael Doran

PUNCTUALITY

The early bird gets the worm,
but the second mouse gets the cheese.
Anon.

—To catch a Hardy they've got to get up very early in the morning.
—What time?
—Oh, about half pas— "What time?"—Hmph!

Oliver Hardy and Stan Laurel, *Sons of the Desert*

You have to get up early if you want to get out of bed.

Groucho Marx

He's a guy who gets up at six o'clock in the morning regardless of what time it is.

Lou Duva

—Shouldn't you have been here two hours ago?
—Why, what happened?

George Burns and Gracie Allen

I usually take a two-hour nap, from one o'clock to four.

Yogi Berra

The late start is due to the time.

David Coleman

I'm so sorry. Mercury is in retrograde, and that messes with technology, and I was trying to get on e-mail to approve something, and my computer kept crashing.

Cameron Diaz, arriving late for an interview

I've been on a calendar but never on time.

Marilyn Monroe

I'm never late. If I'm late, it's because I'm dead.

Robert MacDougal, *Entrapment*

Let's synchronize our watches. It's now ... threeish.
The Major, *Soap*

[*looking at his watch*] This sundial is ten minutes slow.
Harold Bissonette, *It's a Gift*

I'm late to everything. I've always wanted to have it written in my will that when I die, the coffin shows up a half-hour late and says on the side, like, in gold: SORRY I'M LATE.
Axl Rose, of Guns N' Roses

Some people are always late, like the late King George V.
Spike Milligan

HAPPINESS

To be stupid, selfish and have good health are three requirements
for happiness, though if stupidity is lacking,
all is lost.
Gustave Flaubert

I'm happy as a Frenchman who's invented a pair of self-removing trousers.
Prince George, *Blackadder The Third*

I'm probably one of the happiest blokes you will ever meet. I have bluebirds flying out of every orifice.
David Coverdale, frontman for Whitesnake

Any time I can look a little taller ... I'm happy.
Jennifer Aniston

I feel my best when I'm happy.
Winona Ryder

I'm absolutely thrilled and over the world about it.
Tessa Sanderson

I haven't felt this relaxed and carefree since I was watch commander at Pearl Harbor.
Grampa Simpson, *The Simpsons*

MISCELLANEOUS

"The time has come," the walrus said, "to talk of many things; of shoes and ships and sealing wax, of cabbages and kings, and why the sea is boiling hot, and whether pigs have wings."
Lewis Carroll

—Eccles, it's me, Bluebottle! Why don't you open the door?
—Okay, how do you open a door?
—You turn the knob on your side.
—But I haven't got a knob on my side!

Bluebottle and Eccles, *The Goon Show*

[*Liz enters the room and stands behind Jack*]
—You've been avoiding me.
—How do you do that without turning around?
—To be perfectly honest, the first couple of people I did that to were not you, but ... here we are.   **Jack Donaghy and Liz Lemon, *30 Rock***

It was so dark, you couldn't see your face in front of you.

Bunny McLeod

Watch closely, I'm only going to do this once ...   **Kamikaze pilot**

There's a paratrooper coming down now. Let's see if he's going to land ...
Tony Blackburn

[*sitting high up in the branches of a tree*]
—I'm up here!
—How did you get up there?
—I fell.   **Andy and Lou, *Little Britain***

There *is* someone called Sherlock Holmes! I thought he was Mother Teresa's son but I know better now. I thought it was around those lines—husband or son.
Jade Goody, *Big Brother 3* (U.K.)

I woke up the other morning and found that everything in my room had been replaced by an exact replica.   **Steven Wright**

—Didn't I meet you in Rumbellipore, sir?
—You did not, sir. I was never there.
—Then you must have a double.
—Thanks, I will.   **Tommy Handley and the Colonel, *ITMA***

Do I not like that.

Graham Taylor

I am shocked! Sort of.

Donald Rumsfeld, Secretary of Defense (YT)

Jesus would be rolling over in his grave.

Homer Simpson, *The Simpsons*

[*judging at the village festival*] This competition is "How many things you can fit in a matchbox." Rosie fitted the most in, with 72 things.
—Seventy-two?!
—... matches.

Judge #1 and Judge #2, *Jam and Jerusalem*

Shut up, brain, or I'll stab you with a Q-Tip!

Homer Simpson, *The Simpsons*

I spoke to Karl the other day. He said, "I got up and then I was washing up and then I noticed there was no milk. So I went to the shop."

He went, "I had a conversation with a woman in the corner shop and everything. I came back, I had my breakfast, walked past a mirror ..." He had a cotton bud still in his ear. And he went, "So why didn't she tell me I had a cotton bud in my ear?"

I said, "What, you're angry with someone who didn't tell you you had a cotton bud stuck in your ear? Surely that's your responsibility, Karl ... How can you forget there's a cotton bud in your ear?" ... His take on the story, the reason he was telling me that story, was how stupid the woman in the shop was for not telling him.

Ricky Gervais, on Karl Pilkington, Quick Stop Entertainment

I was trying to daydream, but my mind kept wandering.

Steven Wright

I told you to make one longer than the other and instead you made one shorter than the other—the opposite.

Sir Boyle Roche

—Operating a crane is just like making love—left, down, rotate 62 degrees, engage rotor ...
—I know how to make love!

Bender and Amy, *Futurama*

If you must make a noise, make it quietly.

Stan Laurel, *Brats*

Don't go away and leave me alone ... You stay and I'll go away.

Groucho Marx

—Are you still here, Basil?
—No, I went a few minutes ago, dear, but I expect I'll be back shortly.

Sybil and Basil Fawlty, *Fawlty Towers*

I don't remember leaving, so I guess we didn't go.

Andrew Berra

—Say good night, Gracie.
—Good night, Gracie.

George Burns and Gracie Allen

Good night. Go to sleep, honey. Pray for brains!

Dorothy Zbornak, *The Golden Girls*

INDEX

A Bug's Life, 403
A Fish Called Wanda, 31
A Funny Thing Happened on the Way to the Forum, 105, 419
Abbot and Costello, 207, 347, 418, 431
Abrams, Elliot, 155
Absolutely Fabulous, 388
According to Jim, 216, 449
Ace, Goodman, 254
Acord, Charlie, 110
Adams, Douglas, 55, 208, 342, 361, 411
Adams, Joey, 115
Adams, Scott, 417
Ade, George, 168
Adler, Jerry, 212
Adler, Peter, 230
Affleck, Ben, 375
After the Fox, 275
Aglionby, Francis, 295
Aguilera, Christina, 229, 371, 409, 433
Ahern, Bertie, 37, 56, 58, 68
Ahmadinejad, Mahmoud, 107
Ahmed, Ahmed, 112
Airplane!, 30, 58, 335, 336, 338
Aitken, Jonathan, 219
Alexander, Alistair, 68
ALF, 141, 191, 212
Ali, Muhammad, 303
All in the Family, 68, 104, 109, 130, 139, 192, 293, 343
All-American Murder, 448
Allcock, Tony, 247
Allen, Dave, 41, 72, 73, 80, 129, 130, 144, 150, 350, 353, 409 411, 421
Allen, Florence, 371
Allen, Fred, 389
Allen, Gracie, 94, 135, 137, 145, 166, 192, 253, 255, 359, 399, 400, 410, 412, 432, 436, 451, 456
Allen, Herbert, 307
Allen, Steve, 193, 237, 249, 366
Allen, Vanessa, 88
Allen, Woody, 105, 128, 157, 172, 176, 189, 203, 210, 222, 227, 242, 243, 275, 298, 331, 344, 345, 349, 388, 94, 416, 420, 421, 426
Allinson, Richard, 211
Alliss, Peter, 183, 383

Alsop, Carlton, 370
American Dad!, 107
Anand, Anita, 412
Anchorman, 248
Anderson, Clive, 366
Anderson, D. H., 52
Anderson, Lindsay, 422
Anderson, Pamela, 89, 94, 127, 434
Andrews, Paul, 336
Andujar, Joaquin, 155, 179
Anger Management, 354
Angle, Jim, 43
Aniston, Jennifer, 452
Annie Hall, 445
Anthony, Andrew, 427
Apply Immediately, 163
Aragon, Ray, 111
"The Archers," 130
Aristophanes, 390
Arkansas Democrat, 99
Armour, Richard, 137
Armstrong, Louis, 221
Army Magazine of Preventive Medicine, 306
Arnold, Andrea, 189
Arron, Bennett, 175
Arsenic and Old Lace, 122
Arthur, 119, 122
Arthur 2: On the Rocks, 164
As Time Goes By, 138
Ash, Mary Kay, 209
Ashman, Kevin, 234
Aspel, Michael, 214
Asquith, Margot, 42, 383
The A-Team, 332
Atkins, Dame Eileen, 414
Atkinson, Ron, 50, 361
Atkinson, Rowan, 239
Atlanta Journal, 303
Atlanta Journal-Constitution, 270
Atlantic City Press, 277
Attell, Dave, 392, 405
Auber, Daniel, 414
Austin, Mark, 237
Austin Powers: The Spy Who Shagged Me, 39, 190, 359
Austin, Warren, 297
The Australian, 47
The A-Z of Being Single, 124

Baby Mama, 135
Bacon, Richard, 267
Bagehot, Walter, 88
Bailey, Bill, 191, 366
Bailey, Covert, 405
Baker, Buddy, 195
Baker, Danny, 435
Ball, Zoë, 122
Banacek, 53
Bananas, 123, 375
The Band Wagon, 375
Bangor Daily News, 419
The Bank Dick, 393
Bankhead, Tallulah, 388
Banks, Chris, 427
Barbellion, W. N. P., 414
Barber, Nadine, 131, 165, 329, 338, 418
Barker, Sue, 44
Barkley, Charles, 97
Barnes, Rosie, 264
Barr, Roseanne, 120
Barraclough, Roy, 224, 402
Barrett, Matt, 310
Barrrymore, Drew, 143
Barry, Dave, 183, 206, 220, 250
Barry, J. J., 157
Barry, Marion, 277
Barry, Mrs. Philip, 146
Barrymore, Drew, 205
Barrymore, Ethel, 149
Basinger, Kim, 166
Bateman, Michael, 448
Bates, Simon, 30, 49, 57, 163, 219, 220, 298, 337, 394, 445
Battista, Orlando A., 100
Beary, Brendan, 306
Beck, Barry, 300
Becker, 381, 40, 433 6
Beckett, Samuel, 430
Beckham, David, 35, 38, 132, 136, 309, 349, 426
Beckham, Victoria, 96, 136, 308, 371, 406
Beckinsale, Kate, 371
Beecham, Sir Thomas, 167
Beefheart, Captain, 109
Beethoven, Ludwig van, 222
Behan, Brendan, 326
Behan, Kathleen, 130

Being There, 106
Beland, Russell, 54, 55, 194, 221, 236, 450
Belasco, Leon, 223
Belo, Brian, 67, 244, 400
Bemrose, Max, 143
Benaderet, Bea, 130
Benaud, Richie, 257
Benchley, Robert, 97, 320, 388, 443
Benitez, John, 224
Benn, Tony, 396
Benn, Tony, 414
Bennett, Sidney, 172
Bennett, Winston, 384
Benny, Jack, 118, 389, 39
The Benny Hill Show, 247
Benson, Beth, 47
Bent, Ned, 352
Bentine, Michael, 157, 240, 348
Bergman, Stefan, 41
Berle, Milton, 91
Berlioz, Hector, 449
Berlusconi, Silvio, 148
Berra, Andrew, 456
Berra, Bridgette, 155
Berra, Carmen, 193, 226
Berra, Gretchen, 372
Berra, Maria, 246
Berra, Tim, 447
Berra, Yogi, 40, 57, 154, 155, 168, 169, 178, 183, 212, 224, 226, 227, 228, 246, 254, 255, 258, 259, 310, 320, 361, 363, 372, 403, 420, 425, 437, 449, 451
Berry, Lynda, 200
Best, Angie, 415
Betten, Richard, 53
The Beverly Hillbillies, 436
Bevin, Ernest, 56
Bewitched, 141
The Bible, 60
Bierce, Ambrose, 295, 433
The Big Chill, 421
The Big Lebowski, 119
The Big Trail, 137
Biggins, Christopher, 392
Billings, Josh, 153
Billington, Arthur, 412
Binder, Mike, 152
Birch, Ellen, 381

Bishop, Joey, 383
Bjayou, Raef, 165
Björk, 166
Black, Cilla, 65, 162
Black, Hugo L., 413
Blackadder, 216
Blackadder Goes Forth, 158
Blackadder II, 216, 246, 400
Blackadder the Third, 96, 313, 431, 452
Blackadder's Christmas Carol, 155
Blackburn, George, 174
Blackburn, Tony, 454
Blackwood, John, 115
Blair, Cherie, 408
Blair, Tony, 63
Blake, Ellen, 68
Blake, Eubie, 413
Blake, Les, 191
Blake, Lilian, 66
Blake, Melanie, 66
Blake, Sir Peter, 248
Blake, Tracey, 370
Blake's, 7, 356
Blier, Vicki, 77
Block Busters, 292
Blofeld, Henry, 367
Bloom, Adam, 205
Bloom, Herschel, 354
The Blues Brothers, 327, 441
Blumberg, Sid, 214
Blunkett, David, 385
Blunt, James, 219
Blyveis, Barry, 164, 300 , 357
Boal, Augusto, 72
The Bob Newhart Show, 199
Bogart, Humphrey, 96
Bogdanovitch, Peter, 93
Bombeck, Erma, 41
Bonaparte, Napoleon, 267
Bond, Chris, 95
Bonney, Kyle, 403
Bonso, Wandryn J., 95
Booth, S., 68
Borat, 106, 302
Borge, Victor, 222, 223, 382
Borgman, Jim, 47
Bosom Buddies, 30
Boston Globe, 102

Boswell, Tom, 449
Bottom, 297, 300
Bottomley, Virginia, 418
Boulton, Adam, 274
Bouvet, Trina, 330
Bowden, Brent, 171
Bowen, Jim, 190
Bowfinger, 228
Bowie, David, 445
Bowman, John, 277
Boxer, Barbara, 414
Boycott, Geoffrey, 40, 57
Boyle, Frankie, 243, 428
The Brady Bunch Movie, 115
Bragg, Melvyn, 238
Brain Donors, 63, 112, 206, 255, 299, 328,
    404, 441
Brand, Jo, 203, 239, 407
Brand, Russell, 335, 365
Brando, Marlon, 199
Branson, Richard, 134
Branson, Sir Richard, 153, 374
Braunstein, Richard, 391
Bray, Elisa, 432
Brazil, Alan, 50
Breenllew, Gill, 95
Brenchley, John, 95
Brennan, Eileen, 130
Brice, Fanny, 384
Brideshead Revisited, 390
Brierly, Stephen, 136
Briggs, Jackie, 68
Bristow, Eric, 128
British Army Journal, 298
Britton, Tony, 51
Broadus, Brian, 54, 302, 375
Brockes, Emma, 418
Bromley, Peter, 48
Brooker, Charlie, 358
Brooks, Mel, 356
Bross, Jack, 54
Brown, A. Whitney, 240, 305
Brown, Bobby, 439
Brown, Douggie, 359
Brown, Ed, 374
Brown, James, 148, 365
Brown, Maggie, 168
Brown, Rita Mae, 414

Brown, Ron, 420
Browne, Des, 150
Browne, Jack, 51
Browning, Guy, 327
Bruggemeier, Franz-Josef, 213
Brunelle, Michael, 78
Bruno, Frank, 47, 168, 185, 186, 418, 436
Bryant, Kelly, 317
Bryer, Robin, 447
Buckley, Alan, 57
Buckley, William F., Jr., 305
Buerk, Michael, 314
Buffett, Warren, 307
Buffy the Vampire Slayer, 92, 380
Bugs Bunny, 347, 437
Bull Durham, 97
Bull, Tom, 420
Bullard, Ronnie, 117
The Bullwinkle Show, 30
Bullock, E. M., 49
Burgess, Anthony, 253
Burke, Alan, 45
Burke, Ron, 102
Burns, George, 126, 145, 166, 253, 255, 410, 427, 432, 451, 456
Burridge, Richard, 187
Burroway, Stanley, 67
Burton, Richard, 392
Bush, George, Sr., 37, 45, 110, 150, 155, 262, 104
Bush, George W., 34, 37, 38, 44, 47, 50, 56, 69, 91, 98, 132, 139, 154, 156, 165, 188, 197, 213, 217, 251, 261, 262, 264, 265, 267, 268, 269 – 70, 296, 297, 299, 301, 302, 301, 302, 305, 306, 307, 310, 311, 312, 317, 323, 335, 341, 342, 343, 359, 360, 377, 383, 407, 409, 409, 410, 414, 424, 427, 429, 437, 440
Bush, Laura, 272
Butler, Bryon, 55
Buttons, Red, 412
Buzzi, Ruth, 157

C, Mel, 236
Cabaret, 355
Caesar, Sid, 253
Cage, John, 218

Caines, Daniel, 175
California Suite, 121, 330, 391, 445
Callahan, John, 397
Calvin and Hobbes, 161, 162, 242, 243, 306, 310, 427, 428, 434 – 35, 445, 447, 447
Cameron, David, 110
Campbell, Joseph, 342
Campbell, Naomi, 280, 325
Campbell, Nicky, 237
Campbell, Sir Menzies "Ming," 133
Campisi, Scott, 90
Can Hieronymus Merkin Ever Forget Mercy Humppe and Find True Happiness?, 228
Capablanca, José Raúl, 189
Caray, Skip, 436
Cardwell, Philip, 58
Carey, Drew, 140
Carey, Mariah, 236
Carl, Jeffrey, 54
Carlin, George, 98, 142, 145, 153, 208, 211, 212, 242, 244, 331, 341, 387
Carnahan, Elden, 75, 217, 298
Carpenter, Harry, 173, 186, 324
Carr, Alan, 104, 142, 389, 410
Carr, J. L., 132
Carr, Jimmy, 31, 116, 185, 193, 201, 248, 335, 409, 417
Carrere, Tia, 364
Carrington, Lord, 351
Carroll, Kevin, 183
Carroll, Lewis, 157, 317, 454
Carry On, Nurse, 384
Carson, Edward, 304
Carson, Frank, 164, 168, 234
Carson, Johnny, 111
Carter, Judy, 357
Cartland, Barbara, 435
Cartmill, Matt, 242
Carville, James, 270
The Cat and the Canary, 347, 348, 357, 444
The Catered Affair, 127
Cavanagh, Tim, 163
Cavett, Dick, 135
Chandler, Raymond, 54
Chapman, Graham, 334
Charlotte Observer, 100
Charlton, Jack, 367
Chase, Ilka, 96

Cheers, 34, 35, 62, 92, 93, 94, 113, 126, 136, 204, 227, 230, 300, 306, 319, 359, 369, 390, 430, 445

Cher, 57, 370

Chernomyrdin, Viktor, 266

Chester Daily News, 415

Chesterton, G. K., 149, 447

Chiafullo, Lou, 72

Chicago Tribune, 99

Chico and the Man, 437

China Seas, 189

Chong, Sue Lin, 368

Christian Herald, 208

Church Bulletin, 62

Church, Charlotte, 317

Church News, 62

Churchill, Adeye, 153

Churchill, Winston, 40, 266, 323

CI5: The New Professionals, 436

Cioc, Mark, 213

Cioran, E. M., 418

Clancy, Tom, 268

Clare, Anthony, 141

Clark, Jennifer, 113

Clarke, Arthur C., 338

Clarke, Genevieve, 119

Clarke, Lou, 118

Clarke, Oz, 163, 390

Clarke, Paul, 69

Clarke, Victoria, 386

Clarkson, Jeremy, 330, 393

Cliff, Josie, 79

Clinton, Bill, 41, 45, 112, 259, 261, 326

Clinton, Hillary, 441

Clooney, George, 370

Close, Chuck, 413

Clough, Brian, 39, 148

Clough, Gordon, 176

Clough, Melissa, 376

Clueless, 426

Coates, Alison, 376

Coates, Craig, 147

Cobb, Irvin S., 372

Cobram, Justin D., 334

Cochrane, Matthew, 128

Cocker, Jarvis, 142

Cocktail, 163

Cocteau, Jean, 123, 437

Coe, Cynthia, 111

Cohen, Bernard H., 45

Cohen, John, 299

Cohn, Harry, 229

Colbert, Stephen, 33, 106, 207, 368

Colchester Gazette, 163

Cole, Bert, 65

Coleman, David, 48, 167, 174, 175, 211, 343, 367, 412, 435, 451

Coleman, Jerry, 179

Collier, Barbara, 218

Collins, Doug, 177

The Commitments, 225

Confetti, 87

Conlon, Marty, 430

Conner, P. J., 67

Constantine, Susannah, 373

Contra Costa Independent, 258

Conway, Tim, 130

Cook, Auggie, 140

Cook, Marv, 181

Cook, Peter, 141, 157

Cook, Robin, 413

Cook, Valerie, 205

Coolidge, Calvin, 165

Cooper, Grace, 199

Cooper, Jilly, 64, 89

Cooper, Robert, 158

Cooper, Tommy, 144, 192, 395

Cope, Julian, 220, 221

Cope, Wendy, 52

Copp, Jim, 374

Corbett, Ronnie, 359, 360

Coren, Alan, 252, 303

Cornwell, Rupert, 272

Coronation Street, 41, 147, 230, 231, 390

Corrado, David, 45, 113, 153, 231

Corso, Lee, 182

Cosby, Bill, 52, 140, 180, 337, 352

The Cosby Show, 126

Coslet, Bruce, 182

Cotswold Life, 190

Cotter, Tom, 204

Cottrill, Judith E., 369

County Down Spectator, 76

Coupling, 107, 108, 110, 114, 151

Courier-Journal, 99

Coverdale, David, 452

Coward, Noël, 366, 367, 418
Cowell, Simon, 149, 248
Cowher, Bill, 181
Cox, Bradford, 79
Cox, David, 78
Cox, Mark, 169, 412
Cox, V. Earnest, 53
Craig, Kim, 255
Crawford, Cindy, 434
Crenshaw, Richard N., 422
Crick, Jamie, 223
Cripps, Seddon, 295
Crisp, Quentin, 355
Crosby Herald, 421
Cross, Clare, 70
Cross, David, 307
Cross, Randy, 181
Cross My Heart, 117
Crow, Sheryl, 213
Crowe, Russell, 139, 205
Cruise, Tom, 349
Cruse, Heloise, 166
The Crying Game, 115
Crystal, Billy, 167
Cullen, John, 187
Cumberland News, 131
Currano, Luke, 366
Currie, Edwina, 52, 436
Curtis, Alan, 231
Curtis, Dave, 250, 359
Curtis, Lilian, 323
Curtiz, Michael, 431

Da Ali G Show, 110, 119, 124, 197, 245, 263, 278, 301, 307, 388
Dagenham Post, 101
Daily Express, 191
Daily Mail, 58
Daily Mirror, 95, 122
Daily Sport, 233
Daily Star, 59
Daily Telegraph, 59, 62, 99, 131, 263, 419
Dale, Lady Elizabeth, 444
Dalehite, Melinda, 110
Daley, Richard, 278
Daley, Richard J., 38
Dallas Morning News, 99

Danco, Leon A., 411
Dane, Michael, 108
Dangerfield, Rodney, 114, 125, 129, 133, 141, 206, 275, 336, 374, 407
Daniel, Judith, 75
Danielson, George, 38
Darg, Constance, 349
Darian, Ron, 209
The Dark Corner, 210
Darke, Ian, 247
Darwin, Anne, 415
Darwin, Charles, 393
Davies, Alan, 431
Davies, Dickie, 169
Davies, Robertson, 411
Davies, Sharron, 173
Davis, Carrie, 127
Davis, E. Gene, 422
Davis, Gary, 33
Davis, Steve, 247
Dawson, Andre, 179
Dawson, Gary, 75
Dawson, Les, 30, 114, 115, 142, 224, 313, 359, 364, 238, 402, 407
Dawson's Creek, 121
Day, Clarence, 350
Day, Doris, 128
Day, Robin, 152
de Balzac, Honoré, 203
de Chamfort, Nicolas, 161
de Gaulle, General Charles, 257
de Gramont, Sanche, 401
de Montaigne, Michel, 349
de Nerval, Gérard, 204
de Régnier, Henri, 123
De Forest, John W., 126
De Sutter, Hank, 78
De Vries, Peter, 46, 47, 70, 108, 119, 130, 140, 255, 395, 403, 436
Deacon, John, 56
Dead Men Don't Wear Plaid, 63, 114
Deadwood, 449
Dean, Dizzy, 376
Dee, Jack, 176
DeGeneres, Ellen, 162, 188, 239, 345
Delany, G., 297
Dembina, Ivor, 119, 145
Dempsey, Jack, 186

Dennis, Jerry, 408
Dentinger, Ron, 40
Denton, Andrew, 191, 308
Depp, Johnny, 335
Dern, Laura, 229
Designing Women, 47, 119
Dessau, Bruce, 240
Dettori, Frankie, 262, 361
The Devil's Dictionary X, 48
Diaz, Cameron, 242, 326, 451
DiCaprio, Leonardo, 115, 124
The Dick Van Dyke Show, 366
Dickinson, Janice, 33
Diekmann, Kai, 267
Dietz, Jeannie, 145
Diller, Phyllis, 117, 276, 375
DiMaggio, Joe, 35
Dinnerladies, 129, 377
Dion, Céline, 138
Disney, Walt, 229
Divac, Vlade, 404
Dizzy Dean, 332
Dr. Who, 39, 450
Dodd, Christopher, 261
Dodd, Ken, 118, 140, 161, 191, 198, 240, 245, 273, 324, 364, 372, 380, 396, 398, 425
Dole, Bob, 251
Dole, Elizabeth, 265
Donachie, W., 297
Donleavy, J. P., 49
Donovan, Jason, 203
Doolan, Ed, 257
Doran, Michael, 451
Dorest Echo, 163
The Doughgirls, 315
Douglas, Jack, 141
Douglas, Norman, 440
Douglas, Sherman, 177
Dover Reporter, 413
Dowd, Larry, 243
Dowling, Brian, 365, 431
Downey, Robert, Jr., 393
Dowtin, Helen, 70
Dowtin, Miriam, 70
Doyle, Chris, 47, 201
Drechsler, Paula, 46
Drew, Carol, 46

Drew, Weldon, 177
The Drew Carey Show, 69, 120, 123, 144, 146, 152, 164, 165, 166, 171, 375, 396, 444
Drury, Mary, 106
Duchess Camilla of Cornwall, 304
Duckman, 51, 52
Dud and Pete, 218, 222, 223, 273
Dudzik, Stephen, 195
Duell, Charles H., 253
Duff, Mickey, 185
Duffield, Bill, 65
The Dukes, 200
Dumas, Alexandre, 274
Dumb & Dumber, 320
Dunn, Daniel, 381
Durocher, Leo, 179
Durrell, Gerald, 64, 246, 371
The Dutch Elm Conservatoire, 294
Dutta, Mo, 66
Duva, Lou, 187, 451
Duvall, E., 95
Dyer, Kieron, 412
Dykes, Sandra J., 123

Early Doors, 245
EastEnders, 151, 432
Eastern Evening News, 274
Easy Living, 52
Eclair, Jenny, 400
Eco, Umberto, 438
Eden, Sir Anthony, 296
Educating Rita, 92
Edward, Jonathan, 174
Edwards, Ian, 58
Edwards, Valerie, 106
Eichorn, Eddie, 178
Einstein, Albert, 209, 233, 311, 435
Eisenhower, Dwight D., 259, 361
Electra, Carmen, 242
The 11 O'Clock Show, 350
Elford, Janet, 244
Elliott, Missy, 424
Ellis, Paul, 43
Ellison, Brenda, 50
Ellison, Harlan, 34
Ely Standard, 101

Eminem, 126, 325
Emperor Hirohito, 297
Emperor Sigismund, 48
Empty Nest, 151
The End, 93
England, Chris, 36
Engvall, Bill, 188, 190, 404
Eno, Brian, 391
Entourage, 125
Entrapment, 451
Ervin, Samuel James, Jr. 32
Esiason, Boomer, 182
Etchingham, Julie, 110
Eton College Chronicle, 190
Eubank, Chris, 96
Eubanks, Bob, 33
Eugene Register, 99
European Vacation, 332
Evangelista, Linda, 233, 368, 406
Evans, Jill, 144
Evening Chronicle, 320
Evening Standard, 76, 131, 217
Everage, Dame Edna, 171, 234, 252
Eyre, Sir Richard, 163

Fahey, Brian A., 66
Fairchild, Mary, 349
Falk, Peter, 165
Fallon, Jimmy, 322, 370
Family Fortunes, 164
Family Guy, 69, 203
Fanshawe, Simon, 410
Farquhar, Michael, 92
Farrell, Colin, 433
The Fast Show, 92, 400
Father Knows Best, 373
Father Ted, 55, 68, 227, 243, 348, 353, 358, 385, 390
Fawlty Towers, 255, 257, 321, 39, 456
Fay, Peter, 75
Feeley, Michelle, 46
Feherty, David, 156
Feldman, Marty, 311
Feldman, Marty, 400
Fergie, 38, 221
Ferguson, Cindy, 370
Ferguson, Craig, 417

Ferguson, Sarah, 30, 88
Ferrari, Nick, 104
Ferry, Otis, 188
Feynman, Richard, 252
Fickling, David, 77
Fidrych, Mark, 179
Fiebig, Jim, 225
Fields, W. C., 56, 192, 327, 363, 376, 379, 440
Fiennes, Joseph, 231
Fine, Annette, 67
Finks, Jim, 181
Finn, Lucy, 348
Finnerty, Pete, 52
Finnes, Sir Ranulph, 377
Finnigan, Judy, 133, 141
Firhad, Mohd, 48
Firth, Carl, 376
Fischer, Martin H., 185
Fitzgerald, Mick, 187
Fitzgerald, Ray, 204
Fitzgerald, Tom, 416
Fitzwater, Marlin, 264
Flaubert, Gustave, 452
Fleiss, Heidi, 294
Fleschner, Malcolm, 55
Fletcher, Bert, 64
The Flintstones, 431
Flood, Willo, 259
Flynn, Carolyn, 198
Flynn, Errol, 310
Flynn, Gladys, 32
For the Love of Mike, 397
Ford, Gerald, 184
Ford, John, 93
Fordham, E. W., 49
Foreman, Don, 309
Foreman, George, 162, 186
Forrest Gump, 152, 153, 154
42nd Street, 139
Foster, Brendan, 174
Foster, Phil, 146
Fox, Samantha, 108, 413
Foxworthy, Jeff, 147, 326, 336
Foxx, Redd, 53
Francis, Tony, 396
Frank, Alan, 417
Frank, Sue, 79

Fraser, Kenneth, 325
Fraser, Lady Antonia, 93
Frasier, 63, 189, 199, 201, 206, 223, 314, 443
French Kiss, 329
Freud, Sir Clement, 200, 329
Friedman, George, 90
Friedman, Kinky, 154, 354
Friends, 113, 154, 192, 226, 358, 387, 434
Frith, Holden, 233
Frost, David, 185, 437
Frost, Jenny, 445
Frost, Robert, 349
Frost, Sir David, 310, 394
Fry, Stephen, 30, 118, 152, 197, 203, 233, 238, 330, 390, 431
Frye, David, 268
Fudd, Elmer, 437
Fuentes, Tito, 178
Furturama, 455

G., Matt, 256
Gaarder, Jostein, 348
Gaffigan, Jim, 201, 250, 254
Gaffney, Jim, 75
Galifianakis, Zach, 89, 228, 408
Gallagher, 236
Gallagher, Liam, 387
Gallagher, Noel, 35, 40, 147, 235, 277
Gallois, Pierre, 249
Garnett, Kevin, 177
Garnett, Stephen, 324
Garvey, Jane, 1376
Gary the Rat, 383
Gavin & Stacy, 115
Gavin, James, 204
Gay, Emmy, 117
Geldof, Peaches, 30
Geller, Uri, 141
Genser, David, 50, 347
Genz, Michael A., 311
George, Boy, 220, 239
George, Dave, 143
Gerkin, Heidi, 64
Gervais, Ricky, 77, 434, 443, 455
Get Smart, 301
Gielgud, Sir John, 232

Gildea, Kevin, 399
Gill, Frank, 397
Gilman, Charlotte Perkins, 138
Gilmore, Artis, 176
Gilmore Girls, 430
Gimme, Gimme, Gimme, 206, 227, 248
Gingold, Hermione, 33
Glasgow, Arnold, 142
Glover, Lucas, 51
The Glums, 379
Gobel, George, 53
Goin' to Town, 111
Gold Diggers of 1933, 404
Goldberg, Isaac, 48
The Golden Girls, 33, 54, 65, 117, 125, 127, 139, 145, 164, 200, 262, 276, 294, 354, 379, 382, 392, 415, 427, 433, 456
Goldman, William, 226
Goldwyn, Sam, 31, 65, 68, 70, 71, 92, 96, 187, 217, 228, 231, 310, 384, 414, 417, 436, 445
Goll, Jeff, 243
Golub, Evan, 90
Gomez, Lefty, 179
Goncourt brothers, 98
Gooden, Drew, 110, 176, 182
Goodge, Eliza, 98
Goodman, Mark S., 229
Goodman, Marvin, 45
Goody, Jade, 39, 64, 65, 128, 144, 149, 155, 203, 208, 217, 242, 251, 261, 317, 323, 324, 389, 398, 407, 432, 454
The Goon Show, 158, 112, 173, 211, 276, 277, 310, 318, 454
The Goons, 245
Goris, Jeff, 250
Gorky, Maxim, 246
Gorman, Teresa, 135
Gottfried, Gilbert, 434
Gottlieb, Theodore, 356
Gough, Sharon, 65
Gould, Bobby, 197
Gourlay, Maureen, 66
Goward, Pru, 57
Grace, Brendan, 338
Graham, Danny, 212
Graham, Errol, 187
Graham, Jane, 212

The Graham Norton Show, 66
Grant, Hugh, 89
Grant, Russell, 56
Grant, Stephen, 145
Gray, Clifton J., 343
Gray, Daniel, 281
The Great Train Robbery, 274
Green, Bill, 56
Green, Green Grass, 41
Green, Hubert, 184
Green, Jean, 52
Green, Jeff, 375
Green, Michael, 95
Green Wing, 373, 385
Greenberg, Leonard, 355
Greene, Laura, 318
Greening, Jonathan, 244
Greening, Kevin, 57
Greenwell, Bill, 53
Greenwood, Emma, 256
Greenwood, Ron, 54
Gregg, Hubert, 447
Greitzer, Mark, 53
Griffin, Archie, 386
Griffiths, T., 52
Grinath, Art, 75, 123, 256, 357, 404
Grizzard, Lewis, 150
Groening, Matt, 268
Groom, Simon, 70
Grose, Francis, 447
Gross, Milton, 184
Grossmith, George, 158
Grossmith, Weedon, 158
Grove, Robin D., 50, 249
Grove, Valerie, 201
Guardian, 59, 76, 77, 100, 101, 102, 165
Gunter, David, 360

Haberman, Philip W., Jr., 395
Hackett, Buddy, 183
Hagen, Walter, 184
Hagman, Larry, 249, 392, 416
Hague, William, 268
Haig, Alexander, 65
Hair Wars, 365
Halbert, Stanley, 194
Half Baked, 201

Hall, Jerry, 364
Hall, Rich, 368
Hall, Stuart, 175, 411
Hamilton, Natasha, 373
Hamilton, Neil 51
Hampton, Mike, 30
Hancock, Tony, 191
Handey, Jack, 122, 154, 186, 190, 206, 207, 212, 238, 239, 244, 252, 301, 303, 305, 306, 311, 330, 331, 337, 342, 347, 425, 445, 450
Hanson, Gerry, 78
Hapgood, J. B., 46
Happy Days, 328
Harding, Mike, 391
Hardy, Jeremy, 46, 224, 337
Hardy, Mark, 249
Hari, Johann, 105
Harlow, Jean, 42
Harman, Harriet, 247
Harrington, Al, 177
Harrison, Dan, 78
Harrison, David T., 195
Harrison, Rachel, 444
Harry Enfield and Chums, 413
Hart, Gary, 129
Hart, Jennifer, 46, 50, 54, 226, 418
Hartman, Ed, 229
Harvey, 445
Harvey, Kieron, 147, 151, 432
Hastings, Gavin, 437
Hattenstone, Simon, 96
Have I Got News for You, 217, 425
Hawking, Stephen, 430
Hawkins, Ronnie, 120
Hawn, Goldie, 104, 197, 293, 309
Hay, James N. D., 77
Haydn, Glyn, 322
Hayes, Brian, 257
Hayes, Chanelle, 163
Haynes, Homer, 373
Hayridge, Hattie, 172
Healey, Denis, 116
Hedberg, Mitch, 166, 193, 210, 226, 252, 319, 329, 390, 435
Hedegaard, Erik, 77
Hedges, John, 420
Heffer, Eric, 258

Hefner, Hugh, 217
Hegel, Georg Wilhelm Freidrich, 435
Hein, Piet, 55
Heinlein, Robert A., 341
Held, John, 184
Heller, Joseph, 214, 322
Hellman, Lillian, 363
Hellzapoppin', 347
Helm, John, 70
Helms, Jesse, 261
Hendrickson, Kyle, 171
Hendrix, Jimi, 415
Henman, Tim, 139, 169
Henry, Andrea, 138
Henry, Dan, 109
Henry, Tony, 157
Hepburn, Katharine, 369
Here Come the Girls, 148
Herniman, Joan, 95
Heseltine, Michael, 264, 266
Hewett, Andrew J., 134
Hewitt, Jennifer Love, 163
Hewitt, Patricia, 247
Heyhoe-Flint, Rachael, 49
Hickman, Joe, 91
Higgins, Alex, 440
Hightower, Jim, 268
Hill, Benny, 114, 371
Hill, Harry, 120, 138, 140, 145, 150, 167,
   193, 203, 208, 209, 331, 332, 351, 360,
   367, 388, 425 – 26, 433
Hill, Jimmy, 247
Hill, Tyrone, 125
Hilton, Paris, 30, 31, 32, 149, 153, 155, 194,
   199, 221, 236, 254, 266, 294, 312, 314,
   318, 322, 354, 364, 365, 370, 432, 434,
   444, 445
Hinchliffe, Andy, 436
Hinton, John, 31
Hislop, Ian, 292
Hit the Ice, 222
Hitchens, Christopher, 268
Hitler, Adolf, 261
Hockney, David, 393
Hoddle, Glenn, 412, 438
Hoest, Bill, 156
Hoffenstein, Samuel, 97
Hoffman, Dustin, 167, 232, 239

Holden, Amanda, 413
Hollywood Squares, 231
Holmes, E. F., 128
Holmes, Eamonn, 127
Holmes, Oliver Wendell, 445
Home Improvement, 93, 151, 152, 194
Honig, William, 46
Hooper, Katherine, 394
Hope, Anthony, 97
Hope, Bob, 116, 184, 186, 226
Hope, Bob, 324, 325
Hopkins, Anthony, 392
Hopkins, Sir Anthony, 232
Hopkinson, Simon, 198
Horne, Lena, 219
Hot Metal, 278
Hot Shots, 112, 298, 384, 448
Houghton, Chantelle, 255 – 56
House, 374
Houston Chronicle, 172
Hovis, Larry, 363
How to Steal a Million, 275
Howard, Dale, 113
Hoying, Bob, 181
Hoyle, Angela, 199
Hubbard, Elbert, 196, 347
Hubbard, Gardiner Green, 252
Huckleberry Finn, 358
Hudson, Kate, 395
Hugo, Victor, 356
Hulford, Colin, 66
Hull, Sandra, 46, 150
Humphreys, John, 57, 211
Hung, Nguyen Thanh, 374
Hunniford, Gloria, 96
Hunt, David, 351
Hunt, James, 38
Hunt, Jonathan, 268
Hurd, Douglas, 276
Hynde, Chrissie, 235
Hyson, Kelly, 149

I Dream of Jeannie, 332
I Dream Too Much, 320
I Love Lucy, 194
I'd Do Anything, 93
I'm Alan Partridge, 404

I'm No Angel, 152
I'm Sorry I Haven't a Clue, 45, 46, 357, 381, 392, 408
I'm Sorry, I'll Read That Again, 407
Iacocca, Lee, 213
Ignatieff, Michael, 272
Ikemoto, Howard, 218
In & Out, 107
Indiana Evening Gazette, 100
The Independent, 102, 273
Indianapolis Star, 259
Innes, Jocasta, 397
International House, 319, 389
Inverdale, John, 237
The Invisible Man Returns, 343
Ionesco, Eugéne, 53
Ireland, Kathy, 354
Irimia, Gabriela, 341, 370
The IT Crowd, 396, 424
It's a Gift, 330, 452
ITMA, 454
Izaguirre, Cynthia, 43
Izzard, Eddie, 32, 104, 209

Jackson, Andrew, 62
Jackson, Glenda, 314
Jagger, Jade, 369
Jagger, Mick, 220
Jahr, Michael, 358
Jam and Jerusalem, 455
James, Alex, 386
James, Clive, 180
James, Kevin, 443
James, Lady Serena, 65
Jameson, Derek, 223, 360, 382, 432
Janssen, David, 228
Januszczak, Waldemar, 449
Jarski, Rosemarie, 42, 75, 376
Jay, Sir Anthony, 79
Jeni, Richard, 248, 402
Jenkins, Roy, 294
Jenkins, Simon, 2452
Jensen, Ashley, 127, 371
Jensen, David, 449
The Jerk, 165, 363
Jerome, Jerome K., 158
Jimeoin, 36, 325

John, Elton, 148
Johnny Carson, 366
Johnny Dangerously, 112
Johns, Daniel, 448
Johnson, Boris, 55, 91, 105, 106, 107, 124, 129, 130, 155, 156, 157, 188, 261, 262, 263, 271, 302, 314, 324, 374, 387, 402, 431, 439
Johnson, Carl, 381
Johnson, Lyndon B., 268
Johnson, Magic, 176
Johnson, Serena, 231
Johnson, William J., 63
Johnston, Brian, 211
Jolie, Angelina, 136
Jones, Ann, 180
Jones, Franklin P., 55
Jones, Mark, 56
Jones, Milton, 164, 167, 198, 226, 274, 277, 331, 372, 375, 424
Jones, Peter, 52
Jons, Milton, 348
Jordan, Michael, 319
Jordan, Paul, 449
Joseph, Sir Keith, 208
Journal Star, 353
Jowett, Benjamin, 349
Joyce, Heidi, 368
Julien, Cathy, 78
Jungle Fever, 139
Jupitus, Phill, 197

Kamen, Milt, 209
Kammer, John, 54
Kane, Charles, 105
Kath & Kim (U.K.), 70, 312
Katona, Kerry, 89
Katz, Jonathan, 135, 410, 415
Kaufman, George S., 449
Kay, Peter, 65, 439
Kaylor, Mark, 185
Keating, Ronan, 235
Keech, Maja, 409
Keegan, Kevin, 168, 187, 247, 367, 412
Kelly, John, 434
Kelly, Lorraine, 236
Kemp, Keith, 79

The Ken Bruce Show, 227
Kennedy, Charles, 406, 441
Kennedy, Edward, 314
Kennedy, Geraldine, 57
Kennedy, Tara, 150
Kerr, Jean, 383
Kerry, John, 296
Keyes, Richard, 57
Khorsandi, Shappi, 323
Kidd, Jason, 176
Kilborn, Craig, 205
Kiley, Brian, 409
Kiner, Ralph, 45
King, Don, 40, 68, 148
King, Jan, 35
King, Jonathan, 294
King, Larry, 445
Kingston, Alex, 138
Kington, Miles, 120, 450
Kirby-Lee, Annabelle, 350
Kissinger, Henry, 301, 303
Kleinbard, David, 142, 311
Kline, Kevin, 230
Kline, Rufus, 68
Knanishu, Joel, 90
Knight, India, 425
Knight News Wire, 59
Knocked Up, 134, 136
Knowles, Beyoncé, 232, 234
Koch, Ed, 293
Kouts, Ann, 229
Krakowski, Jane, 232
Krattenmaker, Ken, 195
Kraus, Karl, 117
Krisciunas, Kevin, 341
Kulwicki, Alan, 258

L.A. Story, 118, 218
Lacy, Pauline, 134
Ladman, Cathy, 141
Lamarr, Hedy, 367
Lancashire Evening Post, 276
Landells, Pete, 95
Landry, Tom, 182
Lara, Adair, 137
Lardner, Ring, 133, 312
Largent, Steve, 182

Larry the Cable Guy, 114
Larson, Doug, 36
Larson, Gary, 205
Larwood, Marek, 192
Laud, Derek, 146
Laurel and Hardy, 124, 125, 140, 144, 151,
    157, 162, 165, 293, 390, 398, 402, 403,
    417, 420, 431, 433, 437, 441, 443, 451,
    455
Laurie, Hugh, 106, 107, 116, 164, 233, 239,
    254, 320, 360, 385, 404, 417
LaVey, Anton Szandor, 374
Lawless, Terry, 436
Lawrence, Steve, 421
Lawrenson, Helen, 119
Lawson, Nigella, 162, 395
Layden, Frank, 177
Le Blanc, Jacques, 305
Le Bon, Simon, 114, 220
Leacock, Stephen, 308
Leahy, Frank, 147
Lec, Stanislaw J., 293
Lee, Ben, 335
Lee, Bill, 179
Lee, Spike, 234
Lee, Tommy, 247
Légaré, Pierre, 212, 383
Lehmann-Haupt, Christopher, 79
Leibert, Marc, 256
Leibman, Wendy, 118
Leifer, Carol, 117, 125
Lennon, John, 148, 257
Leno, Jay, 64, 210, 271, 272, 368
Leonard, Hugh, 256, 393
Lesko, Mark, 195
Leslie, Shane, 448
Letterman, David, 58, 140, 178, 212, 239,
    250, 262, 271 – 72, 336, 345, 407
Levant, Oscar, 76, 233
Levenson, Sam, 417
Levinson, Hank, 45
Levy, Michael, 422
Lewis, Gib, 68
Lewis, Linda, 219
Lewis, Richard, 119, 120
Lewis-Francis, Mark, 175
Lewis-Smith, Victor, 403
Liberace, Wladziu Valentino, 223

Lichtenberg, Georg Christoph, 348
Lieberman, Gerald F., 115
Liebert, Marc, 120
Liebman, Wendy, 133, 138, 198, 205, 320
Life on Mars, 294
Liggett, Phil, 49, 172
Limmer, Alan, 391
The Lion in Winder, 439
Little Britain, 90, 127, 136, 145, 171, 173,
   180, 193, 216, 324, 387, 404, 454
The Little Engine That Could, 333
Littlejohn, Richard, 449
Littlewood, Sidney, 326
L. L. Cool J, 117
Llewelyn-Bowen, Laurence, 327
Lloyd, Danielle, 266
Lock, Sean, 91
Locker-Lampson, Frederick, 88
Lockridge, Rocky, 435
Logan, Johnny, 64
Lohan, Dina, 166
Lohan, Lindsay, 314, 387
Lombardi, Vince, 182
London, Brian, 68
London, Jay, 113, 136, 365, 366, 372, 374
Long, William R., 379
The Longest Yard, 171
Longford, Lord, 96
Longoria, Eva, 77
Loose Women, 67, 198, 221
Lopez, Jennifer, 428
Lord Albemarle, 118
Lord Gowrie, 234
Lord Grenfell, 415
Lord Hailsham, 258
Lord Riddell, 421
Lord Snowdon, 428
The Los Angeles Times, 99, 410
Louisville Courier, 314
Love, Adrian, 161
Love and Death, 124, 292, 299, 304
Love at First Bite, 347
Love, Jason, 404
Love Life, 114
Love Me Tonight, 381
Lowe, Ted, 412
Lucas, Matt, 223
Lulu, 415

Lush, Peter, 58
Lyall, John, 88, 169
Lydon, John, 370
Lynam, Des, 57, 185
Lynde, Paul, 203
Lyneham, Paul, 56
Lyttelton, Humphrey, 53

*M*A*S*H*, 31, 70, 253, 255, 303, 304, 351,
   375, 380, 397, 402, 437, 444, 445
Mabley, Moms, 417
Macauley, Alastair, 153
MacDonald, Sarah, 56
Machado, Antonio, 193 193
Macintyre, Ben, 78
Maclain, John, 153, 165, 194, 245, 253, 355,
   399
MacManus, Seumas, 366
Maconie, Stuart, 365
Macpherson, Archie, 168, 413
Macpherson, Elle, 372
Madden, Dave, 305
Madeley, Richard, 105, 111, 133, 173, 236,
   237, 389
Madonna, 148, 234, 326, 353, 355
Mahaffy, John P., 355
Maher, Bill, 271
Maine, Robert, 329
Mair, Dorothy, 375
Maitland, Lady Olga, 412
Major, John, 324
Making the Grade, 391
Malcolm in the Middle, 400
Malcolm, Linda K., 195
Malia, Carol, 333
Malloy, Jack, 78
Maltz, Ellen, 422
The Man with Two Brains, 384
Manchester Guardian, 281
Maney, Mabel, 353
Manson, Marilyn, 351, 399
Mantle, Mickey, 151
Marchand, Amanda, 346, 399
Marchant, Samantha, 395
Marcos, Imelda, 311
Margolyes, Miriam, 191, 308
Marion, Frances, 166

Marks, Vic, 169
Marquis, Don, 88
Marr, Andrew, 248
Married...With Children, 395
Marsden, Luke, 117
Marsh, Jodie, 398
Marsh, John, 74
Marshall, Peter, 203
Martin, Dean, 219
Martin, Demetri, 32, 36, 46, 63, 168, 173, 193, 201, 234, 252, 372, 373, 394, 396, 405, 409, 443
Martin, Dick, 116
Martin, Judith, 146
Martin, Steve, 40, 89, 110, 143, 188, 227
Martins, Serena, 50
Marvin, Hank, 31
Marx, Chico, 223, 300, 343
Marx, Groucho, 70, 92, 97, 111, 121, 133, 144, 188, 218, 226, 300, 321, 328, 346, 366, 369, 416, 432, 450, 451, 456
Marx, Karl, 438
Marx, Patricia, 229
Marx, Zeppo, 183
Mary Hartman, Mary Hartman, 221
Mary Tyler Moore, 117, 437, 450
Maskell, Dan, 180
Mason, Alan, 50
Mason, Hugh, 243
Mathis, Andrew W., 346
Matthau, Walter, 343
Mawhinny, Brian, 388
Maxwell, Elsa, 405
Maxwell, Robert, 56
May, Brian, 245, 365
McAleer, Kevin, 135, 236, 326, 332, 356, 437, 445
McCann, Charlie, 187
McCartney, Paul, 90
McClarnon, Liz, 235
McClatchly News Service, 99
McClintock, Annie, 321
McCormac, Dr. J., 382
McCourt, Malachy, 406
McCrory, Glenn, 186
McCunnie, Frances, 77
McDonald, Sir Trevor, 417
McEnroe, John, 161

McFarland, Roy, 436
McGowan, Alistair, 357
McGrady, Tracy, 177
McGrath, Rory, 198
McGraw, Tug, 169, 178
McGregor, Ewan, 44
McGuire, Terry, 176
McLeod, Bunny, 454
McLoughlin, Coleen, 371, 403
McNally, Frank, 325
McVicar, John, 294
Mecham, Evan, 109
Mecklenburg, Karl, 181
Mellema, Kevin, 90
Melly, George, 414
Melville, Herman, 338
Men Behaving Badly, 130, 136, 143, 350
Mencken, H. L., 295, 345
Merchant, Stephen, 401
Mercury, Freddie, 319
Merkley, Greg, 78
Merton, Paul, 167, 337
Meschkow, Sanford, 53
Metro, 89
Michael, George, 323
Michener, James A., 437
Midhurst and Petworth Observer, 416
Midler, Bette, 121, 210, 440
Mighty Aphrodite, 185
Miley, 91
Milford Connecticut Citizen, 99
Milhem, Damon R., 424
Miller, Albert G., 46
Miller, Dennis, 216, 270, 350
Miller, George, 195
Miller, Henry, 95
Miller, Johnny, 184
Miller, Mick, 224
Miller, Zell, 299
Milligan, Spike, 39, 40, 72, 153, 172, 208, 230, 299, 280, 303, 304, 320, 325, 339, 358, 372, 424, 452
Mills, Heather, 122, 401
Mills, Paul, 327
Mills, Sara, 359
Minter, Alan, 186
Mirren, Dame Helen, 123
Miss Piggy, 335

The Missoulian, 397
Mitchell, Stitch, 180
Moffat, Douglas, 450
Molière, 415
Mondale, Walter, 150
Monkhouse, Bob, 33, 118, 156, 380, 405, 411
Monroe, Marilyn, 451
Montague, Julian, 93
Montague, Sarah, 88
Montand, Yves, 130
Montgomery, Carol, 134
Monty Python, 93
Monty Python's Flying Circus, 91, 205, 403
Monty Python's Life of Brian, 313
Moon, Keith, 224
Moonlightling, 439
Moore, George, 131, 310, 244
Moore, Rick, 201
Mor, Martin, 298
Moran, Dylan, 311, 326, 387, 394
Morecambe and Wise, 89, 111, 212, 222, 273
Morecambe, Eric, 128, 152, 210, 222, 231, 280, 313, 327
Morely, Julia, 368
Morgan, Cliff, 246
Morgan, J., 150
Morgan, Matthew, 330
Morgan, Rhodri, 435
Mork & Mindy, 34, 405, 439
Morley, Robert, 40
Morris, Chris, 222
Morris, Dewi, 172
Morris, John, 450
Morris, Mike, 34
Morris-Marsham, David, 398
Morrison, Joe, 63
Mortimer, Bob, 418
Morton, J. B., 52, 205
Mosley, Don, 450
Mourinho, José, 147, 149
Moyles, Chris, 127
Mr. Arkadin, 278
Mr. KVL 41, 311
Mrs. Doubtfire, 416
Mrs. Merton, 174, 220, 298, 368
The Mrs. Merton Show, 130

Muggeridge, Kitty, 234
Muggeridge, Malcolm, 116
Muhammad, Muard, 324
Muhammad, Wali, 186
Mull, Martin, 407
Mulligan, Andy, 312
Munnery, Simon, 118, 153, 175, 207, 209, 311, 323, 363, 386
The Muppet Show, 399
Murder by Death, 435
Murphy, Eric, 336
Murphy, Vivien, 200
Murray, Al, 109, 245
Murray, Chic, 439
Murray, Gill 96
My Favorite Blonde, 111
My Name is Earl, 201, 323, 392, 394
My So-Called Life, 199

Nagle, Florence, 427
The Naked Gun, 117, 389, 440
The Naked Gun 2½: The Smell of Fear, 56, 111
Naked Gun 33 1/3, 278
Napolento, Doctor Louis, 120
Nathan, George Jean, 345
Naughtie, James, 450
Neal, William "Cody," 292
Neff, Tom, 346
Negus, Arthur, 258
Neill, Terry, 346
Neilly, Jim, 406
Nelly, 33
Nelms, Cynthia, 133
New, Chris, 377
New Jersey News, 299
New London Connecticut News, 100
New Mexican, 99
New Scientist, 64
New Statesman, 447
New York Post, 100
The New York Times, 60, 100, 101, 102, 231, 307, 372, 420
Newport Daily Press, 100
Newsweek, 357
Nichol, Phil, 302
Nicholas, Max, 255

Nielsen, Leslie, 183
Night Court, 440
Nissalke, Tom, 30
Niven David, 298
Nixon, Richard, 261, 266, 421, 441
Noble, Ross, 443
Noone, Peter, 42
Norman, Greg, 132
North, Colonel Oliver, 441
North, Lieutenant Colonel Oliver, 304
Notes on a Scandal, 390
Nove, Charles, 219
Nuns on the Run, 350
Nursing Newsletter, 58
Nutley, Buzz, 165, 210, 249, 318

O'Brien, Bill, 319
O'Brien, Conan, 42, 272, 305, 418
The Observer, 100, 135
O'Callaghan, Ken, 121
O'Carroll, Brendan, 198
O'Connor, Joseph, 213, 343
The Odd Couple, 150
O'Doherty, David, 384
O'Faolain, Sean, 107
The Office, 37, 55
The Office (U.K.), 107
Ogilvy, Angus, 147
Oglesby, Dave, 230
O'Grady, Paul, 70, 105
O'Hanlon, Ardal, 135, 140
Oh, Mr. Porter!, 333
O'Neal, Eamonn, 450
O'Neal, Shaquille, 176, 177, 320
One Good Turn, 310
The Onion, 346
Only Fools and Horses, 137, 370, 389
Ontario Record, 294
Openshaw, Peter, 295
Opik, Lembit, 341
The Oregonian, 79, 99
O'Reilly, Tony, 172
O'Rourke, P. J., 146, 158
Orwell, George, 89
Osbourne, Kelly, 132, 142
Osbourne, Ozzy, 142

O'Shea, Kelvin, 330
O'Sullevan, Sir Peter, 187
O'Toole, Peter, 32
Ovett, Steve, 174
Owen, Ieuan, 57
Ozark, Danny, 169

Paige, Elaine, 373
Pal Joey, 346
The Paleface, 111
The Palm Beach Story, 300
Palmer, Samuel, 51
Palmer-Tomkinson, Tara, 149
Paltrow, Gwyneth, 31
Panettiere, Hayden, 364
Pannullo, Jerry, 31, 47, 195
Papa's Delicate Condition, 314
Papier, Steven, 219
Parfitt, Rick, 359
Parker, Colonel Tom, 308
Parker, Dorothy, 39, 69, 110, 216, 392, 425
The Parallax View, 388
Parris, Matthew, 191
Parrott, E. O., 95
Parry, Mike, 49, 65
Parsons, Nicholas, 415
Partington, Jonathan R., 53
Parton, Dolly, 312, 364
Pasack Valley Community Life, 100
Pascoe, Alan, 174
Patterson, Bruce, 52
Patterson, Floyd, 187
Patterson, Robert, 295
Paul, Jonathan, 54, 232, 243
The Paul O'Grady Show, 167
Pauli, Wolfgang, 428
Payne, D., 311
Peanuts, 162, 230, 342, 365, 385, 424, 426, 444
Pearce, Ralph, 95
Pearce-Higgins, John, 347
Peebles, Andy, 172, 438
Peel, John, 158
Peel, Martin, 381
Peep Show, 279
Pennis, Dennis, 96
Peoria Journal Star, 99

Perelman, S. J., 68, 120, 333
Perfect Strangers, 381
Perle, Richard N., 296
Perret, Gene, 369
Perry, Grayson, 167
Peterson, Bill, 181
Philips, Emo, 138, 143, 235, 300, 350, 360,
   408, 416
Phillips, Tracy, 68
Phoenix Nights, 67, 155
Piazza, Mike, 179
Picasso, Pablo, 412
Pickering, Ron, 174, 175
Pike, Harry, 75
Pilkington, Karl, 200
Pink, 134
The Pink Panther Strikes Again, 206
Pinocchio, 58
Pinter, Harold, 438
Pitcher, Al, 246
Planet Earth, 32
Planojo, 407
Platt, Carol, 138
Plauger, P. J., 154
Pleat, David, 168
Poggendorff, Johann, 253
Police Squad!, 276, 278, 279, 280, 383, 394
Polk, Torrin, 182
Pool, Chris, 187
Poole, E. B., 188
Poplin, Sally, 32
Porridge, 294, 428
Potter, James, 413
Potts, Ryan, 51
Poundstone, Paula, 173, 309
Powell, Florence, 79
Powell, Gail, 332
Powell, Peter, 123
Powell, Sue, 229
Prescott, John, 66, 98, 171, 261, 338
Presley, Elvis, 109, 219, 228
Previn, André, 222
Price, Katie, 89, 137
Prince Charles, 162
Prince Edward, 48
Prince Philip, 42, 104, 189, 213, 234, 243,
   262, 320, 337, 338, 397, 410
The Princess Bride, 413

Princess Margaret, 273
Princess Michael of Kent, 273
Private Benjamin, 303, 304
The Private Life of Samuel Pepys, 218
The Producers, 292
Pulman, John, 346
Punch magazine, 401
Punt & Dennis, 133
Punt, Steve, 198

Quayle, Dan, 50, 58, 63, 139, 244, 258, 265,
   327, 360, 361
Queen Elizabeth II, 44
Quigley, Sheila, 92
Quincy, 376
Quinn, Micky, 49
Quirke, Pauline, 402

Radcliffe and Maconie, 235
Radcliffe, Mark, 204, 373
Radner, Gilda, 240
Raeburn, Anna, 137
Rafferty, Sean, 222, 237
Rand, Ayn, 356
Raphael, Sally Jessy, 449
Rappaport, Dennis, 441
Ratner, Gerlad, 307
Ratoff, Gregory, 50
Rayburn, Gene, 43
Read, Mike, 55
Reagan, Ronald, 44, 134, 262, 265, 296,
   297, 300, 317, 358
Reality Bites, 355
The Rebel, 217, 218
Red Dwarf, 249, 428, 429, 431
Redknapp, Jamie, 140
Redmond, Michael, 193, 341, 353
Reed, Lou, 220, 429
Rees, Ann, 141
Reese, Susan, 54
Reeves, Keanu, 348, 428
Reeves, Vic, 418
Regan, Donald, 432
Reid, Tara, 328, 431
Reilly, Shanessa, 354
Reucassel, Craig, 98

Rhea, Caroline, 164
Rhys Joes, Griff, 312
Riback, Billy, 133
Ricardo, Benny, 178
Rice, Anneka, 410
Rice, Condoleezza, 44
Rice, Jerry, 182
Rich, Jeffrey, 46
Richards, Keith, 387
Richardson, Gary, 258
Richie, Nicole, 387
Richie, Shane, 357
Riley, Pauline, 126
Ringo Starr, 235
Rippon, Angela, 87
Rising Damp, 121
Ritchard, Cyril, 366
Rivers, Joan, 134, 137, 142, 152, 246, 247,
    369, 371
Rizzo, Frank, 277, 299
Roach, Joan, 56
Roach, Sir Boyle, 254, 435, 437, 438
Road to Morocco, 147
The Road to Singapore, 405
Road to Utopia, 36, 122
The Road to Wellville, 406
Roanoak Times, 389
Roberston, Max, 180
Roberts, Adele, 436
Roberts, Elaine, 48
Roberts, Ted, 245
Robertson, Max, 70
Robinson, Anne, 368, 383
Robinson, David, 53
Robinson, Edward G., 231
Robinson, Gene, 124
Robson, Bobby, 57, 223
Robson, Linda, 402
Roche, Maruice, 413
Roche, Sir Boyle, 56, 455
Rock, Chris, 234, 238
Rockford Files, 114
Rodman, Dennis, 425
Rodriguez, Alex, 258
Rodriguez, Chi Chi, 183, 184, 405
Rogell, Gregg, 271, 382
Rogers, Clive, 448
Rogers, General, 297

Rogers, George, 181
Rogers, Gladys, 66
Rogers, Robert L., 398
Romm, Joseph, 35, 299
Ronka, David, 444
Room 101, 393
Rooney, Mickey, 117, 367
Rose, Axl, 114, 452
Rose, Kenneth, 256
Rose, Pete, 68
Rosenburg, Jim, 124
Rosenthal, Jim, 174
Roslin, Gaby, 35
Ross, Jonathan, 31, 89, 219
Rosten, Leo, 48, 51, 66, 90, 240, 431
Rowan & Martin's Laugh-In, 219, 313
Roxanne, 449
The Royle Family, 115, 403
Rubin, Bob, 134
Ruffing, Twink, 195
Ruggles of Red Gap, 389
Rugrats, 67, 68, 148, 233, 343, 443
Rumsfeld, Donald, 94, 232, 264, 265, 302,
    317, 343, 361, 438 – 49, 455
Rushdie, Salman, 131
Rushton, Willy, 379
Russell, Bertrand, 350, 415
Russell, Michael, 53
The Russell Brand Show, 66
Rut-Brown, Jan, 53
Ryan, Tom, 331
Ryder, Winona, 276, 452
Rykan, 66

Sacchi, Arrigo, 52
Sagan, Carl, 41, 243
St. Elsewhere, 433
St. Louis Post-Dispatch, 60
Saki, 104
Sales, Soupy, 194
Salinger, J. D., 327
Salisbury Journal, 62
San Francisco Chronicle, 59, 101, 211
Sanderson, Tessa, 452
Sanderson, Wimp, 176
Sansome, Al, 65
Santos, Cleberson Souza, 116

Sasso, Peter, 407
Satie, Erik, 224, 405
Sayer, Leo, 148
Schacht, Hjalmar, 298
Schiff, Richard, 266
Schmich, Mary, 414
Schmidt, Rod, 194
Schroeder, Pat, 268
Schulz, Charles M., 370
Schwarz, Claire, 78
Schwarz, Thomas L., 194
Schwarzenegger, Arnold, 124, 257, 261, 264, 307
Scott, Brough, 48, 433
Scott, David R., 46
Scott, Jerry, 47
Scott, Ralph, 151
Scott, Ray, 163
Scowcroft, Brent, 301
The Scranton Tribune, 59
Seabiscuit, 87
Seabrook, Peter, 210
Seattle Times, 99
Seaver, Tom, 449
Sedaris, David, 73
Sedgwick, General John, 306
Seinfeld, 95
Seinfeld, Jerry, 98, 187, 207, 248, 322, 359
Sénéchal, Héloïse, 231
The Seven Year Itch, 211
Shackleford, Charles, 178
Shakespeare, William, 431
Shameless, 63
Shandling, Garry, 139, 143, 296, 331, 368, 381
Shankly, Bill, 424
Sharp, Rhod, 428
Shaw, George Bernard, 32, 139, 154, 178, 266, 353, 429, 439
Shepherd, Joe, 195
Sheridan, Richard, 263
Sheridan, Tom, 263
Shetland Times, 421
Shields, Brooke, 310, 394
Shirley Valentine, 118
The Shop Around the Corner, 445
Short, Shelley, 235
Showbiz, 42

Sibley, Alex, 342
Sillett, John, 50
Silverman, Sarah, 109, 134, 279, 355, 364, 377, 408
Silvers, Sid, 39
Silverstone, Alicia, 227
Simon & Simon, 375
Simon, Neil, 94
Simpson, Jessica, 42, 236, 267, 39, 401
Simpson, John, 302
The Simpsons, 32, 34, 41, 45, 75, 91, 93, 105, 107, 109, 110, 140, 141, 142, 147, 150, 154, 158, 162, 163, 183, 190, 192, 194, 198, 200, 203, 208, 213, 217, 219, 220, 227, 228, 232, 244, 248, 249, 252, 255, 275, 276, 279, 280, 294, 305, 308, 309, 311, 313, 318, 319, 329, 332, 333, 338, 341, 344, 349, 355, 361, 363, 369, 381, 384, 394, 396, 400, 416, 424, 426, 427, 428, 432, 433, 441, 443, 444, 452, 455
Sims, Robert, 94
Sinatra, Frank, 220
Sing Your Troubles Away, 402
Sinha, Paul, 301
Sipress, David, 88, 93
Sisk, Joseph, 90
Sisqó, 106
Sissons, Peter, 405
Six Feet Under, 129
Skelton, Red, 149
"Sketcherism Spoon," 69, 70
Skinner, Frank, 30, 207, 393
Skinner, Jane, 43
Sledge, Tommy, 416
Sleeper, 143, 249
Small Talk, 205, 412
Smirnoff, Yakov, 127
Smith, Alan, 51, 56
Smith, Anna Nicole, 302
Smith, Arthur, 36
Smith, Bob, 216
Smith, Chuck, 75, 90, 111, 119, 150, 298, 307, 398, 430
Smith, Emmitt, 181
Smith, J. Calvin, 75
Smith, Jon Patrick, 246
Smith, Linda, 221, 224

Smith, Rev. Sydney, 408
Smith, Ron, 401
Smith, Shepard, 43
Smith, Tim, 413
Snagge, John, 173
Snepsts, Harold, 171
Soap, 106, 108, 324, 452
Solomon, Hilary, 46
Some Like It Hot, 173, 372
Son of Paleface, 105
Sone, Paul A., 195
Sonnenberg, Ben, 71
The Sopranos, 65, 92, 346, 421, 445
Sorenson, Jean, 151
Southern, Gordon, 238
Spaceballs, 207
Spaced, 115
Spafford, Gene, 251
Spanky, 330
Sparkes, John, 384
Spears, Britney, 229, 232, 293, 318
Spellar, John, 45
Spikey, Dave, 314, 318, 345
Spinks, Leon, 432
SpongeBob SquarePants, 434
Spooner, Rev. William Archibald, 69, 127, 448
Spurrier, Steve, 182
Stage Door Canteen, 345
Stallone, Sylvester, 122
The Star-Democrat, 277
Starling, Marlon, 186
Starr, Dave, 207
Starr, Ringo, 223, 235
Steel Magnolias, 94
Steele, Edna, 374
Stein, Joel, 226
Steinhorn, Jason, 371
Stengel, Casey, 178, 411
Stephanopolous, George, 265
Steptoe and Son, 231
Stergiopoulos, Gerry, 318
Stevens, Lester, 233
Stevens, Shakin', 219
Stevenson, Adlai, 309
Stevenson, David, 32
Stewart, Jackie, 39
Stewart, Jon, 271, 302

Stewart, Les, 192
Stewart, Rod, 219, 273
Stinnett, Caskie, 381
Stir Crazy, 292
Stockman, David, 265
Stone, Doug, 78
Stone, Norman, 199
Stott, Richard, 417
Stover, Hermine, 51, 52
Streep, Meryl, 44
Streisand, Barbra, 148
Stren, Jonty, 354
Strider, Bill, 121
Strike Me Pink, 116
Stroustrup, Bjarne, 254
Stubbs, Ray, 172
Stupak, Michelle, 335
Suder, Nicholas, 229
Sues, Alan, 104, 309
Sugar, Bert R., 171
Sullivan, Meg, 47, 408
Sullivan's Travels, 192
Summerall, Pat, 364
Summerfield, Arthur, 254
Summers, Lawrence, 213
The Sun, 384
Sunday Express, 206
Sunday Mirror, 389
Sunday Patriot News, 59
The Sunday Times, 275, 277, 331
Surrender, 118
Sussex Press, 59
Suter, Brad, 90
Sutton Coldfield Observer, 59
Sutton, Don, 178
Sutton, Marty, 67
Swan, Jane, 183
Swanson, Gloria, 96
Sweeny Todd: The Demon Barber of Fleet Street, 398
Swift, Jonathan, 434
Swinburn, Walter, 433
Sykes, Eric, 189

Taft, Mrs. Robert A., 248
Take the Money and Run, 225, 274, 292
Talk Radio, 39

Tarantino, Quentin, 226, 357
Tarrant, Chris, 141
Tatchell, Peter, 371
Taxi, 126 237, 428, 433
Taylor, Dennis, 57
Taylor, Graham, 35, 234, 247, 455
Teachers, 112
Temple-Morris, Peter, 436
10 Things I Hate About You, 35
Tequila, Tila, 119
Terminator, 276
Terry-Thomas, 69
Thapar, Karan, 270
That '70s Show, 121, 244, 393
That's My Boy, 363
Thatch, Nguyen Co, 266
Thatcher, Denis, 128
Thatcher, Margaret, 264
Theismann, Joe, 434
Theroux, Louis, 294
The Thin Blue Line, 152, 249, 432
Third Watch, 121, 419
30 Rock, 38, 90, 125, 148, 151, 156, 349,
    367, 370, 373, 392, 426, 441, 454
This Is Spinal Tap, 221
Thomas, Warren, 114
Thompson, Derek, 367, 48
Thompson, Hunter S., 331
Thompson, Mychal, 439
Thompson, Richard, 436
Thomson, Garrett, 402
Thorndike, Sybil, 420
Three Amigos!, 116, 430
The Three Stooges, 36, 113, 123, 203, 217,
    298, 381
Thurber, James, 274
Thurman, Blair, 195
Thurman, Uma, 248
Timberlake, Justin, 92
The Times, 59, 127, 196, 197, 302, 396
Titchmarsh, Alan, 334
Toksvig, Sandi, 271
Tolstoy, Leo, 414
Tomlin, Lily, 314, 437
Toms, Caroline, 67
Tonawanda News, 99
Took, Barry, 325
Top Gear, 400

Torch Song Trilogy, 108
Townsend, Andy, 50
The Travel Show, 48
Travis, John, 261
Travolta, John, 31, 50
Trenton Times, 300
Trevino, Lee, 184
Trillin, Calvin, 35, 281
Trueman, Fred, 31, 55
Truman, Harry, 268
Trump, Donald, 257, 307, 366
Trump, Ivana, 89, 117
Tsongas, Paul, 266
Tulip, Paul, 148
Turtle Diary, 394
Twain, Mark, 38, 91, 253, 304, 419, 431,
    448
Tweddle, Elizabeth, 37
The 25 Most Nonsensical Protest Signs, 59
Tyler, Steven, 387
Tynan, Kenneth, 46
Tyson, Mike, 151, 358, 411

Uchea, Carley, 318
Udall, Morris K., 262
Ullman, Tracey, 199
Unfaithfully Yours, 223, 300
Unforgiven, 415
Untamed Heart, 206
Updike, John, 183
Updike, Mark, 420
Ustinov, Peter, 303, 336, 399

Valdez, Jeff, 205
Valentine, Bobby, 179
Valley Newsletter, 58
Van Damme, Jean-Claude, 242, 258
Van Doren, Mamie, 157
Van Schaick, George, 52
Veeck, Bill, 182
Venables, Terry, 50, 247, 359
Venison, Barry, 346
Verba, John, 422
The Vermonter, 62
Vernon, Jackie, 406, 420
The Vicar of Dibley, 137, 154, 210, 218, 368

Vicious, Sid, 225
Vick, Michael, 181
Vidal, Gore, 268
Vider, Gary, 271
Vincent, Peter, 309
Vincent, Robbie, 57, 382, 408
Vine, David, 51
Vine, Jeremy, 96
Vine, Tim, 93, 188, 220, 255, 333, 345, 380, 397, 401, 407
Violen, W. R., 67
Viz magazine, 175, 197, 204, 207, 213, 221, 256, 274, 276, 279, 280, 297, 311, 328, 330, 380, 381, 394, 397, 398, 409, 418, 221, 244, 256, 274, 276, 279, 280
Voltaire, 224
von Zell, Harry, 70
von Zell, Howard, 399
Vosburgh, Dick, 68

Waddell, Sid, 57
Wade, Virginia, 180
Wadsworth, Jerry, 200
Waiting for God, 350
Wakefield, Tim, 330
Walker, Antoine, 177
Walker, Murray, 37, 69, 154, 156, 169, 209, 430, 438
Walker, Woody, 120
Wall Street Journal, 250
Wallace, Danny, 261
Walliams, David, 173
Wallis, Nick, 346
Wallsten, Peter, 409
Walpole, Robert, 153
Walsh, Ted, 187
Walsh-Atkins, Alex, 171
Walters, Barbara, 33
Wang, Wally, 376
Ward, Artemus, 297
Ward, E. M., 447
Warner, Harry, 263
Watson, Mark, 227
Watt, Jim, 186
Wax, Ruby
Way Out West, 112
Wayne, John, 326

Wayne's World, 122
Weah, George, 236
Webb, Alan, 50
Webster, Geoff, 49
Webster, Gregory, 321
The Wedding Date, 437
Weekly World News, 99
Weinstock, Lotus, 117, 354, 450
Welcome Back, Kotter, 125, 349
Weller, Nicola, 77, 281, 401
Welsh Press, 223
Welwyn and Hatfield Herald and Post, 448
West Lancashire Visitor, 59
West, Mae, 149, 436
West, Rebecca, 144
The West Wing, 245
Westrum, Wes, 179
What's New Pussycat?, 34, 113, 190
Wheeler, Bert, 238
When Harry Met Sally, 358, 361
White Girls Are Easy, 112
White, Paula, 413
Whitehorn, Katharine, 353, 414
Whitelaw, William, 263, 264, 294, 389
Widdecombe, Ann, 45, 308
Wilde, Oscar, 146, 399, 432
Wilkinson, Anne, 335
Will & Grace, 113, 124, 164, 314, 360, 387, 434
Willcox, Toyah, 235
Willey, Dean, 51
Williams, J. P. R., 51
Williams, Kenneth, 77
Williams, Pat, 177
Williams, Robbie, 89, 219
Williams, Robin, 40, 107, 273, 438
Williams, Steve, 375
Willoughby, Carina, 309
Wills, Maury, 406
Wilson, Jack, 411
Wilson, Lori, 80
Windsor, John, 416
Winfield, Julian, 176
Winfrey, Oprah, 235
Wings, 36, 107, 122, 139, 152, 153, 158, 199, 210, 337, 338, 426
Winn, Cindy, 66
Winner, Michael, 385

Winslet, Kate, 93
Winstead, Lizz, 113
Winters, Shelley, 233
Wire in the Blood, 218
Wisconsin State Journal, 99
Witcher, Jerrold M., 403
Witte, Tom, 75, 263
Wittgenstein, Ludwig, 293, 438
The Wizard of Oz, 154, 430
WKRP in Cincinnati, 109
Wodehouse, P. G., 39, 97, 189, 211, 230,
    306, 338, 343, 391, 425, 430
Wogan, Sir Terry, 97, 436
Wolff, Isabel, 317
Wolski, 135
Wood, Jason, 108
Wood, Leon, 133
Wood, Victoria, 113, 382
Woodward, A., 186
Woolsey, Robert, 238
Worcester, Sarah, 195
Worley, Jo Anne, 113, 116, 313, 424
Wright, Gill, 68
Wright, Steven, 33, 40, 91, 96, 132, 163,
    167, 194, 195, 207, 208, 209, 211, 212,
    216, 218, 227, 228, 238, 239, 255, 262,
    262, 275, 309, 318, 329, 330, 331, 332,
    335, 337, 341, 342, 346, 373, 386, 396,

410, 414, 416, 418, 420, 443, 444, 445,
    454, 455
Wrongfully Accused, 196, 279, 305, 326
Wurtzel, Joan, 229
Wyndham, Iris, 111
Wyndham, Joan, 111

Yates, Paula, 233
Yes, Minister, 267
York Daily Record, 272
York Evening Press, 275
You Can't Cheat an Honest Man, 363
Young, Dusty, 325
Young Frankenstein, 347
The Young Ones, 36, 146, 156, 198, 228,
    300
Youngman, Henny, 116, 151, 189, 194, 214,
    31, 327, 374, 380, 406, 417
Yow, David, 94

The Zambian Times, 60
Zappa, Frank, 221, 365, 394
Zeller, Thomas, 213
Zephaniah, Benjamin, 107
Ziglar, Zig, 172
Zorba the Greek, 125

Other Books by Ulysses Press

The Dirtiest, Most Politically Incorrect Jokes Ever
Allan Pease, $12.95
This book is packed with no-holds-barred gags for those who are fed up with others telling them what to say, how to think and what is allowed to be funny.

The Big Ass Book of Jokes
Rudy A. Swale, $14.95
The thousands of jokes in this huge volume range from clean enough to tell at work to too off-color for corporate e-mail. With so many jokes in one book, there is something for everyone.

Blonde Walks into a Bar: The 4,000 Most Hilarious, Gut-Busting Gags, One-Liners and Jokes
Jonathan Swan, $14.95
Unapologetically funny and irreverent, this book holds nothing back as it delivers laugh after laugh.

The Ginormous Book of Dirty Jokes: Over 1000 Sick, Filthy and X-Rated Jokes
Rudy A. Swale, $12.95
This masterpeice offers the biggest, baddest, badassest collection of off-color quips.

The Girl's-Only Dirty Joke Book
Karen S. Smith, $10.95
From under-sized penises and unfaithful men to over-sized breasts and less-than-brilliant blondes, this book serves up the filthiest female humor ever put into print.

Man Walks into a Bar: Over 6,000 of the Most Hilarious Jokes, Funniest Insults and Gut-Busting One-Liners
Stephen Arnott & Mike Haskins, $14.95
This book is packed full of quick and easy jokes that are as simple to remember and repeat as they are funny.

The Sassy Bitch's Book of Dirty Jokes
Katie Reynolds, $10.95
This no-holds-barred joke book features outrageous one-liners, stories and punch lines on everything from romance, one-nighters and dirty talk to foreplay, penis size and between-the-sheets mishaps.

Seriously Sick Jokes: The Most Disgusting, Filthy, Offensive Jokes from the Vile, Obscene, Disturbed Minds of b3ta.com
Compiled by Rob Manuel, $10.95
Without a single suitable joke to tell one's mother, *Seriously Sick Jokes* is a lewd, crude and absolutely filthy collection that will have readers cringing between bouts of uncontrollable laughter.

The Ultimate Dirty Joke Book
Mike Oxbent & Harry P. Ness, $11.95
This joke collection holds back nothing and guarantees outrageous laughs.

To order these books call 800-377-2542 or 510-601-8301, fax 510-601-8307, e-mail ulysses@ulyssespress.com, or write to Ulysses Press, P.O. Box 3440, Berkeley, CA 94703. All retail orders are shipped free of charge. California residents must include sales tax. Allow two to three weeks for delivery.

Rosemarie Jarski is a blonde of Irish-Polish parents, living in Essex. She hasn't the foggiest why she was asked to compile this collection.